The Goffman Reader

Edited with introductory essays by

Charles Lemert

and

Ann Branaman

First published 1997

2 4 6 8 10 9 7 5 3 1

Blackwell Publishers Inc.
350 Main Street
Malden, Massachusetts 02148
USA

Blackwell Publishers Ltd
108 Cowley Road
Oxford OX4 1JF
UK

Library of Congress Cataloging-in-Publication Data

Goffman, Erving.
 The Goffman reader / edited and with preface and introduction by Charles Lemert and Ann Branaman.
  p. cm.
 Includes bibliographical references and index.
 ISBN 1–55786–893–X (hardcover). — ISBN 1–55786–894–8 (pbk.)
 1. Goffman, Erving. 2. Sociologists—United States—Biography.
 3. Sociology—United States—History. I. Lemert, Charles C., 1937–.
  II. Branaman, Ann. III. Title.
HM22.U6G643 1997
301'.0973—dc20   96–26921
                                                   CIP

British Library Cataloguing in Publication Data

A CIP catalogue record for this book is available from the British Library.

Printed in Great Britain by Hartnolls Limited, Bodmin, Cornwall

This book is printed on acid-free paper

The Goffman Reader

"Ervi[n] [p]ossessed the most distinctive voice among the social scienti[sts] [gen]eration . . . This is an excellent selection from his varied writing[s] introduce a new generation to his unique vision of the social

Nathan Glazer, Harvard University

"The [ha]ve assembled a very coherent and defensible set of selections f[rom] [ke]y works. No sociologist can make these connections better
than [Charles] [L]emert. Right now he is the preeminent social theorist in
Ameri[ca]

Norman Denzin, University of Illinois-Urbana

"Goff[man] [cert]ainly seems to be on everyone's lips these days. It is true that
most [of his b]ooks are still in print, but there is not an anthology of this sort.
It shou[ld] [prov]e a great boon in teaching."

Krishan Kumar, University of Virginia

To Wesleyan University

of which we are both children by adoption,
and from whose students, teachers, and alumni
we have learned much of what we know about how to learn.

Note

Stars are used in the selections from Goffman's writings to indicate the end and start of each extract. The correspondence of extracts to the original publication can be determined by reference to the page numbers in the footnote at the start of each selection.

Contents

"Goffman"
by Charles Lemert

There was a time, and in some quarters there still is, when the word "Goffman" evoked an understanding so distinctive that one hardly knew what to do with it. To read Goffman was, and is today, to be thus evoked—called out into a netherworld in which the peculiar and the familiar are perfectly joined. As he once said, reflecting as much his own nature as on that of social things:

> *Universal human nature is not a very human thing.*
> *("On Face-work," 1955; reprinted in Interaction Ritual, 1967, p. 45)*

Goffman forces readers out of the convenient illusion that their experience is uniquely theirs. He requires them to tolerate the prospect that, far from being unique, individual human experience may be so insidiously true as to be outside the sphere of things truly human.

In his day (a short one of barely two decades, from about 1960 when his books were first widely noticed until his death in 1982), Goffman's proper name had become an improper word. It was not that, in one of the ill-conceived notions of the concept "word," his name stood for something outside itself such as a particular brand of sociology, or an unusually evocative manner of writing. In the usual senses of "word," "*Goffman*" stood for little. It was rather that he made something happen; as when a shudder of recognition won't let go of the misery of being a single:

> *To be alone, to be a "solitary" in the sense of being out of sight and sound of everyone, is not to be alone in another way, namely, as a "single," a party of one, a person not in a with, a person unaccompanied "socially" by others in some public undertaking (itself often crowded), such as sidewalk traffic, shopping in stores, and restaurant dining.*
> *("Response Cries," 1978; reprinted in Forms of Talk, 1981, p. 79)*

Fortunately for us today, Goffman's genius was every bit as much literary as observational. Indeed, his fame as a microscope of human nuance may rest entirely on the manner by which he presented those observations in

writing. One of the most unimaginative complaints against him is that he
had no replicable method. It is certainly true, as the first-time reader will
soon see, that what Goffman observed in us and how he observed it are
found exclusively in what he says. He abjured all the self-authorizing
manners of scientists and community organizers of various other
kinds—appeals to protocols, laws, proofs, techniques, road maps, evidences,
recipes, instruction manuals, rules for use, schedules, and the like. For that
matter, there are in Goffman no facts as we normally construe them. At best,
there are definitions, but these are always quirky like universal human nature
itself. Goffman's definitions are really moves against the grain of readerly
expectations. When all is said and done, there is not much more than what
Goffman says—and this is composed in and around a bewildering collection
of newspaper clippings, anecdotes, informal field notes, references to
student papers alongside books and articles by those of presumably established repute, and such like. Goffman, the writer, evoked without
stipulation; as when he turns so familiar a concept as "action" on its defin-
itional ear:

> Serious action is a serious ride, and rides of this kind are all but arranged
> out of everyday life. As suggested, every individual engages in consequential
> acts, but most of these are not problematic, and when they are (as when career
> decisions are made that affect one's life) the determination and settlement of
> these bets will often come after decades, and by then will be obscured by
> payoffs from many of his other gambles. Action, on the other hand, brings
> chance-taking and resolution into the same heated moment of experience; the
> events of action inundate the momentary now with their implications for the
> life that follows.
>
> ("Where the Action Is" in Interaction Ritual, 1967, p. 261)

But, of course, this is all to the advantage of those of us who read him so
long after his passing. He wrote in such a way that, even where the anecdotes are worn out, today's readers can in most instances experience what
Goffman conjures up. This magic transpires in the reading of an author
whose effect is enlarged by its mysterious location somewhere between
incredible fact and certifiable fiction. This collection of readings from
Goffman's most important writings relies on this condition and promise of
his excellent literary graces, of which just one small instance is found among
the opening lines of Goffman's undelivered 1982 presidential address to the
American Sociological Association:

> For an evening's hour, it is given to each current president of the Association
> to hold captive the largest audience of colleagues that sociology can provide.
> For an hour then, within the girdle of these walls, a wordy pageantry is re-

enacted. A sociologist you have selected from a very short list takes to the center of this vasty Hilton field on a hobby horse of his own choosing. (One is reminded that the sociologically interesting thing about Hamlet is that every year no high school in the English-speaking world has trouble finding some clown to play him.) In any case, it seems that presidents of learned societies are well enough known about something to be elected because of it. Taking office, they find a podium attached, along with encouragement to demonstrate that they are indeed obsessed by what their election proved they were already known to be obsessed by. Election winds them up and sets them loose to set their record straight; they rise above restraint and replay it.

("The Interaction Order," 1983, p. 1)

Even if Goffman were no longer able to evoke anything plausible in our world today, it would still be worth the while to read him just as today a reader derives delights aplenty from reading Homer. Few of us know, nor are we among, those whose odysseys are menaced or protected by otherworldly monsters and nymphs. Yet *The Odyssey* is read still by those who journey the face of their worlds longing for a lost home. The genre Goffman created was far from epic. Yet those who travel under the illusions of everyday life are bound to find illumination in the social wonders he creates. The essence of artistic genius is just this: to create verisimilitude enough to draw the client out from what dulls the ability to feel, thus to consider all that life offers. The surprises of social life are there, after all, around and before us at every turn, waiting. Whatever may be concluded about the exact place and value of his social science, Goffman is surely one of the most disturbing guides we shall ever have to the social everpresent; as in the way he uncovers the layers of hidden expiatory functions behind an act each of us performs daily, the apology:

Note that the offender's willingness to initiate and perform his own castigation has certain unapparent values. Were others to do to him what he is willing to do to himself, he might be obliged to feel affronted and to engage in retaliatory action to sustain his moral worth and autonomy. And he can overstate or overplay the case against himself, thereby giving to the others the task of cutting the self-derogation short—this latter, in turn, being a function that is safer to lodge with the offended since they are not likely to abuse it, whereas he, the offender, might. . . . Apologies represent a splitting of the self into a blameworthy part and a part that stands back and sympathizes with the blame giving, and, by implication, is worthy of being brought back into the fold.

(Relations in Public, 1971, p. 113)

This Goffman-effect may well be why he has had so very many interpreters and why, more to the point, many of them have sought to normalize
him. Even those who so clearly respect the man and his ideas seek to rope
him back into range. Anthony Giddens, for example, suggests that
Goffman, the least systematic of sociologists, was in fact a "systematic social
theorist."[1] (What he meant, rather, was that in spite of it all, there is a common thread to Goffman's wild mix of stuff.) William Gamson, setting
himself partly against Alvin Gouldner's famous criticism of Goffman's lack
of politics, insists that Goffman's legacy did not exclude political sociology.[2]
(This may be, but Gamson strains to demonstrate the point which, in the
end, is more that political sociology ought to consider the microevents out
of which political action is contrived.) Pierre Bourdieu, a persistent inventor
of rare methods, thinks of Goffman as a kin of sorts, as one who produced
"one of the most original and rarest methods of doing sociology."[3] (True,
but only upon taking "methods" with a grain of salt.) Randall Collins, than
whom none is more devoted, thinks of Goffman as above all else a
Durkheimian who, among much else, conveyed a reliable account of class
difference and conflict.[4] (True also, but only partly so.) Plus which, there
are those like Norman Denzin who are called to abandon Goffman because
he had abandoned them—as in the case of Denzin's famous rebuke of
Goffman's *Frame Analysis* for its alleged structuralist departure from the
more interactive Chicago traditions.[5] (More later.) Some others, like Gary
Marx, remember the man with awe and gratitude for his intellectual finesse
but often too with revulsion for the all-too-human Goffman who on occasion held himself above his own notorious interactive offenses.[6] Marx's
reminiscences of Goffman are thus analogous to Alasdair Macintyre's well-
known ambivalences toward him: "brilliant," but also a sponsor of "grave
cultural loss."[7]

Whether it is praise or complaint, a very great number of the most astute
social critics want Goffman to be other than he was—and other than, in most
instances, he professed himself to be. Goffman, for all his studied complex-
ities, thought of himself (and his field) in simple terms: a working sociologist,
restless before categories and bold to do what analytic work can be done.

*From the perspective of the physical and biological sciences, human social life
is only a small irregular scab on the face of nature, not particularly amenable
to deep systematic analysis. And so it is. . . . Indeed I have heard it said that
we should be glad to trade what we've so far produced for a few really good
conceptual distinctions and a cold beer. But there's nothing in the world we
should trade for what we do have: the bent to sustain in regard to all elements
of social life a spirit of unfettered, unsponsored inquiry, and the wisdom not
to look elsewhere but ourselves and our discipline for this mandate. That is*

our inheritance and what so far we have to bequeath. If one must have warrant addressed to social needs, let it be for unsponsored analyses of the social arrangements enjoyed by those with institutional authority—priests, psychiatrists, school teachers, police, generals, government leaders, parents, males, whites, nationals, media operators, and all the other well-placed persons who are in a position to give official imprint to versions of reality.

("The Interaction Order," 1983, p. 17)

It is not so much that Goffman was not what interpreters wish he had been, but that Goffman was, as I said, just "Goffman"—if not quite *sui generis*, at least other than anything else to which we are accustomed, thus always more than he can be taken to be. His brilliance at making things happen with words is most disconcertingly at play in the way his writing actually creates the reader—in much the same way that Goffman describes all selves as subject to transcending relationships:

Each moral career, and behind this, each self, occurs within the confines of an institutional system, whether a social establishment such as a mental hospital or a complex of personal and professional relationships. The self, then, can be seen as something that resides in the arrangements prevailing in a social system for its members. The self in this sense is not a property of the person to whom it is attributed, but dwells rather in the pattern of social control that is exerted in connection with the person by himself and those around him. This special kind of institutional arrangement does not so much support the self as constitute it.

(Asylums, 1961, p. 168)

The experience Goffman effects is that of colonizing a new social place into which the reader enters, from which to exit never quite the same. To have once, even if only once, seen the social world from within such a place is never after to see it otherwise, ever after to read the world anew. In thus seeing differently, we are other than we were. Only resisting fear keeps us the same as we thought we were.

Though Goffman was surely the sociologist he professed to be, he was every bit as much, simply, a writer. This may be why, in certain crucial respects, literary and cultural theorists are sometimes more able to take Goffman on his own terms. Those accomplished in the art of reading intended fictions realize that reading is about letting go, thus to allow the evocations to do their work. Consider the following passage:

He pulled down over his eyes a black straw hat the brim of which he extended with his hand held out over it like an eye-shade, as though to

*see whether someone was coming at last, made the perfunctory gesture
of annoyance by which people mean to show that they have waited
long enough, although they never make it when they are really waiting,
then . . . he emitted the loud panting breath that people exhale not
when they are too hot but when they wish it to be thought that they are too
hot.*

Is this not pure Goffman? In essence it is, but in reality it is pure Proust.
These lines from *Remembrance of Things Past* were among those used by the
British playwright Alan Bennett to illustrate Goffman's essentially literary
attitude. Bennett is among a good many literary people who find some
kinship with Goffman's writing.[8] Pursuing these affinities, Bennett further
remarks on Goffman's artistic response to the staff at the Shetlands hotel
where he stayed in 1950 while researching his University of Chicago doctoral
thesis. Goffman had been sent by his teacher Lloyd Warner to study the
social structure of this Scottish island. Instead he studied the characters
staffing his hotel and their manner of dealing with outsiders, himself
included. From this, of course, came eventually his first great book, *The
Presentation of Self in Everyday Life* (1959), of which Bennett says: "It was a
novel beginning. And a novel."[9] Bennett is among those who have likened
Goffman to Kafka, in which reference he makes the twist I recommend:
"Much of Goffman could be a commentary on Kafka. One puts it that way
round, the artist before the academic, but the truth one finds in Goffman's
work is the truth one goes to fiction for."[10]

*Similarly, I have been told by Shetlanders that their grandfathers used to
refrain from improving the appearance of the cottage lest the laird take such
improvements as a sign that increased rents could be extracted from them.
. . . More important, there are male islanders today who have long since
given up the subsistence farming and stringent pattern of endless work, few
comforts and a diet of fish and potatoes, traditionally the islander's lot. Yet
these men frequently wear in public places the fleece-lined leather jerkin and
the high rubber boots that are notoriously symbolic of crofter status.*
                                        (The Presentation of Self, 1959, p. 39)

The self-consciously informal "I have been told" excuses the account from
factual certification. It invites the reader to trust the text's uncertifiable
claims, as do many of his other expressions—"but of course," "as in," and
the like—which in effect are necessary to the effect he desires.[11] One is thus
brought in, just as in reading fiction, to a reality with scant footing outside
the narrator's line. There the reader, deprived of the right of independent
judgment as to the facts of the matter, must enter or quit the story being

told. Impression management, the concept for which the book is justly famous, is itself a managed impression.

If, then, it is so that Goffman's truth is close to fiction, what is one to make of Goffman's sociology? Just as sociologists seek to appropriate Goffman to their own categories of sociological prejudice, many outside the field are tempted to claim him unto their own affiliations. At one extreme, this is done out of foolish disdain for sociology and done according to the proposition: Sociology being a degraded manner of inquiry, then Goffman's genius must be something other. Even so well-regarded a literary man as Christopher Ricks inhumanely transposes his own "unprincipled dissatisfaction with sociology" into an unwarranted characterization of Goffman: "As is frequent in Goffman's work, one of his humane impulses is a principled dissatisfaction with his profession, not merely in his judging that some of his colleagues don't do well enough by delicacy and by interrelationship, but in his knowing that they and he couldn't ever do well *enough*."[12] Ricks wants Goffman for his own use. Like Bennett, Ricks draws Goffman into the literary, most notably in his much acclaimed *Keats and Embarrassment* (1974).

At the other extreme of interpretative decency, Karl Scheibe, one of academic psychology's most appreciative readers of Goffman, is anything but dissatisfied with sociology. Yet, Scheibe observes with plausible justification that, after the early books, *The Presentation of Self* (1959) and *Asylums* (1961), sociologists grew cold toward Goffman inversely to the warmth of his reception outside sociology.[13] It is indeed true that sociologists never quite knew what to make of *Frame Analysis* (1974) and other later works implicated in Goffman's own linguistic turn, while it is precisely *Frame Analysis* and *Forms of Talk* (1981) that drew the most attention outside the field.

All this raises the vexing question of Goffman's true relation to sociology and, in turn, of sociology's to the wider world of human studies. Surely, one of the most remarkable events in the history of social and humanistic study in the last generation is its famous linguistic turn. There is scarcely a field properly concerned with investigating human culture in which a major number of its adherents have failed to address themselves to language and its forms of manifestation in order, thus, to rethink their ways. Consider just the names that come readily to mind: Austin, Asante, Rorty, Searle, Habermas, Foucault, Derrida, Lacan, Gadamer, Garfinkel, Morrison, Jameson, Said, Althusser, Sedgwick, Smith, Denzin, Williams, Hall, Gouldner, Lévi-Strauss, Lyotard, Butler, Bourdieu, Baudrillard, Bernstein, Anzaldúa, Gates—names constituting a membership that would embarrass many of them. But none could deny that in some crucial way their work includes a meditation on language. One could just as easily compose a list, no less irregular, of those (for starters: Thompson, Giddens, Collins, Anderson, Coleman, Bate, Bloom, Thorne, Gitlin) who have made room in their work for the exercise of objections to the linguistic turn. One need not recognize more than a few on either list to see immediately that, however much he might have protested his inclusion, Goffman belongs among the former. What is of particular interest is that sociology, for the large part, has been perplexed not just by Goffman's linguistic turn but by the phenomenon itself. But the subject of this observation is not so much the vexations of officially organized sociology as Goffman's ready identification with it in spite of his discipline's principled objection to the literature of language, texts, and discourse.

I am myself convinced that the outsider who best understood Goffman's relation to sociology was Dell Hymes, the distinguished anthropological linguist (and Goffman's colleague at the University of Pennsylvania): "Erving's greatness, I think, is this. In a period in which linguistics was stumbling from syntax into semantics and discourse, and sociology was reeling from renewed zeal for qualitative analysis of interaction, he saw clearly from the beginning what the meeting point would have to be, and that for all the charm and fascination of linguistics, the ground in which the linguistics of social life could flower would have to be sociological ground."[14] At no place is this more true than in Goffman's most linguistic, least sociological paper, "Felicity's Condition," which concludes:

> *The general constraint that an utterance must satisfy, namely, that it connect acceptably with what recipient has in, or can bring to, mind, applies in a manner to nonlinguistic acts in wordless contexts. These acts, too, insofar as they can be perceived by individuals in the vicinity, will have to be styled so as provide evidence that their doer is engaged in something that perceivers find understandable, even if they are not favored thereby. . . . Whenever we come in contact with another through the mails, over the telephone, in face-to-face talk, or even merely through immediate co-presence, we find ourselves with one central obligation: to render our behavior understandably relevant to what the other can come to perceive is going on. Whatever else, our activity must be addressed to the other's mind, that is, to the other's capacity to read our words and actions for evidence of our feelings, thoughts, and intent. This confines what we say and do, but it also allows us to bring to bear all the world to which the other can catch allusions.*
>
> *("Felicity's Condition," 1983, pp. 50–1)*

The felicitous condition that accounts for competent linguistic performances is, ultimately, sociological.

It would be wrong, I think, to construe Goffman as some kind of interdisciplinary magpie, building intellectual nests here and there, from anthropology to psychology and linguistics, talking things up so noisily that even literary people notice him. But of course it is true, as Clifford Geertz proposes, that Goffman is among those who have blurred genre distinctions in the human sciences.[15] Just the same, even when Goffman expressed reservations about his own field, he remained just what Hymes said he was, a sociologist at heart.

I have no universal cure for the ills of sociology. A multitude of myopias limit the glimpse we get of our subject matter. To define one source of blindness and bias as central is engagingly optimistic. Whatever our substantive focus and whatever our methodological persuasion, all we can do I believe is to keep faith with the spirit of natural science, and lurch along, seriously kidding ourselves that our rut has a forward direction. We have not been given the credence and weight that economists lately have acquired, but we can almost match them when it comes to the failure of rigorously calculated predictions. Certainly our systematic theories are every bit as vacuous as theirs: we manage to ignore almost as many critical variables as they do. We do not have the esprit that anthropologists have, but our subject matter at least has not been obliterated by the spread of the world economy. So we have an undiminished opportunity to overlook the relevant facts with our very own eyes. We can't get graduate students who score as high as those who go into Psychology, and at its best the training the latter get seems more professional and more thorough than what we provide. So we haven't managed to produce in our students the high level of trained incompetence that psychologists have achieved in theirs, although, God knows, we're working on it.

("The Interaction Order," 1983, p. 2)

★

Those who are willing at this later date to take up a systematic reading of Goffman would be right, therefore, to wonder about Goffman's relation to sociology. I do not for a minute assume, and we certainly do not desire, that the group of readers interested in this book would comprise only those willing and able to identify themselves as professional sociologists. Rather, noting the far-flung intellectual territories to which an interest in Goffman traveled in his lifetime, this book is organized against the expectation that an interest in Goffman remains either alive in fact or is in prospect of being awakened.

Speaking for myself, I believe (and have elsewhere advertised[16]), that sociology suffers when it is narrowly identified with the work of professionals by whose names it is most commonly recognized. There would be no sociology in the professional sense of the word were there not, prior to any of its sustaining institutional arrangements, a natural and ubiquitous practical sociology with which all competent members of any enduring social entity are thoroughly familiar. That their familiarity is often naive and generally insusceptible of being called to mind in order to be put into talk, does nothing to contradict this assumption. Indeed, there are those who consider this naivety a kind of perverse evidence of the very ubiquity of the practical sociology of, if I may say it this way, ordinary people. More to the point, Goffman himself stood out among those who believed this to be so. This was one of the premises that activated his most famous general sociological principle: That deviants, who do their devious deeds with consummate social skill, operate necessarily according to the same social rules as the normals whose norms are violated as much by studied ignorance of their own covered-over degradations of the values they espouse as by violence done against them, and their norms, by deviants.

> *It should be seen, then, that stigma management is a general feature of society, a process occurring wherever there are identity norms. The same features are involved whether a major differentness is at question, of the kind traditionally defined as stigmatic, or a picayune differentness, of which the shamed person is ashamed to be ashamed. One can therefore suspect that the role of the normal and the role of stigmatized are parts of the same complex, cut from the same standard cloth. . . . One can assume that the stigmatized and the normal have the same mental make-up, and that this necessarily is the standard one in our society; he who can play one of these roles, then, has exactly the required equipment for playing out the other, and in fact in regard to one stigma or another is likely to have developed some experience in doing so.*
>
> (Stigma, 1963, pp. 130–1)

In short, professional sociologists, least of all Goffman, would have little to say if they were unable to rely on the native reports of ordinary members of society, including themselves when out of uniform.

However much the idea that sociology is a practical resource of persons without official training and certification may offend professional sociologists, it is not an idea that would be lost on other practitioners of the human sciences. Physicians, writers, composers, undertakers, comedians, anthropologists, screen writers, news reporters, historians, TV producers, beauticians, poets, parents, dentists are but a few of those who draw their material for creative work out of the mundane culture to which they play. Sociology, being different in many good ways, is not different in this respect.

If I am granted this largely unexplained assumption, I would go on to say that the discovery of it is one of the more important and general convictions to have emerged, alongside and mixed up with, the linguistic turn of the last generation or so—since, say, the 1960s. It could well be said that the most important, lingering, and unresolved argument in and among studies of human culture is the one over the status of language in social life and, conversely, of the social once the status of language is taken seriously.

Among those who take discourse, text, talk in general, or conversation seriously as, if not models, means for construing the social, there is the tendency to write and speak in ways that create the impression that these various epiphanies of language-use are the only true reality there is. This is not always what is meant, though it is indeed meant in some extreme cases of those who have read up on the subject too little or too late. Among those on the other side, who consider themselves proponents of the fundamental reality of the social, there is an understandable (if not excusable) readiness to caricature proponents of the linguistic turn as nihilists bent upon destroying, if not the real world, at least the promise that we can understand it realistically. I have personally been witness to sessions of learned societies in which the most sophisticated people money can sponsor have fought tooth and nail over the meaning of a single line written nearly thirty years ago by the *bête noir* of the linguistic turn. That line, as it is quoted without benefit of reading, is: "There is nothing outside the text." The same line, as it was written in 1967, is: "*There is nothing outside the text* [there is no outside text; *il n'y a pas de hors-texte*.]"[17] Though the bracketed words will do no good for those unfamiliar with Jacques Derrida's painstaking play with the delicacies of the French language, it is plain at least that the text as quoted is something quite different from the text as written. Those repelled by Derrida's linguistic turn may be surprised to learn that the line actually does not mean there is nothing but text, or language. Rather it refers (admittedly in a complicated way) to the complexity of the text's relation to the realities exterior to it. Conversely, there is an equal number of ridiculous versions of the linguistic turn which ignore the real concerns of proponents of the social. If you have not personally witnessed such debates, you have missed very little.

What you ought not miss, however, is the point that one of the most important questions of our day is a question of this mysterious relation. Though their way of talking may sometimes suggest otherwise, students of culture are not, I think, hell-bent on escaping reality by either the linguistic or sociologic route. In fact, one need not have read a word of these controversies to be alarmed by the ever rising confusions that subsist in the dirty waters between social reality and what is *said* about it. What is said in public has very little to do with actual social behaviors. Inspired rhetoric defending American civilization is uttered by individuals who behave, and legislate, in the most uncivilized ways imaginable. The media, which provide the only instruction most citizens ever hope to get, communicate the most unreal, garbled truths about social life. Heroes are made to be sellers of shoes. And on it goes. One has no need any longer to return to the locus classicus of this phenomenon: "We had to destroy the village to save it." Language's extension into media has turned back on language itself, somehow undercutting social reality.

> *The central example here of what might be called "commercial realism," the standard transformation employed in contemporary ads, in which the scene is conceivable in all detail as one that could in theory have occurred as pictured, providing us with a simulated slice of life; but although the advertiser does not seem intent on passing the picture off as a caught one, the understanding seems to be that we will not press him too far to account for just what sort of reality the scene has. (The term "realistic," like the term "sincerity" when applied to a stage actor, is self-contradictory, meaning something that is praiseworthy by virtue of being something else, although not that something else.)*
>
> *(Gender Advertisements, 1976, p. 15)*[18]

Commercial realism is a fact of social life whereby what is said (including what we say) about what is real and true bears less and less on the social world as it is.

It is possible, therefore, to say that the social critics, Goffman included, who have turned abruptly and insistently to the study of language have done so in order to account for an observable fact of social life: that social reality is oddly, perhaps pathologically, formed out of discourses, including talk and especially media, that bear little direct responsibility to the truth of things. Just as most proponents of the linguistic turn are seeking critical and analytic ways out, around, or over this fact, so their opponents fear that too much attention to the reality of language is part of the very problem whereby talk has no footing in reality, not to mention truth. This, again, is a concern shared widely by most practical sociologists of wildly different cultural and political attitudes. What else is at the bottom of the confusion created today by shifting political alliances on the right and left of most industrial societies if it is not a deeply felt, and evidently justified, suspicion that those in charge do not, indeed they cannot, tell truth from fiction?

> *"One and a half hours after the President's suite had been cleared of student demonstrators, Grayson Kirk stood in the center of his private office looking at the blankets, cigarette butts and orange peels that covered his rug. Turning to A.M. Rosenthal of* The New York Times *and several other reporters who had come into the office with him he murmured, 'My God, how could*

human beings do a thing like this?' . . . *"Jerry L. Avorn et al.,* Up Against
the Ivy Wall *(New York: Atheneum Publishers, 1969), p. 100. The great
sociological question, of course, is not how could it be that human beings do
a thing like this, but rather how it is that human beings do this sort of thing
so rarely. How come persons in authority have been so overwhelmingly
successful in conning those beneath them into keeping the hell out of their
offices.*

(*Relations in Public*, 1971, p. 288, note 44)[19]

In this, one among Goffman's many famous footnotes, he refers to an incident in the 1968 student rebellions at Columbia University. That was a time
when the culture at large was just waking up to the central fact of relations
in public: that public relations turn on the misplaced authority of deceitful
presentations. One could say that, for better or worse, today we have all
learned the lesson Goffman was among the first to teach.

★

To read Goffman's writing today with the expectation that it is pertinent to
the present requires some settled judgment on the times in which he began
to write and their relation to the times in which we now read, no less than
to Goffman's own coming to terms with a way of writing about the world.

Goffman was born 1922, Jewish and Canadian. It is tempting to account
his insistent outsider point of view to the ethnic and national conditions
of his birth. This is possible. But it is certain that the date of his birth meant
he came of age during the Depression and World War II, completing his
undergraduate studies at the University of Toronto in 1945. Goffman's
graduate work at the University of Chicago was pursued, thereby, during
the absolute high water mark of sociology in America, but in a school that,
though well regarded and influential, was considered at odds with the then
dominant, professional schools at Columbia and Harvard. Even so,
Goffman's student work inclined at odds with a school that was itself at odds
with the dominant mode of sociology, most notably in his abandonment of
his advisor's recommendation in order to study the social interactions of the
Shetlands people. In spite of this rebellion, Goffman completed his
doctorate in 1953.

It was not that Goffman put himself utterly outside sociology. To the end
of his life he considered himself an "empiricist" and, simply, a "social
psychologist."[20] Goffman's readiness to be in, if not of, sociology is evident
in the very first papers he published before completing his doctoral work.
"Symbols of Class Status" (1951) is pretty standard sociology by contrast
to "On Cooling the Mark Out" (1952) in which he first displays the method
of writing from his own distinctive position to the subject at hand with scant

regard for the niceties of scholarly ritual. There he moved, with daring for a
student without immediate prospect of employment, from the mechanisms
of the con to the nuances of status maintenance.

> *But perhaps the most important movement of those who fail is one we never
> see. Where roles are ranked and somewhat related, persons who have been
> rejected from the one above may be difficult to distinguish from persons who
> have risen from the one below. For example, in America, upper-class women
> who fail to make a marriage in their own circle may follow the recognized
> route of marrying an upper-middle class professional. Successful lower-
> middle class women may arrive at the same station in life, coming from the
> other direction. Similarly, among those who mingle with one another as
> colleagues in the profession of dentistry, it is possible to find some who have
> failed to become physicians and others who have succeeded at not becoming
> pharmacists or optometrists. No doubt there are few positions in life that do
> not throw together some persons who are there by virtue of failure and other
> persons who are there by virtue of success. In this sense, the dead are sorted
> but not segregated, and continue to walk among the living.*

> ("On Cooling the Mark Out," 1952, p. 463)

One might suppose that the more traditional "Symbols of Class Status" was
but a first experiment with normal sociological behavior. In the sense that
he never after abandoned the distinctive style of "On Cooling the Mark
Out," it was. But, remember, the last two papers of his life (both published
posthumously) fell on either side of the same divide. The one, "The Interaction Order" (1983), his undelivered ASA presidential address was,
stylistics notwithstanding, a ringing defense not just of sociology but of its
(and his own!) commitments to the study of social structures. The other,
"Felicity's Condition" (also 1983), quite possibly his most brilliant (and
certainly most systematic) theoretical exposition, took on the central issue
in sociolinguistics of just how assumptions work to fill the gaps in expressed
meanings. But still he wrote from the eccentric style and vision nurtured
over the years.

That his career took the form of, and provided the condition for, his
orthogonal relation to his professional field is evident in the major academic
appointments he held. His first regular position at the National Institute of
Mental Health in Bethesda, Maryland, preceded appointment in 1957 to a
post in the Department of Sociology at the University of California. Berkeley
then, like Chicago in his student days, was a major department in the field
outside the more traditional Harvard and Columbia programs. There
Goffman remained for a decade through the unusual years of 1960s student
and civil rights movements in which Berkeley figured prominently. In 1968

he left for the University of Pennsylvania to assume a chair that explicitly excluded sociology from its name: Benjamin Franklin Professor of Anthropology and Psychology. He was there when he died in 1982, in the year of his presidency of the ASA.

It has been said "that it is against the Sixties as a whole that Goffman's work must be seen."[21] Insofar as the observation refers to the reception of Goffman as a character to be reckoned with, this is correct. Though he never became a must-read cult figure of the counterculture resistance—as did Fanon, Marcuse, McLuhan, and Goodman—Goffman was certainly influential, particularly through *Asylums* (1961) which was read as part of the anti-psychiatry movement. But, I think, it is wrong to interpret Goffman as having been formed somehow by the events of the 1960s. He was already forty in 1962, a full decade after "On Cooling the Mark Out," and even longer since he had executed the field studies that led to *The Presentation of Self in Everyday Life*. Goffman's intellectual formation took place in the 1940s and 1950s. The early work that came to define his method (if that is the word) was much more a product of the 1950s.

Though the 1960s draw more attention among the general public, they having been more sensational, the 1950s are vastly more important for an understanding of what came to be in America and the world in the last half of the twentieth century. More exactly, the 1960s hardly make sense without an understanding of the preceding years. All of the spectacular countercultural and political movements that occurred in the 1960s had their roots in the contradictions of the 1950s.

The 1950s could be accurately described as that moment when Americans reached boldly to assert the proud prospects of their military and economic triumphs in the 1940s, but in reaching they met resistance at every turn—from the Soviet "menace," the early civil rights movement, the first signs of youth rebellion in music and film, the coming out of the truth of sexual possibility promoted by the Kinsey reports, the growing uneasiness with the good life in empty suburbs. All these, and much more, were felt within, as a crisis at the heart of the American soul in which millions of Americans suspected that their dreams of the good life were founded on false circumstances. Few knew for certain that this was so, and fewer still could offer an account of it, at least not until a new wave of social critics began the painful process of studying the troubles in American life. Though, so far as I know, Goffman never wrote a word that would be recognized as explicit social criticism of American society, he cannot be understood, I think, apart from those movements and events that the new social critics sought to explain.

A social establishment is any place surrounded by fixed barriers to perception in which a particular kind of activity regularly takes place. I have suggested that any social establishment may be studied profitably from the point of view of impression management. Within the walls of a social establishment we find a team of performers who cooperate to present to an audience a given definition of the situation. This will include the concept of own team and of audience and assumptions concerning the ethos that is to be maintained by the rules of politeness and decorum. We often find a division into back region, where the performance of a routine is prepared, and front region, where the performance is presented. . . . Among members of the team we find that familiarity prevails, solidarity is likely to develop, and that secrets that could give the show away are shared and kept. A tacit agreement is maintained between performers and audience to act as if a given degree of opposition and of accord existed between them. Typically, but not always, agreement is stressed and opposition is underplayed.

(*The Presentation of Self*, 1959, p. 238)

Consider the terms and their cognates and concerns: impression management, teamwork, tacit agreement, familiarity, performance. In the late 1950s these were terms the new social criticism took with some scorn from the bureaucratic culture that was then transforming middle-class America. Goffman did the thinking through that led to his use of them in the early 1950s—at about the same time as Erik Erikson's first studies of identity crisis (1950), David Riesman's *Lonely Crowd* (1950), C. Wright Mills's, *White Collar* (1951), William Whyte's *The Organization Man* (1956), John Keats's, *Crack in the Picture Window* (1957), and Vance Packard's *Hidden Persuaders* (1957). It was not, I suppose, so much that Goffman did what no one else was doing, but that, contrary to the impression that he lacked a social consciousness, he actually worked out his own, admittedly perverse and muted, social critique of America in the 1950s.

This is where Alvin Gouldner's criticism of Goffman is at least somewhat unjust.[22] From the point of view of the late 1960s when Gouldner wrote, Goffman did seem very little concerned with political and social issues. But from the point of view of the 1950s Goffman was out there doing no less than others, while Gouldner (just two years older than Goffman) was writing his Weberian thesis for Robert K. Merton on industrial bureaucracy, and others were similarly suppressing their more radical instincts in the face of McCarthyism. It is not that Goffman was a closet political sociologist, as Gamson wants him to be. He was not. But he was attuned to something deeply wrong in American life and, in this, he resonated with others whose social critiques were more overt.

It may seem a very long way from the 1950s to the prospect of relevance for Goffman's ideas in the 1990s. But, I think not. In fact, and this will be shocking to some, I believe that it is impossible to understand the events that are producing the end culture of the 20th century, including the linguistic turn and all the variant forms of social criticism current today, without a thoughtful consideration of the 1950s.

★

It is always difficult for people to appreciate the changes going on about them, especially so when the changes are as fundamental as those that were beginning in the 1950s in the United States. While Europe and Asia were still recovering from World War II, and while much of the rest of the world was seizing the opportunity of the disabilities in Europe and Japan and the distractions of affluence in the USA to free itself from the colonial system, changes too small to notice were giving first notices.

But how does one describe these changes as they first appeared? Even to mention, or list, them as they were in those days is to take the risk of any causal retrospective: that of naming events then so small that one supposes they could not possibly have led to conditions today so huge and obvious. That the events to which I am about to refer might have had a beginning in this earlier time might be easier to swallow by mentioning them first as we now know them.

Which are the most salient characteristics of the world as it is at the end of the twentieth century? These would have to be: (1) the lack of prospect of any ultimate source of moral or political authority in world affairs and the countervailing prevalence of political and economic uncertainty; (2) the epidemic of hunger, poverty, and disease which disappoint the most basic hope of progress that modern society once held so brashly; (3) and, in spite of these, the incongruous fact that most human beings, even those in the globe's remotest places, are, one way or another, electronically tethered to the rest and the whole.

Moral discord, failure of progress, and the electronic revolution—the list is so parsimoniously obvious that one underestimates the degree to which it also summarizes the very short list of facts upon which people of otherwise incommensurable attitudes can and do agree. In fact, in America, politicians of the right take at least the first two of these as signs of the pending (or actual) collapse of civilization (while equivocating somewhat on the third which some see as both a cause of moral degradation and a device for moral reformation). More precisely Allan Bloom, most cogently, and Newt Gingrich, most recently, assign the cause of these three facts of our time to the 1960s. To them, the 1960s produced the moral failure that causes poverty and is accentuated by the sexual immorality of television and the movies. The political left, such as it is, interprets these facts differently: the 1960s freed oppressed peoples, thus provoking the backlash that depletes the political generosity which in turn aggravates poverty and hunger, the facts of which are maliciously hidden behind the mindlessness of the media. The two sides come together, if at all, over a grudging concession that the answer, if any, lies somewhere down the electronic superhighway. These are the defining extremes of what passes for a debate on national culture and future prospects for the United States. Both extremes return to the three basic facts. Where, in addition to their simplifications, they are most wrong is in locating the facts in the 1960s.

It was, rather, in the 1950s, just when Goffman was coming into his own, that the foundations of the present situation were laid in three at first obscure events which can be offered as symbols of what would come to pass.

February 9th, 1950 and Moral Discord. That February Goffman was still a graduate student at the University of Chicago. "On Cooling the Mark Out" would not appear for another two years. On the 9th of the month an obscure United States Senator from Wisconsin addressed the Ohio County Women's Republican Club in no less obscure Wheeling, West Virginia. Joseph McCarthy flashed before his startled audience a "list" of 205 names of those in high places who were "known" to be Communists working with the United States State Department. In the days following, word of McCarthy's claims spread across the nation, but no reliable list was ever produced. Yet from this peculiar event came McCarthyism and years of internal terrorism that ruined many innocent lives. In those years, television, still new and available to few, would be enlivened by Senator McCarthy's public hearings into the role of communist sympathizers in the US Army. This was also the year of David Riesman's *Lonely Crowd* and Erik Erikson's *Childhood and Society*—both social studies of the decline of the "inner directed" character in American life.

Though some forty years later the Cold War would be declared over, American culture never recovered from the moral chaos with which that war and McCarthyism divided the American soul. Chaos, of course, is by its nature relative. One need not have believed the simple pieties of American faith in the immediate World War II years to have trusted America's spectacular and exceptional achievements. Those years were a brief moment during which it truly seemed that America was promising everyone everything they could hope for. It was the American Century—a figure of speech presidents still work, though feebly. The United States was supreme. Everyone else was weak. The world's best hope was, then, America whose social values were considered all but self-evidently true. Few realized that these values were weakly based in reality. They were due less to American virtues than to the lack of any serious rival—military, economic, or cultural. Until the election of Bill Clinton all post-War American Presidents, and most political leaders, came of age in, or were shaped by, the false glory of that period. So strong were expectations that, in retrospect, one can hardly blame them for failing to understand how devastating McCarthyism and the wider war over Communism would be to the fragile American spirit.

Sociologically, the most important consequence of the Cold War terrors was its inducement to conformity, to keeping quiet, to seeking out the officially safe line in public opinion—an inducement already offered by the requirements of success in the growing bureaucratic world of business that the early social critics attacked. It was a time of compromise for the independent spirit of the American entrepreneur, a compromise to which one sought to provide a good face. But the face work was never thereafter sufficient to sustain the illusion of the old American individualism which would never again be what it was once imagined to have been.

A second general solution to the problem of cooling the mark out consists of offering him a status which differs from the one he has lost or failed to gain but which provides at least a something or a somebody for him to become. Usually the alternative presented to the mark is a compromise of some kind, providing him with some of the trappings of his lost status as well as with some of its spirit. A lover may be asked to become a friend; a student of medicine may be asked to switch to the student of dentistry; a boxer may become a trainer; a dying person may be asked to broaden and empty his worldly loves so as to embrace the All-Father that is about to receive him. Sometimes the mark is allowed to retain his status but is required to fulfil it in a different environment: the honest policeman is transferred to a lonely beat; the too zealous priest is encouraged to enter a monastery; an unsatisfactory plan manager is shipped off to another branch. Sometimes the mark is "kicked upstairs" and given a courtesy status such as "Vice President." In the game for social roles, transfer up, down, or away may all be consolation prizes.

("On Cooling the Mark Out," 1952, p. 457)

Thereafter the American Century would offer good consolation prizes, but never the real thing as it had been dreamed for a short while after World War II. One could just as easily associate the date of McCarthy's Wheeling speech with December 1, 1955, the day Rosa Parks refused to move to the back of a bus in Montgomery, Alabama. The Civil Rights Movement, which at its beginnings seemed to offer very much more than a consolation prize, turned within a decade into the most visible, unyielding sign of moral separation in the USA. The failure of the society to give what it promised came from under the same rocks out from which Joseph McCarthy had crept. Americans, whatever the content of their dreams, would never again achieve the level of moral accord they thought they had cemented during and just after World War II.

July 24, 1959 and the Depression of Social Hope. In 1959 Erving Goffman was just beginning his first academic appointment at the University of California. A new edition of *The Presentation of Self in Everyday Life* was shipped to booksellers. Goffman was just then becoming a figure of note in American sociology. Those alive and alert that year, whatever they knew of Goffman, would surely have seen or heard about one of its most dramatic political moments: when then Vice-President Richard Nixon debated with the Soviet Premier Nikita Khrushchev in Moscow. At the end of the decade, America had suffered a number of humiliating defeats in its world struggle with Communism, among them: its failure to act against the Soviet Union's brutal suppression of the Hungarian revolution (1956); the USSR's brilliant success in the space race—Sputnik I being the first orbiting space vehicle (1957); the first major Soviet diplomatic victory in Africa with the acceptance of its offer of support for the building of Egypt's Aswan Dam project (1958); Fidel Castro's defeat of corporate America's puppet dictator of Cuba, Fulgencio Batistá, and Cuba's prompt incorporation into the economic and political sphere of the Communist world powers (1959). The decade that had begun with a Communist victory in China (1949) and the Korean War (1950–3), which had fed the fires of McCarthyism, ended in a worsening of America's world position in the struggle against the "evil empire."

Thus, in 1959 Richard Nixon, already anticipating his run for the presidency in 1960, traveled to Moscow as part of the American delegation to a world trade exposition. The US exhibit was a model kitchen in which were displayed the consumer products that Americans of even modest means could afford for the first time—dishwashers, electric mixers, and all the rest. In the demonstration kitchen, Nixon confronted Khrushchev with a challenge that the USA and the USSR ought to compete not over military matters but in the production of consumer goods of benefit to ordinary people. What seemed a bold move was in fact weak. True, the Soviet production system was so over-burdened with technological and armament expenditures that it was unable to satisfy consumer needs and demands for just such products. But, what was inconceivable then was that the American economy would eventually face limits of its own. Though always the leader in the manufacture and purchase of consumer products, the appearance of widespread affluence in the United States in the 1950s only masked the false prospects of continuous economic growth and equality. Within five years, in 1964, President Lyndon Johnson would act in the same American self-confidence that had moved Nixon's challenge by proposing, and largely enacting, the most massive program of social welfare spending in American history. The War on Poverty, however, was soon undermined by the war in Vietnam, again a venture entered into in the belief that America's economic prowess was such that it could easily afford both guns and butter. The miscalculations that brought Johnson down in 1968 were not, as it may have seemed, a mere mistake in judgment that any other American leader is likely to have avoided—not Nixon had he beaten Kennedy in 1964, not Kennedy had he lived. Much later, in the 1980s, President Ronald Reagan embarked on a similar sort of welfare program for the already wealthy and soon to be well-off, and hatched it with huge defensive expenditures as well. Though the principles and concerns were different, Reaganomics had the same effects as all the other American economic politics since the 1950s: declining economic growth, falling personal income for the masses (but rising differentially for a smaller and smaller privileged class), disappearing jobs, collapsing social welfare programs for the poor (but not for corporations and the well-off), stagnating educational attainment, destroying social hope.

The first steps in the sad story of disillusionment so well known today were taken after the 1950s. They too were founded on the false security of that earlier decade. The stupid confidences of Nixon, like those of Johnson and Reagan, all derived from an overextended faith in the social perfection of the American economic and social system. It is not that the system was (or is) bad, but that it simply never was what, in the 1950s, so many thought it was. Poverty in America was discovered in the first years of the 1960s by the Kennedy–Johnson administrations. Then, in discovering poverty, it was believed that it could be overcome. Today, a good forty years after, poverty, hunger, homelessness, disease are, in relative terms, as bad as ever and much worse than in the days of Nixon's bold gambit in Moscow.

Nixon, always a ready object for political contempt, should not be judged too sternly on this matter. His naive faith in his system was little different from that of most Americans, including even the most marginal. Many American blacks, for example, began then to feel that their day too had come. It was not a bad dream, and there were surely good reasons to believe in it, but from an economic point of view it was, simply, false. It demanded too much of the already limited natural and human resources of even the American system.

Growth of the sort required to produce even a semblance of the social equality then thought possible would have had to be sustained through the rest of the century. Vietnam, and the oil crises of the early 1970s, hurt. But, again, they were not mistakes, just the first signs of the economic and political facts of life. America, no more than any other truly stratified and diversified society, was unable to keep the promises it made to itself. It would be extreme to say that all this was illusion, but much of it, including the core assumptions, was.

A good deal of social thinking shared the optimism of the times—most notable the sociology of Talcott Parsons and closely allied public intellectuals like Seymour Martin Lipset and Daniel Bell who were then announcing the end of ideology. But, at the same time, in the years on either side of

Nixon's kitchen debate, the social criticism that had begun with Riesman, Erikson, Mills and others in the early 1950s was now intensified and increasingly projected into mass-market journalism. Michael Harrington's *The Other America* (1962), Rachel Carson's *Silent Spring* (1962), Betty Friedan's *The Feminine Mystique* (1963), Ralph Nader's *Unsafe At Any Speed* (1965) were among the most enduring classics of the mass-market social criticism. Each of these books, and hundreds of others, had one common theme: things were not as good as they seemed. Each was a probe behind the line of illusion that was already weakened by the confusing signs that interposed themselves throughout the 1950s.

Taken as a whole, the then new social criticisms invited a conclusion that went even beyond the fear that America had lost its moral way. Now, more pungently, one could smell the odor of something in the American system that was, if not rotten, as least over-ripe. Then one got the first undeniable whiffs of the notion that the system was at best unable to provide for all, at worst that it never was intended to do so. Then, the illusions of social life became a first topic of consideration. The serious truth behind the fun of the fifties was there to be told.

> *In daily life, games are seen as part of recreation and "in principles devoid of important repercussions upon the solidity and continuity of collective and institutional life." Games can be fun to play, and fun alone is the approved reason for playing them. The individual, in contrast to his treatment of "serious" activity, claims a right to complain about a game that does not pay its way in immediate pleasure and, whether the game is pleasurable or not, to plead a slight excuse, such as an indisposition of mood, for not participating. Of course, those who are tactful, ambitious, or lonely participate in recreation that is not fun for them, but their later private remarks testify that it should have been. Similarly, children, mental patients, and prisoners may not have an effective option when officials declare game-time, but it is precisely in being thus constrained that these unfortunates seem something less than persons.*
>
> *("Fun in Games" in Encounters, 1961, p. 17)*[23]

Already, in the mid 1950s, what we now know for certain was becoming apparent: even the most frivolous of the pleasures broadcast throughout the land were the false face of another story altogether, of other truths that could no longer be contained.

September 9th, 1956 and the Electronic Revolution. Early September 1956 found Goffman beginning the last year of his assignment at the Laboratory of Socio-developmental Studies of the National Institute of Mental Health, during which he prepared the important early essays on face work, deference and demeanor, and embarrassment. His first full-time position as a professor of sociology was still a year away. On the evening of September 9th, Elvis Presley made his first and famously truncated appearance on CBS television's *The Ed Sullivan Show*. Elvis was already a recording star of such magnitude that a rival network, NBC, canceled its regularly scheduled program (it showed a movie instead rather than compete in the time slot against Elvis). Sullivan himself was sick in bed that night but his show swept the ratings. More than 80 percent of all television viewers watched and heard Elvis sing his opening number, "Love Me Tender." Though he was, at first, shy and subdued, the studio audience went crazy. But Elvis began to rock in his second number (a rendition of Little Richard's "Ready Teddy"). The television cameras panned in such a way as to screen Elvis's sexy pelvis from those watching at home. The censoring of his sex had the predictable effect of making just that the next day's talk of the town—and of the nation.[24]

Though they occurred earlier in the fifties, the US Senate's televised Army–McCarthy Hearings had been a television sensation, breaking the tired routines of early television programming only to bring ordinary Americans into the spectacle of a foolish attempt to purify political morality. The hearings were variations on a traditional theme of American righteousness, even if the observer could well see (as many did) what was wrong. The Elvis appearance, by contrast, symbolized something else, something deeper, more enduring, and troubling. One could already see the tremendous power of this new medium: the power to enter the homes of millions and there, amid the untidied disarray of daily life, to present, with little cost and trouble, realities to which a good bit of the culture was devoted to denying. In the case of Elvis, the reality was the ubiquity of a near-universal sexual thrall, in contrast to the official puritanism. What the Kinseys had documented about sex in America in their academic books in 1948 and 1953 was flashed in the instant of television's attempt to censor. Sex of all kinds was everywhere—in all homes, among all people, even the kids. Today this is not news. It was not really news in the 1950s, but it was shocking, or at least bracing, that it could become such readily available news. As things turned out, sex was hardly the worst of it.

As television rapidly developed into the popular medium of choice that it is today, more of America and the world that had been held in illusion became perfectly, inexorably visible. One need only mention the most unforgettable images: President Kennedy's televisual charm on his election; his and the other assassinations; police dogs and water hoses set upon civil rights protesters in the South; and, surely most significantly, Walter Cronkite's visit to Vietnam early in 1968, when he declared the war unwinnable. Once this most respected of television's journalists declared his opinion, the war was in fact unwinnable, at least from the point of view of public opinion. Within just more than a decade, from the mid 1950s to the late 1960s, television had come to be the sole source of information for most Americans. It was, of course, and is, a source that shows no mercy, not even in what it hides.

Strictly speaking the age of the visual media, which began in the mid 1950s, is an age in which reality literally came to be a mediated reality. To borrow the old sociological line, what people came to define as real was real in fact to the extent that it was itself defined by the mystery of millions of tiny, invisible dots projected somehow through space into the homes of all alike. Everyone in America, regardless of social rank, saw the same invisible pelvis in 1956, just as after 1968 the illusive victory and inevitable defeat in Vietnam came similarly, if more gradually, into view.

From 1956, it would be still another eight years before the publication of Marshall McLuhan's sensational (and still respected) *Understanding Media*, the first important social analysis of television as a unique medium of communication and social relations. Except for a few tempting pages near the end of *Frame Analysis* (1974) and suggestions here and there in *Gender Advertisements* (1976), Goffman himself never examined the mediating effects of television as distinct from the other dramatic forms that were so crucial to his writing—theater, radio, the newspaper, and the novel. Just the same, it would be difficult to account for the most unusual features of his sociology without reference to the growing influence of visual media on American society. Before McLuhan's important essay in 1964, few understood the special power of television. Indeed, television programming itself was so technically immature by today's standards that it was easy to misperceive television as a kind of radio with pictures, as indeed early news broadcasting and sitcoms largely were. But the distinctive nature of television had less to do with what appeared on the screen than with how the images on those screens intruded upon, and changed, the habits of daily life, the structure of family relations, and the very nature of entertainment and information.

Goffman was among those who understood, at some basic level, that social relations were already by then organized more around the appearance than the content of things. The common theme of the most famous social criticisms of the 1950s was the concern that conformism (or, as David Riesman put it, "other-directedness") in ordinary life was at odds with traditional American and Western patterns of personal self-understanding and social interaction. Vance Packard's books, *The Hidden Persuaders* and *Status Seekers*, developed related ideas crudely. In the latter, for example, Packard argued that Americans were more preoccupied with the superficial symbols expressing their newly won status than with the inner values of personal life. Goffman's *The Presentation of Self in Everyday Life* (first published in Scotland in 1956) is nothing if it was not concerned with the role of expressive strategies in the management of a socially creditable impression.

Every person lives in a world of social encounters, involving him either in face-to-face or mediated contact with other participants. In each of these contacts, he tends to act out what is sometimes called a line—that is, a pattern of verbal and nonverbal acts by which he expresses his view of the situation and through this his evaluation of the participants, especially himself. Regardless of whether a person intends to take a line, he will find that he has done so in effect. The other participants will assume that he has more or less willfully taken a stand, so that if he is to deal with their response to him he must take into consideration the impression they have possibly formed of him. . . . The term face *may be defined as the positive social value a person effectively claims for himself by the line others assume he has taken during a particular contact. Face is an image of self delineated in terms of approved social attributes—albeit an image that others may share, as when a person makes a good showing for his profession or religion by making a good showing of himself.*

("On Face Work," 1955; reprinted in Interaction Ritual, 1967, p. 5)

Today many live in virtual reality and travel on an information super-highway. Even if one only vaguely understands to what state of informational affairs these terms refer, hardly anyone would dare doubt that, whatever they are, they refer to a state in which information technologies have somehow moved through a visual warp and turned back in time and space upon what we once optimistically considered "real" life.

It is possible to consider Goffman a televisual genius before the fact, and it is certain that he was one of the first social critics fully to appreciate the tenuous grip that our most common social interactions have on what we still prefer to call reality. Goffman was truly a man of his day in that his social ideas covered, if at a certain remove, the basic facts of late modern times: that both moral consensus and social hope are imaginary constructs; and that the essence of social reality has little to do with essences, least of all with essential values. Though he did not judge these conditions one way or another, he was possibly the first to tell us what we hated to hear. Appearances count for more than do truth, beauty, freedom, the good self, and all the other foundational virtues of modern life. More, I think, than anyone in his day (and certainly more than any sociologist) Goffman was a thinking product of those basic facts of our times which had their beginnings in his. This is why he should be read today.

★

Still, one might ask, why was it necessary for this televisual genius Goffman to participate in the notorious linguistic turn? Was not a book such as *Frame*

Analysis (1974) one of those rare instances when a truly independent thinker fell incautiously into the faddish structuralist language mania then emerging in all quarters of social theory? First, inasmuch as Goffman was, in the 1950s, an undercover social critic of postwar society, the turn to a more intentional investigation of language was appropriate, if not completely necessary. And, secondly, even granting (as I would) that *Frame Analysis* was his only mostly failed work, the turn to language was anything but fad-following—neither for Goffman, nor the many others. The linguistic turn (so poorly named!) is not about language so such as much as it is that to which social theory and politics must turn as a consequence of the changes that devolved from the 1950s. This can be seen in the extent to which language and culture have become today a central consideration, the importance of which far exceed the precious habits of academic discourse.

In a 1995 speech to American war veterans, Senator Robert Dole of Kansas, who became the choice of conservatives in the 1996 American presidential campaign, bitterly denounced "intellectual elites" who advocate multiculturalism, including multilingual education: "We need the glue of language to help hold us together. We must stop the practice of multilingual education as a means of instilling ethnic pride or as a therapy for low self-esteem or out of elitist guilt over a culture built on the traditions of the West."[25] Behind the chanting of a right-wing creed is Dole's telling confession of the reality of things American: "We need the glue of language to help hold us together." His admission of the tenuousness of the social whole expresses the fear he would wish away. Senator Dole, like most politicians, was doing little more than mouthing a widespread cultural anxiety, one so terrifying that it excites left and right to similar extremes.[26]

Political differences aside, the facts of our time come down to a bitter, urgent debate over the nature of social reality, behind which one finds the troubling question of language. In the USA there are those who say that America is still what it always was; and those whom conservatives attack who say that the reality of differences today are just those that were suppressed by the old America. Or, to rephrase with reference to language, there are those who insist, as they always have done, that the only basis for social unity is that all speak the same language; and those who believe that the integrity of social groups can only be sustained by giving voice to all its members. It is not by accident that many who believe the former, in addition to favoring a one-language policy, are also inclined to contradict their own patriotic rhetorics by undervaluing the importance of individual rights and free speech. They tend to favor limits on women's rights to abortion, on the writ of habeas corpus, on the rights of media people and teachers to speak their minds however offensively. Conversely, those who believe the social whole lives off the differences of its parts are more likely (in spite of their reputed liberal, closet socialist habits of mind) to believe in due process, free speech, and multicultural expression. It is not necessary at the moment to judge between the two perspectives (and their many subvariations) to see that language and speech are absolutely central to the arguments over the truth of social reality.

It can be said simply that the linguistic turn in social theory was not the cause but the result of the social changes that emerged as early as the 1950s. It was then, as I have suggested, that the old verities of a single, real and true society began to come apart. A scarce half-century later we see very well the results of the divisions that were then only fissures on the margins of a delicate crystal which, now, having been turned to a different light refracts a thousand points of social color. The alabaster cities gleam differently now. This is more strikingly true in the USA, the most multicultural of the major world societies, but it is just as true, in relative terms, in all the world societies influenced by European culture.

Language is what societies are left with when their members can no longer agree on the nature of social reality. When, by contrast, an official theory of social reality imposes itself over large sectors of a population, then the few voices of dissent will be taken with less seriousness and the majority will be content to trust whatever is considered real. These are the stable times when sciences, economies, and political cultures consolidate and refine advances. These are the times when truths are certain, when all men consider themselves equal, and when the men who count can be counted upon to speak the same language. When such times are shaken, as today they are in the USA and even more terrifyingly in Russia and many of its neighbor states, language is what matters most. In short, when there is little accord as to the society's essential verities, then public debate is forced back into controversies over the rules of the language games in which unbridgeable differences are played out. As a result, in the former Soviet Union the Russian language is losing its universal hold, just when the USA is becoming a bilingual society in a sea of multilingual enclaves.[27]

This is why there was a linguistic turn beginning in the late 1950s and early 1960s and why, necessarily, Goffman was a part of it. It was not, one presumes, that Goffman was first of all interested in speech and language (though these interests are evident in the earliest writings), but that he was above all else interested in social reality. It was this prior interest that led him, later in his career, to the more formal study of talk, semiotics, and conversation that was hidden but evident in *Relations in Public* (1971), overt but ill-formed in *Frame Analysis* (1974) and *Gender Advertisements* (1976), explicit and well organized in *Forms of Talk* (1981), and primary and formal in "Felicity's Condition" (1983). But a reader of Goffman must never forget that his interest in language and expressive strategies was always there from the beginning *because* the basic question of his life's work was, as he repeatedly said: How does social reality sustain itself?

A character staged in a theater is not in some ways real, nor does it have the same kind of real consequences as does the thoroughly contrived character performed by a confidence man; but the successful *staging of either of these types of false figures involves use of* real *techniques—the same techniques by which everyday persons sustain their real social situations. Those who conduct face to face interaction on a theater's stage must meet the key require-ment of real situations: they must expressively sustain a definition of the situation: but this they do in circumstances that have facilitated their devel-oping an apt terminology for the interactional tasks that all of us share.*

(*The Presentation of Self, 1959, pp. 254–5)*

I close with a call to arms. To utter something and to not disconfirm that we are sane requires that our saying be heard to draw appropriately on one array of presuppositions—that sustained by our hearers—and avoid being heard to make others—those which are not, although they may be by persons not present. Responding to another's words, we must find a phrasing that answers not merely to the other's words but to the other's mind—so the other can draw both from the local scene and from the distal, wider worlds of her or his experience.

(*"Felicity's Condition," 1983, p. 48)*

These lines from Goffman's first book and his last essay may reverse the emphasis on language in the maintenance of social reality, but both were, like all of his writings, preoccupied with a sociology of real social things.

He may not have been as much a Durkheimian as Randall Collins believes, but he did share, as he admits,[28] an early enthusiasm for Durkheim. This was, I believe, nothing more than his abiding concern for the work of good sociology. How indeed do social facts arise and sustain themselves? In the face of the social realities that were slowly shifting just below the surface of appearances in the 1950s, Goffman's prescient attentions to these matters, though focused at the exceedingly microscopic, were, as things turned out, very much more enduring than the attentions of Parsons and his followers (as well as those of the soon to emerge cohort of Marxian sociol-ogists) to the most macroscopic. Who today would bet that the best sociology of reality is one that attends primarily to the functional prerequi-sites of social action (as did Parsons) or to the exhaustive force of class conflict (as did that day's more vulgar Marxists)? Action and class conflict certainly are still important features of social life in the industrial nations, but increasingly their importance must be measured against a prior fact that, in those societies, action is felt to be stymied precisely by the deadlines of tired ways of functioning while the class wars are tangled inextricably in overlaying and undermining struggles arising from ethnic, racial, and sexual differences. It is exactly this once unimaginable coming together of the bureaucratic function of which Weber first warned and a thoroughly countervailing, thus shocking, breaking out of world-encompassing velvet revolutions—revolutions of such vitality that even political conservatives may long for the good old days when the only overt conflict was that between the classes. Those in power today know very well how to break unions and marginalize the poor. What leaves them wondering is how to deal with all the many varieties of protest by gays, blacks, and feminists.

Goffman, to be sure, has nothing explicit to say to us about these details of the present situation, though a close reading of him will likely reveal that even in these respects he was ahead of his contemporaries.[29] Where, already in the 1950s, he was miles ahead of everyone else was in his fine understanding that reality was not just (as we say all too casually today) "constructed" but constructed by definite, precise, and surprisingly universal social mechanisms—and constructed in ways that can be appreciated *only* on condition of abandonment of the dogmatic insistence that the reality of social things is a given, as distinct from being part of the fateful action of daily life. Once that dogma is stared down, straight and honestly, then a sociology can begin imaginatively to reconstruct the rules by which people, in their many differences, and by means of their expressive capacities, make social arrangements work on many occasions, if only for a while.

Earlier I referred to Goffman as a televisual genius before the fact, by which I meant that his sociology was, in a certain sense, televisual in spite of the fact that he himself had no explicit social theory of the new medium that came into its own in his lifetime.[30] How can this be? First off, consider the unusual style of writing. What Goffman was doing in writing as he did was to create an imaginative form in its own right. He was not attempting, as were many social scientists and other purveyors of the truth of social things, to *represent* social reality in what he wrote. He was not so much speaking *for* the reality to which he referred, as speaking *in* it at a remove. Goffman never sought to situate himself as the teller of the world's truths which is perfectly obvious from the fact that his was a sociology based on the premise that world reality was fragile, changing, uncertain, vulnerable, and always, always mediated. This was the quality of his writing that caught the attention of literary people. Goffman's sociology was a kind of fiction, but a televisual fiction as much as a literary one. As controversial as the thought may be, the still tougher question is: Which kind?

To say that Goffman's sociological form was akin to fiction is not to say that he was uninterested in the nature of social reality. Hardly this. Rather, the idea is that his view of social reality was such that he could write about it in no other way but one that approaches fiction. This is a more simple proposition than at first it must seem. There are but two choices in the matter. Those who think of the social world as *ultimately* (if not immediately) coherent, stable, and waiting to be discovered are relatively free to think of their research and writing as the vehicle by which world reality is conveyed. Alternately, those who think of the social world as a more tricky, sometimes thing are less free to indulge in realism. It is all too easy to forget that "reality" is little more than a proposition about the nature of things. One can live happily without ever questioning the proposition, but those who make it their business to ask such questions must eventually ask: Which reality?—the confident kind?—or the tricky one? Both are attitudes worthy of respect. Goffman was among those who chose the latter, as did Sigmund Freud, Max Weber in his more gloomy moments, Marcel Proust, and Oprah Winfrey. Others, including Emile Durkheim, Karl Marx, Charles Dickens, and Kevin Costner, chose the former, more confident one. Either can be entertaining and informative. It is a choice, however, and a choice that determines how a sociologist or any other person charged with similar interpretative responsibilities will write, speak, and otherwise present to others what they think is going on.

So, though Goffman believed in the tricky kind of world, he believed in reality. And, though he was a sociologist, he was a literary one for reason of what he believed about reality. But, still, the question remains: What kind of fiction is this, and in what sense is it televisual?

In arguing that everyday activity provides an original against which copies of various kinds can be struck, the assumption was that the model was something that could be actual and, when it was, would be more closely enmeshed in the ongoing world than anything modeled after it. However, in many cases, what the individual does in serious life, he does in relationship to cultural standards established for the doing and for the social role that is built up out of such doings. Some of these standards are addressed to the maximally approved, some to the maximally disapproved. The associated lore itself draws from the moral traditions of the community as found in folk tales, characters in novels, advertisements, myth, movie stars and their famous roles, the Bible, and other sources of exemplary representation. So everyday life, real enough in itself often seems to be a laminated adumbration of a pattern or model that is itself a typification of quite uncertain real status. (A famous face who models a famous-name dress provides in her movements a keying, a mock-up, of an everyday person walking about in everyday dress, something, in short, modeled after actual wearings; but obviously she is also a model for everyday appearance-while-dressed, which appearance is, as it were, always a bridesmaid but never a bride.) Life may not be an imitation of art, but ordinary conduct, in a sense, is an imitation of the properties, a gesture at the exemplary forms, and the primal realization of these ideals belongs more to make-believe than to reality.

(*Frame Analysis, 1974, p. 562*)[31]

In this passage amid his summary of *Frame Analysis* Goffman makes clear just what he thought of reality and the expressive means by which it is sustained. However much what is real may be an original, we copy as we conduct our personal affairs, and that which we copy is itself a transformation (that is, a keying), or make-believe, or simulation of the real we copy. Mothers who mother as their mothers mothered them are mothering after an imaginary recollection.[32] Mothering in this sense is make-believe in just the same way as a teenage boy wears the shoes of Michael Jordan as a way of keying up a sense of social status against the one with which he must live. And so on. There is very little that goes on in daily life that is not, in some basic sense, at least a fabrication of what we imagine we ought to be or do in such and such a situation. Fabrications and their variants are, in effect, all we have to guide us in Goffman's view. In this sense Goffman was still a Durkheimian. Societies are, fundamentally, collective representations. In no other way can they be *sui generis*. We are and do what we are and do by playing against the reality presented to us, which plays are provided from collective representations or what can be called, at some risk of misunderstanding, culture. The only other way to think about this is to assume we are provided with certain automatic faculties (let us call them, for want of a better term, *roles*) that signal how and what he ought to think and do given the reality presented. For a long while sociologists took seriously this overly realistic (and overly socialized) view of human conduct. Fewer do today because it entails the assumption that the reality of the world is neat, available, and kind—an assumption hard to sustain in the face of the evening news.

More than any of his interpreters, even more than Fredric Jameson, Patricia Clough has gotten Goffman's relation to reality right, and its effect of his writing style. "Since the 'actual' is always already framed," says Clough, "as the 'real' and in such a way that makes keying and fabrication probable, the kind of rereading suggested by Goffman's writings is a matter of grasping simulations in terms of each other, as if a typology of simulations were possible."[33] What matters in reading Goffman is most importantly, his view of reality as always mediated in this way, always displaced; from which derives his distinctive way of writing, which in turn led him to his linguistic turn. He wrote more and more reflexively about talk and language as the years went by because, as I have said, he surely understood what was going on in the world and how it demanded such a view of the nature of things.

But how does this make Goffman televisual? And why bother with the allusion? Certainly many of Goffman's most appreciative readers have been put off by the later books, especially *Frame Analysis*. Norman Denzin effectively broke with him because of the structuralism in that book[34] and others, like Fredric Jameson, who much respected its semiotic turn, were just as critical of its "structuralist ideology,"[35] as were others. It is surely true that *Frame Analysis* was one of Goffman's intellectually least successful efforts because, at the least, it was, even for him, so extraordinarily messy. But fortunately he eventually came back to his literary sensibilities in *Forms of Talk* (the book that so enchanted the literary critics) and in the last two essays, especially "Felicity's Condition."

Here, in "Felicity's Condition," Goffman develops his view of social reality and its necessary relation to talk. The essay offers itself as a highly technical (which it is) disquisition on a most important issue in the sociolinguistics of conversation. Drawing upon, but moving beyond, speech act theory, Goffman advances the argument that was already well-formulated in *Forms of Talk*. Conversation works not through the utterances presented in turns of talk so much as through the ability of speakers to tolerate presuppositions. Talk is not clear. Or, we might say, ordinary language in spoken conversation does not tell the truth of the speakers as such (to say nothing of the truth of the world). Conversation involves an endless number of pauses, questions, breaks, uncertain points. And even when its language is clear, utterances are never complete in themselves. Talk relies heavily on presuppositions, as in one of Goffman's examples: "What did you think of the movie last night?" which presumes that the movie scheduled actually ran, that Mary actually attended it, that John is in a state of relation to Mary that permits the asking of the question, and much more. None of this is conveyed by the words themselves. Yet, the words depend on it all and, amazingly, conversation works most of the time. It does because, as Goffman says in the lines at the end of the essay: "Whatever else, our activity must be addressed to the other's mind, that is, to the other's capacity to read our words and actions for evidence of our feelings, thoughts, and intent. This confines what we say and do, but it also allows us to bring to bear all the world to which the other can catch allusions."[36] In other words, even in conversation we are forced beyond that which appears to be the primary surface of meaning, the utterances themselves. We must address not an other's words, but their mind, their capacity to understand what is going on. But this is not a mind-to-mind interaction, rather it is one mediated, as he says, by a shared capacity to "bear all the world to which the other can catch allusions."

Thus, a conversation builds up a fund of matters that can be referred to succinctly, providing one of the reasons why we are inclined to "fill in" a latecomer. The problem, then, is that one passages by degree from what can be taken to be in immediate consciousness to what can be more or less readily

recalled thereto, the given *changing gradually to the* recallable.... *Further,
when one turns from brief interchanges to, say, longish narratives, the locater
format becomes somewhat complicated. Instead of laying the groundwork
with one utterance ("Ya remember Harry?"), the narrator may feel that a
whole informational prologue must be provided before hearers will be able to
properly follow along with the unfolding drama and properly frame described
events. .... And, of course, within the narrative frame, characters in the
replayed events will provide us through their reported utterances with
embedded examples of the new and the given, which in fact cannot quite
function that way for us listeners; for we, in information state terms, are situated at a higher level. We are situated as listeners to the teller's story, not as
listeners to the utterances of characters in the teller's story.*

("Felicity's Condition," 1983, p. 14)

Just as life is a copy of an original we imagine, so talk proceeds by the ability
of those who speak to each other to imagine the worlds in the other's minds
and to compose utterances or narratives that speak or attend, not to what is
said about what was said, but to what our conversational partner is meaning
to say. Talk, thus, is like reality. Both require attention less to what is, or is
said, than to the imaginary worlds: that is, to the worlds we copy in our
attempts to sustain reality, to the worlds into which we are invited when
others speak to us as though we were thoroughly sane. This is the felicitous
condition upon which, Goffman proposes, talk and social reality depend.

★

If you still wonder why read Goffman today, then ask yourself how you, and
others you know, work in the world as it is. If all your relations are primary,
all your data are clear and clean, all your news thoroughly trustworthy just
as it is told you, then Goffman is not for you. If, contrariwise, there is a telephone ringing, a stereo playing, or television running itself off somewhere in
your neighborhood, perhaps in your place; and, if you have been brought
up out of the place of your reading to attend to some interruption that
required attention to another's world, so different at the moment from
that to which you are attending; and, if you believe the world, in the larger
sense of the word, is today one in which the moral discord, social depression, and mediated intrusions are the working stuff of lively social
participation, then Goffman is for you.

Goffman may not be for everyone, but his incongruous relation to his
times nearly a half-century ago explain why so many of his writings are
congruent with the reality most of us face today, whether we like it or not.

Notes

1   Anthony Giddens, "Goffman As a Systematic Social Theorist," in Paul Drew and Anthony Wooton, eds., *Erving Goffman* (Polity Press, 1988), chapter 9.

2   William Gamson, "Goffman's Legacy to Political Sociology," *Theory and Society*, 14 (1985): pp. 605–22.

3   Pierre Bourdieu, "Erving Goffman, Discoverer of the Infinitely Small," *Theory, Culture and Society*, 2 (1983): pp. 112–13.

4   Randall Collins, "The Passing of Intellectual Generations: Reflections on the Death of Erving Goffman," *Sociological Theory*, 4:1 (1986): p. 109.

5   Norman Denzin and Charles Keller, "Frame Analysis Reconsidered," *Contemporary Sociology*, 10:1 (1981): pp. 52–60.

6   Gary Marx, "Role Models and Role Distance," *Theory and Society*, 13 (1984): pp. 649–61.

7   See Alasdair Macintyre, "The Self as Work of Art," *New Statesman* (28 March 1969), p. 447, for "brilliant"; and idem, *After Virtue* (University of Notre Dame Press, 1981), pp. 31–2 for the "cultural loss" idea. Macintyre, in effect, reads Goffman as giving up on the self and thus giving up on this staple of modernity. On this see Karl Scheibe, *Self Studies* (Praeger, 1995), p. 51.

8   Alan Bennett, "Cold Sweat," *London Review of Books* (15 October–4 November 1981), p. 12; reprinted in idem, *Writing Home* (Faber and Faber, 1994), pp. 302–3.

9   "Cold Sweat," ibid.; *Writing Home*, p. 303.

10   "Cold Sweat," p. 13; *Writing Home*, p. 311.

11   On "but, of course," and similar locutions, see Christopher Ricks, "Phew! Oops! Oof!" in *The New York Review of Books* (July 16, 1981), p. 42. I confess to my own use of such expressions after Goffman or, better put, an inability to resist using them when writing of him.

12   Christopher Ricks, "Phew! Oops! Oof!" p. 42.

13   Karl Scheibe, *Self Studies* (Praeger, 1995), p. 50.

14   Dell Hymes, "On Erving Goffman," *Theory and Society*, 13 (1984): p. 630.

15   Clifford Geertz, *Local Knowledge* (Basic Books, 1983), p. 34 I owe this point to Tom Burns, *Erving Goffman* (Routledge, 1992), p. 3.

16   Charles Lemert, *Sociology After the Crisis* (Harper Collins, 1995).

17   Jacques Derrida (trans. Gayatri Chakravorty Spivak), *Of Grammatology* (Johns Hopkins University Press, 1974), p. 158.

18   For a discussion see Patricia Clough, *End(s) of Ethnography* (Sage, 1992), chapter 6.

19   For a discussion see William Gamson, "Goffman's Legacy to Political Sociology," *Theory and Society*, 14 (1985), especially p. 606.

20   For "empiricist," see "A Reply to Denzin and Keller," *Contemporary Sociology*, 10:1 (1981): p. 62, where Goffman remarks that the structuralism of Claude Lévi-Strauss runs contrary to "the crude empiricism in which I was raised." For "social psychologist," see Jef Verhoeven, "An Interview With Erving Goffman, 1980," *Research on Language and Social Interaction*, 26:3 (1993): p. 322, where Goffman says "what I am doing is structural Social Psychology."

21   Fredric Jameson, "On Goffman's Frame Analysis," *Theory and Society*, 13 (1976): p. 122.

22   Alvin Gouldner, *Coming Crisis of Western Sociology* (Basic Books, 1970), pp. 378–90.

23   Goffman's long quotation is from Roger Callois, "Unity of Play: Diversity of Games," *Diogenes*, No. 19 (1957), p. 99.

24   On Elvis see Peter Guralnick, *Last Train to Memphis: The Rise of Elvis Presley* (Little, Brown and Company, 1994), pp. 337–8.

25   See *The New York Times* (September 5, 1995), especially p. A15.

26 For a particularly disheartening instance of the left anxiety with the new cultural theories, see Todd Gitlin, *The Twilight of Common Dreams: Why America is Wracked by Culture Wars* (Henry Holt, 1995).

27 See Ryszard Kapuscinski, *Imperium* (Vintage Books, 1994).

28 "An Interview with Erving Goffman, 1980," pp. 325–8.

29 One example is that by the late 1950s Goffman had already carefully read Simone de Beauvoir's feminist classic, *The Second Sex* (first published 1949, published in the USA 1953), one of the most often cited works in *The Presentation of Self*, and a work the sociological establishment ignored (and ignores) altogether.

30 One example of just how puny his *explicit* theory of television was is the meager notice he gives it in *Frame Analysis*, p. 550.

31 In the use of the phrase "realm status" Goffman cites Alfred Schutz, "Symbol, Reality and Society," *Collected Papers*, vol. 1 (Martinus Nijhoff, 1962), p. 328.

32 As Nancy Chodorow explained not long after *Frame Analysis*, in *Reproduction of Mothering* (University of California Press, 1978).

33 Patricia Ticineto Clough, *The End(s) of Ethnography* (Sage, 1992), pp. 108–9.

34 See Norman Denzin and Charles Keller, "Frame Analysis Reconsidered," *Contemporary Sociology*, 10:1 (1981): pp. 52–60.

35 "On Goffman's *Frame Analysis*," *Theory and Society*, 13 (1976): p. 130.

36 "Felicity's Condition," p. 511.

Goffman's Social Theory
by Ann Branaman

Erving Goffman is the quintessential sociologist of everyday social life. The self, social interaction, social order, deviance, social inequality, calculation, morality—all are matters taken up in Goffman's writings. Goffman's major contribution is to portray the interdependence of these phenomena by painting them into a complex portrait.

The writings of Erving Goffman include eight books, three collections of essays, and at least twenty-eight essays, published in the period from 1951 to 1983. Goffman has been and continues to be widely read. However, he is typically read and appropriated in a piecemeal fashion, as can be seen by a review of entries in the social science citation index and the secondary literature on Goffman. Because there is no comprehensive collection of Goffman's writings, students typically first learn about him by reading one of his books or essays. Introductory sociology or social psychology students are often assigned *The Presentation of Self in Everyday Life*, *Stigma*, or *Interaction Ritual*. Students of deviance or medical sociology might read *Stigma* or one or more of the essays collected in *Asylums*. Sociologists of gender might read *Gender Advertisements* and "The Arrangement Between the Sexes." Theory students may read *Frame Analysis* or "Felicity's Condition." Communications students sometimes read *Forms of Talk*. Most of Goffman's writings get read by somebody, though seldom are they studied as a whole. However he is read, Goffman's depiction of the details of social life in any one of his works demonstrates his penetrating style of analysis and offers an insider/outsider's angle on the depicted social realm. Yet, fragmentary reading of Goffman is inadequate to put Goffman's snapshots of social life together in such a way that the larger portrait of Goffman the social theorist can be appreciated.

In this collection, we divide Goffman's writings into four categories: (1) The Production of Self; (2) The Confined Self; (3) The Nature of Social Life; and (4) Frames and the Organization of Experience. The categories represent distinct aspects of Goffman's thought and usually pull together writings of roughly the same time period in Goffman's career. Yet, as this introduction to Goffman's ideas will indicate, the categories blend together in a way that makes it possible to identify the most consistent and illuminating social theoretical ideas.

Corresponding to each of the four categories into which we divide Goffman's work, four main ideas of sociological import can be identified, each of which will be discussed in more detail below. The first, and probably the most central, idea in Goffman's thought is that the self is a social product. The self is a social product in two senses. First, it is a product of the performances that individuals put on in social situations. There is no essence that exists inside an individual, waiting to be given expression in social situations. Rather, the sense of self arises as a result of publicly validated performances. Yet, secondly, even though individuals play an active role in fashioning these self-indicating performances, they are generally constrained to present images of themselves that can be socially supported in the context of a given status hierarchy. Thus, the self is a social product in the sense that it depends upon validation awarded and withheld in accordance with the norms of a stratified society.

The second main idea in Goffman's thought is that the degree to which the individual is able to sustain a respectable self-image in the eyes of others depends on access to structural resources and possession of traits and attributes deemed desirable by the dominant culture. *Asylums* poignantly illustrates that the capacity to sustain a dignified image of oneself depends on access to personal possessions, privacy, and autonomy. As Goffman points out in "The Territories of Self," a chapter in Goffman's book *Relations in Public* (1971), access to such resources varies inversely with social status. Not only does self depend on structural props associated with power and status, but Goffman's argument in *Stigma* is that sustaining a viable self also depends on possession of traits and attributes deemed by the dominant society to be requisite of full-fledged humanity.

The third idea that can be drawn from Goffman's work concerns his view of the nature of social life. Goffman's analysis oscillates between metaphors of drama, ritual, and game, metaphors that draw attention to both the manipulative and the moral aspects of social life. The point indicated by Goffman's oscillation, however, is that manipulation and morality are not as separable as we might like to think. Morality does not reside within us or above us but rather is manufactured through performances and interaction rituals designed to affirm human dignity. Yet, on the other side, the seemingly manipulative and self-serving focus on enhancing one's self-image in the eyes of others is the most essential way in which we commit ourselves to the moral order of society. We are attached to the moral order of society, according to Goffman, by means of attachment to face. We affirm the ritual order by taking care to maintain face—our own face and the faces of others. Thus, morality and manipulation, according to Goffman's portrayal, are matters not all that separate.

The fourth of Goffman's key theoretical ideas is that social experience is governed by "frame," or principles of organization which define the meaning and significance of social events. Framing involves bracketing an activi providing some sort of cue as to what the bracketed activity means. For instance, I can frame my words as my own or as an imitation of someone else, or I could frame a performance as the real thing or as practice. The key relevance of this idea in Goffman's social theory is that events, actions, performances, and selves do not always speak for themselves but rather depend on framing for their meaning. Although the meaning of experience relies on framing, however, individuals are not free to frame experience as they please. Goffman emphasizes that framing is constrained by social structure and social organization, explicitly stating that he considers social structure and social organization primary relative to the framing of experience in everyday social situations (*Frame Analysis*, p. 13). On the other hand, Goffman suggests that the importance of the analysis of frame is limited not only to an understanding of how social life is *experienced*. Rather, the framing of experience at the interactional level is sufficiently autonomous relative to social structure and organization that it is possible for framing to strengthen *or* loosen structural arrangements. In fact, some social arrangements are supported in large part by the framing of experience in everyday life. The social construction of gender, according to Goffman's analysis, is a case in point, as we shall see.

The Production of Self

In Goffman's work, two seemingly contradictory sets of definitions, or images, of the self appear. First, Goffman suggests, on the one hand, that the self is entirely a social product, with no underlying personal core. On the other hand, he presents a dualistic image of self when he argues that there is an unsocialized component to the self that drives the individual into and out of social intercourse and sometimes impels the individual to behave in ways out of keeping with social norms. Secondly, Goffman suggests that individuals are not entirely determined by society insofar as they are able to manipulate strategically the social situation and others' impressions of themselves, fashioning themselves in much the same way as they would a character in a theatrical production. Yet, on the other hand, Goffman emphasizes that individuals are not able to choose freely the images of self they would have others accept, but rather are constrained to define themselves in congruence with the statuses, roles, and relationships they are accorded by the social order.

The rudiments of these ideas about the nature of the self that Goffman developed early in his career are already presented in Goffman's 1952 essay "On Cooling the Mark Out." Here, he makes three main points about the nature of the self. First, the self is built out of public claims made by individuals concerning possession of values or properties. Secondly, although there is some room for individual manipulation, the extent to which a person is able to defend self-claims is dependent on the structure of social life. Most self claims, in other words, involve claims to roles, statuses, and relationships and thus require validation by social organizations and other social participants. Finally, Goffman thinks that the process of "cooling the mark out" indicates something more general about the nature of the self. "Cooling the mark out" is the process whereby the person whose self claims cannot be socially sustained is aided in coming to a comfortable resignation to a lesser self. Goffman points out that the fact that "cooling the mark out" occurs with such regularity and ease suggests that the self is not a unitary entity. A person's self is generally built out of multiple, loosely-integrated social roles. When one is destroyed, an individual in most cases finds consolation in others ("On Cooling the Mark Out", 1952, p. 461).

In the work following "On Cooling the Mark Out"—especially *The Presentation of Self in Everyday Life* and *Interaction Ritual*—these themes are further developed. The following, seemingly contradictory, sets of images of self are explored: (1) the self as socially determined and the dualistic socialized/unsocialized self; (2) the individual as a strategic manipulator of impressions and the socially constrained, script-following social actor.

Although the idea that the self is a social product persists throughout Goffman's career, dualistic images of the self are especially evident in Goffman's early work. In "On Face-work" (1955; reprinted in *Interaction Ritual* [*IR*, 1967), Goffman defines self, first, as an "image pieced together from the expressive implications of the full flow of events in an undertaking"; but self also denotes a "kind of player in a ritual game who copes honorably or dishonorably, diplomatically or undiplomatically, with the judgmental contingencies of the situation" (*IR*, p. 31). In other words, the self is the mask the individual wears in social situations, but it is also the human being behind the mask who decides which mask to wear.

In *The Presentation of Self in Everyday Life* [*PS*] (Doubleday, Anchor Books edition, 1959), Goffman implies a similar duality to the self in his distinction between the "all-too-human self" and the "socialized self" (*PS*, p. 56), or between the "self-as-performer" and the "self-as-character" (*PS*, p. 252). The all-too-human self is the human being as a psychobiological organism with impulses, moods, and variable energies (*PS*, p. 56), but also is the self which engages in the "all-too-human task of staging a performance" (*PS*, p. 252). Goffman suggests that the self-as-performer is not merely a social product. The individual as performer is the thinking, fantasizing, dreaming, desiring human being whose capacity to experience pride and shame motivates him or her not only to perform for others but also to take precautions against embarrassment. The attributes of the self-as-performer are psychobiological in nature yet "seem to arise out of intimate interaction with the contingencies of staging performances" (*PS*, pp. 253–4).

It is the self-as-performer which could properly be considered to be housed within the individual organism and not entirely determined by social contingencies. When we define our own or another person's self, however, we usually have in mind much more than these basic energies, desires, and impulses. Goffman emphasizes that the self-as-performer is not the same as the self as such, but rather is the basic motivational core which motivates us to engage in the performances with which we achieve selfhood. Thus, dualistic images of self do not contradict his idea that the self is socially constructed. As Goffman sees it, the socialized self, or the self-as-character, represents a person's unique humanity. It is the socialized self or the character performed, not the self-as-performer, which is equated with self in our society. But this part of the self, according to Goffman, is a social product. Paradoxically, it is the self performed outwardly in social life and not the inner motivational core that we think of as the *inner* self. Goffman states the case quite eloquently in a passage from *The Presentation of Self*.

A correctly staged and performed character leads the audience to impute a self to a performed character, but this imputation—this self—is a *product* of a scene that comes off, and is not a *cause* of it. The self, then, as a performed character, is not an organic thing that has a specific location, whose fundamental fate is to be born, to mature, and to die; it is a dramatic effect arising diffusely from a scene that is presented, and the characteristic issue, the crucial concern, is whether it will be credited or discredited.

(*The Presentation of Self*, 1959, pp. 252–3)

Despite Goffman's acknowledgement of the human being behind the mask, he consistently downplays its significance. In fact, Goffman suggests that the sole importance of the self-as-performer is that it propels individuals to attend the social scenes at which they become social constructs. Although many readers (probably more at the time Goffman wrote than now) would like to save a certain human dimension of the self from the grip of the social, Goffman states quite explicitly in "On Face-work" that universal human nature is nothing more than the capacity and propensity to be bound by moral rules and to become a social construct.

Universal human nature is not a very human thing. By acquiring it, the person becomes a kind of construct, built up not from inner psychic propensities but from moral rules that are impressed upon him from without. These rules, when followed, determine the evaluation he will make of himself and of his fellow-participants in the encounter, the distribution of his feelings, and the kinds of practices he will employ to maintain a specified and obligatory kind of ritual equilibrium. The general capacity to be bound by moral rules may

well belong to the individual, but the particular set of rules which transforms
him into a human being derives from requirements established in the ritual
organization of social encounters.

("On Face-work," 1955; reprinted in *Interaction Ritual*,
1967, p. 45)

Not only is there little substance to that universally human part of the self
Goffman sets apart from the social construct, but Goffman further under-
mines the significance of the duality by pointing out that the distinction
people so much want to make between the "real" and the "contrived" self
does not correspond to his own distinction between the all-too-human
self and the socialized self. Even while conceding that individuals in our
society distinguish between the real and the contrived self, Goffman's point
is to challenge such dichotomous conceptions (*PS*, p. 72). Both the real *and*
the contrived self are contingent upon performance in social situations. The
successful staging of a contrived self, Goffman points out, involves the use
of the same *real* "techniques by which everyday persons sustain their real
social situations" (*PS*, pp. 254–5). Both honest and dishonest performers
"must take care to enliven their performances with appropriate expressions,
exclude from their performances expressions that might discredit the
impression being fostered, and take care lest the audience impute unintended meanings" (*PS*, p. 66). The very structure of the self, he argues, "can
be seen in terms of how we arrange for such performances in our Anglo-
American society" (*PS*, p. 252).

In arguing that the self is a product of performances in social situations,
Goffman is not suggesting that a person is no more than any particular situationally defined role. Admitting a distinction between the person and the
situationally defined role, however, he points out that the distinction itself
is a social product. For instance, the college student who works as a janitor
during the summer does not identify and is not identified by others with the
role because of the social meaning of his student status and social class position. While several early interpreters of Goffman criticized his failure to
distinguish the person and the situationally defined role, as well as his weak
understanding of the continuity of personal biography,[1] certain comments
of Goffman's in *Frame Analysis* [*FA*] (1974) appear to answer these criticisms. First, Goffman gives his "three cheers for the self," in acknowledging
the case to be made for a continuous self. The first is his acknowledgement
of the distinction between person and role. "It is a basic assumption of any
particular role performance that the performer has a continuing biography,
a single continuing personal identity, beyond that performance, albeit one
that is compatible and consistent with the role in question" (*FA*, p. 286).
Secondly, he acknowledges the continuity of the individual's life. A person's
continuing biography insures, to an important degree, a "traceable life" (*FA*,

p. 287). The activities and events of an individual's life generally leave a permanent tracing which increase the possibility of uncovering a true record of it (*FA*, p. 288). Thirdly, Goffman points out that people are able to distance themselves from some of the activities, events, and roles in which they are involved by defining them as accidental or otherwise unrelated or insignificant to personal identity (*FA*, p. 292). With this point, Goffman makes reference to his earlier discussion of "role distance"—the process by which the individual effectively expresses separateness between himself and his putative role ("Role Distance" in *Encounters* [*E*], 1961, p. 108). Finally, Goffman acknowledges the "human being" peeking out behind all of the person's immediate roles (*FA*, pp. 293–4). He thus concludes: "So three cheers for the self." But then he adds, "Now let us reduce the clatter" (*FA*, p. 294).

He reduces the clatter by pointing out, as he had already in *The Presentation of Self* and in other works, that the difference between role and person is itself socially framed. A distinction is made between the person, individual, or player and the role, capacity, or function. The nature of the distinction, however, depends on the particular person–role formula generated by the frame which sustains it (*FA*, p. 269).

> There is a relation between person and role. But the relationship answers to the interactive system—to the frame—in which the role is performed and the self of the performer glimpsed. Self, then, is not an entity half-concealed behind events, but a changeable formula for managing oneself during them. Just as the current situation prescribes the official guise behind which we will conceal ourselves, so it provides for where and how we will show through, the culture itself prescribing what sort of entity we must believe ourselves to be in order to have something to show through in this manner.
>
> (*Frame Analysis*, 1974, pp. 573–4)

Goffman's point is not that the person is no more or less than the situationally defined role, but rather that neither is essential. Both person and role are equally dependent on social definition (*FA*, p. 270). As he argued earlier in "Role Distance," the individual's expressions of a self behind a role are as much subject to role analysis as the roles themselves (*E*, p. 152).

One of Goffman's most persistent points (made repeatedly in *The Presentation of Self*, in "Role Distance," and *Frame Analysis*) is that what a person "really is" is seldom discoverable and, in any case, is not really the issue. "What is important is the sense he provides them through his dealings with them of what sort of person he is behind the role he is in" (*FA*, p. 298). This is not, of course, to attribute sovereignty to the individual over the self-manufacturing process.

Several passages throughout Goffman's work, if taken out of context, might seem to indicate that Goffman accords individuals undue control over the images that others receive. In "Role Distance," Goffman depicts the individual as the manager of a "holding company" of multiple selves, employing techniques designed to determine how others perceive the significance and relative importance of these selves (*E*, p. 91). He points out, furthermore, that while the individual cannot completely control the information about himself that becomes available in the situation, he does "actively participate in sustaining a definition of the situation that is stable and consistent with his image of himself" (*E*, p. 104).

Though in none of Goffman's work does he outrightly suggest that individuals are masters of the process by which they attempt to persuade themselves and others to accept given self-conceptions, *The Presentation of Self in Everyday Life* does focus on the individual's active role in advancing a particular conception of self to others. Because of the very basic fact that social life must be organized largely on the basis of inference concerning facts which lie beyond the time and place of interaction (*PS*, pp. 1–3), individuals are afforded a certain amount of leeway to control how others see them (*PS*, p. 8). "Dramatic realization" is a technique individuals use to "fill in the truth" of their selves. "Dramatic realization" denotes the signs used by individuals to infuse otherwise unapparent or obscure activity with the meaning they wish to convey (*PS*, p. 30). A student nodding her head to reveal otherwise unapparent attentiveness is one example. Although there is nothing inherently deceptive about such activity, Goffman does point out that "dramatic realization" often entails a diversion from effective action (*PS*, p. 33), as when vigorous head-nodding interferes with note-taking and further attentiveness. In addition, Goffman points out that "idealization," the presentation of oneself as living up to ideal standards, actually makes the person better from the outside in. Yet, at the same time, it entails a certain amount of concealment of inconsistencies (*PS*, p. 41).

Though the individual exercises a certain amount of liberty in the management of impressions, Goffman does not accord the individual complete autonomy in deciding the images of self to be conveyed. In general, person–role formulas are socially, not individually, determined. Personal identity, furthermore, is perhaps more commonly constituted by the framing of an individual's experience by others than it is by the individual. In *Stigma* [*S*] (1963), Goffman defines personal identity in terms which require no corresponding subjective experience of the individual at all. What matters is not how the individual identifies him or herself but rather how he or she is identified by others. By "personal identity," Goffman refers to those characteristics and facts which set off the individual person in the minds of other people (*S*, p. 56). He explicitly points out, however, that he does not include in his definition of personal identity the idea that "what distinguishes an individual from all others is the core of his being" (*S*, p. 56). Goffman does set "self-identity" or "ego-identity"—the "subjective sense of his own situation and his own continuity and character" (*S*, p. 105)—apart from social and personal identity. The self-identity of individuals, however, bears a close relation to their various social experiences (*S*, p. 105). The individual, Goffman points out, "constructs an image of himself out of the same materials from which others first construct a social and personal identification, although he exercises important liberties in regard to what he fashions" (*S*, p. 106).

For all the talk of the individual's self-determining power, there is much more of the socially determined limitations on this power. The self, as Goffman defines it in *Relations in Public [RP]* (1971), is "the code that makes sense out of almost all the individual's activities and provides a basis for organizing them. This self is what can be read about the individual by interpreting the place he takes in an organization of social activity, as confirmed by expressive behavior" (*RP*, p. 366). The individual, however, is socially constrained to express through this code a "workable definition of himself"—in other words, a definition which is closely attuned to the one that others can accord him (*RP*, p. 366). In *The Presentation of Self*, Goffman emphasizes that the effectiveness of the individual's management of impressions depends on the projected agreement of others (*PS*, p. 9). The fact that the individual's impression management may rarely be contested attests not to the individual's sovereignty as much as it does to the fact that the individual is conservative in the liberties he or she takes in overreaching the bounds of the "interactional modus vivendi" (*PS*, p. 9). The mutual acceptance of "lines" is a basic structural feature of interaction which constrains the person to stick to the line initially presented ("On Face-work" in *IR*, p. 11). The individual's social "face" is "only on loan to him from society"; "approved attributes and their relation to face make of every man his own jailer; this is a fundamental social constraint even though each man may like his cell" (*IR*, p. 10).

The Confined Self

Sometimes, the cell can be quite constraining. In many of his early works and essays, Goffman defines the social construction of self without focusing on its constraining aspects. That is, he defines the dramatic techniques and social processes which produce the self and describes the nature of ritual order and the games played to maintain and manipulate it. Under ordinary (or perhaps ideal) circumstances, individuals have access to sufficient resources to produce a respectable self and stand in sync with the social order to such an extent that they honor its rules and accept their allotted places in it. In works published about the same time as *The Presentation of Self* and several of the essays in *Interaction Ritual*—namely, the essays collected in *Asylums* and the short book *Stigma*—Goffman shifts the focus of analysis from "normal" experience to examine the experience of self and social inter- action from the perspective of individuals deprived of the institutional supports and claims to normal identity taken for granted by most. In the context of an environment which imposes upon an individual a degraded status, it is easy to view the individual's attachment to self as a prison. Goffman is trying to say something about the structure of the self in general, however, and not just about the selves of individuals living under abnormal constraints.

In the mid 1950s, at the same time when Goffman was writing about the self and social interaction *in general*, he was engaged in a three-year study of the life of psychiatric inmates at St Elizabeth's Hospital in Washington, DC (*Asylums* [*A*], p, ix). Though apparently divergent in topic from the depic- tion of normal interactional rituals and impression management techniques of everyday life in his other works, his concerns are, in fact, quite congruent. As he states in the introduction to the collection *Asylums*, "A chief concern is to develop a sociological version of the structure of the self" (*A*, p, xiii).

By examining the effects of total institutions on the experience of self, "On the Characteristics of Total Institutions," an essay in *Asylums*, exposes the dependence upon social arrangements of the self-experience of individuals not so constrained. Goffman defines total institutions as social arrangements which regulate, under one roof and according to one rational plan, all spheres of individuals' lives—sleeping, eating, playing, and working (*A*, pp. 5–6). As he sees it, total institutions are "forcing houses for changing persons; each is a natural experiment on what can be done to the self" (*A*, p. 12). Individuals who enter a total institution are stripped of the supports provided by the social arrangements of their home worlds and suffer a series of mortifications of self. Analyzing these fairly standard processes by which a person's self is mortified in total institutions, Goffman says, "can help us to see the arrangements that ordinary establishments must guarantee if members are to preserve their civilian selves" (*A*, p. 14).

The processes by which an individual's self is mortified include:

(1) *Role Dispossession.* In civil life, individuals are free to schedule their lives such that they can play a sequence of roles throughout the day and the life-cycle. Life is structured such that no single role prohibits performing other roles. In the total institution, on the other hand, membership disrupts role-scheduling, since the separation of the inmate from the wider world may continue indefinitely (*A*, p. 14).

(2) *Programming and identity-trimming.* Admissions procedures (such as taking a life history, searching, bathing, and instructing as to rules) function to shape and code the individual into "an object that can be fed

into the administrative machinery of the establishment." Such programming necessarily involves exclusion of most of the individual's previous
bases of self-identification (*A*, p. 16).

(3)   *Dispossession of name, property, and "identity kit."* Upon admission
to a total institution, individuals are deprived of certain possessions in
which self feelings are invested. They typically lose their full name (*A*,
p. 18), are deprived of personal possessions (*A*, p. 19), and are denied
access to the cosmetic and clothing supplies or "identity kit" necessary
for managing personal image (*A*, p. 20). Without these resources, individuals lose the ability to present their usual image to others (*A*, pp.
21–2).

(4)   *Imposition of degrading postures, stances, and deference patterns.* The
inmate is frequently required to adopt postures and stances—such as
standing at attention or submitting to strip searches—that mortify the self
(*A*, p. 21). In addition, the necessity of begging or asking for cigarettes,
matches, water, or permission to use the telephone as well as staff expectations of verbal deference force the inmate into undignified verbal
postures (*A*, p. 22). Corresponding to the indignities the inmate must
enact are the indignities he or she must suffer from others, such as teasing,
poking at negative attributes, and name-calling (*A*, pp. 22–3). Whether
the indignities are enacted by the individual or imposed from without,
they result in individuals adopting a stance incompatible with their
conception of self (*A*, p. 23).

(5)   *Contaminative exposure.* Contaminative exposure is both physical
and interpersonal. Outside of total institutions, an individual is able to
"hold objects of self-feeling—such as body, his immediate actions, his
thoughts, and some of his possessions—clear of contact with alien and
contaminating things. But in total institutions these territories of the self
are violated; the boundary that the individual places between his being
and the environment is invaded and the embodiments of self profaned"
(*A*, p. 23). First, the individual's information preserve is violated, as
facts about the inmate's social statuses and past behaviors are collected
in a file available to staff (*A*, pp. 23–4). Further, since the total institution offers no private spaces to conceal ordinarily private activities, the
inmate is forced to expose himself in humiliating circumstances (*A*,
p. 24).

   The inmate is contaminated not only by these physical exposures but
also by forced interpersonal contact (*A*, p. 28). Forced submission to strip
searches is the most direct and obvious example. More pervasive is the
status-contamination inmates endure by being mixed with inmates of
different ages and statuses (*A*, p. 29), and the denial of the right to hold
oneself above others through a formal style of address (*A*, p. 31).

(6)   *Disruption of usual relation of individual actor and his acts.* In ordinary

life, an individual is generally able to separate self from disrespectful treatments of it by others (*A*, pp. 35–6). Through certain face-saving reactive expressions, the individual is able to establish a distance between the mortifying situation and the self (*A*, p. 36). Such expressions—sullenness, failure to express deference, subtle expressions of irony or contempt—on the part of the inmate, however, are taken to be actions revealing the self rather than actions revealing the self's separateness from the degrading circumstances. Goffman calls this a "looping effect": "an agency that creates a defensive response on the part of the inmate takes this very response as the target of its next attack. The individual finds that his protective response to an assault upon self is collapsed into the situation" (*A*, pp. 35–6).

(7)   *Restrictions on self-determination, autonomy, and freedom of action.* The net result of each of the previous defilements of the self is to disrupt the actions that in civil society serve as indications of adult self-determination, autonomy, and freedom (A, p. 43).

The completely mortified person has access to none of the resources, freedoms, and territories necessary for sustaining a viable self. The mortifications of the self that Goffman describes in *Asylums* are the inverse of the "territories of the self" that Goffman later describes in *Relations in Public* (1971). Central to maintenance of self, according to Goffman, is the preservation of "territories of the self." Territories of the self are simultaneously material and ideal, consisting of the physical spaces over which a person can command use as well as the rights to privacy and the claims on social space that a person is entitled to make. Goffman outlines eight types of territories of the self: personal space, the stall, use space, the turn, the sheath, possessional territory, information preserve, and conversation preserve (*RP*, pp. 29–40). Although most people can take for granted the capacity to make most of these claims at least some of the time, Goffman emphasizes that one's place in various stratification orders determines when, where, and to what degree one can claim the territorial preserves necessary for sustaining self. "In general, the higher the rank, the greater the size of all territories of the self and the greater the control across the boundaries" (*RP*, pp. 40–1).

The condition of the mental patient is one in which the territories of the self are most minuscule and control over them nearly nonexistent. Goffman summarizes the conditions of the mental patient and their implications for the self most poignantly in "The Moral Career of the Mental Patient," an essay in *Asylums*.

> Like the neophyte in many of these total institutions, the new inpatient finds himself cleanly stripped of many of his accustomed affirmations, satisfactions,

and defenses, and is subjected to a rather full set of mortifying experiences: restriction of free movement, communal living, diffuse authority of a whole echelon of people, and so on. Here one begins to learn about the limited extent to which a conception of oneself can be sustained when the usual setting of supports for it are suddenly removed.

(*Asylums*, 1961, p. 148)

The self-experience of the inmate illuminates the fact that the "self arises not merely out of its possessor's interactions with significant others, but also out of the arrangements that are evolved in an organization for its members" (*A*, p. 148).

People can separate themselves from some settings or distance themselves from some of their actions and roles. Other settings, such as living rooms, are viewed as extensions of the self of their owner but are under the individual's control to design for the express purpose of influencing others' impressions. There are still other settings, however, that are taken as expressions of the individual's status but over which the individual has little or no control. A work setting is one example, but a psychiatric hospital is a more extreme one since the self is more explicitly at stake.

And this is due not merely to their uniquely degraded living levels, but also to the unique way in which significance for self is made explicit to the patient, piercingly, persistently, and thoroughly. Once lodged on a given ward, the patient is firmly instructed that the restrictions and deprivations he encounters are not due to such blind forces as tradition or economy—and hence dissociable from the self—but are intentional parts of his treatment, part of his need at the time, and therefore an expression of the state that his self has fallen to.

(*Asylums*, 1961, p. 149)

The self of the mental patient is defined by these institutional conditions to such an extent that there is little room for maneuvers aimed at maintaining a viable self-image in the eyes of others. In the terms he later used in *Frame Analysis*, the mental patient is "framed." In this latter work, Goffman notes that certain kinds of power generate persistent misframing: "When the overall treatment of an individual hinges on judgments of his competence, and when his protestations regarding judgment can themselves be discounted, then misframing can be common and long-lasting" (*FA*, p. 445). The mental patient, for instance, is identified by the institution, and has little hope of combatting the framework by which his experience is interpreted.

The experience of the mental patient, however, is the extreme case of a more general experience of "normals." "The divination of moral character by adducing indicators from the past is one of the major preoccupations of everyday life. And the treacherous feature is that 'a case can be made,' and at the same time there is no foolproof way of determining whether it is made correctly" (*FA*, p. 453). Such a vulnerability of experience opens the possibility for the individual to be contained in what Goffman calls a "frame trap"—an arrangement of the world in such a way that "incorrect views, however induced, are confirmed by each bit of new evidence or each effort to correct matters, so that, indeed, the individual finds that he is trapped and nothing can get through" (*FA*, p. 480).

So, it is not that inmates are ignorant or neglectful of the techniques of self-presentation, as is sometimes attributed to them. Rather, participation in the impression-management games employed by people in ordinary life can work against, rather than in favor of, the chances of sustaining a desired conception of self-identity—as when any claim to self the mental patient makes is quickly deflated by the staff (*A*, p. 162). For an inmate or other stigmatized person, there are definite limits to the claims about oneself that will be accepted by others—no matter how strategically they are made or how authentic the claims may be.

The essays collected in *Asylums* deal with a delimited realm of existence, even as their purpose is to shed light on the social supports necessary for sustaining self in general. In a sense, it could be said the *Stigma* [S] (1963) broadens the analysis and makes a total institution out of the whole of society. Society could be considered a total institution insofar as it is the basis of a single, universal system of honor that determines the complement of attributes individuals must possess in order to be accorded full-fledged humanity. Stigma refers to an attribute that is generally considered to be deeply discrediting. A stigmatized person, at least in respect of their stigma, is often not considered to be a human being at all. Stigmatized individuals typically are denied the respect and regard from others that the uncontaminated aspects of their existence would lead them to expect (*S*, pp. 8–9). Obviously, some attributes are more stigmatizing than others, yet Goffman delineates three types of stigma in such a way that it has some relevance to the personal experience of most people.

> Three grossly different types of stigma may be mentioned. First there are the abominations of the body—the various physical deformities. Next there are blemishes of individual character perceived as weak will, domineering or unnatural passions, treacherous and rigid beliefs, and dishonesty, these being inferred from a known record of, for example, mental disorder, imprisonment, addiction, alcoholism, homosexuality, unemployment, suicidal attempts, and radical political behavior. Finally there are the tribal stigma of race, nation, and religion . . .
>
> (*Stigma*, 1963, p. 4)

"Normals" are people who do not depart negatively from the particular expectations at issue. Goffman points out, however, that few of us are normals in every respect. Most are not crippled or criminals. But not many, if even any, are entirely free from the tribal stigmas to which Goffman refers. Goffman's category of tribal stigma can be extended in such a way as to include most of us. Goffman himself makes a remark in his book *Stigma* that would support this extension.

> In an important sense there is only one complete unblushing male in America: a young, married, white, urban, northern, heterosexual Protestant father of college education, fully employed, of good complexion, weight and height, and a recent record in sports.
>
> (*Stigma*, 1963, p. 128)

The rest—women, people of color, gays and lesbians, children, and more generally most human beings—are negated by this set of standards and are thus considerably less equipped to sustain self-images accorded honor, or even humanity, by the societal system. Like normals, stigmatized individuals must engage in self-presentation, but of a different sort. Instead of trying to present themselves favorably, they are required to present themselves in such a way that indicates that they accept their inferior status and don't intend to make claims to full-fledged humanity by treading on ground reserved for normals.

Individuals may deny their failure. They may develop identity beliefs of their own, living an existence alienated from society and defining the normals as the ones who are not quite human (*S*, p. 6). Or, they might join a supportive group of fellow deviants with different standards of humanity (*S*, p. 114). Yet, Goffman suggests that the development of alternative systems of honor is rare in society, at least in the 1963 American society of which he spoke. "In America at present, however, separate systems of honor seem to be on the decline. The stigmatized individual tends to hold the same beliefs about identity that we do" (*S*, p. 7).

In the same way that the psychiatric institution disallows the patient to separate himself from mortifying treatment, society defines "good adjustment" to possession of stigmatizing attributes in such a way that challenge to the world of normals will not occur. A good adjustment involves acceptance of the standards of normals and willingness to underplay the significance of one's difference, while at the same time voluntarily staying away from situations in which normals would find it difficult to demonstrate acceptance (*S*, p. 121). The good-adjustment line garners a "phantom acceptance" for the stigmatized (*S*, p. 122). But, more importantly, it protects the world of normals from challenge.

It means that the unfairness and pain of having to carry a stigma will never be presented to them; it means that normals will not have to admit to themselves how limited their tactfulness and tolerance is; and it means that normals can remain relatively uncontaminated by intimate contact with the stigmatized, relatively unthreatened in their identity beliefs.

(Stigma, 1963, p. 121)

Asylums and *Stigma* may be read as an analysis of the hopeless plight of inmates, the stigmatized, and persons otherwise suffering abnormal constraints and deprived of basic social resources. Yet, even as Goffman's major purpose in *Asylums* and *Stigma* is to demonstrate the self's entanglement with institutionally based supports and constraints, at the same time he suggests that certain resistant stances are available to even the most marginalized members of society. As Goffman puts it in "The Underlife of a Public Institution," another essay in *Asylums*, a certain recalcitrance to complete social determination is an essential constituent of the self (*A*, p. 319). Here, he defines self as a "stance-taking entity, a something that takes up a position somewhere between identification with an organization and opposition to it" (*A*, pp. 319–20). Elsewhere, furthermore, Goffman has made reference to the "selfhood [which] resides in the cracks of the solid buildings of the world" (*A*, p. 320) and the "naked spasms of the self at the end of the world" ("Where the Action Is" in *Interaction Ritual*, 1967, pp. 267–70).

The theme of "The Underlife of a Public Institution" is precisely these opposing stances, cracks in institutional arrangements, and resistant elements of the self. He begins the essay by stating that the other side of the commitment and attachment entailed by involvement in a social entity concerns the limits to the claims on the self that may be made by a social entity (*A*, p. 174). With regard to the claims of any social entity, an individual may adopt one of the following extreme stances:

He can openly default his obligations, separate himself from what he has been tied to, and brazen out the redefining looks that people give him. He can reject the bond's implication for his conception of himself but prevent this alienation from being apparent in any of his actions. He can privately embrace the self-implications of his involvement, being to himself what the others who are involved feel he ought to be.

(Asylums, 1961, p. 175)

Individuals rarely, however, adopt one of these extreme positions. Usually, individuals adopt a middle position. People avoid complete self-identification with their affiliation, allow some disaffection to be seen, while at the same time fulfilling major obligations (*A*, p. 174). It is through this dialectic of identification and distancing that the identity of a participant in a social organization is defined (*A*, p. 180). Individuals adopt what Goffman calls a "primary adjustment" to an organization when they identify with and cooperate with the goals of a social organization; "he becomes the 'normal', 'programmed', or built-in member" (*A*, p. 189). "Secondary adjustments," on the other hand, "represent ways in which the individual stands apart from the role and the self that were taken for granted for him by the institution" (*A*, p. 189). Although they represent the individual's preservation of a self independent of any particular social institution, secondary adjustments typically "arise in connection with the individual's bondage to other types of social entity" (*A*, p. 197). Goffman refers to the distancing practices sustained in connection with a group of others as "the underlife of an institution" (*A*, p. 199). In the context of the mental hospital, the underlife of the institution consists of adjustments patients make using resources of the institution officially designed for other purposes to re-establish territories of the self, spheres of autonomy, separate social structures, and separate systems of status (*A*, pp. 201–3). A richly developed underlife is bred by conditions of extreme poverty—as in the mental institution which denies patients the basic tools for building a life. Yet, Goffman believes that the process which is accentuated in the total institution is a more extreme version of a theme intrinsic to all social establishments.

> Whenever we look at a social establishment, we find a counter to this first theme: we find that participants decline in some way to accept the official view of what they should be putting into and getting out of the organization and, behind this, of what sort of self and world they are to accept for themselves. . . . We find a multitude of homely little histories, each in its way a movement of liberty. Whenever worlds are laid on, underlives develop.
>
> (*Asylums*, 1961, p. 305)

This practice of reserving something of oneself from the clutch of an institution, Goffman argues, is not an incidental mechanism of defense but an essential constituent of the self (*A*, p. 316). Hence, Goffman's definition of the self as "a stance-taking entity, a something that takes up a position somewhere between identification with an organization and opposition to it" (*A*, p. 320).

The underworld-self that is fashioned in and through these secondary adjustments, however, isn't exactly a self—or at least not an officially recognized one. Paradoxically, it seems that the sort of self-preservation Goffman considers to be an essential constituent of the self is achieved precisely by surrendering attachment to the self. Goffman's analyses in *Asylums* and *Stigma* suggest that attachment to self can be itself a source of mortification for individuals confined within oppressive institutions and/or less than favorably defined according to the standards of normals. The mental patient learns that he has little capacity to sustain solid claims about himself; he learns "that a defensible picture of self can be seen as something outside oneself that can be constructed, lost, and rebuilt, all with great speed and some equanimity" ("The Moral Career of the Mental Patient" in *A*, p. 165). Moral commitment to a vision of self, which can be so easily and regularly built up and destroyed, is thus not very practical. He concludes "The Moral Career of the Mental Patient" with a strategy by which individuals can combat this mortification by an alienating institutional environment—"moral loosening" from attachment to self. According to Goffman, the mental patient learns to adopt a separate identity from the one that the hospital can give and take away (*A*, p. 165). The patient comes to be apathetic towards the moral game of defending the self, to treat the matter of selfhood with indifference. He treats the self not as "a fortress, but rather a small open city" and becomes "weary of having to show displeasure when held by the enemy." He learns that society does not define nor allow him the conditions for sustaining a viable self, and with this knowledge the threat that attaches people to self is weakened (*A*, p. 165).

> The moral career of the mental patient has unique interest, however; it can illustrate the possibility that in casting off the raiments of the old self—or in having this cover torn away—the person need not seek a new robe and a new audience before which to cower. Instead he can learn, at least for a time, to practice before all groups the amoral arts of shamelessness.
>
> (*Asylums*, 1961, p. 169)

Perhaps Goffman was merely describing in these passages the institutional conquest of human dignity and the resultant psychic withdrawal, as he is generally read.[2] On the other hand, perhaps Goffman was illuminating a viable strategy for anyone who would like to break the grip of a constraining institution or society. To remain firmly attached to self is to engage the ritual order on its own grounds, grounds on which gains are rarely made by those not already endowed with societally valued attributes. Rather than representing merely a description of the attitude that the inmate of a psychiatric institution learns to take toward his institutionally defined moral failure, perhaps it could also represent a strategy of resistance for all human beings whose selves are inevitably doomed to failure according to the standards of societally defined universal humanity. The elements of the strategy, as revealed by the previously-quoted passages, are: (1) the adoption of a standpoint outside the moral field defined by "normals"; (2) apathy towards the self-image management techniques and interaction rituals effectively carried out by the socially powerful; and (3) disinvestment in self.

Whether or not Goffman meant to imply an extension of the mental patient's anti-self stance beyond the domain of the extreme mortifying conditions of the total institution is certainly questionable, and the viability of an anti-self stance as an effective human response to mortifying social conditions might also be debated. Yet, Goffman's theory of the self as social product, taken as a whole, surely does challenge us to consider our moral relation to self and to recognize the resources on which it depends. We have seen two main components of Goffman's ideas concerning the production of self: first, that the self is a product of performances in social life; secondly, that the self that an individual is able to perform and have accepted by others is in large part determined by the social status and resources to which an individual has access.

A third aspect of Goffman's thinking about self, however, is inseparable from his analysis of social life. The self, as Goffman portrays it, is simultaneously a product of dramatic performance, an object of social ritual, and a field of strategic gamesmanship—in other words, a focal point for each of Goffman's three major metaphors for describing social life. The interplay of these three metaphors can clearly be seen in Goffman's theory of the self. The self is a product of performances staged in social life, and most of the time these performances are constrained by the ritual order of social life. It is through our attachment to self that we are attached to society. We maintain face by following social norms, showing deference for and affirming the dignity of others, and presenting ourselves in accordance with our own places in the status hierarchy. The main function of "face-work"—interactional work oriented towards affirming and protecting the dignity of social participants—is to maintain the ritual order of social life. Yet, even though conservatism is the rule and the maintenance of social order the primary goal, Goffman does assume a human propensity to maximize social esteem and suggests that we make game-like calculations to determine when and where to make face-gaining maneuvers. Our conservatism with respect to the status quo can, in large part, be explained by our strategic determinations that we stand to lose more than we might gain by engaging in face-gaining maneuvers. The interrelation of each of the metaphors Goffman uses to describe social life is perhaps most apparent in Goffman's theory of the self, although it is also evident in Goffman's more general analysis of social life.

The Nature of Social Life: Drama, Ritual, and Game

Goffman uses three metaphors for viewing social life: drama, ritual, and game. Interpretations of Goffman tend to vary according to relative emphasis on the ritual or the game metaphor. Readers who emphasize Goffman's ritual metaphor argue that he was primarily concerned with the maintenance of morality and social order, while those who emphasize the game metaphor see in Goffman's analyses of social life a world of perpetual one-upmanship and manipulative con-artistry. Goffman's drama metaphor seems to be amenable to both readings and is interpreted according to whether the reader sees Goffman's conception of social life as moral or manipulative. Evidence exists to support both readings. Goffman's emphasis on the strategic planning of performances, the game-like calculations underlying decisions about whether to risk loss of face in an attempt to gain face in social situations, and the control and manipulation of information in attempts to gain the upper hand in competitive interactions certainly suggest that Goffman sees manipulative aspects of social life. On the other hand, Goffman presents a view of social life as a realm in which morality is affirmed by means of everyday-life interaction rituals. Our performances in social life are not, according to this view, primarily oriented to personal gain but rather to affirmation of respect for the social order. Although the images might seem contradictory, Goffman describes social life in a way that reveals the interplay of manipulation and morality. The following presentation of Goffman's metaphors of social life will demonstrate this interplay within each of the three metaphors.

Social life as drama

In *The Presentation of Self in Everyday Life* (1959), Goffman employs the model of theatrical performance, or the dramaturgical perspective, to study the organization of social life (*PS*, p. xi). Goffman assumes that individuals inevitably have a variety of interests in attempting to control the impression others receive of their actions in social situations (*PS*, p. 4). As any single social encounter can never contain enough direct evidence to support the guiding definition of the situation, the smooth flow of social life depends upon participants accepting the impressions others attempt to convey concerning their identities and the meaning of their actions (*PS*, p. 3).

The Presentation of Self in Everyday Life is concerned with the techniques by which such impressions are conveyed (*PS*, p. 15). The book outlines six dramaturgical principles: performances, teams, regions, discrepant roles, communication out of character, and impression management. Performance entails individuals' attempt to impress upon others and often themselves that their character is what they claim, that actions mean what is intended, and that the definition of the situation is what is implicitly claimed (*PS*, p. 17). Goffman defines performance as "the activity of an individual which occurs during a period marked by his continuous presence before a particular set of observers and which has some influence on the observers" (*PS*, p. 22). Components of the performance include the front, dramatic realization, idealization, expressive control, misrepresentation, and mystification. The front is the equipment, including physical props of the social setting as well as personal expressive equipment such as rank, clothing, sex, or age, that functions to define the performance for observers (*PS*, pp. 22–4). Dramatic realization is the process whereby individuals infuse their activity during a particular interaction with signs to convey facts that otherwise might remain obscure (*PS*, p. 30). Idealization is the tendency of actors to present idealized impressions for their audience (*PS*, p. 35), involving forgoing or concealing action inconsistent with the idealized standards (*PS*, p. 40). The capacity for idealization is enhanced by audience segregation (*PS*, p. 49). Performers rely on expressive control to keep inconsistent moods and energies from disrupting the performance. As Goffman puts it, "A certain bureaucratization of the spirit is expected so that we can be relied upon to give a perfectly homogenous performance at every appointed time" (*PS*, p. 56). Because orientation to situations requires acceptance of performed cues, few of which are invulnerable to misuse, misrepresentation is a possibility (*PS*, p. 58). Goffman points out, however, that the distinction between a true and a false performance concerns not the actual performance as much as it does whether or not the performer is authorized to give the performance in question (*PS*, p. 59). Finally, mystification involves the maintenance of a social distance which holds the audience in a state of awe in regard to the performer (*PS*, p. 67).

Rarely is it the case that a performance is concerned solely with the presentation of an individual's character, but rather performances commonly involve cooperation of a team which works together to express the characteristics of a social situation (*PS*, p. 77). Performances often depend upon the segregation of social space into "front regions" and "back regions." The front region is the place where the performance is given and standards maintained (*PS*, p. 107); the back region is the place "where the impression fostered by the performance is knowingly contradicted as a matter of course" (*PS*, p. 112). "Discrepant roles," on the other hand, pose a problem to the maintenance of the credibility of the performance (*PS*, p. 141), as when the same individual occupies roles which place him or her in the audience in one instance and in the performers' back region in the other. "Communication out of character" involves the expression of sentiments which are discrepant with the official performance (*PS*, p. 169). Most frequently, communication out of character occurs backstage among teammates; treatment of the absent, staging talk, and team collusion are examples of such. In the case of "realigning actions," however, communication-out-of-character occurs between performers and audience. Realigning actions are unofficial communications used to shift the official working consensus of the interaction (*PS*, p. 190).

In order to prevent embarrassment and disruption in social interaction, participants are required to possess certain attributes and engage in certain practices. Goffman categorizes these "arts of impression management" under three headings: defensive attributes and practices, protective practices, and "tact regarding tact." Goffman outlines three types of defensive practices. First, in order to successfully defend their own show, performers must exhibit "dramaturgical loyalty" among themselves. That is, they must adhere to the moral obligation of protecting the secrets of their team (*PS*, p. 212). Secondly, they must maintain "dramaturgical discipline," avoiding becoming so carried away by the show that they forget to attend to the techniques of staging a successful performance (*PS*, p. 216). Third, it is useful if team members are "dramaturgically circumspect"; that is, if they "exercise foresight and design in determining in advance how best to stage a show" (*PS*, p. 218). These defensive practices have their counterpart in certain protective practices of the audience (*PS*, p. 229). The audience voluntarily avoids the secret areas of the performers (*PS*, p. 229), tactfully avoids introducing contradictions to the performance (*PS*, p. 231), and pretends to "not see" flaws (*PS*, p. 231). Finally, the performer must exercise "tact regarding tact." In other words, the performer must tactfully respond to the tact of the audience—by reading the hints and modifying the performance (*PS*, p. 234).

Goffman is wary of pushing the dramaturgical model of social life too far. In the theater, performances are consciously planned and intended to be received as make-believe. The actions, responses, and modes of self-presentation of individuals in real life, on the other hand, are thought to be unconscious, genuine, and closely tied to reality. Goffman admits that "all the world is not, of course, a stage" (*PS*, p. 72). But then he adds, "but the crucial ways in which it isn't are not easy to specify" (*PS*, p. 72). Ultimately, Goffman debunks the distinction between reality and contrivance.

> We tend to see real performances as something not purposely put together at all, being an unintentional product of the individual's unselfconscious response to the facts in his situation. And contrived performances we tend to see as something painstakingly pasted together, one false item on another, since there is no reality to which the items of behavior could be a direct response. It will be necessary to see now that these dichotomous conceptions are by way of being the ideology of honest performers, providing a strength to the show they put on, but a poor analysis of it.
>
> (*The Presentation of Self*, 1959, p. 70)

A person's status or self or character cannot be distinguished from the performance. "To *be* a given kind of person, then, is not merely to possess the required attributes, but also to sustain the standards of conduct and appearance that one's social grouping attaches thereto" (*PS*, p. 75). It is the success of the performance, that is its credibility to oneself and to others, that leads the audience and the performer to impute a self to a performed character (*PS*, p. 252). The self, in other words, is a product of performance rather than a cause of it (*PS*, p. 253).

In employing the dramaturgical metaphor, Goffman does not intend to characterize social life as a realm of manipulative play-acting in which morality plays no role. In fact, Goffman does not hold manipulation and morality in opposition at all. As social beings, Goffman points out, individuals are concerned with living up to the many moral standards of the social world. But, *as performers*, they are "concerned not with the moral issue of realizing these standards, but with the amoral issue of engineering a convincing impression that these standards are being realized" (*PS*, p. 251).

Social life as ritual

That Goffman does not oppose manipulation and morality in his depictions of social life can be seen by examining the relationship between his "strategic game" and "ritual" metaphors of social life. Goffman's analyses of interaction can be divided into one or the other category, although the oscillation between metaphors that his work sometimes exhibits indicates the interpenetration of ritualistic and game-like qualities of social life. Those works in which ritual analysis predominates include "On Face-work" (1955), "The Nature of Deference and Demeanor" (1956), "Embarrassment and Social Organization" (1956), "Alienation from Interaction" (1957) (all collected in *Interaction Ritual*), *Behavior in Public Places* (1963), and *Relations in Public* (1971). The game metaphor, on the other hand, is the organizing principle in "Fun in Games" (1961) (in *Encounters*), "Where the Action Is" (in *Interaction Ritual*) (1967), and *Strategic Interaction* (1969).

Explicitly drawn connections to Durkheim's ideas about religious ritual and social solidarity are found in "The Nature of Deference and Demeanor" and *Relations in Public*, and allusions to Durkheim's *The Elementary Forms of Religious Life* can be seen in nearly all of his early works. He concludes the third section of his dissertation with the remark: "An idol is to a person as a rite is to etiquette" ("Communication Conduct in an Island Community", 1953, p. 104). And he directly quotes Durkheim's *Sociology and Philosophy* in *The Presentation of Self* in support of his view of the self as an object of ritual care (*PS*, p. 69). As Goffman suggests in "On Face-work" and *The Presentation of Self in Everyday Life*, the self has become the sacred object of modern interpersonal life that symbols of the social collectivity were in Durkheim's analysis of primitive societies.

The main function of "face-work" is to maintain the ritual order of social

life. For the most part, an individual's "face" is not something freely chosen but is something accorded by society. Individuals are due respect
consistent with their social status. Interaction rituals serve to affirm the
"faces" of individuals variously positioned within the status order. The task
of individuals is to present themselves in a way that shows acceptance of
their social station. Because of the basic rules of self-respect and considerateness that operate in social interaction, mutual acceptance of the lines
taken in social interaction is a basic structural feature of interaction ("On
Face-work" in *IR*, p. 11).

This argument parallels the one made in "The Nature of Deference and
Demeanor." A person conveys social desirability through demeanor, that is
through attributes such as discretion, sincerity, modesty, self-control, and
poise (*IR*, p. 77). One key way in which a person expresses demeanor,
however, is through the giving and withholding of deference to others. A
properly demeaned individual is one who accords deference in congruence
with his or her own and others' social station, thus maintaining the ritual
order (*IR*, p. 81). In this essay, the connections to Durkheim are explicitly
drawn at beginning and end. He concludes the essay:

> Many gods have been done away with, but the individual himself stubbornly
> remains as a deity of considerable importance. He walks with some dignity
> and is the recipient of many little offerings. He is jealous of the worship due
> him, yet, approached in the right spirit, he is ready to forgive those who may
> have offended him. Because of their status relative to his, some persons will
> find him contaminating while others will find they contaminate him, in either
> case finding that they must treat him with ritual care. Perhaps the individual
> is so viable a god because he can actually understand the ceremonial signifi-
> cance of the way he is treated, and quite on his own can respond dramatically
> to what is proffered him. In contacts between such deities there is no need
> for middlemen; each of these gods is able to serve as his own priest.
>
> (*Interaction Ritual*, 1967, p. 95)

A significant portion of social life, then, is devoted to the accordance of
proper levels of worship to selves variously positioned in status hierarchies.
Not unrelated to the norms that define demeanor and guide allocation of
deference are the numerous unspoken social traffic rules that pervade
everyday existence yet seem to have little significance either for communicating status or for matters of interpersonal loss or gain at all. Indicating the
significance Goffman accords to the maintenance of ritual independently of
strategic concerns over gain and loss of status, both *Behavior in Public Places*
(1963) and *Relations in Public* (1971) are devoted to examining the traffic
rules of social life. In both works, Goffman defines "social order" as
the ground rules of social life, the conditions and constraints placed on the

manner in which activity is carried out and ends are sought but not on the *choice* of ends (*RP*, pp. x–xi).

Behavior in Public Places (*BPP*) outlines the "situational proprieties" of various forms of social interaction, including access, involvement obligations, attention, and tactful leavetaking. Though situational proprieties may not have any clearly visible instrumental function for the participants, Goffman believes that they function to "give body to the joint social life . . ." (*BPP*, p. 196). Respect for situational proprieties is essential for providing the social order necessary for peaceful and secure coexistence. Although no individual social situation is representative of the institution in which it is embedded, the behavior of individuals in social situations does say something about their regard for broader units of social life (*BPP*, p. 220). Situational improprieties, for instance, may serve to express alienation from a class, community, social establishment, or institution (*BPP*, p. 223).

Relations in Public examines the social routines and practices—territories of the self, supportive interchanges, remedial interchanges, tie-signs, and normal appearances—used to maintain social order. A central component of social organization involves the claims that individuals make to personal and public spaces, possessions, information, and conversation (*RP*, pp. 28–41). Each of these forms of territoriality, Goffman points out, is socially determined; that is, the size of and control of territories of the self depends upon social rank (*RP*, pp. 40–41). Individuals affirm social order by marking out their own territories and respecting those of others in a manner consistent with respective social rank. Supportive interchanges are "interpersonal rituals" which "affirm and support the social relationship between doer and recipient" (*RP*, p. 63). Remedial interchanges are interpersonal practices, such as accounts or apologies, which attempt to rectify an offense to a social relationship (*RP*, p. 109). Tie-signs, such as handholding, are signs that indicate the nature of relationships between persons (*RP*, p. 194). Finally, a portion of social life is devoted to maintenance of "normal appearances," providing and looking for signs from others that nothing in the world is out of the ordinary and routines may be followed as usual (*RP*, p. 239). Goffman draws an analogy between Durkheim's analysis of religious ritual and these various interpersonal rituals.

> In contemporary society rituals performed to stand-ins for supernatural entities are everywhere in decay, as are extensive ceremonial agendas involving long strings of obligatory rites. What remains are brief rituals one individual performs for and to another, attesting to civility and good will on the performer's part and to the recipient's possession of a small patrimony of sacredness. What remains, in brief, are interpersonal rituals.
>
> (*Relations in Public*, 1971, p. 63)

Although strategy, manipulation, and gamesmanship hardly seem apt words for describing what goes on in these sorts of interpersonal rituals, game-like qualities are never entirely absent from even the most ritualistic realms of social life. Especially in "On Face-work," one can see the interplay of ritual and game-like aspects of social life. On the one side, face is the central object of interpersonal rituals. Protecting, defending, and maintaining the social hierarchy of face is the norm, as opposed to game-like moves and challenges. On the other side, the stability of the ritual order and the attachment of individuals to their socially allotted faces is a function of game-like considerations. The interpenetration of ritual and game is most clearly apparent when Goffman characterizes the self as "a kind of player in a ritual game . . ." ("On Face-work" in *IR*, p. 31). Sometimes a person will engage in aggressive face-work practices, attempting to make points by introducing information favorable to himself and unfavorable to others (*IR*, p. 25). At other times, a person will strategically avoid contacts which might pose a threat to an established and desirable image of self (*IR*, p. 15). At still other times, face-work will be oriented towards correcting assaults and reestablishing the ritual equilibrium of the hierarchy of face (*IR*, p. 19). Even when no challenges to or transformations of the social hierarchy of face occur, however, game-like considerations are nonetheless in play. In fact, Goffman suggests that strategic calculations are a determining factor in the maintenance of ritual order. It is because individuals determine that more is to be lost than to be gained by challenging the social status quo that most affirm the ritual order.

> Social life is an uncluttered, orderly thing because the person voluntarily stays away from the places and topics and times where he is not wanted and where he might be disparaged for going. He cooperates to save his face, finding that there is much to be gained from venturing nothing.
>
> (*Interaction Ritual*, 1967, p. 43)

Social life as game

The interpenetration of ritualistic and game-like qualities of social life can likewise be seen when Goffman shifts to a focus on the game metaphor in "Fun in Games" (1961) (in *Encounters*), "Where the Action Is" (1967) (in *Interaction Ritual*), and *Strategic Interaction* (1970). Goffman's express intention in "Fun in Games," in fact, is to analyze fun and games in a way that sheds light on interaction in general (*E*, p. 17). Games are not so different from social encounters in general. Both involve rules as to what aspects of the situation, events, the material environment, and the attributes of individuals should be considered relevant and meaningful. Games and serious activities alike are "world-building activities" (*E*, p. 27). The parallel between games and the more serious activities of maintenance of ritual order is revealed most poignantly in the concluding section to this essay in which Goffman examines the conditions that promote fun or easeful interaction (*E*, p. 66). Goffman identifies two conditions which generate engrossment among participants in games: first, problematic outcome; secondly, opportunities to exhibit attributes valued in the wider social world (*E*, p. 68). From one angle, problematic outcome seems *not* to be a prevalent condition of the ritual procession of social life. Rather than being a forum for competition and display, informal social participation could be seen to be a forum for "ultimate validation of relationships of intimacy and equality" (*E*, p. 78). Goffman suggests, however, that the conditions of vital social encounters are not that different from the conditions of a fun game. Sociable gatherings depend upon a certain level of status endogamy to ensure the provision of ceremonial affirmation of externally based status characteristics. Too much status inequality among participants would require the sacrifice of either intimacy or proper sacralization. On the other hand, too little difference among participants makes social encounters boring. As in games, engrossment in social encounters depends upon a certain degree of problematic outcome. The vitality of social relationships depends upon enough social difference as to permit at least a little loss or gain.

> A dissolution of some externally based social distance must be achieved, a penetration of ego-boundaries, but not to an extent that renders the participants fearful, threatened, or self-consciously concerned with what is happening socially. Too much potential loss and gain must be guarded against, as well as too little.
>
> (*Encounters*, 1961, p. 79)

Even though practices oriented towards maintenance of the ritual order may predominate in the everyday existence of most people most of the time, the excitement and adventure of social life often derives from realms which involve a level of risk and invite gamesmanship. "Where the Action Is" (1967) defines "action" as activity that involves fatefulness. Fateful activity is "activity that is both problematic and consequential" (in *IR*, p. 164). Although social life is orchestrated such as to minimize fatefulness, the "human condition is such that some degree of fatefulness will always be found" (*IR*, p. 164). The maintenance of the ceremonial order that individuals are pledged to uphold by means of interpersonal rituals is never quite as unproblematic as it might appear (*IR*, pp. 168–9). Character is inevitably gambled in any interpersonal interaction (*IR*, p. 217). On the one side, character refers to the capacity to maintain composure and self-sameness in the face of challenge (*IR*, p. 217). On the other side, however, character is something that can be gained by putting oneself on the line and making a good showing (*IR*, p. 237). Character and the ritual order of which it is part are renewed only in moments of fatefulness (*IR*, p. 239). The establishment of the boundaries of the ritual order, indeed, occurs by means of a special kind of moral game—"character contests" (*IR*, p. 240).

Character contests are interpersonal disputes over whose status claims and conception of proper treatment of self and others will be allowed to prevail (*IR*, p. 241). On the one hand, character contests often pose little threat to the interactional status quo, as immaturity is attributed to the aggressor and character to the one who refuses to be drawn into a fray of honor (*IR*, p. 253). For the most part, people try to avoid chance-taking with regard to their characters (p. 260). On the other, however, "there is some ambivalence about safe and momentless living" (*IR*, p. 260). There are certain prized attributes that can not be expressed or affirmed without exposure to fatefulness. To create a forum for affirmation of these, individuals must engage in fateful action (*IR*, p. 261). Goffman suggests that such fateful action is outside the normal round of social life, but that our moral fantasies impute honor to this activity (*IR*, p. 267). "These naked little spasms of the self occur at the end of the world, but there at the end is action and character" (*IR*, p. 270).

Taking the condition of mutual fatefulness as its starting point, *Strategic Interaction* [*SI*] (1969) analyzes the structure and strategies of interaction so oriented. "Expression Games" outlines the structure of interactions contingent upon the control of information (*SI*, p. 4). The more that is at stake in the interaction, the greater the possibility of deception (*SI*, pp. 68–9). Expression games involve an observer with an interest in gaining information from a subject and a subject with an interest in controlling the information the observer may glean. The subject makes moves—some unwitting and others intentionally designed to be observed—while the observer attempts to discern the reality behind the observations (*SI*, pp. 11–20). The possibility of faking and of faking of faking on the part of the subject leaves the observer in a state of uncertainty as to the reality of the subject's moves, as the possibility that the observer may penetrate the subject's show leaves the subject in a state of uncertainty as to how his moves are being interpreted by the observer. The distinction between the observer and subject roles, however, breaks down under conditions of mutual suspicion. As the observer attempts to penetrate the subject's show, the subject is concerned to discern the observer's trust and reading of moves. "Each seeker is therefore doubly a concealer, and each concealer is doubly a seeker" (*SI*, p. 72). Goffman suggests that expression games are a part of almost every social situation.

In every social situation we can find a sense in which one participant will be an observer with something to gain from assessing expressions, and another will be a subject with something to gain from manipulating this process. A single structure of contingencies can be found in this regard which renders agents a little like us all and all of us a little like agents.

(*Strategic Interaction*, 1969, p. 81)

"Strategic interaction" differs from expression games in that it involves not merely manipulation of information but also assessment of courses of action (*SI*, p. 145). The essay "Strategic Interaction" outlines the matters players must consider in planning rational action. These include: (1) the opponent's moves; (2) the operational code, or orientation to gaming that influences how the players play; (3) the opponent's resolve to proceed with the game at whatever cost; (4) the information state, or knowledge that the opponent may possess about his own and the other's situation; (5) the opponent's resources or capacities; (6) the players' attributes; (7) the gameworthiness of the players; and (8) the players' integrity, or commitment to continued loyalty to the party's interests once play has begun (*SI*, pp. 95–7). Strategic interaction is a mutual assessment in which opponents attempt to chart their own best course of action on the basis of an enumeration of the opponent's possibilities of action (*SI*, p. 100) and "in light of one's thoughts about the others' thoughts about oneself" (*SI*, p. 101). The contribution of the concept of strategic interaction, as Goffman sees it, is that it moves beyond symbolic interactionism's limited focus on communication by analyzing interactions involving mutual fatefulness, awareness of interdependence of outcomes, and the capacity to structure action on the basis of a calculative assessment of the other's possible moves and considerations (*SI*, pp. 136–7).

Clearly, Goffman's ritual and game metaphors diverge widely in certain of his works. "The Nature of Deference and Demeanor" is probably the most pure source of his ritual analysis, while there are hardly any hints of Goffman's ritual metaphor in *Strategic Interaction*. Yet, it is important to see that the metaphors are not contradictory, as the amenability of the drama metaphor to either reading indicates. A performance is simultaneously an expression of deference to the social order as well as a move in a strategic game, according to Goffman. We strategically chart our performances and courses of action and interaction, often with an aim of being a viable member of a morally cohesive social order. On the one side, the performance of morality requires strategy. On the other side, the ritual order constrains our performances and strategic moves.

Frames and the Organization of Experience

Frame analysis

Goffman's later work shifts from a more concrete analysis of the self–society relation to a seemingly more abstract analysis of the principles that organize our experience. Though different from his earlier work, however, his analysis of frames (especially in *Frame Analysis* [*FA*], 1974) adds an important dimension to his social theory that is certainly important for thinking about self and society.

Goffman's later work emphasizes that social experience is organized by frames, which he defines as principles of organization which govern the subjective meaning we assign to social events (*FA*, p. 11). For example, we might frame an activity as a hobby or an occupation. The way we and others relate to the activity depends on the way it is framed. Goffman does not believe that individual participants in social encounters create the frames that determine the meaning of their experience (*FA*, p. 1), nor does he accord frames a constitutive function relative to social structure and social organization (*FA*, p. 13). He does, however, think that definitions of situations and, generally, human subjective experience are built up in accordance with frames (*FA*, p. 10). Thus, even though he does not claim to explain the organization of society on the basis of frame, he considers frame analysis essential to understanding the organization of experience (*FA*, p. 13).

The greater part of *Frame Analysis* is devoted to defining and outlining the principles by which experience is subjectively organized. These principles include: primary frameworks, keys and keyings, and designs and fabrications. For instance, events may be interpreted according to one of two primary frameworks, natural or social. Events interpreted according to natural frameworks are perceived as unguided and not subject to moral judgment. Actions interpreted according to social frameworks, on the other hand, are described as "guided doings" and are subject to social appraisals (*FA*, p. 22). An earthquake, for instance, is explained by a natural framework, while an interpersonal dispute is interpreted according to a social framework. The "key" transforms the meaning of an activity from what it literally appears to be to something else (*FA*, pp. 43–4). For instance, an utterance may be taken as a genuine expression of a person's thoughts and feelings or it may be "keyed" as sarcasm. A design or a fabrication is an "intentional effort of one or more individuals to manage activity so that a party of one or more others will be induced to have a false belief about what it is that is going on" (*FA*, p. 83). Unlike keyings which are presumably understood as such by the participants, fabrications are intended to induce a false sense of reality and are subject to discrediting (*FA*, pp. 84–5).

Goffman suggests that frames are often simply functional. In general, individuals can be guided by frames and find that the ongoing world supports their interpretations because framed activity is anchored in some way or another in the everyday unstaged world (*FA*, pp. 247–8). The framing of an activity as work, for example, may be anchored in the reality of the pay received or any number of other background factors that function to distinguish work from play. Goffman notes, however, that frames are often not very tightly anchored to any objective reality. The framing of experience is usually anchored by layers of other frames. For instance, the framing of an interaction between two individuals as a superordinate–subordinate interaction is anchored in the respective positions of the persons within an organization. Yet, the meaning of the positions themselves depend on layers of social meanings.

Chapter 8 of *Frame Analysis* considers the question of how framed activity is anchored in ongoing reality (*FA*, p. 250), or, in William James's words, the question: "Under what circumstances do we think things real?" (*FA*, p. 250). The anchoring of activity in the ongoing world, according to Goffman, allows us to generate a *sense* of reality but does not render activity unframed and invulnerable to misconstruction. Indeed, Goffman suggests that the significance of frames for anchoring social life and the vulnerability to which they expose us are two sides of the same coin. On the one hand, Goffman states that he assumes that our interpretative frameworks are more or less adequate (*FA*, p. 440). Even though every individual faces various ambiguities and possibilities of error and deception with regard to frames, it is presumed that these troubles can be resolved fairly easily. Errors are generally short-lived, because action on the basis of an erroneous framework will generally create contradictions within a complexly interconnected social realm which lead the individual to detect the error (*FA*, p. 321). On the other hand, Goffman says that the very sources we use to generate certitude are typically left unanalyzed and thus may easily be the sources of our deception (*FA*, p. 444).

> The delicate issue, it seems, is that in certain matters, often socially important ones, no very effective check may be available in the society regarding the validity or invalidity of a framework. A specific belief may not be crucial and a specific confrontation of competing frames of reference not possible. Or there may be little interest in pressing such alternative accountings as exist, or little attention paid to such as are presented.
>
> (*Frame Analysis*, 1974, p. 200)

The anchoring of frames is especially loose when we are framing informal interpersonal experience and defining people. Goffman points out, in contradiction to the common sense view that intimate relations afford deeper access to the "truth" of the person than do formal relations, that "formal relations might be less subject to the play of doubts than are intimate ones" (*FA*, p. 458). Informal social relations are more subject to the contingencies of subjective framing because there is not formal institutional apparatus to constrain the way individuals frame themselves, others, and the social situation.

Judgments of character are particularly subject to framing because self is not a stable substance. Not only are our selves a product of performances, but our actions and performances do not always speak for themselves. A self is not simply a product of performance, but is a product of the framing of a person's actions and performances. When we are operating at the level of informal social relations and are concerned to make judgments of moral character, framing is especially consequential because the framing is least anchored to any hard reality. Thus, there is no unambiguous way to check the accuracy of a judgment as to the character of another human being, and no fail-safe way for a judged person to combat an ill-fitting frame.

Why should this be a problem, if it is simply the inevitable nature of the self and social life? As long as people are able to communicate openly with one another regarding the fit of the interpretative frames they apply to social experience, to themselves, and others, frames should supply a helpful and mutually acceptable orientation to social life. Yet, Goffman suggests that the selection of frames does not proceed so democratically. Goffman argues that social power is a condition of persistent misframing. People with little social power have little power to frame events or to combat interpretive frameworks applied to them. A person judged to be incompetent, for example, carries no weight in combating the judgment. The protests can be discounted, taken as evidence of incompetence (*FA*, p. 445). This vulnerability of informal social life makes it possible for individuals to be contained in what Goffman calls a "frame trap."

> When an individual is misunderstood and others misframe his words and actions, he is likely to provide a corrective account. In this way matters get straight. So, too, when an individual errs for other reasons in defining the world, contrary evidence is likely soon to appear. . . . What I want to suggest here is that the world can be arranged (whether by intent or default) so that incorrect views, however induced, are confirmed by each bit of new evidence or each effort to correct matters, so that, indeed, the individual finds that he is trapped and nothing can get through.
>
> (*Frame Analysis*, 1974, p. 480)

Indeed, everyday conduct tends in the same direction: routinely, the character we impute to another allows us to discount his criticisms and other professions of belief, transforming these expressions into "what can only be expected" of someone of that character. Thus are interpretative vocabularies self-sealing. In these cases, truly, we deal with the myth of the girl who spoke toads; every account releases a further example of what it tries to explain away.

(Ibid., p. 482)

Although the notion of being "framed" implies the existence of a reality behind the misconstruction, Goffman suggests that there is no original behind the frame. A sincere person, for instance, is not one who expresses his or her true inner reality, but rather one who acts "in such a way as to convince others that the apparent frame is in fact the actual one" (*FA*, p. 487). Goffman argues that the reality against which we impute unreality is itself a construction (*FA*, p. 560). It might even be said that Goffman views the social world itself as the context of a very complex and encompassing frame trap that defines the identities and experiences of all participants – only, a frame trap that is not taken as such.

The frame analysis of talk

A portion of social life is oriented towards the pursuit of concrete goals within the context of structured social organizations and resilient physical environments. Within such realms, the framing of experience is constrained by more or less hard realities. Interpretative license is limited. A greater proportion of social life—more or less significant, depending on a person's view of life—is, however, informal and not explicitly oriented towards concrete social projects. Intimate interpersonal bonds as well as many other forms of informal social relationships are developed and maintained primarily out of informal talk. When people engage in informal talk, they are less often trying to stir others towards action in a collective project as they are trying to gain appreciation of themselves and their experiences (*FA*, p. 503). As Goffman sees it, informal talk is inherently dramatic in nature. Generally, it consists of a dramatic recounting of a person's life experiences and self, with the teller granted an extensive license to select and interpret as he or she sees fit. As was suggested above, informal talk is less firmly anchored than formal social relations to the ongoing world. For this reason, informal talk is more vulnerable than other types of experience to the manipulations of frame. Thus, frame analysis is especially apt with regard to informal talk.

The essays collected in *Forms of Talk* are an extension and application of the ideas put forth in *Frame Analysis*, especially in the chapter "The Frame Analysis of Talk." The essays illustrate three main points: first, that talk is governed by social rules and common understandings; secondly, that talk is always a form of social interaction; and thirdly, that talk is a loosely anchored performance aimed at establishing the alignment of a participant in social interaction.

The first point, that talk is governed by social rules and common understandings that go beyond and sometimes even conflict with linguistic norms, is one that he had made many years before in the short essay "The Neglected Situation" (1964, p. 136) and which he elaborated in a subsequently published essay, "Felicity's Condition" (1983). In this essay, Goffman argues that meaningful and felicitous talk depends on common understanding and shared presuppositions derived not only from prior utterances but also from a stock of shared social knowledge. "Felicity's Condition," as Goffman defines it, is "any arrangement which leads us to judge an individual's verbal acts to be not a manifestation of strangeness" ("FC," p. 27). Noting that there is nothing new to the argument that meaningful spoken interaction depends upon appropriate drawing from an array of presuppositions, Goffman argues that detailed *analysis* of the taken-for-granted is something that has yet to be undertaken by sociologists. While linguists have illuminated the formal presuppositions of utterances, social presuppositions of talk—e.g., about who can speak to whom in what circumstances—have yet to be examined ("FC," p. 48).

A similar point is made in "Replies and Responses," the first essay collected in *Forms of Talk* [*FT*] (1981). Here, Goffman argues that understanding spoken interaction in terms of the constraints of a communication system is inadequate. Not only is spoken interaction directed towards linguistic system constraints, but it is also constrained by social norms concerning how to handle oneself with respect to others (*FT*, p. 16). Sometimes, such ritual constraints are closely tied to linguistic system constraints. For instance, saving one's face is accomplished by preserving orderly communication (*FT*, p. 19). Goffman's main point in this essay, however, is that ritual constraints do not always reinforce linguistic system constraints. Often, the social context can call for certain forms of spoken interaction that do not correspond to the formal rules and dialogic structures of communication systems (*FT*, p. 25). Furthermore, there are certain utterances—those which Goffman calls "response cries" in his second essay in *Forms of Talk*—which do not qualify as conventionally directed talk and which can be understood only by reference to the social situation outside states of talk (*FT*, p. 122).

The second and third ideas, that talk is always a form of social interaction and that it is a loosely anchored performance aimed at establishing the alignment of a person in a social interaction, runs through each of the essays in *Forms of Talk* but is especially emphasized in "Response Cries." Goffman demonstrates this by considering forms of talk and utterances not generally understood to be intended for public consumption—self-talk and response cries. Self-talk is typically thought to be a breach of civility. The general rule is "no talking in public." Goffman points out, however, that there are exceptions to the rule that indicate that self-talk is as much a form of social interaction as are more explicitly directed statements. One important way in which self-talk functions as a form of social interaction is when an individual employs it to reestablish moral character or self-respect. Faced with the embarrassment of appearing foolish, a person might engage in self-talk to let others know what he had intended and/or that he is himself impressed with his apparent foolishness. Goffman generalizes that self-talk frequently arises out of the need to reestablish ourselves as honest, competent persons, and that it serves to indicate to others that we are alive to the demands of the social situation even if we momentarily slip (*FT*, p. 96). Curse words serve a similar function. Often thought to be an unconscious, emotional reaction to unfortunate events, Goffman believes that curse words are rarely uttered except in the presence of others because their function is primarily social (*FT*, p. 97). Like curse words, "response cries"—non-words used in response to various dramatic moments in life—are not mere emotional over-flowings but rather display evidence of the alignment we take toward social events (*FT*, pp. 100–1). A person who utters a revulsion sound ("Eeuw!") during a moment of contact with a defiling substance, for instance, demonstrates vocally what she cannot express in action—distance from the degradation associated with contamination by the defiling substance (*FT*, p. 104). By means of talk, response cries, and nonverbal modes of communication, we are able to establish our relationship to social events and to our utterances. That such framing of events and utterances occurs routinely and profoundly influences the meaning of these events and utterances is, according to Goffman, a fact that must be taken seriously by both sociologists and linguists. Neither the objective study of social events nor the study of the formal structure of utterances, Goffman argues, can capture the meanings that we establish in these various informal ways (*FT*, p. 147). The remaining essays in *Forms of Talk*—"Footing," "The Lecture," and "Radio Talk"—provide additional illustration of these points.

The framing of gender

Another application of frame analysis can be found in Goffman's analysis of gender in "The Arrangement Between the Sexes" (ABS) and *Gender Advertisements* (*GA*). Differences between men and women are often thought to be a direct outcome of biological sex differences, a product of differential social structural opportunities, or some combination of both. Although Goffman acknowledges the limited impact of biological constraints and certainly does not deny the significance of social structure, his own approach is to look at how the frames that organize social interaction produce the meaning of gender. Rather than providing the forum for the expression of natural differences, he argues that the organization of interaction itself produces the differences between the sexes (ABS, p. 324).

One of the key ways in which gender is given its significance in society is by means of the process of institutional reflexivity. Institutional reflexivity is the process whereby the social environment is organized in such a way as to make whatever natural sex differences there are significant (ABS, p. 313). One example given by Goffman is that of toilet practices. Despite insignificant differences in men's and women's processes of elimination, the segregation of public restrooms is a means whereby differences are reaffirmed and reestablished in the face of sexual integration of much of public space (ABS, p. 316). Goffman suggests that one of the basic things that children are taught as part of their gender socialization is how to use social situations to express gender (ABS, pp. 324–5).

Gender is given expression in social situations through what Goffman calls "displays." A display provides "evidence of the actor's *alignment* in a gathering, the position he seems prepared to take up in what is about to happen in the social situation" (*GA*, 1979, p. 1). Displays "tentatively establish the terms of the contact, the mode or style or formula for the dealings that are to ensue between the persons providing the display and the persons perceiving it" (*GA*, p. 1). Although gender displays are ordinarily thought to express the respective natures of women and men, Goffman thinks that cultural resources are the primary sources of gender displays (*GA*, pp. 3–4). A very significant source of gender displays, according to Goffman, is the parent–child relationship complex (*GA*, p. 4). In our culture, male–female relations are typically patterned on the model of the parent–child relationship. According to this model, the subordinate receives paternalistic care and protection from some of the harsh realities of social life in exchange for acceptance of the nonperson treatment and violation of privacy and autonomy that go along with a child-like status (*GA*, pp. 4–5). Goffman suggests that the extension of this frame from its original source to that of gender relations indicates that it has little to do with any real human nature of males and females. By contrast, the only human nature of males and females is the "capacity to learn to provide and to read depictions of masculinity and femininity and a willingness to adhere to a schedule for presenting these pictures . . ." (*GA*, p. 8).

The interaction order

Goffman's analysis of gender points to a theoretical issue that comes up in the introduction to *Frame Analysis* and which is considered more systematically in "The Interaction Order" [IO] (1983)—that is, the relationship between interactional frames and social structure. In the introduction to *Frame Analysis*, Goffman is quick to point out that interactional participants are not at liberty to create the frames that will define their situations. He separates his own analysis from a misreading of the famous dictum of W.I. Thomas: "If men define situations as real, they are real in their consequences." Goffman states that the statement is "true as it reads but false as it is taken" (*FA*, p. 1). It is taken falsely when, as some theorists have implied, it is assumed that an individual or group of individuals in a social encounter can manufacture reality at will simply by redefining it. On the contrary, frames are given by society and typically predate the social situations in which they are employed (*FA*, p. 1). Here, Goffman states explicitly that he considers social organization and social structure to be primary relative to the framed experience individuals have in social encounters (*FA*, p. 13). Yet his more systematic treatment of the issue in "The Interaction Order" indicates that he may have overstated the case in his introduction to *Frame Analysis*. His main point in "The Interaction Order" is to "make up the case for considering the interaction order as a substantive domain in its own right" (IO, p. 2). He echoes his earlier claim in pointing out that this does not imply considering the relatively autonomous interactional order as prior to or constitutive of macrostructural phenomena and identifies various social structural phenomena which cannot be reduced to an aggregate of particular social encounters (IO, p. 9). Yet, he clarifies his position by indicating that he does not, on the other hand, take macrostructural phenomena to be necessarily prior to or constitutive of the interactional order. In some respects, the interaction order is autonomous relative to social structure. Although he admits socially structured differences in resources and advantages within the interaction order, he argues that the forms and processes of the interaction order are independent of these inequalities—"the central theme remains of a traffic of use, and of arrangements which allow a great diversity of projects and intents to be realized through unthinking recourse to procedural forms" (IO, p. 6).

Not only is the interaction order not necessarily determined by macrostructural processes, but there are features of the interaction order which themselves bear on social structures (IO, p. 8). Goffman gives three examples in which situational effects have direct impact on social structure. First, the dependency of organizations on personnel who partake in a multitude of social situations on and off the job render the organizations themselves vulnerable to the injuries or abductions that individuals suffer in social situations (IO, p. 8). Secondly, agents of social organization can be influenced in face-to-face dealings to act in ways that affect the organization as a whole (IO, p. 8). Thirdly, organizational life depends on "people-processing encounters . . . in which 'impressions' subjects make during the interaction affects their life chances" (IO, p. 8). "It is in these processing encounters, then, that the quiet sorting can occur which, as Bourdieu might have it, reproduces the social structure" (IO, p. 8). While the covert values given to structural variables (e.g., class, gender, race, age) are not generated situationally, the actual weighing of attributes occurs in a social situation—a situation which may consolidate *or* loosen structural arrangements (IO, p. 8).

Conclusion

In the preceding, I have elaborated four of Goffman's main ideas. First, he analyzes many facets of the self–society relation and challenges common thinking about the self with his view of the self as a social product. Secondly, he exposes the link between power, status, performance, and self and provides an implicit critique of the exclusiveness of the world of "normals." Thirdly, in oscillating between three metaphors for describing social life—the drama, ritual, and game metaphors—Goffman demonstrates the inherent interplay between manipulation and morality in social life, challenging us to recognize the everyday techniques upon which morality is based. Finally, Goffman argues that frames play a powerful role in guiding the interpretation of experience, determining the meaning of social events, and defining the personal identities of individuals. Even though he holds that frames are secondary to and often derivative of social structure and social organization, he also thinks that situationally based interpretative patterns can actively influence social structural arrangements.

As the preceding introduction to Goffman's social theory should indicate, Goffman's work read as a whole, coheres into a rich and concrete theory of the self and social life. He articulates the interdependence of self and social life with detail, poignancy, and insight matched by no other social theorist.

Notes

1. For example, Alasdair Macintyre, "The Self as Work of Art," *New Statesman* (28 March 1969); Alvin Gouldner, "Other Symptoms of the Crisis: Goffman's Dramaturgy and Other New Theories," in idem, *The Coming Crisis of Western Sociology* (Heinemann, 1970); Alan Dawe, "The Underworld View of Erving Goffman," *British Journal of Sociology*, 24 (1973): pp. 246–53.

2. For example, Alan Dawe, "The Underworld View of Erving Goffman," *British Journal of Sociology*, 24 (1973): pp. 246–53; Eliot Friedson, "Celebrating Erving Goffman," *Contemporary Sociology*, 12 (1983), pp. 359–62; Mary Rogers, "Goffman on Power, Hierarchy, and Status," in Jason Ditton, ed., *The View from Goffman* (Macmillan, 1980); Michael Schudson, "Embarrassment and Erving Goffman's Idea of Human Nature," *Theory and Society*, 13 (1984): p. 646.

PART I

The Production of Self

1

Self Claims

"On Cooling the Mark Out: Some Aspects of Adaptation to Failure"*

In cases of criminal fraud, victims find they must suddenly adapt themselves to the loss of sources of security and status which they had taken for granted. A consideration of this adaptation to loss can lead us to an understanding of some relations in our society between involvements and the selves that are involved.[1]

In the argot of the criminal world, the term "mark" refers to any individual who is a victim or prospective victim of certain forms of planned illegal exploitation. The mark is the sucker—the person who is taken in. An instance of the operation of any particular racket, taken through the full cycle of its steps or phases, is sometimes called a play. The persons who operate the racket and "take" the mark are occasionally called operators.

The confidence game—the con, as its practitioners call it—is a way of obtaining money under false pretenses by the exercise of fraud and deceit. The con differs from politer forms of financial deceit in important ways. The con is practiced on private persons by talented actors who methodically and regularly build up informal social relationships just for the purpose of abusing them; white-collar crime is practiced on organizations by persons who learn to abuse positions of trust which they once filled faithfully. The one exploits poise; the other, position. Further, a con man is someone who accepts a social role in the underworld community; he is part of a brotherhood whose members make no pretense to one another of being "legit." A white-collar criminal, on the other hand, has no colleagues, although he may have an associate with whom he plans his crime and a wife to whom he confesses it.

The con is said to be a good racket in the United States only because most Americans are willing, nay eager, to make easy money, and will engage in action that is less than legal in order to do so. The typical play has typical

* Originally published in *Psychiatry*, 1952, 15 (4), pp. 451–63. Reprinted by permission of Guilford Publications, Inc.

phases. The potential sucker is first spotted, and one member of the working team (called the outside man, steerer, or roper) arranges to make social contact with him. The confidence of the mark is won, and he is given an opportunity to invest his money in a gambling venture which he understands to have been fixed in his favor. The venture, of course, is fixed, but not in his favor. The mark is permitted to win some money and then persuaded to invest more. There is an "accident" or "mistake," and the mark loses his total investment. The operators then depart in a ceremony that is called the blowoff or sting. They leave the mark but take his money. The mark is expected to go on his way, a little wiser and a lot poorer.

Sometimes, however, a mark is not quite prepared to accept his loss as a gain in experience and to say and do nothing about his venture. He may feel moved to complain to the police or to chase after the operators. In the terminology of the trade, the mark may squawk, beef, or come through. From the operators' point of view, this kind of behavior is bad for business. It gives the members of the mob a bad reputation with such police as have not yet been fixed and with marks who have not yet been taken. In order to avoid this adverse publicity, an additional phase is sometimes added at the end of the play. It is called cooling the mark out. After the blowoff has occurred, one of the operators stays with the mark and makes an effort to keep the anger of the mark within manageable and sensible proportions. The operator stays behind his team-mates in the capacity of what might be called a cooler and exercises upon the mark the art of consolation. An attempt is made to define the situation for the mark in a way that makes it easy for him to accept the inevitable and quietly go home. The mark is given instruction in the philosophy of taking a loss.

When we call to mind the image of a mark who has just been separated from his money, we sometimes attempt to account for the greatness of his anger by the greatness of his financial loss. This is a narrow view. In many cases, especially in America, the mark's image of himself is built up on the belief that he is a pretty shrewd person when it comes to making deals and that he is not the sort of person who is taken in by anything. The mark's readiness to participate in a sure thing is based on more than avarice; it is based on a feeling that he will now be able to prove to himself that he is the sort of person who can "turn a fast buck." For many, this capacity for high finance comes near to being a sign of masculinity and a test of fulfilling the male role.

It is well known that persons protect themselves with all kinds of rationalizations when they have a buried image of themselves which the facts of their status do not support. A person may tell himself many things: that he has not been given a fair chance; that he is not really interested in becoming something else; that the time for showing his mettle has not yet come; that the usual means of realizing his desires are personally or morally distasteful, or require too much dull effort. By means of such defenses, a person saves himself from committing a cardinal social sin—the sin of defining oneself in terms of a status while lacking the qualifications which an incumbent of that status is supposed to possess.

A mark's participation in a play, and his investment in it, clearly commit him in his own eyes to the proposition that he is a smart man. The process by which he comes to believe that he cannot lose is also the process by which he drops the defenses and compensations that previously protected him from defeats. When the blowoff comes, the mark finds that he has no defense for not being a shrewd man. He has defined himself as a shrewd man and must face the fact that he is only another easy mark. He has defined himself as possessing a certain set of qualities and then proven to himself that he is miserably lacking in them. This is a process of self-destruction of the self. It is no wonder that the mark needs to be cooled out and that it is good business policy for one of the operators to stay with the mark in order to talk him into a point of view from which it is possible to accept a loss.

In essence, then, the cooler has the job of handling persons who have been caught out on a limb—persons whose expectations and self-conceptions have been built up and then shattered. The mark is a person who has compromised himself, in his own eyes if not in the eyes of others.

Although the term, mark, is commonly applied to a person who is given short-lived expectations by operators who have intentionally misrepresented the facts, a less restricted definition is desirable in analyzing the larger social scene. An expectation may finally prove false, even though it has been possible to sustain it for a long time and even though the operators acted in good faith. So, too, the disappointment of reasonable expectations, as well as misguided ones, creates a need for consolation. Persons who participate in what is recognized as a confidence game are found in only a few social settings, but persons who have to be cooled out are found in many. Cooling the mark out is one theme in a very basic social story.

For purposes of analysis, one may think of an individual in reference to the values or attributes of a socially recognized character which he possesses. Psychologists speak of a value as a personal involvement. Sociologists speak of a value as a status, role, or relationship. In either case, the character of the value that is possessed is taken in a certain way as the character of the person who possesses it. An alteration in the kinds of attributes possessed brings an alteration to the self-conception of the person who possesses them.

The process by which someone acquires a value is the process by which he surrenders the claim he had to what he was and commits himself to the conception of self which the new value requires or allows him to have. It is the process that persons who fall in love or take dope call getting hooked. After a person is hooked, he must go through another process by which his new involvement finds its proper place, in space and time, relative to the other calls, demands, and commitments that he has upon himself. At this point certain other persons suddenly begin to play an important part in the individual's story; they impinge upon him by virtue of the relationship they happen to have to the value in which he has become involved. This is not the place to consider the general kinds of impingement that are institutionalized in our society and the general social relationships that arise: the personal relationship, the professional relationship, and the business relationship. Here we are concerned only with the end of the story, the way in which a person becomes disengaged from one of his involvements.

In our society, the story of a person's involvement can end in one of three general ways. According to one type of ending, he may withdraw from one of his involvements or roles in order to acquire a sequentially related one that is considered better. This is the case when a youth becomes a man, when a student becomes a practitioner, or when a man from the ranks is given a commission.

Of course, the person who must change his self at any one of these points of promotion may have profound misgivings. He may feel disloyal to the way of life that must be left behind and to the persons who do not leave it with him. His new role may require action that seems insincere, dishonest, or unfriendly. This he may experience as a loss in moral cleanliness. His new role may require him to forgo the kinds of risk-taking and exertion that he previously enjoyed, and yet his new role may not provide the kind of heroic and exalted action that he expected to find in it. This he may experience as a loss in moral strength.

There is no doubt that certain kinds of role success require certain kinds of moral failure. It may therefore be necessary, in a sense, to cool the dubious neophyte in rather than out. He may have to be convinced that his doubts are a matter of sentimentality. The adult social view will be impressed upon him. He will be required to understand that a promotional change in status is voluntary, desirable, and natural, and that loss of one's role in these circumstances is the ultimate test of having fulfilled it properly.

It has been suggested that a person may leave a role under circumstances that reflect favorably upon the way in which he performed it. In theory, at least, a related possibility must be considered. A person may leave a role and at the same time leave behind him the standards by which such roles are judged. The new thing that he becomes may be so different from the thing he was that criteria such as success or failure cannot be easily applied to the change which has occurred. He becomes lost to others that he may become himself; he is of the twice-born. In our society, perhaps the most obvious example of this kind of termination occurs when a woman voluntarily gives up a prestigeful profession in order to become a wife and a mother. It is to be noted that this illustrates an institutionalized movement; those who make it do not make news. In America most other examples of this kind of termination are more a matter of talk than of occurrence. For example, one of the culture heroes of our dinner-table mythology is the man who walks out on an established calling in order to write or paint or live in the country. In other societies, the kind of abdication being considered here seems to have played a more important role. In medieval China, for instance, anchoretic withdrawal apparently gave to persons of quite different station a way of retreating from the occupational struggle while managing the retreat in an orderly, face-saving fashion.[2]

Two basic ways in which a person can lose a role have been considered; he can be promoted out of it or abdicate from it. There is, of course, a third basic ending to the status story. A person may be involuntarily deprived of his position or involvement and made in return something that is considered a lesser thing to be. It is mainly in this third ending to a person's role that occasions arise for cooling him out. It is here that one deals in the full sense with the problem of persons' losing their roles.

Involuntary loss seems itself to be of two kinds. First, a person may lose a status in such a way that the loss is not taken as a reflection upon the loser. The loss of a loved one, either because of an accident that could not have been prevented or because of a disease that could not have been halted, is a case in point. Occupational retirement because of old age is another. Of course, the loss will inevitably alter the conception the loser has of himself and the conception others have of him, but the alteration itself will not be treated as a symbol of the fate he deserves to receive. No insult is added to injury. It may be necessary, none the less, to pacify the loser and resign him to his loss. The loser who is not held responsible for his loss may even find himself taking the mystical view that all involvements are part of a wider con game, for the more one takes pleasure in a particular role the more one must suffer when it is time to leave it. He may find little comfort in the fact that the play has provided him with an illusion that has lasted a lifetime. He may find little comfort in the fact that the operators had not meant to deceive him.

Secondly, a person may be involuntarily deprived of a role under circumstances which reflect unfavorably on his capacity for it. The lost role may be one that he had already acquired or one that he had openly committed himself to preparing for. In either case the loss is more than a matter of ceasing to act in a given capacity; it is ultimate proof of an incapacity. And in many cases it is even more than this. The moment of failure often catches a person acting as one who feels that he is an appropriate sort of person for the role in question. Assumption becomes presumption, and failure becomes fraud. To loss of substance is thereby added loss of face. Of the many themes that can occur in the natural history of an involvement, this seems to be the most melancholy. Here it will be quite essential and quite difficult to cool the mark out. I shall be particularly concerned with this second kind of loss—the kind that involves humiliation.

It should be noted, parenthetically, that one circle of persons may define a particular loss as the kind that casts no reflection on the loser, and that a different circle of persons may treat the same loss as a symbol of what the loser deserves. One must also note that there is a tendency today to shift certain losses of status from the category of those that reflect upon the loser to the category of those that do not. When persons lose their jobs, their courage, or their minds, we tend more and more to take a clinical or naturalistic view of the loss and nonmoral view of their failure. We want to define a person as something that is not destroyed by the destruction of one of his selves. This benevolent attitude is in line with the effort today to publicize the view that occupational retirement is not the end of all active capacities but the beginning of new and different ones.

A consideration of consolation as a social process leads to four general problems having to do with the self in society. First, where in modern life does one find persons conducting themselves as though they were entitled to the rights of a particular status and then having to face up to the fact that they do not possess the qualification for the status? In other words, at what points in the structures of our social life are persons likely to compromise themselves or find themselves compromised? When is it likely that a person will have to disengage himself or become disengaged from one of his involvements? Secondly, what are the typical ways in which persons who find themselves in this difficult position can be cooled out; how can they be made to accept the great injury that has been done to their image of themselves, regroup their defenses, and carry on without raising a squawk? Thirdly, what, in general, can happen when a person refuses to be cooled out, that is, when he refuses to be pacified by the cooler? Fourthly, what arrangements are made by operators and marks to avoid entirely the process of consolation?

In all personal-service organizations customers or clients sometimes make complaints. A customer may feel that he has been given service in a way that is unacceptable to him—a way that he interprets as an offense to the conception he has of who and what he is. The management therefore has the problem of cooling the mark out. Frequently this function is allotted to specialists within the organization. In restaurants of some size, for example, one of the crucial functions of the hostess is to pacify customers whose self-conceptions have been injured by waitresses or by the food. In large stores the complaint department and the floorwalker perform a similar function.

One may note that a service organization does not operate in an anonymous world, as does a con mob, and is therefore strongly obliged to make some effort to cool the mark out. An institution, after all, cannot take it on the lam; it must pacify its marks.

One may also note that coolers in service organizations tend to view their own activity in a light that softens the harsher details of the situation. The cooler protects himself from feelings of guilt by arguing that the customer is not really in need of the service he expected to receive, that bad service is not really deprivational, and that beefs and complaints are a sign of bile, not a sign of injury. In a similar way, the con man protects himself from remorseful images of bankrupt marks by arguing that the mark is a fool and not a full-fledged person, possessing an inclination towards illegal gain but not the decency to admit it or the capacity to succeed at it.

In organizations patterned after a bureaucratic model, it is customary for personnel to expect rewards of a specified kind upon fulfilling requirements of a specified nature. Personnel come to define their career line in terms of a sequence of legitimate expectations and to base their self-conceptions on the assumption that in due course they will be what the institution allows persons to become. Sometimes, however, a member of an organization may fulfill some of the requirements for a particular status, especially the requirements concerning technical proficiency and seniority, but not other requirements, especially the less codified ones having to do with the proper handling of social relationships at work. It must fall to someone to break the bad news to the victim; someone must tell him that he has been fired, or that he has failed his examinations, or that he has been by-passed in promotion. And after the blowoff, someone has to cool the mark out. The necessity of disappointing the expectations that a person has taken for granted may be infrequent in some organizations, but in others, such as training institutions, it occurs all the time. The process of personnel selection requires that many trainees be called but that few be chosen.

When one turns from places of work to other scenes in our social life, one finds that each has its own occasions for cooling the mark out. During informal social intercourse it is well understood that an effort on the part of one person (ego) to decrease his social distance from another person (alter) must be graciously accepted by alter or, if rejected, rejected tactfully so that the initiator of the move can save his social face. This rule is codified in books on etiquette and is followed in actual behavior. A friendly movement in the direction of alter is a movement outward on a limb; ego communicates his belief that he has defined himself as worthy of alter's society, while at the same time he places alter in the strategic position of being able to discredit this conception.

The problem of cooling persons out in informal social intercourse is seen most clearly, perhaps, in courting situations and in what might be called de-courting situations. A proposal of marriage in our society tends to be a way in which a man sums up his social attributes and suggests to a woman that hers are not so much better as to preclude a merger or partnership in these matters. Refusal on the part of the woman, or refusal on the part of the man to propose when he is clearly in a position to do so, is a serious reflection on the rejected suitor. Courtship is a way not only of presenting oneself to alter for approval but also of saying that the opinion of alter in this matter is the opinion one is most concerned with. Refusing a proposal, or refusing to propose, is therefore a difficult operation. The mark must be carefully cooled out. The act of breaking a date or of refusing one, and the task of discouraging a "steady" can also be seen in this light, although in these cases great delicacy and tact may not be required, since the mark may not be deeply involved or openly committed. Just as it is harder to refuse a proposal than to refuse a date, so it is more difficult to reject a spouse than to reject a suitor. The process of de-courting by which one person in a marriage maneuvers the other into accepting a divorce without fuss or undue rancor requires extreme finesse in the art of cooling the mark out.

In all of these cases where a person constructs a conception of himself which cannot be sustained, there is a possibility that he has not invested that which is most important to him in the soon-to-be-denied status. In the current idiom, there is a possibility that when he is hit, he will not be hit where he really lives. There is a set of cases, however, where the blowoff cannot help but strike a vital spot; these cases arise, of course, when a person must be dissuaded from life itself. The man with a fatal sickness or fatal injury, the criminal with a death sentence, the soldier with a hopeless objective—these persons must be persuaded to accept quietly the loss of life itself, the loss of all one's earthly involvements. Here, certainly, it will be difficult to cool the mark out. It is a reflection on the conceptions men have—as cooler and mark—that it is possible to do so.

I have mentioned a few of the areas of social life where it becomes necessary, upon occasion, to cool a mark out. Attention may now be directed to some of the common ways in which individuals are cooled out in all of these areas of life.

For the mark, cooling represents a process of adjustment to an impossible situation—a situation arising from having defined himself in a way which the social facts come to contradict. The mark must therefore be supplied with a new set of apologies for himself, a new framework in which to see himself and judge himself. A process of redefining the self along defensible lines must be instigated and carried along; since the mark himself is frequently in too weakened a condition to do this, the cooler must initially do it for him.

One general way of handling the problem of cooling the mark out is to give the task to someone whose status relative to the mark will serve to ease the situation in some way. In formal organizations, frequently, someone who is two or three levels above the mark in line of command will do the hatchet work, on the assumption that words of consolation and redirection will have a greater power to convince if they come from high places. There also seems to be a feeling that persons of high status are better able to withstand the moral danger of having hate directed at them. Incidentally, persons protected by high office do not like to face this issue, and frequently attempt to define themselves as merely the agents of the deed and not the source of it. In some cases, on the other hand, the task of cooling the mark out is given to a friend and peer of the mark, on the assumption that such a person will know best how to hit upon a suitable rationalization for the mark and will know best how to control the mark should the need for this arise. In some cases, as in those pertaining to death, the role of cooler is given to doctors or priests. Doctors must frequently help a family, and the member who is leaving it, to manage the leave-taking with tact and a minimum of emotional fuss. A priest must not so much save a soul as create one that is consistent with what is about to become of it.

A second general solution to the problem of cooling the mark out consists of offering him a status which differs from the one he has lost or failed to gain but which provides at least a something or a somebody for him to become. Usually the alternative presented to the mark is a compromise of some kind, providing him with some of the trappings of his lost status as well as with some of its spirit. A lover may be asked to become a friend; a student of medicine may be asked to switch to the study of dentistry; a boxer may become a trainer; a dying person may be asked to broaden and empty his worldly loves so as to embrace the All-Father that is about to receive him. Sometimes the mark is allowed to retain his status but is required to fulfill it in a different environment: the honest policeman is transferred to a lonely beat; the too zealous priest is encouraged to enter a monastery; an unsatisfactory plant manager is shipped off to another branch. Sometimes the mark is "kicked upstairs" and given a courtesy status such as "Vice President." In the game for social roles, transfer up, down, or away may all be consolation prizes.

A related way of handling the mark is to offer him another chance to qualify for the role at which he has failed. After his fall from grace, he is allowed to retrace his steps and try again. Officer selection programs in the army, for example, often provide for possibilities of this kind. In general, it seems that third and fourth chances are seldom given to marks, and that second chances, while often given, are seldom taken. Failure at a role removes a person from the company of those who have succeeded, but it does not bring him back—in spirit, anyway—to the society of those who have not tried or are in the process of trying. The person who has failed in a role is a constant source of embarrassment, for none of the standard patterns of treatment is quite applicable to him. Instead of taking a second chance, he usually goes away to another place where his past does not bring confusion to his present.

Another standard method of cooling the mark out—one which is frequently employed in conjunction with other methods—is to allow the mark to explode, to break down, to cause a scene, to give full vent to his reactions and feelings, to "blow his top." If this release of emotions does not find a target, then it at least serves a cathartic function. If it does find a target, as in "telling off the boss," it gives the mark a last-minute chance to re-erect his defenses and prove to himself and others that he had not really cared about the status all along. When a blow-up of this kind occurs, friends of the mark or psychotherapists are frequently brought in. Friends are willing to take responsibility for the mark because their relationship to him is not limited to the role he has failed in. This, incidentally, provides one of the less obvious reasons why the cooler in a con mob must cultivate the friendship of the mark; friendship provides the cooler with an acceptable reason for staying around while the mark is cooled out. Psychotherapists, on the other hand, are willing to take responsibility for the mark because it is their business to offer a relationship to those who have failed in a relationship to others.

It has been suggested that a mark may be cooled out by allowing him, under suitable guidance, to give full vent to his initial shock. Thus the manager of a commercial organization may listen with patience and understanding to the complaints of a customer, knowing that the full expression of a complaint is likely to weaken it. This possibility lies behind the role of a whole series of buffers in our society—janitors, restaurant hostesses, grievance committees, floorwalkers, and so on—who listen in silence, with apparent sympathy, until the mark has simmered down. Similarly, in the case of criminal trials, the defending lawyer may find it profitable to allow the public to simmer down before he brings his client to court.

A related procedure for cooling the mark out is found in what is called stalling. The feelings of the mark are not brought to a head because he is given no target at which to direct them. The operator may manage to avoid the presence of the mark or may convince the mark that there is still a slight chance that the loss has not really occurred. When the mark is stalled, he is given a chance to become familiar with the new conception of self he will have to accept before he is absolutely sure that he will have to accept it.

As another cooling procedure, there is the possibility that the operator and the mark may enter into a tacit understanding according to which the mark agrees to act as if he were leaving of his own accord, and the operator agrees to preserve the illusion that this was the case. It is a form of bribery. In this way the mark may fail in his own eyes but prevent others from discovering the failure. The mark gives up his role but saves his face. This, after all, is one of the reasons why persons who are fleeced by con men are often willing to remain silent about their adventure. The same strategy is at work in the romantic custom of allowing a guilty officer to take his own life in a private way before it is taken from him publicly, and in the less romantic custom of allowing a person to resign for delicate reasons instead of firing him for indelicate ones.

Bribery is, of course, a form of exchange. In this case, the mark guarantees to leave quickly and quietly, and in exchange is allowed to leave under a cloud of his own choosing. A more important variation on the same theme is found in the practice of financial compensation. A man can say to himself and others that he is happy to retire from his job and say this with more conviction if he is able to point to a comfortable pension. In this sense, pensions are automatic devices for providing consolation. So, too, a person who has been injured because of another's criminal or marital neglect can compensate for the loss by means of a court settlement.

I have suggested some general ways in which the mark is cooled out. The question now arises: what happens if the mark refuses to be cooled out? What are the possible lines of action he can take if he refuses to be cooled? Attempts to answer these questions will show more clearly why, in general, the operator is so anxious to pacify the mark.

It has been suggested that a mark may be cooled by allowing him to blow his top. If the blow-up is too drastic or prolonged, however, difficulties may arise. We say that the mark becomes "disturbed mentally" or "personally disorganized." Instead of merely telling his boss off, the mark may go so far as to commit criminal violence against him. Instead of merely blaming himself for failure, the mark may inflict great punishment upon himself by attempting suicide, or by acting so as to make it necessary for him to be cooled out in other areas of his social life.

Sustained personal disorganization is one way in which a mark can refuse to cool out. Another standard way is for the individual to raise a squawk, that is, to make a formal complaint to higher authorities obliged to take notice of such matters. The con mob worries lest the mark appeal to the police. The plant manager must make sure that the disgruntled department head does not carry a formal complaint to the general manager or, worse still, to the Board of Directors. The teacher worries lest the child's parent complain to the principal. Similarly, a woman who communicates her evaluation of self by accepting a proposal of marriage can sometimes protect her exposed position—should the necessity of doing so arise—by threatening her disaffected fiancé with a breach-of-promise suit. So, also, a woman who is de-courting her husband must fear lest he contest the divorce or sue her lover for alienation of affection. In much the same way, a customer who is angered by a salesperson can refuse to be mollified by the floorwalker and demand to see the manager. It is interesting to note that associations dedicated to the rights and the honor of minority groups may sometimes encourage a mark to register a formal squawk; politically it may be more advantageous to provide a test case than to allow the mark to be cooled out.

Another line of action which a mark who refuses to be cooled can pursue is that of turning "sour." The term derives from the argot of industry but the behavior it refers to occurs everywhere. The mark outwardly accepts his loss but withdraws all enthusiasm, good will, and vitality from whatever role he is allowed to maintain. He complies with the formal requirements of the role that is left him, but he withdraws his spirit and identification from it. When an employee turns sour, the interests of the organization suffer; every executive, therefore, has the problem of "sweetening" his workers. They must not come to feel that they are slowly being cooled out. This is one of the functions of granting periodic advancements in salary and status, of schemes such as profit-sharing, or of giving the "employee" at home an anniversary present. A similar view can be taken of the problem that a government faces in times of crisis when it must maintain the enthusiastic support of the nation's disadvantaged minorities, for whole groupings of the population can feel they are being cooled out and react by turning sour.

Finally, there is the possibility that the mark may, in a manner of speaking, go into business for himself. He can try to gather about him the persons and facilities required to establish a status similar to the one he has lost, albeit in relation to a different set of persons. This way of refusing to be cooled is often rehearsed in phantasies of the "I'll show them" kind, but sometimes it is actually realized in practice. The rejected marriage partner may make a better remarriage. A social stratum that has lost its status may decide to create its own social system. A leader who fails in a political party may establish his own splinter group.

All these ways in which a mark can refuse to be cooled out have consequences for other persons. There is, of course, a kind of refusal that has little consequence for others. Marks of all kinds may develop explanations and excuses to account in a creditable way for their loss. It is, perhaps, in this region of phantasy that the defeated self makes its last stand.

The process of cooling is a difficult one, both for the operator who cools the mark out and for the person who receives this treatment. Safeguards and strategies are therefore employed to ensure that the process itself need not and does not occur. One deals here with strategies of prevention, not strategies of cure.

From the point of view of the operator, there are two chief ways of avoiding the difficulties of cooling the mark out. First, devices are commonly employed to weed out those applicants for a role, office, or relationship who might later prove to be unsuitable and require removal. The applicant is not given a chance to invest his self unwisely. A variation of this technique, that provides, in a way, a built-in mechanism for cooling the mark out, is found in the institution of probationary period and "temporary" staff. These definitions of the situation make it clear to the person that he must maintain his ego in readiness for the loss of his job, or, better still, that he ought not to think of himself as really having the job. If these safety measures fail, however, a second strategy is often employed. Operators of all kinds seem to be ready, to a surprising degree, to put up with or "carry" persons who have failed but who have not yet been treated as failures. This is especially true where the involvement of the mark is deep and where his conception of self had been publicly committed. Business offices, government agencies, spouses, and other kinds of operators are often careful to make a place for the mark, so that dissolution of the bond will not be necessary. Here, perhaps, is the most important source of private charity in our society.

A consideration of these preventive strategies brings to attention an interesting functional relationship among age-grading, recruitment, and the structure of the self. In our society, as in most others, the young in years are defined as not-yet-persons. To a certain degree, they are not subject to success and failure. A child can throw himself completely into a task, and fail at it, and by and large he will not be destroyed by his failure; it is only necessary to play at cooling him out. An adolescent can be bitterly disappointed in love, and yet he will not thereby become, at least for others, a broken person. A youth can spend a certain amount of time shopping around for a congenial job or a congenial training course, because he is still thought to be able to change his mind without changing his self. And, should he fail at something to which he has tried to commit himself, no permanent damage may be done to his self. If many are to be called and few chosen, then it is more convenient for everyone concerned to call individuals who are not fully persons and cannot be destroyed by failing to be chosen. As the individual grows older, he becomes defined as someone who must not be engaged in a role for which he is unsuited. He becomes defined as something that must not fail, while at the same time arrangements are made to decrease the chances of his failing. Of course, when the mark reaches old age, he must remove himself or be removed from each of his roles, one by one, and participate in the problem of later maturity.

The strategies that are employed by operators to avoid the necessity of cooling the mark out have a counterpart in the strategies that are employed by the mark himself for the same purpose.

There is the strategy of hedging, by which a person makes sure that he is not completely committed. There is the strategy of secrecy, by which a person conceals from others and even from himself the facts of his commitment; there is also the practice of keeping two irons in the fire and the more delicate practice of maintaining a joking or unserious relationship to one's involvement. All of these strategies give the mark an out; in case of failure he can act as if the self that has failed is not one that is important to him. Here we must also consider the function of being quick to take offense and of taking hints quickly, for in these ways the mark can actively cooperate in the task of saving his face. There is also the strategy of playing it safe, as in cases where a calling is chosen because tenure is assured in it, or where a plain woman is married for much the same reason.

It has been suggested that preventive strategies are employed by operator and mark in order to reduce the chance of failing or to minimize the consequences of failure. The less importance one finds it necessary to give to the problem of cooling, the more importance one may have given to the application of preventive strategies.

I have considered some of the situations in our society in which the necessity for cooling the mark out is likely to arise. I have also considered the standard ways in which a mark can be cooled out, the lines of action he can pursue if he refuses to be cooled, and the ways in which the whole problem can be avoided. Attention can now be turned to some very general questions concerning the self in society.

First, an attempt must be made to draw together what has been implied about the structure of persons. From the point of view of this paper, a person is an individual who becomes involved in a value of some kind—a role, a status, a relationship, an ideology—and then makes a public claim that he is to be defined and treated as someone who possesses the value or property in question. The limits to his claims, and hence the limits to his self, are primarily determined by the objective facts of his social life and secondarily determined by the degree to which a sympathetic interpretation of these facts can bend them in his favor. Any event which demonstrates that someone has made a false claim, defining himself as something which he is not, tends to destroy him. If others realize that the person's conception of self has been contradicted and discredited, then the person tends to be destroyed in the eyes of others. If the person can keep the contradiction a secret, he may succeed in keeping everyone but himself from treating him as a failure.

Secondly, one must take note of what is implied by the fact that it is possible for a person to be cooled out. Difficult as this may be, persons regularly define themselves in terms of a set of attributes and then have to accept the fact that they do not possess them—and do this about-face with relatively little fuss or trouble for the operators. This implies that there is a norm in our society persuading persons to keep their chins up and make the best of it—a sort of social sanitation enjoining torn and tattered persons to keep themselves packaged up. More important still, the capacity of a person to sustain these profound embarrassments implies a certain looseness and lack of interpenetration in the organization of his several life-activities. A man may fail in his job, yet go on succeeding with his wife. His wife may ask him for a divorce, or refuse to grant him one, and yet he may push his way onto the same streetcar at the usual time on the way to the same job. He may know that he is shortly going to have to leave the status of the living, but still march with the other prisoners, or eat breakfast with his family at their usual time and from behind his usual paper. He may be conned of his life's savings on an eastbound train but return to his home town and succeed in acting as if nothing of interest had happened.

Lack of rigid integration of a person's social roles allows for compensation; he can seek comfort in one role for injuries incurred in others. There are always cases, of course, in which the mark cannot sustain the injury to his ego and cannot act like a "good scout." On these occasions the shattering experience in one area of social life may spread out to all the sectors of his activity. He may define away the barriers between his several social roles and become a source of difficulty in all of them. In such cases the play is the mark's entire social life, and the operators, really, are the society. In an increasing number of these cases, the mark is given psychological guidance by professionals of some kind. The psychotherapist is, in this sense, the society's cooler. His job is to pacify and reorient the disorganized person; his job is to send the patient back to an old world or a new one, and to send him back in a condition in which he can no longer cause trouble to others or can no longer make a fuss. In short, if one takes the society, and not the person as the unit, the psychotherapist has the basic task of cooling the mark out.

A third point of interest arises if one views all of social life from the perspective of this paper. It has been argued that a person must not openly or even privately commit himself to a conception of himself which the flow of events is likely to discredit. He must not put himself in a position of having to be cooled out. Conversely, however, he must make sure that none of the persons with whom he has dealings are of the sort who may prove unsuitable and need to be cooled out. He must make doubly sure that should it become necessary to cool his associates out, they will be the sort who allow themselves to be gotten rid of. The con man who wants the mark to go home quietly and absorb a loss, the restaurant hostess who wants a customer to eat quietly and go away without causing trouble, and, if this is not possible, quietly to take his patronage elsewhere—these are the persons and these are the relationships which set the tone of some of our social life. Underlying this tone there is the assumption that persons are institutionally related to each other in such a way that if a mark allows himself to be cooled out, then the cooler need have no further concern with him; but if the mark refuses to be cooled out, he can put institutional machinery into action against the cooler. Underlying this tone there is also the assumption that persons are sentimentally related to each other in such a way that if a person allows himself to be cooled out, however great the loss he has sustained, then the cooler withdraws all emotional identification from him; but if the mark cannot absorb the injury to his self and if he becomes personally disorganized in some way, then the cooler cannot help but feel guilt and concern over the predicament. It is this feeling of guilt—this small measure of involvement in the feelings of others—which helps to make the job of cooling the mark out distasteful, wherever it appears. It is this incapacity to be insensitive to the suffering of another person when he brings his suffering right to your door which tends to make the job of cooling a species of dirty work.

One must not, of course, make too much of the margin of sympathy connecting operator and mark. For one thing, the operator may rid himself of the mark by application or threat of pure force or open insult. In Chicago in the 1920's small businessmen who suffered a loss in profits and in independence because of the "protection" services that racketeers gave to them were cooled out in this way. No doubt it is frivolous to suggest that Freud's notion of castration threat has something to do with the efforts of fathers to cool their sons out of oedipal involvements. Furthermore, there are many occasions when operators of different kinds must act as middlemen, with two marks on their hands; the calculated use of one mark as a sacrifice or fall guy may be the only way of cooling the other mark out. Finally, there are barbarous ceremonies in our society, such as criminal trials and the drumming-out ritual employed in court-martial procedures, that are expressly designed to prevent the mark from saving his face. And even in those cases where the cooler makes an effort to make things easier for the person he is getting rid of, we often find that there are bystanders who have no such scruples. Onlookers who are close enough to observe the blowoff but who are not obliged to assist in the dirty work often enjoy the scene, taking pleasure in the discomfiture of the cooler and in the destruction of the mark. What is trouble for some is Schadenfreude for others.

This paper has dealt chiefly with adaptations to loss; with defenses, strategies, consolation, mitigations, compensations, and the like. The kinds of sugar-coating have been examined, and not the pill. I would like to close this paper by referring briefly to the sort of thing that would be studied if one were interested in loss as such, and not in adaptations to it.

A mark who requires cooling out is a person who can no longer sustain one of his social roles and is about to be removed from it; he is a person who is losing one of his social lives and is about to die one of the deaths that are possible for him. This leads one to consider the ways in which we can go or be sent to our death in each of our social capacities, the ways, in other words, of handling the passage from the role that we had to a state of having it no longer. One might consider the social processes of firing and laying-off; of resigning and being asked to resign; of farewell and departure; of deportation, excommunication, and going to jail; of defeat at games, contests, and wars; of being dropped from a circle of friends or an intimate social relationship; of corporate dissolution; of retirement in old age; and, lastly, of the deaths that heirs are interested in.

And, finally, attention must be directed to the things we became after we have died in one of the many social senses and capacities in which death can come to us. As one might expect, a process of sifting and sorting occurs by which the socially dead come to be effectively hidden from us. This movement of ex-persons throughout the social structure proceeds in more than one direction.

There is, first of all, the dramatic process by which persons who have died in important ways come gradually to be brought together into a common graveyard that is separated ecologically from the living community. For the dead, this is at once a punishment and a defense. Jails and mental institutions are, perhaps, the most familiar examples, but other important ones exist. In America today, there is the interesting tendency to set aside certain regions and towns in California as asylums for those who have died in their capacity as workers and as parents but who are still alive financially.[3] For the old in America who have also died financially, there are old-folks' homes and rooming-house areas. And, of course, large cities have their Skid Rows which are, as Park put it, "full of junk, much of it human, i.e., men and women who, for some reason or other, have fallen out of line in the march of industrial progress and have been scrapped by the industrial organization of which they were once a part."[4] Hobo jungles, located near freight yards on the outskirts of towns, provide another case in point.

Just as a residential area may become a graveyard, so also certain institutions and occupational roles may take on a similar function. The ministry in Britain, for example, has sometimes served as a limbo for the occupational stillborn of better families, as have British universities. Mayhew, writing of London in the mid-nineteenth century, provides another example: artisans of different kinds, who had failed to maintain a position in the practice of their trade, could be found working as dustmen.[5] In the United States, the jobs of waitress, cab driver, and night watchman, and the profession of prostitution, tend to be ending places where persons of certain kinds, starting from different places, can come to rest.

But perhaps the most important movement of those who fail is one we never see. Where roles are ranked and somewhat related, persons who have been rejected from the one above may be difficult to distinguish from persons who have risen from the one below. For example, in America, upper-class women who fail to make a marriage in their own circle may follow the recognized route of marrying an upper-middle class professional. Successful lower-middle class women may arrive at the same station in life, coming from the other direction. Similarly, among those who mingle with one another as colleagues in the profession of dentistry, it is possible to find some who have failed to become physicians and others who have succeeded at not becoming pharmacists or optometrists. No doubt there are few positions in life that do not throw together some persons who are there by virtue of failure and other persons who are there by virtue of success. In this sense, the dead are sorted but not segregated, and continue to walk among the living.

Notes

1   Terminology regarding criminal activity is taken primarily from D.W. Maurer, *The Big Con* (New York, Bobbs-Merrill, 1940), and also from E. Sutherland, *The Professional Thief* (Chicago, Univ. of Chicago Press, 1937). The approach that this paper attempts to utilize is taken from Everett C. Hughes of the University of Chicago. The sociological problem of failure was first suggested to me by James Littlejohn of the University of Edinburgh.

2   See, for example, Max Weber, *The Religion of China* (H. H. Gerth, tr.); Glencoe, Ill., Free Press, 1951; p.178.

3   Some early writers on caste report a like situation in India at the turn of the nineteenth century. Hindus who were taken to the Ganges to die, and who then recovered, were apparently denied all legal rights and all social relations with the living. Apparently these excluded persons found it necessary to congregate in a few villages of their own. In California, of course, settlements of the old have a voluntary character, and members maintain ceremonial contact with younger kin by the exchange of periodic visits and letters.

4   R. E. Park, *Human Communities;* Glencoe, Ill.; Free Press. 1952; p.60

5   Henry Mayhew, *London Labour and the London Poor;* London, Griffin, Bohn, 1861; Vol. II, pp. 177–8.

2

Self-Presentation

From *The Presentation of Self in Everyday Life*[*]

Underlying all social interaction there seems to be a fundamental dialectic. When one individual enters the presence of others, he will want to discover the facts of the situation. Were he to possess this information, he could know, and make allowances for, what will come to happen and he could give the others present as much of their due as is consistent with his enlightened self-interest. To uncover fully the factual nature of the situation, it would be necessary for the individual to know all the relevant social data about the others. It would also be necessary for the individual to know the actual outcome or end product of the activity of the others during the interaction, as well as their innermost feelings concerning him. Full information of this order is rarely available; in its absence, the individual tends to employ substitutes—cues, tests, hints, expressive gestures, status symbols, etc.—as predictive devices. In short, since the reality that the individual is concerned with is unperceivable at the moment, appearances must be relied upon in its stead. And, paradoxically, the more the individual is concerned with the reality that is not available to perception, the more must he concentrate his attention on appearances.

The individual tends to treat the others present on the basis of the impression they give now about the past and the future. It is here that communicative acts are translated into moral ones. The impressions that the others give tend to be treated as claims and promises they have implicitly made, and claims and promises tend to have a moral character. In his mind the individual says: "I am using these impressions of you as a way of checking up on you and your activity, and you ought not to lead me astray." The peculiar thing about this is that the individual tends to take this stand even though he expects the others to be unconscious of many of their expressive behaviors and even though he may expect to exploit the others on the basis of the

* First published 1956; this extract from the edition of 1959, pp. 249–55. Copyright © 1959 by Erving Goffman. Used by permission of Doubleday, a division of Bantam Doubleday Dell Publishing Group, Inc.

information he gleans about them. Since the sources of impression used by the observing individual involve a multitude of standards pertaining to politeness and decorum, pertaining both to social intercourse and task-performance, we can appreciate afresh how daily life is enmeshed in moral lines of discrimination.

Let us shift now to the point of view of the others. If they are to be gentlemanly, and play the individual's game, they will give little conscious heed to the fact that impressions are being formed about them but rather act without guile or contrivance, enabling the individual to receive valid impressions about them and their efforts. And if they happen to give thought to the fact that they are being observed, they will not allow this to influence them unduly, content in the belief that the individual will obtain a correct impression and give them their due because of it. Should they be concerned with influencing the treatment that the individual gives them, and this is properly to be expected, then a gentlemanly means will be available to them. They need only guide their action in the present so that its future consequences will be the kind that would lead a just individual to treat them now in a way they want to be treated; once this is done, they have only to rely on the perceptiveness and justness of the individual who observes them.

Sometimes those who are observed do, of course, employ these proper means of influencing the way in which the observer treats them. But there is another way, a shorter and more efficient way, in which the observed can influence the observer. Instead of allowing an impression of their activity to arise as an incidental by-product of their activity, they can reorient their frame of reference and devote their efforts to the creation of desired impressions. Instead of attempting to achieve certain ends by acceptable means, they can attempt to achieve the impression that they are achieving certain ends by acceptable means. It is always possible to manipulate the impression the observer uses as a substitute for reality because a sign for the presence of a thing, not being that thing, can be employed in the absence of it. The observer's need to rely on representations of things itself creates the possibility of misrepresentation.

There are many sets of persons who feel they could not stay in business, whatever their business, if they limited themselves to the gentlemanly means of influencing the individual who observes them. At some point or other in the round of their activity they feel it is necessary to band together and directly manipulate the impression that they give. The observed become a performing team and the observers become the audience. Actions which appear to be done on objects become gestures addressed to the audience. The round of activity becomes dramatized.

We come now to the basic dialectic. In their capacity as performers, individuals will be concerned with maintaining the impression that they are living up to the many standards by which they and their products are judged.

Because these standards are so numerous and so pervasive, the individuals who are performers dwell more than we might think in a moral world. But, *qua* performers, individuals are concerned not with the moral issue of realizing these standards, but with the amoral issue of engineering a convincing impression that these standards are being realized. Our activity, then, is largely concerned with moral matters, but as performers we do not have a moral concern with them. As performers we are merchants of morality. Our day is given over to intimate contact with the goods we display and our minds are filled with intimate understandings of them; but it may well be that the more attention we give to these goods, then the more distant we feel from them and from those who are believing enough to buy them. To use a different imagery, the very obligation and profitability of appearing always in a steady moral light, of being a socialized character, forces one to be the sort of person who is practiced in the ways of the stage.

Staging and the Self

The general notion that we make a presentation of ourselves to others is hardly novel; what ought to be stressed in conclusion is that the very structure of the self can be seen in terms of how we arrange for such performances in our Anglo-American society.

In this report, the individual was divided by implication into two basic parts: he was viewed as a *performer,* a harried fabricator of impressions involved in the all-too-human task of staging a performance; he was viewed as a *character,* a figure, typically a fine one, whose spirit, strength, and other sterling qualities the performance was designed to evoke. The attributes of a performer and the attributes of a character are of a different order, quite basically so, yet both sets have their meaning in terms of the show that must go on.

First, character. In our society the character one performs and one's self are somewhat equated, and this self-as-character is usually seen as something housed within the body of its possessor, especially the upper parts thereof, being a nodule, somehow, in the psychobiology of personality. I suggest that this view is an implied part of what we are all trying to present, but provides, just because of this, a bad analysis of the presentation. In this report the performed self was seen as some kind of image, usually creditable, which the individual on stage and in character effectively attempts to induce others to hold in regard to him. While this image is entertained *concerning* the individual, so that a self is imputed to him, this self itself does not derive from its possessor, but from the whole scene of his action, being generated by that attribute of local events which renders them interpretable by witnesses. A correctly staged and performed scene leads the audience to impute a self to a performed character, but this imputation—this self—is a *product* of a scene that comes off, and is not a *cause* of it. The self, then, as a performed character, is not an organic thing that has a specific location, whose fundamental fate is to be born, to mature, and to die; it is a dramatic effect arising diffusely from a scene that is presented, and the characteristic issue, the crucial concern, is whether it will be credited or discredited.

In analyzing the self then we are drawn from its possessor, from the person who will profit or lose most by it, for he and his body merely provide the peg on which something of collaborative manufacture will be hung for a time. And the means for producing and maintaining selves do not reside inside the peg; in fact these means are often bolted down in social establishments. There will be a back region with its tools for shaping the body, and a front region with its fixed props. There will be a team of persons whose activity on stage in conjunction with available props will constitute the scene from which the performed character's self will emerge, and another team, the audience, whose interpretive activity will be necessary for this emergence. The self is a product of all of these arrangements, and in all of its parts bears the marks of this genesis.

The whole machinery of self-production is cumbersome, of course, and sometimes breaks down, exposing its separate components: back region control; team collusion; audience tact; and so forth. But, well oiled, impressions will flow from it fast enough to put us in the grips of one of our types of reality—the performance will come off and the firm self accorded each performed character will appear to emanate intrinsically from its performer.

Let us turn now from the individual as character performed to the individual as performer. He has a capacity to learn, this being exercised in the task of training for a part. He is given to having fantasies and dreams, some that pleasurably unfold a triumphant performance, others full of anxiety and dread that nervously deal with vital discreditings in a public front region. He often manifests a gregarious desire for teammates and audiences, a tactful considerateness for their concerns; and he has a capacity for deeply felt shame, leading him to minimize the chances he takes of exposure.

These attributes of the individual *qua* performer are not merely a depicted effect of particular performances; they are psychobiological in nature, and yet they seem to arise out of intimate interaction with the contingencies of staging performances.

And now a final comment. In developing the conceptual framework employed in this report, some language of the stage was used. I spoke of performers and audiences; of routines and parts; of performances coming off or falling flat; of cues, stage settings and backstage; of dramaturgical needs, dramaturgical skills, and dramaturgical strategies. Now it should be admitted that this attempt to press a mere analogy so far was in part a rhetoric and a maneuver.

The claim that all the world's a stage is sufficiently commonplace for readers to be familiar with its limitations and tolerant of its presentation, knowing that at any time they will easily be able to demonstrate to themselves that it is not to be taken too seriously. An action staged in a theater is a relatively contrived illusion and an admitted one; unlike ordinary life, nothing real or actual can happen to the performed character—although at another level of course something real and actual can happen to the reputation of performers *qua* professionals whose everyday job is to put on theatrical performances.

And so here the language and mask of the stage will be dropped. Scaffolds, after all, are to build other things with, and should be erected with an eye to taking them down. This report is not concerned with aspects of theater that creep into everyday life. It is concerned with the structure of social encounters—the structure of those entities in social life that come into being whenever persons enter one another's immediate physical presence. The key factor in this structure is the maintenance of a single definition of the situation, this definition having to be expressed, and this expression sustained in the face of a multitude of potential disruptions.

A character staged in a theater is not in some ways real, nor does it have the same kind of real consequences as does the thoroughly contrived character performed by a confidence man; but the *successful* staging of either of these types of false figures involves use of *real* techniques—the same techniques by which everyday persons sustain their real social situations. Those who conduct face to face interaction on a theater's stage must meet the key requirement of real situations; they must expressively sustain a definition of the situation: but this they do in circumstances that have facilitated their developing an apt terminology for the interactional tasks that all of us share.

3

The Self as Ritual Object

From "The Nature of Deference and Demeanor"*

Deference and demeanor are analytical terms; empirically there is much overlapping of the activities to which they refer. An act through which the individual gives or withholds deference to others typically provides means by which he expresses the fact that he is a well or badly demeaned individual. Some aspects of this overlapping may be cited. First, in performing a given act of presentational deference, as in offering a guest a chair, the actor finds himself doing something that can be done with smoothness and aplomb, expressing self-control and poise, or with clumsiness and uncertainty, expressing an irresolute character. This is, as it were, an incidental and adventitious connection between deference and demeanor. It may be illustrated from recent material on doctor–patient relationships, where it is suggested that one complaint a doctor may have against some of his patients is that they do not bathe before coming for an examination,[1] while bathing is a way of paying deference to the doctor it is at the same time a way for the patient to present himself as a clean, well demeaned person. A further illustration is found in acts such as loud talking, shouting, or singing, for these acts encroach upon the right of others to be let alone, while at the same time they illustrate a badly demeaned lack of control over one's feelings.

The same connection between deference and demeanor has had a bearing on the ceremonial difficulties associated with intergroup interaction: the gestures of deference expected by members of one society have sometimes been incompatible with the standards of demeanor maintained by members of another. For example, during the nineteenth century, diplomatic relations between Britain and China were embarrassed by the fact that the *Kot'ow* demanded of visiting ambassadors by the Chinese Emperor was felt by some British ambassadors to be incompatible with their self-respect.[2]

A second connection between deference and demeanor turns upon the

* First published 1956; this extract from *Interaction Ritual: Essays on Face-to-Face Behavior*, 1967, pp. 81–95. Copyright © 1967 by Erving Goffman. Reprinted by permission of Pantheon Books, a division of Random House, Inc.

fact that a willingness to give others their deferential due is one of the qualities which the individual owes it to others to express through his conduct, just as a willingness to conduct oneself with good demeanor is in general a way of showing deference to those present.

In spite of these connections between deference and demeanor, the analytical relation between them is one of "complementarity," not identity. The image the individual owes to others to maintain of himself is not the same type of image these others are obliged to maintain of him. Deference images tend to point to the wider society outside the interaction, to the place the individual has achieved in the hierarchy of this society. Demeanor images tend to point to qualities which any social position gives its incumbents a chance to display during interaction, for these qualities pertain more to the way in which the individual handles his position than to the rank and place of that position relative to those possessed by others.

Further, the image of himself the individual owes it to others to maintain through his conduct is a kind of justification and compensation for the image of him that others are obliged to express through their deference to him. Each of the two images in fact may act as a guarantee and check upon the other. In an interchange that can be found in many cultures, the individual defers to guests to show how welcome they are and how highly he regards them; they in turn decline the offering at least once, showing through their demeanor that they are not presumptuous, immodest, or over-eager to receive favor. Similarly, a man starts to rise for a lady, showing respect for her sex; she interrupts and halts his gesture, showing she is not greedy of her rights in this capacity but is ready to define the situation as one between equals. In general, then, by treating others deferentially one gives them an opportunity to handle the indulgence with good demeanor. Through this differentiation in symbolizing function the world tends to be bathed in better images than anyone deserves, for it is practical to signify great appreciation of others by offering them deferential indulgences, knowing that some of these indulgences will be declined as an expression of good demeanor.

There are still other complementary relations between deference and demeanor. If an individual feels he ought to show proper demeanor in order to warrant deferential treatment, then he must be in a position to do so. He must, for example, be able to conceal from others aspects of himself which would make him unworthy in their eyes, and to conceal himself from them when he is in an indignified state, whether of dress, mind, posture, or action. The avoidance rituals which others perform in regard to him give him room to maneuver, enabling him to present only a self that is worthy of deference; at the same time, this avoidance makes it easier for them to assure themselves that the deference they have to show him is warranted.

To show the difference between deference and demeanor, I have pointed out the complementary relation between them, but even this kind of related-

ness can be overstressed. The failure of an individual to show proper deference to others does not necessarily free them from the obligation to act with
good demeanor in his presence, however disgruntled they may be at having
to do this. Similarly, the failure of an individual to conduct himself with
proper demeanor does not always relieve those in his presence from treating
him with proper deference. It is by separating deference and demeanor that
we can appreciate many things about ceremonial life, such as that a group
may be noted for excellence in one of these areas while having a bad reputation in the other. Hence we can find a place for arguments such as De
Quincey's[3] that an Englishman shows great self-respect but little respect for
others while a Frenchman show great respect for others but little respect for
himself.

We are to see, then, that there are many occasions when it would be
improper for an individual to convey about himself what others are ready to
convey about him to him, since each of these two images is a warrant and
justification for the other, and not a mirror image of it. The Meadian notion
that the individual takes toward himself the attitude others take to him seems
very much an oversimplification. Rather the individual must rely on others
to complete the picture of him of which he himself is allowed to paint only
certain parts. Each individual is responsible for the demeanor image of
himself and the deference image of others, so that for a complete man to be
expressed, individuals must hold hands in a chain of ceremony, each giving
deferentially with proper demeanor to the one on the right what will be
received deferentially from the one on the left. While it may be true that the
individual has a unique self all his own, evidence of this possession is thoroughly a product of joint ceremonial labor, the part expressed through the
individual's demeanor being no more significant than the part conveyed by
others through their deferential behavior toward him. . .

Conclusions

The rules of conduct which bind the actor and the recipient together are the
bindings of society. But many of the acts which are guided by these rules
occur infrequently or take a long time for their consummation.
Opportunities to affirm the moral order and the society could therefore be
rare. It is here that ceremonial rules play their social function, for many of
the acts which are guided by these rules last but a brief moment, involve no
substantive outlay, and can be performed in every social interaction.
Whatever the activity and however profanely instrumental, it can afford
many opportunities for minor ceremonies as long as other persons are
present. Through these observances, guided by ceremonial obligations and
expectations, a constant flow of indulgences is spread through society, with

others who are present constantly reminding the individual that he must keep himself together as a well demeaned person and affirm the sacred quality of these others. The gestures which we sometimes call empty are perhaps in fact the fullest things of all.

It is therefore important to see that the self is in part a ceremonial thing, a sacred object which must be treated with proper ritual care and in turn must be presented in a proper light to others. As a means through which this self is established, the individual acts with proper demeanor while in contact with others and is treated by others with deference. It is just as important to see that if the individual is to play this kind of sacred game, then the field must be suited to it. The environment must ensure that the individual will not pay too high a price for acting with good demeanor and that deference will be accorded him. Deference and demeanor practices must be institutionalized so that the individual will be able to project a viable, sacred self and stay in the game on a proper ritual basis.

An environment, then, in terms of the ceremonial component of activity, is a place where it is easy or difficult to play the ritual game of having a self. Where ceremonial practices are thoroughly institutionalized, as they were on Ward A, it would appear easy to be a person. Where these practices are not established, as to a degree they were not in Ward B, it would appear difficult to be a person. Why one ward comes to be a place in which it is easy to have a self and another ward comes to be a place where this is difficult depends in part on the type of patient that is recruited and the type of regime the staff attempts to maintain.

One of the bases upon which mental hospitals throughout the world segregate their patients is degree of easily apparent "mental illness." By and large this means that patients are graded according to the degree to which they violate ceremonial rules of social intercourse. There are very good practical reasons for sorting patients into different wards in this way, and in fact that institution is backward where no one bothers to do so. This grading very often means, however, that individuals who are desperately uncivil in some areas of behavior are placed in the intimate company of those who are desperately uncivil in others. Thus, individuals who are the least ready to project a sustainable self are lodged in a milieu where it is practically impossible to do so.

It is in this context that we can reconsider some interesting aspects of the effect of coercion and constraint upon the individual. If an individual is to act with proper demeanor and show proper deference, then it will be necessary for him to have areas of self-determination. He must have an expendable supply of the small indulgences which his society employs in its idiom of regard—such as cigarettes to give, chairs to proffer, food to provide, and so forth. He must have freedom of bodily movement so that it will be possible for him to assume a stance that conveys appropriate respect for others and appropriate demeanor on his own part; a patient strapped to a bed may find it impractical not to befoul himself, let alone to stand in the presence of a lady. He must have a supply of appropriate clean clothing if he is to make the sort of appearance that is expected of a well demeaned person. To look seemly may require a tie, a belt, shoe laces, a mirror, and razor blades—all of which the authorities may deem unwise to give him. He must have access to the eating utensils which his society defines as appropriate ones for use, and may find that meat cannot be circumspectly eaten with a cardboard spoon. And finally, without too much cost to himself he must be able to decline certain kinds of work, now sometimes classified as "industrial therapy," which his social group considers *infra dignitatem*.

When the individual is subject to extreme constraint he is automatically forced from the circle of the proper. The sign vehicles or physical tokens through which the customary ceremonies are performed are unavailable to him. Others may show ceremonial regard for him, but it becomes impossible for him to reciprocate the show or to act in such a way as to make himself worthy of receiving it. The only ceremonial statements that are possible for him are improper ones.

The history of the care of mental cases is the history of constricting devices: constraining gloves, camisoles, floor and seat chains, handcuffs, "biter's mask," wet-packs, supervised toileting, hosing down, institutional clothing, forkless and knifeless eating, and so forth.[4] The use of these devices provides significant data on the ways in which the ceremonial grounds of selfhood can be taken away. By implication we can obtain information from this history about the conditions that must be satisfied if individuals are to have selves. Unfortunately, today there are still mental institutions where the past of other hospitals can be empirically studied now. Students of interpersonal ceremony should seek these institutions out almost as urgently as students of kinship have sought out disappearing cultures.

Throughout this paper I have assumed we can learn about ceremony by studying a contemporary secular situation—that of the individual who has declined to employ the ceremonial idiom of his group in an acceptable manner and has been hospitalized. In a crosscultural view it is convenient to see this as a product of our complex division of labor which brings patients together instead of leaving each in his local circle. Further, this division of labor also brings together those who have the task of caring for these patients.

We are thus led to the special dilemma of the hospital worker: as a member of the wider society he ought to take action against mental patients, who have transgressed the rules of ceremonial order; but his occupational role obliges him to care for and protect these very people. When "milieu therapy" is stressed, these obligations further require him to convey warmth in response to hostility; relatedness in response to alienation.

We have seen that hospital workers must witness improper conduct without applying usual negative sanctions, and yet that they must exercise disrespectful coercion over their patients. A third peculiarity is that staff members may be obliged to render to patients services such as changing socks, tying shoelaces or trimming fingernails, which outside the hospital generally convey elaborate deference. In the hospital setting, such acts are likely to convey something inappropriate since the attendant at the same time exerts certain kinds of power and moral superiority over his charges. A final peculiarity in the ceremonial life of mental hospitals is that individuals collapse as units of minimal ceremonial substance and others learn that what had been taken for granted as ultimate entities are really held together by rules that can be broken with some kind of impunity. Such understanding, like one gained at war or at a kinsman's funeral, is not much talked about but it tends, perhaps, to draw staff and patients together into an unwilling group sharing undesired knowledge.

In summary, then, modern society brings transgressors of the ceremonial order to a single place, along with some ordinary members of society who make their living there. These dwell in a place of unholy acts and unholy understandings, yet some of them retain allegiance to the ceremonial order outside the hospital setting. Somehow ceremonial people must work out mechanisms and techniques for living without certain kinds of ceremony.

In this paper I have suggested that Durkheimian notions about primitive religion can be translated into concepts of deference and demeanor, and that these concepts help us to grasp some aspects of urban secular living. The implication is that in one sense this secular world is not so irreligious as we might think. Many gods have been done away with, but the individual himself stubbornly remains as a deity of considerable importance. He walks with some dignity and is the recipient of many little offerings. He is jealous of the worship due him, yet, approached in the right spirit, he is ready to forgive those who may have offended him. Because of their status relative to his, some persons will find him contaminating while others will find they contaminate him, in either case finding that they must treat him with ritual care. Perhaps the individual is so viable a god because he can actually understand the ceremonial significance of the way he is treated, and quite on his own can respond dramatically to what is proffered him. In contacts between such deities there is no need for middlemen; each of these gods is able to serve as his own priest.

Notes

1   Ernest Dichter, *A Psychological Study of the Doctor–Patient Relationship* (California Medical Association, Alameda County Medical Association, 1950), pp. 5–6.

2   R. K. Douglas, *Society in China* (Innes, London, 1958), pp. 291–6.

3   Thomas De Quincey, "French and English Manners," *Collected Writings of Thomas De Quincy,* David Mason, ed. (Adams and Charles Black, Edinburgh, 1890), vol. XIV, 327–34.

4   See W.R. Thomas, "The Unwilling Patient," *Journal of Medical Science,* 99 (1953), especially p. 193; and Alexander Walk, "Some Aspects of the 'Moral Treatment' of the Insane up to 1854," *Journal of Medical Science,* 100 (1954), 191–201.

4

The Self and Social Roles

From "Role Distance"*

The role perspective has definite implications of a social-psychological kind. In entering the position, the incumbent finds that he must take on the whole array of action encompassed by the corresponding role, so role implies a social determinism and a doctrine about socialization. We do not take on items of conduct one at a time but rather a whole harness load of them and may anticipatorily learn to be a horse even while being pulled like a wagon. Role, then, is the basic unit of socialization. It is through roles that tasks in society are allocated and arrangements made to enforce their performance.

Recruitment for positions is restrictively regulated in some way, assuring that the incumbents will possess certain minimal qualifications, official and unofficial, technically relevant and irrelevant.[1] Incumbency tends to be symbolized through status cues of dress and manner, permitting those who engage in a situation to know with whom they are dealing. In some cases there will also be a role term of reference and address. Each position tends to be accorded some invidious social value, bringing a corresponding amount of prestige or contamination to the individual who fills it.

For this paper, it is important to note that in performing a role the individual must see to it that the impressions of him that are conveyed in the situation are compatible with role-appropriate personal qualities effectively imputed to him: a judge is supposed to be deliberate and sober; a pilot, in a cockpit, to be cool; a bookkeeper to be accurate and neat in doing his work. These personal qualities, effectively imputed and effectively claimed, combine with a position's title, when there is one, to provide a basis of *self-image* for the incumbent and a basis for the image that his role others will have of him. A self, then, virtually awaits the individual entering a position. . .

★   ★   ★

* Originally published in *Encounters: Two Studies in the Sociology of Interaction*, 1961, pp. 87, 90–1, 106–10, 132–3, 139, 152. Copyright © 1961. All rights reserved. Reprinted by permission of Allyn & Bacon.

It is a basic assumption of role analysis that each individual will be involved in more than one system or pattern and, therefore, perform more than one role. Each individual will, therefore, have several selves, providing us with the interesting problem of how these selves are related. The model of man according to the initial role perspective is that of a kind of holding company for a set of not relevantly connected roles; it is the concern of the second perspective to find out how the individual runs this holding company.

While manifestly participating in one system of roles, the individual will have some capacity to hold in abeyance his involvement in other patterns, thus sustaining one or more dormant roles that are enacted roles on other occasions. This capacity supports a life cycle, a calendar cycle, and a daily cycle of role enactments; such scheduling implies some jurisdictional agreements as to where and what the individual is to be when. This *role-segregation* may be facilitated by *audience-segregation,* so that those who figure in one of the individual's major role-sets do not figure in another, thereby allowing the individual to possess contradictory qualities. Nevertheless, a person such as a surgeon, who keeps his surgical tools off his kitchen table and his wife off his other table, may someday find himself with the role dilemma of treating an other both as kinsman and as a body. The embarrassment and vacillation characteristic of *role conflict* presumably result. The identification of this kind of trouble is not a limitation of role analysis but one of its main values, for we are led to consider mechanisms for avoiding such conflict or dealing with unavoidable conflict. . . .[2]

★   ★   ★

Three matters seem to be involved: an admitted or expressed attachment to the role; a demonstration of qualifications and capacities for performing it; an active *engagement* or spontaneous involvement in the role activity at hand, that is, a visible investment of attention and muscular effort. Where these three features are present, I will use the term *embracement.* To embrace a role is to disappear completely into the virtual self available in the situation, to be fully seen in terms of the image, and to confirm expressively one's acceptance of it. To embrace a role is to be embraced by it. Particularly good illustrations of full embracement can be seen in persons in certain occupations: team managers during baseball games; traffic policemen at intersections during rush hours; landing signal officers who wave in planes landing on the decks of aircraft carriers; in fact, any one occupying a directing role where the performer must guide others by means of gestural signs.

An individual may affect the embracing of a role in order to conceal a lack of attachment to it, just as he may affect a visible disdain for a role, thrice refusing the kingly crown, in order to defend himself against the psychological dangers of his actual attachment to it. Certainly an individual may be attached to a role and fail to be able to embrace it, as when a child proves to have no ticket or to be unable to hang on.

Returning to the merry-go-round, we see that at five years of age the situation is transformed, especially for boys. To be a merry-go-round horse rider is now apparently not enough, and this fact must be demonstrated out of dutiful regard for one's own character. Parents are not likely to be allowed to ride along, and the strap for preventing falls is often disdained. One rider may keep time to the music by clapping his feet or a hand against the horse, an early sign of utter control. Another may make a wary stab at standing on the saddle or changing horses without touching the platform. Still another may hold on to the post with one hand and lean back as far as possible while looking up to the sky in a challenge to dizziness. Irreverence begins, and the horse may be held on to by his wooden ear or his tail. The child says by his actions: "Whatever I am, I'm not just someone who can barely manage to stay on a wooden horse." Note that what the rider is apologizing for is not some minor untoward event that has cropped up during the interaction, but the whole role. The image of him that is generated for him by the routine entailed in his mere participation—his virtual self in the context—is an image from which he apparently withdraws by *actively* manipulating the situation. Whether this skittish behavior is intentional or unintentional, sincere or affected, correctly appreciated by others present or not, it does constitute a wedge between the individual and his role, between doing and being. This "effectively" expressed pointed separateness between the individual and his putative role I shall call *role distance*. A shorthand is involved here: the individual is actually denying not the role but the virtual self that is implied in the role for all accepting performers.

In any case, the term role distance is not meant to refer to all behavior that does not directly contribute to the task core of a given role but only to those behaviors that are seen by someone present as relevant to assessing the actor's attachment to his particular role and relevant in such a way as to suggest that the actor possibly has some measure of disaffection from, and resistance against, the role. Thus, for example, a four-year-old halfway through a triumphant performance as a merry-go-round rider may sometimes go out of play, dropping from his face and manner any confirmation of his virtual self, yet may indulge in this break in role without apparent intent, the lapse reflecting more on his capacity to sustain any role than on his feelings about the present one. Nor can it be called role distance if the child rebels and totally rejects the role, stomping off in a huff, for the special facts about self that can be conveyed by holding a role off a little are precisely the ones that cannot be conveyed by throwing the role over.

At seven and eight, the child not only dissociates himself self-consciously from the kind of horseman a merry-go-round allows him to be but also finds that many of the devices that younger people use for this are now beneath him. He rides no-hands, gleefully chooses a tiger or a frog for a steed, clasps hands with a mounted friend across the aisle. He tests limits, and his antics may bring negative sanction from the adult in charge of the machine. And he is still young enough to show distance by handling the task with bored, nonchalant competence, a candy bar languidly held in one hand.

At eleven and twelve, maleness for boys has become a real responsibility, and no easy means of role distance seems to be available on merry-go-rounds. It is necessary to stay away or to exert creative acts of distance, as when a boy jokingly treats his wooden horse as if it were a racing one: he jogs himself up and down, leans far over the neck of the horse, drives his heels mercilessly into its flanks, and uses the reins for a lash to get more speed, brutally reining in the horse when the ride is over. He is just old enough to achieve role distance by defining the whole undertaking as a lark, a situation for mockery.

Adults who choose to ride a merry-go-round display adult techniques of role distance. One adult rider makes a joke of tightening the safety belt around him; another crosses his arms, giving popcorn with his left hand to the person on his right and a coke with his right hand to the person on his left. A young lady riding sidesaddle tinkles out, "It's cold," and calls to her watching boy friend's boy friend, "Come on, don't be chicken." A dating couple riding adjacent horses holds hands to bring sentiment, not daring, to the situation. Two double-dating couples employ their own techniques: the male in front sits backwards and takes a picture of the other male rider taking a picture of him. And, of course, some adults, riding close by their threatened two-and-a-half-year-old, wear a face that carefully demonstrates that they do not perceive the ride as an event in itself, their only present interest being their child.

And finally there is the adult who runs the machine and takes the tickets. Here, often, can be found a fine flowering of role distance. Not only does he show that the ride itself is not—as a ride—an event to him, but he also gets off and on and around the moving platform with a grace and ease that can only be displayed by safely taking what for children and even adults would be chances.

Some general points can be made about merry-go-round role distance. First, while the management of a merry-go-round horse in our culture soon ceases to be a challenging "developmental task," the task of expressing that it is not continues for a long time to be a challenge and remains a felt necessity. A full twist must be made in the iron law of etiquette: the act through which one can afford to try to fit into the situation is an act that can be styled to show that one is somewhat out of place. One enters the situation to the degree that one can demonstrate that one does not belong.

A second general point about role distance is that immediate audiences figure very directly in the display of role distance. Merry-go-round horsemen are very ingenuous and may frankly wait for each time they pass their waiting friends before playing through their gestures of role distance. Moreover, if persons above the age of twelve or so are to trust themselves to making a lark of it, they almost need to have a friend along on the next horse, since persons who are "together" seem to be able to hold off the socially defining force of the environment much more than a person alone.

A final point: two different means of establishing role distance seem to be found. In one case the individual tries to isolate himself as much as possible from the contamination of the situation, as when an adult riding along to guard his child makes an effort to be completely stiff, affectless, and preoccupied. In the other case the individual cooperatively projects a childish self, meeting the situation more than halfway, but then withdraws from this castoff self by a little gesture signifying that the joking has gone far enough. In either case the individual can slip the skin the situation would clothe him in.

A summary of concepts is now in order. I have tried to distinguish among three easily confused ideas: *commitment, attachment,* and *embracement.* It is to be noted that these sociological terms are of a different order from that of *engagement,* a psychobiological process that a cat or a dog can display more beautifully than man. Finally, the term *role distance* was introduced to refer to actions which effectively convey some disdainful detachment of the performer from a role he is performing.

$$\star \quad \star \quad \star$$

A Simultaneous Multiplicity of Selves

It is common in sociology to study the individual in terms of the conception he and others have of him, and to argue that these conceptions are made available to him through the role that he plays. In this paper, the focus of role is narrowed down to a situated activity system. And it is argued that the individual must be seen as someone who organizes his expressive situational behavior *in relation* to situated activity roles, but that in doing this he uses whatever means are at hand to introduce a margin of freedom and maneuverability, of pointed disidentification, between himself and the self virtually available for him in the situation.

Instead, then, of starting with the notion of a definition of the situation we must start with the idea that a particular definition is *in charge of the situation,* and that as long as this control is not overtly threatened or blatantly rejected, much counter-activity will be possible. The individual acts to say: "I do not dispute the direction in which things are going and I will go along with them, but at the same time I want you to know that you haven't fully contained me in the state of affairs." Thus, the person who mutters, jokes, or responds with sarcasm to what is happening in the situation is nevertheless going along with the prevailing definition of the situation—with whatever bad spirit. The current system of activity tells us what situated roles will be in charge of the situation, but these roles at the same time provide a framework in which role distance can be expressed. Again, it should be noted that face-to-face interaction provides an admirable context for executing a double stance—the individual's task actions unrebelliously adhere to the official definition of the situation, while gestural activity that can be sustained simultaneously and yet noninterferingly shows that he has not agreed to having all of himself defined by what is officially in progress.

In whatever name the individual exerts role distance, it is plain, by definition, that the injected identification will be more or less in opposition to the one available in the situated role. But we must now see that role distance is merely an extreme instance of expressions, not a part of the self virtually available in a role, and that many other, less opposing, expressions can also occur. As long as the dominion of the situated role is not challenged, other role identities, ones different from but not necessarily opposed to the officially available self, can be sustained too. Role distance directs attention to the fact that situated roles allow for nonrelevant expressions but does not tell us much about the range of these expressions.

★   ★   ★

I have argued that the individual does not embrace the situated role that he finds available to him while holding all his other selves in abeyance. I have argued that a situated activity system provides an arena for conduct and that in this arena the individual constantly twists, turns, and squirms, even while allowing himself to be carried along by the controlling definition of the situation. The image that emerges of the individual is that of a juggler and synthesizer, an accommodator and appeaser, who fulfils one function while he is apparently engaged in another; he stands guard at the door of the tent but lets all his friends and relatives crawl in under the flap. This seems to be the case even in one of our most sacred occupational shows—surgery.

I have also argued that these various identificatory demands are not created by the individual but are drawn from what society allots him. He frees himself from one group, not to be free, but because there is another hold on him. While actively participating in an activity system, he is, nevertheless, also obliged to engage in other matters, in relationships, in multi-situated systems of activity, in sustaining norms of conduct that crosscut many particular activity systems. I want now to try to look more closely at some of the cultural influences that seem to be at work determining the expression of role-irrelevant identifications during role performance—influences that are broadly based in the society at large, in spite of the narrow arena in which they are given their due.

★   ★   ★

A situated system of activity and the organization in which this system is sustained provide the individual with that one of his roles that will be given principal weight on this occasion. But even while the local scene establishes what the individual will mainly be, many of his other affiliations will be simultaneously given little bits of credit.

A final comment is to be added. There is a vulgar tendency in social thought to divide the conduct of the individual into a profane and sacred part, this version of the distinction strangely running directly contrary to the one Durkheim gave us. The profane part is attributed to the obligatory world of social roles; it is formal, stiff, and dead; it is exacted by society. The sacred part has to do with "personal" matters and "personal" relationships—with what an individual is "really" like underneath it all when he relaxes and breaks through to those in his presence. It is here, in this personal capacity, that an individual can be warm, spontaneous, and touched by humor. It is here, regardless of his social role, that an individual can show "what kind of a guy he is." And so it is, that in showing that a given piece of conduct is part of the obligations and trappings of a role, one shifts it from the sacred category to the profane, from the fat and living to the thin and dead. Sociologists *qua* sociologists are allowed to have the profane part; sociologists *qua* persons, along with other persons, retain the sacred for their friends, their wives, and themselves.

The concept of role distance helps to combat this touching tendency to keep a part of the world safe from sociology. For if an individual is to show that he is a "nice guy" or, by contrast, one much less nice than a human being need be, then it is through his using or not using role distance that this is likely to be done. It is right here, in manifestations of role distance, that the individual's personal style is to be found. And it is argued in this paper that role distance is almost as much subject to role analysis as are the core tasks of roles themselves.

Notes

1   E.C.Hughes, "Dilemmas and Contradictions of Status," *American Journal of Sociology*, 50 (1945), pp. 353–9.
2   For example, see S. E. Perry and L. C. Wynne, "Role Conflict, Role Redefinition, and Social Change in a Clinical Research Organization," *Social Forces*, 38 (1959), pp. 62–5.

PART II

The Confined Self

5

Status, Territory, and the Self

From "The Territories of the Self"*

At the center of social organization is the concept of claims, and around this center, properly, the student must consider the vicissitudes of maintaining them.

To speak closely of these matters, a set of related terms is needed. There is the "good," the desired object or state that is in question; the "claim," namely, entitlement to possess, control, use, or dispose of the good; the "claimant," that is, the party on whose behalf the claim is made; the "impediment," meaning here the act, substance, means, or agency through which the claim is threatened; the "author" (or "counter-claimant"), namely, the party—when there is one—on whose behalf the threat to claims is intended; and finally, the "agents," these being the individuals who act for and represent the claimant and counter-claimant in these matters involving claims.

When we restrict our attention to activity that can only occur during face-to-face interaction, the claimant tends to be an individual (or a small set of individuals) and to function as his own agent. The same can be said of the counter-claimant, but in addition the impediment that occurs in his name is likely to involve his own activity or body. Therefore, conventional terms such as "victim" and "offender" will often be adequate. And one type of claim becomes crucial: it is a claim exerted in regard to "territory." This concept from ethology seems apt, because the claim is not so much to a discrete and particular matter but rather to a field of things—to a preserve—and because the boundaries of the field are ordinarily patrolled and defended by the claimant.

Territories vary in terms of their organization. Some are "fixed"; they are staked out geographically and attached to one claimant, his claim being supported often by the law and its courts. Fields, yards, and houses are examples. Some are "situational"; they are part of the fixed equipment in

* Originally published in *Relations in Public: Microstudies of the Public Order*, 1971, pp. 28–41. Copyright © 1971 by Erving Goffman. Reprinted by permission of Basic Books, a division of Harper Collins Publishers, Inc.

the setting (whether publicly or privately owned), but are made available to the populace in the form of claimed goods while-in-use. Temporary tenancy is perceived to be involved, measured in seconds, minutes, or hours, informally exerted, raising constant questions as to when the claim begins and when it terminates. Park benches and restaurant tables are examples. Finally, there are "egocentric" preserves which move around with the claimant, he being in the center. They are typically (but not necessarily) claimed long term. Purses are an example. This threefold division is, of course, only valid in degree. A hotel room is a situational claim, yet it can function much like a house, a fixed territory. And, of course, houses in the form of trailers can move around.

The prototypical preserve is no doubt spatial and perhaps even fixed. However, to facilitate the study of co-mingling—at least in American society—it is useful to extend the notion of territoriality into claims that function like territories but are not spatial, and it is useful to focus on situational and egocentric territoriality. Starting, then, with the spatial, we shall move by steps to matters that are not.

1. *Personal Space:* The space surrounding an individual, anywhere within which an entering other causes the individual to feel encroached upon, leading him to show displeasure and sometimes to withdraw.[1] A contour, not a sphere, is involved, the spatial demands directly in front of the face being larger than at back.[2] The fixed layout of seats and other interior equipment may restrictively structure available space around the individual in one dimension, as occurs in line or column organization. When two individuals are alone in a setting, then concern about personal space takes the form of concern over straight-line distance.

Given that individuals can be relied upon to keep away from situations in which they might be contaminated by another or contaminate him, it follows that they can be controlled by him if he is willing to use himself calculatedly to constitute that object that the others will attempt to avoid, and in avoiding, move in a direction desired by him.[3] For example, we read of the engaging action of a pickpocket "stall" who uses his body to "pratt in" a mark, that is to cause the mark to hold himself away from a body that is pressing on him, and incidentally hold himself in a position from which his wallet can be reached; similarly we read of the "pratting out" of one bystander whose position prevents theft from another.[4]

It is a central feature of personal space that legitimate claim to it varies greatly according to the accountings available in the setting and that the bases for these will change continuously. Such factors as local population density, purpose of the approacher, fixed seating equipment, character of the social occasion, and so forth, can all influence radically from moment to moment what it is that is seen as an offense. Indeed, in human studies it is often best to consider personal space not as a permanently possessed, egocentric claim but as a temporary, situational preserve into whose center the individual moves.

Take, for example, the social organization of co-waiting. Obviously, to stand or sit next to a stranger when the setting is all but empty is more of an intrusion than the same act would be when the place is packed and all can see that only this niche remains. In theory we might expect also a continuous process of adjustment whereby each arrival and each departure causes alterations throughout.[5] What seems to occur in middle-class society is that arrival creates sequential reallocation but departure leads to somewhat more complex behavior, since an individual who leaves his current niche to take up a freed one produces an open sign that he is disinclined to be as close to his neighbor as he was. (When the two are of opposite sex, there exists the added complication that failure to move away when possible can be taken as a sign of undue interest.) In consequence, a departure may leave an empty place and no change in the remaining allocation, or at least an appropriator may wait for some tactful moment before making use of the newly available resource. In brief, moving in on someone or having oneself moved in on is a less delicate task than removing oneself from proximity to him. In consequence, as say a streetcar empties, there will be a period when two individuals signal by proximity a relationship that does not in fact exist.

All of this may be seen in miniature in elevator behavior. Passengers have two problems: to allocate the space equably, and to maintain a defensible position, which in this context means orientation to the door and center with the back up against the wall if possible.[6] The first few individuals can enter without anyone present having to rearrange himself, but very shortly each new entrant—up to a certain number—causes all those present to shift position and reorient themselves in sequence. Leave-taking introduces a tendency to reverse the cycle, but this is tempered by the countervailing resistance to appearing uncomfortable in an established distance from another. Thus, as the car empties, passengers acquire a measure of uneasiness, caught between two opposing inclinations—to obtain maximum distance from others and inhibit avoidance behavior that might give offense.

2. *The Stall:* The well-bounded space to which individuals can lay temporary claim, possession being on an all-or-none basis.[7] A scarce good will often be involved, such as a comfortable chair, a table with a view, an empty cot, a telephone booth. In the main, stalls are fixed in the setting, although, for example, at beaches devices such as large towels and mats can be carried along with the claimant and unrolled when convenient, thus providing a portable stall. When seats are built in rows and divided by common armrests (as in theaters), then personal space and stall have the same boundaries. When there is space between seats, then personal space is likely to extend beyond the stall. And, of course, there are stalls such as boxes at the opera which allocate several seats to the exclusive use (on any one social occasion)

of a single "party." The availability of stalls in a setting articulates and stabi-
lizes claims to space, sometimes providing more than would have been
claimed as personal space, sometimes less—as can be seen, for example, in
regard to seats when a class of six-year-olds attends an adult theater or when
parents have a meeting in an elementary school room.

It should be noted that a stall can be left temporarily while the leave-taker
is sustained in a continuing claim upon it; personal space cannot.[8]
Furthermore, often the claimant to a stall will not be an individual but two
or more of them who properly share it, as illustrated nicely in public tennis
courts and commercial bowling alleys, these being designed to provide a
large, well-equipped stall to parties of players for stipulated periods of time.
(In our society the most common multi-person stall is the table, there being
relatively few too small for more than one person or too large to be claimed
by a party of only two.) Personal space, on the other hand, is largely a one-
person possession, although in crowded places, such as packed elevators, a
small child grasped to a parent may be treated as part of the latter's personal
space, and couples engaged in affectional entwinings may also be treated as
claiming a single personal space.

The point about stalls, as suggested, is that they provide external, easily
visible, defendable boundaries for a spatial claim. Stalls provide a contrast
in this regard to personal space, the latter having ever-shifting dimensions.
This points up a problem in the organization of American public places.
Here, for practical considerations, equipment such as picnic tables or park
benches is often built to a size to suggest that each can be claimed as a stall
by a participation unit, a "single" or a "with." However, when crowding is
such that this allocation would leave some individuals standing, then a rule
is understood to apply that gives unaccommodated participation units the
right to enforce a fictional division of a stall into two (and occasionally more
than two) stalls. Obviously, then, as crowding increases, those already
ensconced will begin to have to give up exclusive claim to a stall. An ambiguity results, because there is no well-established principle to order the
sequence in which various claimants, already ensconced, will be obliged to
give up their exclusiveness. A field is thus opened for personal enterprise.
Hence, on buses, streetcars, and trains, seats designed to hold two persons,
and fully recognized to be designed to accommodate two strangers when
necessary, nonetheless establish for the first arrival a territory he may
attempt to retain for himself by standard ruses: he may leave his own possessions on the empty place, thereby marking it for his own and obliging
competitors to move (or ask to have moved) something that symbolizes
another; he may deny his eyes to those seeking a seat, thereby preventing
them from obtaining the fleeting permission that they tend to seek, failure
to receive which can cause them to move on to the next available place; he
may expose some contaminating part of himself, such as his feet, or allow

part of his body to fall on the disputed place, so that those who would use the place must invite contamination; and so forth.

3. *Use Space:* The territory immediately around or in front of an individual, his claim to which is respected because of apparent instrumental needs. For example, a gallery goer can expect that when he is close to a picture, other patrons will make some effort to walk around his line of vision or excuse or minimize their momentarily blocking it. Persons holding a conversation over a distance can expect a similar accommodation from non-participants whose bodies might block the giving and receiving of conversation management cues. Sportsmen of all kind expect some consideration will be given to the amount of elbow room they require in order to manipulate their equipment, as do convicts using pickaxes to break stone. Gymnasts using a vaulting horse expect that others will "stay out of their way." A crewman obliged to scrub and polish a designated portion of the surface of his warship expects, especially on the day before weekly inspection, to be able to keep everyone away during and right after the cleaning.[9] Note that circumstances can allow the individual to offer instrumental grounds for demanding limits on the level of noise and sound, especially when the source is physically close by.

4. *The Turn:* The order in which a claimant receives a good of some kind relative to other claimants in the situation. A decision-rule is involved, ordering participants categorically ("women and children first," or "whites before blacks"), or individually ("smallest first, then next smallest"), or some mixture of both.[10] Typically claimants are required to have been present in order to establish their claim on a turn, but once this has been done and marked in some way, they may be allowed to absent themselves until their turn comes up. In our Western society, perhaps the most important principle in turn organization is "first come, first served," establishing the claim of an individual to come right after the person "ahead" and right before the person "behind."[11] This decision rule creates a dominance ranking but a paradoxical one, since all other forms of preference are thereby excluded.[12]

Turn-taking requires not only an ordering rule but a claiming mechanism as well. This may be formal, for example, number-tickets, names on a receptionist's list, or informal, as when the individual remains close to the place of service and assumes that a tacit consensus will operate. Sometimes a line or row formation (a queue) will be employed as a collective, mnemonic device, and sometimes this formal device allows the participant to sustain a formally unmarked turn during brief absences.[13] Many queues qualify a with as a claimant, especially where one member can transact all of its business (as in movie queues), and this often leads to permission to join an acquaintance ahead of where one otherwise would have been, since in these cases a single already established in line will be able to act as though he is merely the agent for a with that is just now fully arrived. I want only to add that when turns are held by bodies standing in single file, then each participant will be involved both in maintaining his turn and his personal space. However, since the taking of turns provides a clear reading of events, great reductions of personal space can be tolerated along with attendant bodily contact.

5. *The Sheath:* The skin that covers the body and, at a little remove, the clothes that cover the skin. Certainly the body's sheath can function as the least of all possible personal spaces, the minimal configuration in that regard; but it can also function as a preserve in its own right, the purest kind of egocentric territoriality. Of course, different parts of the body are accorded different concern—indeed this differential concern tells us in part how the body will be divided up into segments conceptually. Among the American middle classes, for example, little effort is made to keep the elbow inviolate, whereas orifice areas are of concern. And, of course, across different cultures, the body will be differently segmented ritually.

6. *Possessional Territory:* Any set of objects that can be identified with the self and arrayed around the body wherever it is. The central examples are spoken of as "personal effects"—easily detachable possessions such as jackets, hats, gloves, cigarette packs, matches, handbags and what they contain, and parcels.[14] We must also include a claimant's co-present dependents because, territorially, they function somewhat like his personal possessions. Finally, there are objects that remain tethered to a particular setting but can be temporarily claimed by persons present, much as can stalls: ashtrays, magazines, cushions, and eating utensils are examples. One might also include here regulative command over mechanical creature-comfort devices: control over radio, television sets, temperature, windows, light, and so forth.

7. *Information Preserve:* The set of facts about himself to which an individual expects to control access while in the presence of others.[15] There are several varieties of information preserve, and there is some question about classing them all together. There is the content of the claimant's mind, control over which is threatened when queries are made that he sees as intrusive, nosy, untactful. There are the contents of pockets, purses, containers, letters, and the like, which the claimant can feel others have no right to ascertain. There are biographical facts about the individual over the divulgence of which he expects to maintain control. And most important for our purposes, there is what can be directly perceived about an individual, his body's sheath and his current behavior, the issue here being his right not to be stared at or examined.[16] Of course, since the individual is also a vehicular unit and since pilots of other such units have a need and a right to track him, he will come to be able to make an exquisite perceptual distinction between being looked at and being stared at, and, God help us, learn to suspect, if

not detect, that the latter is being masked by the former; and he will learn to conduct himself so that others come to respond to him in the same way. Incidentally, wherever we find such fine behavioral discriminations, we should suspect that what is at work is the need to keep two different behavioral systems functioning without interference in the same physical area.

8. *Conversational Preserve:* The right of an individual to exert some control over who can summon him into talk and when he can be summoned; and the right of a set of individuals once engaged in talk to have their circle protected from entrance and overhearing by others.

I have touched on eight territories of the self, all of a situational or an egocentric kind: personal space, stalls, use space, turns, sheath, possessional territory, information preserve, and conversational preserve. One general feature of these several forms of territoriality should be noted: their socially determined variability. Given a particular setting and what is available in it, the extensivity of preserves obviously can vary greatly according to power and rank. Patients in a charity hospital may have to wait until dying before being given a privacy screen around their bed; in middle-class private hospitals, the patient may enjoy this privilege at other times, too, for example, when breast feeding a child.[17] Similarly, clinic patients in a hospital may be discussed by physicians by name, while private patients in the same hospital are given the privacy rights of being referred to by room number.[18] In general, the higher the rank, the greater the size of all territories of the self and the greater the control across the boundaries. (Within a given household, for example, adults tend to have vastly larger territorial claims than do children.) Cutting across these differences, however, there is another—the variation that occurs in the understandings sustained by any one set of individuals as they move from situation to situation. For example, middle-class Americans at Western ski lodges allow their bodies to be stared at and touched-in-passing to a degree that would be considered quite intrusive were this to occur in the public places of their home town.[19] Finally, there are group-cultural differences that crosscut these cross cuttings. For example, there is some evidence that lower-class blacks are more concerned to obtain eyeing avoidance than are lower-class Italians.[20]

Notes

1   Sociological versions of this territory of the self are provided by Robert Sommer, "Studies in Personal Space," *Sociometry*, XXII (September 1959): 247–60, and Kenneth B. Little, "Personal Space," *Journal of Experimental Social Psychology*, I (August 1965): 237–47. An ethological source is H. Hediger, *Studies of the Psychology and Behaviour of Captive Animals in Zoos and Circuses* (London: Butterworths Scientific Publications, 1955). A precursive statement is the 1936 paper by Kurt Lewin, "Some Social-Psychological Differences between the United States and Germany," in his *Resolving Social Conflicts* (New York: Harper & Row, Publishers, 1948), pp. 3–33.

2   This is nicely illustrated in Eastern seaboard parlor cars designed with a wide, longitu-
dinal aisle and single seats at intervals on either side, the seats arranged to swivel. When
there is crowding, travelers maximize their "comfort" by turning their seats to exactly that
direction that will allow the eyes, when oriented in the direction of the trunk, to gaze upon
the least amount of passenger flesh. Standing passengers may crowd right up against the
seats but in doing so will find themselves ringed in by two rows of backs. In ordinary
railway or bus seating in America, passengers who feel overcrowded may be able to send
their eyes out the window, thereby vicariously extending their personal space.

3   This argument derives from H. Hediger's well-known discussion of "flight distance" and
"escape distance" and its bearing on lion taming. See his *Studies of the Psychology and
Behaviour of Captive Animals in Zoos and Circuses,* op.cit., pp. 40,123.

4   David W. Maurer, *Whiz Mob* (Publications of the American Dialect Society, No. 24,
Gainesville, Florida, 1955), pp. 62–5.

5   See J. H. Crook, "The Basis of Flock Organization in Birds," and his discussion of arrival
distance, settled distance and distance after departure, in W. H. Thorpe and O. L.
Zangwill, eds., *Current Problems in Animal Behaviour* (Cambridge: Cambridge University
Press, 1961), pp. 140 ff.

6   There are other general features of body behavior in elevators. In a useful unpublished
paper ("Behavior in Elevators," 1965), John Gueldner suggests that the general practice
is for male riders to be somewhat at attention, with hands to the side and no side involvements, with an equivalent posture for women—as if all activity had halted while
individuals were in transit. Gueldner suggests that the seeking of a defensible niche establishes standard priorities: first entrant takes up the corner near the controls or one of the
rear corners; the next entrant is likely to take up the corner diagonally across from
the taken one. The third and fourth passengers take up the remaining corners, the fifth the
middle of the rear wall, the sixth the center of the car. Members of withs, however, tend
to stay together, retaining an ecological expression of their status even though eyes are
front. Gueldner also suggests that there is a point of crowding where effort to maintain
space is rather suddenly given up and something approaching indiscriminate packing
occurs.

7   The term has been used by ethologists who study the daily round of the domestic cow.

8   In gentlemen's clubs, mental hospitals, old folks' homes, and domestic living rooms,
proprietary claims tend to grow up around chairs and other stalls so that although these
start out as part of situationally provided territories available on a first-come basis for any
continuous period of use, they soon take on the character of fixed territories possessed
by one individual whether or not he is present to claim by use. See Michael A. Woodbury,
"Ward Dynamics and the Formation of a Therapeutic Group," *Chestnut Lodge
Symposium,* Rockville, Maryland, mimeo (1958), and Alan Lipman, "Chairs as
Territory," *New Society,* XX (April 1967): 564–6.

9   See Philip D. Roos, "Jurisdiction: An Ecological Concept," *Human Relations,* XXI
(1968): 75–84. Roos provides a case history argument for making a sharper distinction
than I have done between territoriality, involving exclusion and possession, and "jurisdiction," involving only exclusion.

10 Upon fuller consideration, we are likely to find that the means employed to manage the
allocation of a minor good (such as a turn) involve more than one rule. And rules about
rules may develop to cover standard problems, determining what should be done when
no rule seems to apply, or when one that should apply cannot, or when mutually incompatible rules apply. One rule may be defined as overruling another on all occasions when
they both apply, or each may be accorded a sphere where it overrides the other. One rule
may serve to rank categories of persons and another to rank members within a category
thusly ranked. Note, individuals often identify a social order by a well-known rule that

figures in it, but the viability of this rule is often dependent on a complex of associated rules covering the natural range of contingencies. The longer and the more widely a given rule is in force, the more developed, presumably, is the complex of rules that buttresses it.

11   In many cases, a claimant is allowed at will to let the party behind go ahead of him; he may even be allowed to pick any place lower down in the line, presumably on the assumption that those behind his original place and above the place he picks will have gained a turn and those below this point will have lost nothing. And in all cases, the claimant apparently can give up his turn entirely. In brief, turn as here defined is a right but not a duty. This raises the issue of "negative queues," namely, an ordering of persons who are to receive something they do not want, such as a place in a gas chamber. (Similarly, some prisons have seats that cannot be given up for a lady.) A dialectical way of assimilating such organization to the notion of preserves is to describe the good that is involved as a claim to postponement. Naturally, here one would be allowed to take any turn ahead of one's position but disallowed from stepping behind or giving up entirely one's position.

12   It might be said—with apologies to Simmel—that it is the essential character of everyday turn-taking to be a middle ground, the claims of property and contract being held in check at one end, the claims of social rank at the other. To take one's turn is neither to take one's property nor to take one's social place. Utilitarian goods are involved, but typically ones so minor that it would have been easy to put their allocation into the service of ceremonial expression. Whereas ceremonial expression provides bodily expression of social position when things go right, turns in daily life do so only when things go wrong.

13   A useful paper on turn-taking in one type of extremity is Leon Man, "Queue Culture: The Waiting Line as a Social System," *American Journal of Sociology*, DXXV (November 1969): 340–54. Some turn-taking merely involves a decision between two users as to which will use a road or walk first, but in most cases, it appears clear that a service of some kind is the good that must be allocated. Service systems are one of the fundamental organizational devices of public order, and their close study has hardly begun. The complete paradigm involves at least five roles: supervisor, server, served, next-up, member of the line. There are, of course, automated systems without supervisors and servers, and many systems which frequently have neither next-up nor member of the line. A service system is the collective form of which the individual's part is the service stop, this involving one complete cycle whereby a participation unit (a with or a single) moves off from some base of operation, seeks out and obtains some service, and then returns to the base.

    It might be added that many services are provided in such a manner that an encounter, a ritually ratified face-to-face contact, occurs only if something out of the ordinary happens and must be managed, providing us with a clear case where server and served can be in contact but not in conversational touch. (Indeed, the server need not even look at the served, but only at, say, the article chosen for purchase, the customer's money, and perhaps his hand.) This sort of deritualization of transactions is sometimes cited as a mark of incivility and urban impersonality, an allegation that is half true and half nonsense. A great deal of consensus and mutual understanding is required to support service transactions executed without the help of social ritual. In some shops a year or so of patronage is required before patron and server know each knows that talk and eye contact can be dispensed with and actions allowed to do all the speaking. (Of course in other service settings, such as better-cashier dealings at the race tracks, newcomers quickly learn to sustain "blind" transactions.) On the prevalence of deritualized service transactions, I am indebted to a useful paper by Marilyn Merritt, "On the Service Encounter," unpublished (1968).

14   In the matter of territoriality, a distinction in law has some relevance. The issue is that of

possession, not ownership; the exertion of current, not ultimate control. See also Roos, op.cit.

15 Traditionally treated under the heading of "privacy." See the current review by Alan F. Westin in *Privacy and Freedom* (New York: Atheneum, 1967). See also Oscar M. Ruebhausen and Orville G. Brim, Jr., "Privacy and Behavioral Research," *Columbia Law Review*, DXV (November 1965): 1184–1211.

16 No doubt there is a link here between having the body touched and having it seen, as in the biblical sense of "knowing" someone or the legal sense of having carnal knowledge. This is not the only ambiguity. Name, both Christian and family, can function like a bit of discretionary information whose divulgence one would like to be able to control but cannot always do so. Here see, for example A.C. Reich, "Police Questioning of Law-Abiding Citizens," *Yale Law Journal*, DXXV, no. 7 (1966). Name can also function as a self-identified personal possession whose use by others the individual may be prepared to license providing they stand in the right relationship to him. In this regard, note the situation of the English better classes at the turn of the century as described by Harold Nicolson, *Good Behaviour* (London: Constable and Company, 1955), p. 272:

> In my own youth, had I been addressed by my Christian name at my private or even my public school, I should have blushed scarlet, feeling that my privacy had been outraged and that some secret manliness had been purloined from me, as if I had been an Andaman Islander or a Masai.

In general, there is the fact that concern for preserves such as the spatial can be partly based indirectly on a concern for information preserves, the former supporting the latter.

17 David Sudnow, *Passing On* (Englewood Cliffs, N.J.: Prentice-Hall, Inc., 1966). W. Rosengren and S. DeVault report that clinic patients in a studied hospital were obliged to accept having the delivery door open; private patients, however, frequently enjoyed the privacy of a closed door. See W. Rosengren and S. DeVault, "The Sociology of Time and Space in an Obstetrical Hospital," in Eliot Freidson, ed., *The Hospital in Modern Society* (New York: The Free Press, 1965), p.278.

18 W. Rosengren and S. DeVault, op. cit., p. 280.

19 Similarly ski lodges tend to allow more license with respect to the initiation of encounters among the unacquainted than is the case in business settings. Here I am indebted to an unpublished paper, "Ski Resort Behavior Patterns" (1965), by Beatrice Farrar.

20 Gerald D. Suttles, *The Social Order of the Slum* (Chicago: The University of Chicago Press, 1968), p. 67.

6

The Mortified Self

From "The Characteristics of Total Institutions"*

The recruit comes into the establishment with a conception of himself made possible by certain stable social arrangements in his home world. Upon entrance, he is immediately stripped of the support provided by these arrangements. In the accurate language of some of our oldest total institutions, he begins a series of abasements, degradations, humiliations, and profanations of self. His self is systematically, if often unintentionally, mortified. He begins some radical shifts in his *moral career,* a career composed of the progressive changes that occur in the beliefs that he has concerning himself and significant others.

The processes by which a person's self is mortified are fairly standard in total institutions;[1] analysis of these processes can help us to see the arrangements that ordinary establishments must guarantee if members are to preserve their civilian selves.

The barrier that total institutions place between the inmate and the wider world marks the first curtailment of self. In civil life, the sequential scheduling of the individual's roles, both in the life cycle and in the repeated daily round, ensures that no one role he plays will block his performance and ties in another. In total institutions, in contrast, membership automatically disrupts role scheduling, since the inmate's separation from the wider world lasts around the clock and may continue for years. Role dispossession therefore occurs. In many total institutions the privilege of having visitors or of visiting away from the establishment is completely withheld at first, ensuring a deep initial break with past roles and an appreciation of role dispossession. A report on cadet life in a military academy provides an illustration:

This clean break with the past must be achieved in a relatively short period. For two months, therefore, the swab is not allowed to leave the

* First published 1958; this extract from *Asylums,* 1961, pp. 14–28. Copyright © 1961 by Erving Goffman.

base or to engage in social intercourse with non-cadets. This complete isolation helps to produce a unified group of swabs, rather than a heterogeneous collection of persons of high and low status. Uniforms are issued on the first day, and discussions of wealth and family background are taboo. Although the pay of the cadet is very low, he is not permitted to receive money from home. The role of the cadet must supersede other roles the individual has been accustomed to play. There are few clues left which will reveal social status in the outside world.[2]

I might add that when entrance is voluntary, the recruit has already partially withdrawn from his home world; what is cleanly severed by the institution is something that had already started to decay.

Although some roles can be re-established by the inmate if and when he returns to the world, it is plain that other losses are irrevocable and may be painfully experienced as such. It may not be possible to make up, at a later phase of the life cycle, the time not now spent in educational or job advancement, in courting, or in rearing one's children. A legal aspect of this permanent dispossession is found in the concept of "civil death": prison inmates may face not only a temporary loss of the rights to will money and write checks, to contest divorce or adoption proceedings, and to vote but may have some of these rights permanently abrogated.[3]

The inmate, then, finds certain roles are lost to him by virtue of the barrier that separates him from the outside world. The process of entrance typically brings other kinds of loss and mortification as well. We very generally find staff employing what are called admission procedures, such as taking a life history, photographing, weighing, fingerprinting, assigning numbers, searching, listing personal possessions for storage, undressing, bathing, disinfecting, haircutting, issuing institutional clothing, instructing as to rules, and assigning to quarters.[4] Admission procedures might better be called "trimming" or "programming" because in thus being squared away the new arrival allows himself to be shaped and coded into an object that can be fed into the administrative machinery of the establishment, to be worked on smoothly by routine operations. Many of these procedures depend upon attributes such as weight or fingerprints that the individual possesses merely because he is a member of the largest and most abstract of social categories, that of human being. Action taken on the basis of such attributes necessarily ignores most of his previous bases of self-identification.

Because a total institution deals with so many aspects of its inmates' lives, with the consequent complex squaring away at admission, there is a special need to obtain initial co-operativeness from the recruit. Staff often feel that a recruit's readiness to be appropriately deferential in his initial face-to-face encounters with them is a sign that he will take the role of the routinely pliant inmate. The occasion on which staff members first tell the inmate of his deference obligations may be structured to challenge the inmate to balk or to hold his peace forever. Thus these initial moments of socialization may involve an "obedience test" and even a will-breaking contest: an inmate who shows defiance receives immediate visible punishment, which increases until he openly "cries uncle" and humbles himself.

An engaging illustration is provided by Brendan Behan in reviewing his contest with two warders upon his admission to Walton prison:

> "And 'old up your 'ead, when I speak to you."
> "'Old up your 'ead, when Mr. Whitbread speaks to you," said Mr. Holmes.
> I looked round at Charlie. His eyes met mine and he quickly lowered them to the ground.
> "What are you looking round at Behan? Look at me."
>   . . . . . .
> I looked at Mr. Whitbread. "I am looking at you," I said.
> "You are looking at Mr. Whitbread—what?" said Mr Holmes.
> "I am looking at Mr. Whitbread."
> Mr. Holmes looked gravely at Mr. Whitbread, drew back his open hand, and struck me on the face, held me with his other hand and struck me again.
> My head spun and burned and pained and I wondered would it happen again. I forgot and felt another smack, and forgot, and another, and moved, and was held by a steadying, almost kindly hand, and another, and my sight was a vision of red and white and pity-coloured flashes.
> "You are looking at Mr. Whitbread—what, Behan?"
> I gulped and got together my voice and tried again till I got it out. "I, sir, please, sir. I am looking at you, I mean, I am looking at Mr. Whitbread, sir."[5]

Admission procedures and obedience tests may be elaborated into a form of initiation that has been called "the welcome," where staff or inmates, or both, go out of their way to give the recruit a clear notion of his plight.[6] As part of this rite of passage he may be called by a term such as "fish" or "swab," which tells him that he is merely an inmate, and, what is more, that he has a special low status even in this low group.

The admission procedure can be characterized as a leaving off and a taking on, with the midpoint marked by physical nakedness. Leaving off of course entails a dispossession of property, important because persons invest self feelings in their possessions. Perhaps the most significant of these possessions is not physical at all, one's full name; whatever one is thereafter called, loss of one's name can be a great curtailment of the self.[7]

Once the inmate is stripped of his possessions, at least some replacements must be made by the establishment, but these take the form of standard issue, uniform in character and uniformly distributed. These substitute possessions are clearly marked as really belonging to the institution and in some cases are recalled at regular intervals to be, as it were, disinfected of identifications. With objects that can be used up—for example, pencils—the inmate may be required to return the remnants before obtaining a reissue.[8] Failure to provide inmates with individual lockers and periodic searches and confiscations of accumulated personal property[9] reinforce property dispossession. Religious orders have appreciated the implications for self of such separation from belongings. Inmates may be required to change their cells once a year so as not to become attached to them. The Benedictine Rule is explicit:

> For their bedding let a mattress, a blanket, a coverlet, and a pillow suffice. These beds must be frequently inspected by the Abbot, because of private property which may be found therein. If anyone be discovered to have what he has not received from the Abbot, let him be most severely punished. And in order that this vice of private ownership may be completely rooted out, let all things that are necessary be supplied by the Abbot: that is, cowl, tunic, stockings, shoes, girdle, knife, pen, needle, handkerchief, and tablets; so that all plea of necessity may be taken away. And let the Abbot always consider that passage in the Acts of the Apostles: "Distribution was made to each according as anyone had need."[10]

One set of the individual's possessions has a special relation to self. The individual ordinarily expects to exert some control over the guise in which he appears before others. For this he needs cosmetic and clothing supplies, tools for applying, arranging, and repairing them, and an accessible, secure place to store these supplies and tools—in short, the individual will need an "identity kit" for the management of his personal front. He will also need access to decoration specialists such as barbers and clothiers.

On admission to a total institution, however, the individual is likely to be stripped of his usual appearance and of the equipment and services by which he maintains it, thus suffering a personal defacement. Clothing, combs, needle and thread, cosmetics, towels, soap, shaving sets, bathing facilities—all these may be taken away or denied him, although some may be kept in inaccessible storage, to be returned if and when he leaves. In the words of St. Benedict's Holy Rule:

> The forthwith he shall, there in the oratory, be divested of his own garments with which he is clothed and be clad in those of the monastery. Those garments of which he is divested shall be placed in the wardrobe, there to be kept, so that if, perchance, he should ever be persuaded by the devil to leave the monastery (which God forbid), he may be stripped of the monastic habit and cast forth.[11]

As suggested, the institutional issue provided as a substitute for what has been taken away is typically of a "coarse" variety, ill-suited, often old, and the same for large categories of inmates. The impact of this substitution is described in a report on imprisoned prostitutes:

> First, there is the shower officer who forces them to undress, takes their own clothes away, sees to it that they take showers and get their prison clothes—one pair of black oxfords with cuban heels, two pairs of much-mended ankle socks, three cotton dresses, two cotton slips, two pairs of panties, and a couple of bras. Practically all the bras are flat and useless. No corsets or girdles are issued.
> There is not a sadder sight than some of the obese prisoners who, if nothing else, have been managing to keep themselves looking decent on the outside, confronted by the first sight of themselves in prison issue.[12]

In addition to personal defacement that comes from being stripped of one's identity kit, there is personal disfigurement that comes from direct and permanent mutilations of the body such as brands or loss of limbs. Although this mortification of the self by way of the body is found in few total institutions, still, loss of a sense of personal safety is common and provides a basis for anxieties about disfigurement. Beatings, shock therapy, or, in mental hospitals, surgery—whatever the intent of staff in providing these services for some inmates—may lead many inmates to feel that they are in an environment that does not guarantee their physical integrity.

At admission, loss of identity equipment can prevent the individual from presenting his usual image of himself to others. After admission, the image of himself he presents is attacked in another way. Given the expressive idiom of a particular civil society, certain movements, postures, and stances will convey lowly images of the individual and be avoided as demeaning. Any regulation, command, or task that forces the individual to adopt these movements or postures may mortify his self. In total institutions, such physical indignities abound. In mental hospitals, for example, patients may be forced to eat all food with a spoon.[13] In military prisons, inmates may be required to stand at attention whenever an officer enters the compound.[14] In religious institutions, there are such classic gestures of penance as the kissing of feet,[15] and the posture recommended to an erring monk that he

> lie prostrate at the door of the oratory in silence; and thus, with his face to the ground and his body prone, let him cast himself at the feet of all as they go forth from the oratory.[16]

In some penal institutions we find the humiliation of bending over to receive a birching.[17]

Just as the individual can be required to hold his body in a humiliating pose, so he may have to provide humiliating verbal responses. An important instance of this is the forced deference pattern of total institutions; inmates are often required to punctuate their social interaction with staff by verbal acts of deference, such as saying "sir." Another instance is the necessity to beg, importune, or humbly ask for little things such as a light for a cigarette, a drink of water, or permission to use the telephone.

Corresponding to the indignities of speech and action required of the inmate are the indignities of treatment others accord him. The standard examples here are verbal or gestural profanations: staff or fellow inmates call the individual obscene names, curse him, point out his negative attributes, tease him, or talk about him or his fellow inmates as if he were not present.

Whatever the form or the source of these various indignities, the individual has to engage in activity whose symbolic implications are incompatible with his conception of self. A more diffuse example of this kind of mortification occurs when the individual is required to undertake a daily round of life that he considers alien to him—to take on a disidentifying role. In prisons, denial of heterosexual opportunities can induce fear of losing one's masculinity.[18] In military establishments, the patently useless make-work forced on fatigue details can make men feel their time and effort are worthless.[19] In religious institutions there are special arrangements to ensure that all inmates take a turn performing the more menial aspects of the servant role.[20] An extreme is the concentration-camp practice requiring prisoners to administer whippings to other prisoners.

There is another form of mortification in total institutions; beginning with admission a kind of contaminative exposure occurs. On the outside, the individual can hold objects of self-feeling—such as his body, his immediate actions, his thoughts, and some of his possessions—clear of contact with alien and contaminating things. But in total institutions these territories of the self are violated; the boundary that the individual places between his being and the environment is invaded and the embodiments of self profaned.

There is, first, a violation of one's informational preserve regarding self. During admission, facts about the inmate's social statuses and past behavior—especially discreditable facts—are collected and recorded in a dossier available to staff. Later, in so far as the establishment officially expects to alter the self-regulating inner tendencies of the inmate, there may be group or individual confession—psychiatric, political, military, or religious, according to the type of institution. On these occasions the inmate has to expose facts and feelings about self to new kinds of audiences. The most spectacular examples of such exposure come to us from Communist confession camps and from the *culpa* sessions that form part of the routine of Catholic religious institutions.[22] The dynamics of the process have been explicitly considered by those engaged in so-called milieu therapy.

New audiences not only learn discreditable facts about oneself that are ordinarily concealed but are also in a position to perceive some of these facts directly. Prisoners and mental patients cannot prevent their visitors from seeing them in humiliating circumstances.[23] Another example is the shoulder patch of ethnic identification worn by concentration-camp inmates.[24] Medical and security examinations often expose the inmate physically, sometimes to persons of both sexes; a similar exposure follows from collective sleeping arrangements and doorless toilets.[25] An extreme here, perhaps, is the situation of a self-destructive mental patient who is stripped naked for what is felt to be his own protection and placed in a constantly lit seclusion room, into whose Judas window any person passing on the ward can peer. In general, of course, the inmate is never fully alone; he is always within sight and often earshot of someone, if only his fellow inmates.[26] Prison cages with bars for walls fully realize such exposure.

Perhaps the most obvious type of contaminative exposure is the directly physical kind—the besmearing and defiling of the body or of other objects closely identified with the self. Sometimes this involves a breakdown of the usual environmental arrangements for insulating oneself from one's own source of contamination, as in having to empty one's own slops[27] or having to subject one's evacuation to regimentation, as reported from Chinese political prisons:

> An aspect of their isolation regimen which is especially onerous to Western prisoners is the arrangement for the elimination of urine and feces. The "slop jar" that is usually present in Russian cells is often absent in China. It is a Chinese custom to allow defecation and urination only at one or two specified times each day—usually in the morning after breakfast. The prisoner is hustled from his cell by a guard, double-timed down a long corridor, and given approximately two minutes to squat over an open Chinese latrine and attend to all his wants. The haste and the public scrutiny are especially difficult for women to tolerate. If the prisoners cannot complete their action in about two minutes, they are abruptly dragged away and back to their cells.[28]

A very common form of physical contamination is reflected in complaints about unclean food, messy quarters, soiled towels, shoes and clothing impregnated with previous users' sweat, toilets without seats, and dirty bath facilities.[29] Orwell's comments on his boarding school may be taken as illustrative:

For example, there were the pewter bowls out of which we had our porridge. They had overhanging rims, and under the rims there were accumulations of sour porridge, which could be flaked off in long strips. The porridge itself, too, contained more lumps, hairs and unexplained black things than one would have thought possible, unless someone were putting them there on purpose. It was never safe to start on that porridge without investigating it first. And there was the slimy water of the plunge bath—it was twelve or fifteen feet long, the whole school was supposed to go into it every morning, and I doubt whether the water was changed at all frequently—and the always-damp towels with their cheesy smell:. . .And the sweaty smell of the changing-room with its greasy basins, and, giving on this, the row of filthy, dilapidated lavatories, which had no fastenings of any kind on the doors, so that whenever you were sitting there someone was sure to come crashing in. It is not easy for me to think of my school days without seeming to breathe in a whiff of something cold and evil-smelling—a sort of compound of sweaty stockings, dirty towels, fecal smells blowing along corridors, forks with old food between the prongs, neck-of-mutton stew, and the banging doors of the lavatories and the echoing chamberpots in the dormitories.[30]

There are still other sources of physical contamination, as an interviewee suggests in describing a concentration-camp hospital:

We were lying two in each bed. And it was very unpleasant. For example, if a man died he would not be removed before twenty-four hours had elapsed because the block trusty wanted, of course, to get the bread ration and the soup which was allotted to this person. For this reason the dead person would be reported dead twenty-four hours later so that his ration would still be allotted. And so we had to lie all that time in bed together with the dead person.[31]

We were on the middle level. And that was a very gruesome situation, especially at night. First of all, the dead men were badly emaciated and they looked terrible. In most cases they would soil themselves at the moment of death and that was not a very esthetic event. I saw such cases very frequently in the lager, in the sick people's barracks. People who died from phlegmonous, suppurative wounds, with their beds overflowing with pus would be lying together with somebody whose illness was possibly more benign, who had possibly just a small wound which now would become infected.[32]

The contamination of lying near the dying has also been cited in mental-hospital reports,[33] and surgical contamination has been cited in prison documents:

> Surgical instruments and bandages in the dressing-room lie exposed to the air and dust. George, attending for the treatment, by a medical orderly, of a boil on his neck, had it lanced with a scalpel that had been used a moment before on a man's foot, and had not been sterilised in the meantime.[34]

Finally, in some total institutions the inmate is obliged to take oral or intravenous medications, whether desired or not, and to eat his food, however unpalatable. When an inmate refuses to eat, there may be forcible contamination of his innards by "forced feeding."

I have suggested that the inmate undergoes mortification of the self by contaminative exposure of a physical kind, but this must be amplified: when the agency of contamination is another human being, the inmate is in addition contaminated by forced interpersonal contact and, in consequence, a forced social relationship. (Similarly, when the inmate loses control over who observes him in his predicament or knows about his past, he is being contaminated by a forced relationship to these people—for it is through such perception and knowledge that relations are expressed.)

From "The Moral Career of the Mental Patient"*

Like the neophyte in many of these total institutions, the new inpatient finds himself cleanly stripped of many of his accustomed affirmations, satisfactions, and defenses, and is subjected to a rather full set of mortifying experiences: restriction of free movement, communal living, diffuse authority of a whole echelon of people, and so on. Here one begins to learn about the limited extent to which a conception of oneself can be sustained when the usual setting of supports for it are suddenly removed.

While undergoing these humbling moral experiences, the inpatient learns to orient himself in terms of the "ward system."[35] In public mental hospitals this usually consists of a series of graded living arrangements built around wards, administrative units called services, and parole statuses. The "worst" level often involves nothing but wooden benches to sit on, some quite indifferent food, and a small piece of room to sleep in. The "best" level may involve a room of one's own, ground and town privileges, contacts with staff

---

* First published 1959; this extract from *Asylums* 1961, pp. 148–9, 161–9. Copyright © 1961 by Erving Goffman.

that are relatively undamaging, and what is seen as good food and ample recreational facilities. For disobeying the pervasive house rules, the inmate will receive stringent punishments expressed in terms of loss of privileges; for obedience he will eventually be allowed to reacquire some of the minor satisfactions he took for granted on the outside.

The institutionalization of these radically different levels of living throws light on the implications for self of social settings. And this in turn affirms that the self arises not merely out of its possessor's interactions with significant others, but also out of the arrangements that are evolved in an organization for its members.

There are some settings that the person easily discounts as an expression or extension of him. When a tourist goes slumming, he may take pleasure in the situation not because it is a reflection of him but because it so assuredly is not. There are other settings, such as living rooms, which the person manages on his own and employs to influence in a favorable direction other persons' views of him. And there are still other settings, such as a work place, which express the employee's occupational status, but over which he has no final control, this being exerted, however tactfully, by his employer. Mental hospitals provide an extreme instance of this latter possibility. And this is due not merely to their uniquely degraded living levels, but also to the unique way in which significance for self is made explicit to the patient, piercingly, persistently, and thoroughly. Once lodged on a given ward, the patient is firmly instructed that the restrictions and deprivations he encounters are not due to such blind forces as tradition or economy—and hence dissociable from self—but are intentional parts of his treatment, part of his need at the time, and therefore an expression of the state that his self has fallen to. Having every reason to initiate requests for better conditions, he is told that when the staff feel he is "able to manage" or will be "comfortable with" a higher ward level, then appropriate action will be taken. In short, assignment to a given ward is presented not as a reward or punishment, but as an expression of his general level of social functioning, his status as a person. Given the fact that the worst ward levels provide a round of life that inpatients with organic brain damage can easily manage, and that these quite limited human beings are present to prove it, one can appreciate some of the mirroring effects of the hospital.[36]

★   ★   ★

In general, then, mental hospitals systematically provide for circulation about each patient the kind of information that the patient is likely to try to hide. And in various degrees of detail this information is used daily to puncture his claims. At the admission and diagnostic conferences, he will be asked questions to which he must give wrong answers in order to maintain his self-respect, and then the true answer may be shot back at him. An attendant to whom he tells a version of his past and his reason for being in the hospital may smile disbelievingly, or say, "That's not the way I heard it," in line with the practical psychiatry of bringing the patient down to reality. When he accosts a physician or nurse on the ward and presents his claims for more privileges or for discharge, this may be countered by a question which he cannot answer truthfully without calling up a time in his past when he acted disgracefully. When he gives his view of his situation during group psychotherapy, the therapist, taking the role of interrogator, may attempt to disabuse him of his face-saving interpretations and encourage an interpretation suggesting that it is he himself who is to blame and who must change. When he claims to staff or fellow patients that he is well and has never been really sick, someone may give him graphic details of how, only one month ago, he was prancing around like a girl, or claiming that he was God, or declining to talk or eat, or putting gum in his hair.

Each time the staff deflates the patient's claims, his sense of what a person ought to be and the rules of peer-group social intercourse press him to reconstruct his stories; and each time he does this, the custodial and psychiatric interests of the staff may lead them to discredit these tales again.

Behind these verbally instigated ups and downs of the self is an institutional base that rocks just as precariously. Contrary to popular opinion, the "ward system" insures a great amount of internal social mobility in mental hospitals, especially during the inmate's first year. During that time he is likely to have altered his service once, his ward three or four times, and his parole status several times; and he is likely to have experienced moves in bad as well as good directions. Each of these moves involves a very drastic alteration in level of living and in available materials out of which to build a self-confirming round of activities, an alteration equivalent in scope, say, to a move up or down a class in the wider class system. Moreover, fellow inmates with whom he has partially identified himself will similarly be moving, but in different directions and at different rates, thus reflecting feelings of social change to the person even when he does not experience them directly.

As previously implied, the doctrines of psychiatry can reinforce the social fluctuations of the ward system. Thus there is a current psychiatric view that the ward system is a kind of social hothouse in which patients start as social infants and end up, within the year, on convalescent wards as resocialized adults. This view adds considerably to the weight and pride that staff can attach to their work, and necessitates a certain amount of blindness, especially at higher staff levels, to other ways of viewing the ward system, such as a method for disciplining unruly persons through punishment and reward. In any case, this resocialization perspective tends to overstress the extent to which those on the worst wards are incapable of socialized conduct and the extent to which those on the best wards are ready and willing to play the social game. Because the ward system is something more than a resocialization chamber, inmates find many reasons for "messing up" or getting into trouble, and many occasions, then, for demotion to less privileged ward position. These demotions may be officially interpreted as psychiatric relapses or moral backsliding, thus protecting the resocialization view of the hospital; these interpretations, by implication, translate a mere infraction of rules and consequent demotion into a fundamental expression of the status of the culprit's self. Correspondingly, promotions, which may come about because of ward population pressure, the need for a "working patient," or for other psychiatrically irrelevant reasons, may be built up into something claimed to be profoundly expressive of the patient's whole self. The patient himself may be expected by staff to make a personal effort to "get well," in something less than a year, and hence may be constantly reminded to think in terms of the self's success and failure.

In such contexts inmates can discover that deflations in moral status are not so bad as they had imagined. After all, infractions which lead to these demotions cannot be accompanied by legal sanctions or by reduction to the status of mental patient, since these conditions already prevail. Further, no past or current delict seems to be horrendous enough in itself to excommunicate a patient from the patient community, and hence failures at right living lose some of their stigmatizing meaning. And finally, in accepting the hospital's version of his fall from grace, the patient can set himself up in the business of "straightening up," and make claims of sympathy, privileges, and indulgence from the staff in order to foster this.

Learning to live under conditions of imminent exposure and wide fluctuation in regard, with little control over the granting or withholding of this regard, is an important step in the socialization of the patient, a step that tells something important about what it is like to be an inmate in a mental hospital. Having one's past mistakes and present progress under constant moral review seems to make for a special adaptation consisting of a less than moral attitude to ego ideals. One's shortcomings and successes become too central and fluctuating an issue in life to allow the usual commitment of concern for other persons' views of them. It is not very practicable to try to sustain solid claims about oneself. The inmate tends to learn that degradations and reconstructions of the self need not be given too much weight, at the same time learning that staff and inmates are ready to view an inflation or deflation of a self with some indifference. He learns that a defensible picture of self can be seen as something outside oneself that can be constructed, lost, and rebuilt, all with great speed and some equanimity. He learns about the viability of taking up a standpoint—and hence a self—that is outside the one which the hospital can give and take away from him.

The setting, then, seems to engender a kind of cosmopolitan sophistication, a kind of civic apathy. In this unserious yet oddly exaggerated moral context, building up a self or having it destroyed becomes something of a shameless game, and learning to view this process as a game seems to make for some demoralization, the game being such a fundamental one. In the hospital, then, the inmate can learn that the self is not a fortress, but rather a small open city; he can become weary of having to show pleasure when held by troops of his own, and weary of having to show displeasure when held by the enemy. Once he learns what it is like to be defined by society as not having a viable self, this threatening definition—the threat that helps attach people to the self society accords them—is weakened. The patient seems to gain a new plateau when he learns that he can survive while acting in a way that society sees as destructive of him.

A few illustrations of this moral loosening and moral fatigue might be given. In state mental hospitals currently a kind of "marriage moratorium" appears to be accepted by patients and more or less condoned by staff. Some informal peer-group pressure may be brought against a patient who "plays around" with more than one hospital partner at a time, but little negative sanction seems to be attached to taking up, in a temporarily steady way, with a member of the opposite sex, even though both partners are known to be married, to have children, and even to be regularly visited by these outsiders. In short, there is licence in mental hospitals to begin courting all over again, with the understanding, however, that nothing very permanent or serious can come of this. Like shipboard or vacation romances, these entanglements attest to the way in which the hospital is cut off from the outside community, becoming a world of its own, operated for the benefit of its own citizens. And certainly this moratorium is an expression of the alienation and hostility that patients feel for those on the outside to whom they were closely related. But, in addition, one has evidence of the loosening effects of living in a world within a world, under conditions which make it difficult to give full seriousness to either of them.

The second illustration concerns the ward system. On the worst ward level, discreditings seem to occur the most frequently, in part because of lack of facilities, in part through the mockery and sarcasm that seem to be the occupational norm of social control for the attendants and nurses who administer these places. At the same time, the paucity of equipment and rights means that not much self can be built up. The patient finds himself constantly toppled, therefore, but with very little distance to fall. A kind of jaunty gallows humor seems to develop in some of these wards, with considerable freedom to stand up to the staff and return insult for insult. While these patients can be punished, they cannot, for example, be easily slighted, for they are accorded as a matter of course few of the niceties that people must enjoy before they can suffer subtle abuse. Like prostitutes in connection with sex, inmates on these wards have very little reputation or rights to lose and can therefore take certain liberties. As the person moves up the ward system, he can manage more and more to avoid incidents which discredit his claim to be a human being, and acquire more and more of the varied ingredients of self-respect; yet when eventually he does get toppled—and he does—there is a much farther distance to fall. For instance, the privileged patient lives in a world wider than the ward, containing recreation workers who, on request, can dole out cake, cards, table-tennis balls, tickets to the movies, and writing materials. But in the absence of the social control of payment which is typically exerted by a recipient on the outside, the patient runs the risk that even a warmhearted functionary may, on occasion, tell him to wait until she has finished an informal chat, or teasingly ask why he wants what he has asked for, or respond with a dead pause and a cold look of appraisal.

Moving up and down the ward system means, then, not only a shift in self-constructive equipment, a shift in reflected status; but also a change in the calculus of risks. Appreciation of risks to his self-conception is part of everyone's moral experience, but an appreciation that a given risk level is itself merely a social arrangement is a rarer kind of experience, and one that seems to help to disenchant the person who undergoes it.

A third instance of moral loosening has to do with the conditions that are often associated with the release of the inpatient. Often he leaves under the supervision and jurisdiction of his next-of-relation or of a specially selected and specially watchful employer. If he misbehaves while under their auspices, they can quickly obtain his readmission. He therefore finds himself under the special power of persons who ordinarily would not have this kind of power over him, and about whom, moreover, he may have had prior cause to feel quite bitter. In order to get out of the hospital, however, he may conceal his displeasure in this arrangement, and, at least until safely off the hospital rolls, act out a willingness to accept this kind of custody. These discharge procedures, then, provide a built-in lesson in overtly taking a role without the usual covert commitments, and seem further to separate the person from the worlds that others take seriously.

The moral career of a person of a given social category involves a standard sequence of changes in his way of conceiving of selves, including, importantly, his own. These half-buried lines of development can be followed by studying his moral experiences—that is, happenings which mark a turning point in the way in which the person views the world—although the particularities of this view may be difficult to establish. And note can be taken of overt tacks or strategies—that is, stands that he effectively takes before specifiable others, whatever the hidden and variable nature of his inward attachment to these presentations. By taking note of moral experiences and overt personal stands, one can obtain a relatively objective tracing of relatively subjective matters.

Each moral career, and behind this, each self, occurs within the confines of an institutional system, whether a social establishment such as a mental hospital or a complex of personal and professional relationships. The self, then, can be seen as something that resides in the arrangements prevailing in a social system for its members. The self in this sense is not a property of the person to whom it is attributed, but dwells rather in the pattern of social control that is exerted in connection with the person by himself and those around him. This special kind of institutional arrangement does not so much support the self as constitute it.

In this paper, two of these institutional arrangements have been considered, by pointing to what happens to the person when these rulings are weakened. The first concerns the felt loyalty of his next-of-relation. The pre-patient's self is described as a function of the way in which three roles are related, arising and declining in the kinds of affiliation that occur between the next-of-relation and the mediators. The second concerns the protection required by the person for the version of himself which he presents to others, and the way in which the withdrawal of this protection can form a systematic, if unintended, aspect of the working of an establishment. I want to stress that these are only two kinds of institutional rulings from which a self emerges for the participant; others, not considered in this paper, are equally important.

In the usual cycle of adult socialization one expects to find alienation and mortification followed by a new set of beliefs about the world and a new way of conceiving of selves. In the case of the mental-hospital patient, this rebirth does sometimes occur, taking the form of a strong belief in the psychiatric perspective, or, briefly at least, a devotion to the social cause of better treatment for mental patients. The moral career of the mental patient has unique interest, however; it can illustrate the possibility that in casting off the raiments of the old self—or in having this cover torn away—the person need not seek a new robe and a new audience before which to cower. Instead he can learn, at least for a time, to practice before all groups the amoral arts of shamelessness.

Notes

1   An example of the description of these processes may be found in Gresham M. Sykes, *The Society of Captives* (Princeton: Princeton University Press, 1958), ch. iv, "The Pains of Imprisonment," pp. 63–83.

2   Sanford M. Dornbusch, "The Military Academy as an Assimilating Institution," *Social Forces*, XXXIII (1955), p. 317. For an example of initial visiting restrictions in a mental hospital, see D. McI. Johnson and N. Dodds, eds., *The Plea for the Silent* (London: Christopher Johnson, 1957), p. 16. Compare the rule against having visitors which has

often bound domestic servants to their total institution. See J. Jean Hecht, *The Domestic Servant Class in Eighteenth-Century England* (London: Routledge and Kegan Paul, 1956), pp. 127–8.

3 A useful review in the case of American prisons may be found in Paul W. Tappan, "The Legal Rights of Prisoners," *The Annals*, CCXCIII (May 1954), pp. 99–111.

4 See, for example, J. Kerkhoff, *How Thin the Veil: A Newspaperman's Story of His Own Mental Crack-up and Recovery* (New York: Greenberg, 1952), p. 110; Elie A. Cohen, *Human Behaviour in the Concentration Camp* (London: Jonathan Cape, 1954), pp. 118–22; Eugen Kogon, *The Theory and Practice of Hell* (New York: Berkley Publishing Corp., n.d.), pp. 63–8.

5 Brendan Behan, *Borstal Boy* (London: Hutchinson, 1958), p. 40. See also Anthony Heckstall-Smith, *Eighteen Months* (London: Allan Wingate, 1954), p. 26.

6 For a version of this process in concentration camps, see Cohen, op. cit., p. 120, and Kogon, op.cit., pp. 64–5. For a fictionalized treatment of the welcome in a girls' reformatory see, Sara Harris, *The Wayward Ones* (New York: New American Library, 1952), pp. 31–4. A prison version, less explicit, is found in George Dendrickson and Frederick Thomas, *The Truth About Dartmoor* (London: Gollancz, 1954), pp. 42–57.

7 For example, Thomas Merton, *The Seven Storey Mountain* (New York: Harcourt, Brace and Company, 1948), pp. 290–1; Cohen, op. cit., pp. 145–7.

8 Dendrickson and Thomas, op. cit., pp. 83–4, also *The Holy Rule of Saint Benedict*, ch. 55.

9 Kogon, op. cit., p. 69.

10 *The Holy Rule of Saint Benedict*, ch. 55.

11 *The Holy Rule of Saint Benedict*, ch. 58.

12 John M. Murtagh and Sara Harris, *Cast the First Stone* (New York: Pocket Books, 1958), pp. 239–40. On mental hospitals see, for example, Kerkhoff, op. cit., p. 10. Mary Jane Ward, *The Snake Pit* (New York: New American Library, 1955), p. 60, makes the reasonable suggestion that men in our society suffer less defacement in total institutions than do women.

13 Johnson and Dodds, op. cit., p. 15; for a prison version see Alfred Hassler, *Diary of a Self-Made Convict* (Chicago: Regnery, 1954), p. 33.

14 L.D. Hankoff, "Interaction Patterns Among Military Prison Personnel," *U.S. Armed Forces Medical Journal*, X (1959), p. 1419.

15 Kathryn Hulme, *The Nun's Story* (London: Muller, 1957), p. 52.

16 *The Holy Rule of Saint Benedict*. ch. 44.

17 Dendrickson and Thomas, op. cit., p. 76.

18 Sykes, op. cit., pp. 70–72.

19 For example, T.E. Lawrence, *The Mint* (London: Jonathan Cape, 1955), pp. 34–5.

20 *The Holy Rule of Saint Benedict*, ch. 35.

21 Kogon, op. cit., p. 102.

22 Hulme, op. cit., pp. 48–51.

23 Wider communities in Western society, of course, have employed this technique too, in the form of public floggings and public hangings, the pillory and stocks. Functionally correlated with the public emphasis on mortifications in total institutions is the commonly found strict ruling that staff are not to be humiliated by staff in the presence of inmates.

24 Kogon, op. cit., pp. 41–2.

25 Behan, op. cit., p. 23.

26 For example, Kogon, op. cit., p. 128; Hassler, op. cit., p. 16. For the situation in a religious institution, see Hulme, op. cit., p. 48. She also describes a lack of aural privacy since thin cotton hangings are used as the only door closing off the individual sleeping cells (p. 20).

27 Heckstall-Smith, op. cit., p. 21; Dendrickson and Thomas, op. cit., p. 53.

28   L. E. Hinkle, Jr. and H. G. Wolff, "Communist Interrogation and Indoctrination of 'Enemies of the State,'" *A.M.A. Archives of Neurology and Psychiatry,* LXXVI (1956), p. 153. An extremely useful report on the profanizing role of fecal matter, and the social necessity of personal as well as environmental control, is provided in C. E. Orbach et al., "Fears and Defensive Adaptations to the Loss of Anal Sphincter Control," *The Psychoanalytic Review,* XLIV (1957), pp. 121–75.

29   For example, Johnson and Dodds, op. cit., p. 75; Heckstall-Smith, op. cit., p. 15.

30   George Orwell, "Such, Such Were the Joys," *Partisan Review,* XIX (September–October 1952), P. 523.

31   David P. Boder, *I Did Not Interview the Dead* (Urbana: University of Illinois Press, 1949), P. 50.

32   Ibid., p. 50

33   Johnson and Dodds, op. cit., p. 16.

34   Dendrickson and Thomas, op. cit., p. 122

35   A good description of the ward system may be found in Ivan Belknap, *Human Problems of a State Mental Hospital* (New York: McGraw-Hill, 1956), ch. ix, especially p. 164.

36   Here is one way in which mental hospitals can be worse than concentration camps and prisons as places in which to "do" time; in the latter, self-insulation from the symbolic implications of the settings may be easier.

7

The Stigmatized Self

From *Stigma: Notes on the Management of Spoiled Identity**

Three grossly different types of stigma may be mentioned. First there are abominations of the body—the various physical deformities. Next there are blemishes of individual character perceived as weak will, domineering or unnatural passions, treacherous and rigid beliefs, and dishonesty, these being inferred from a known record of, for example, mental disorder, imprisonment, addiction, alcoholism, homosexuality, unemployment, suicidal attempts, and radical political behavior. Finally there are the tribal stigmas of race, nation, and religion, these being stigmas that can be transmitted through lineages and equally contaminate all members of a family.[1] In all of these various instances of stigma, however, including those the Greeks had in mind, the same sociological features are found: an individual who might have been received easily in ordinary social intercourse possesses a trait that can obtrude itself upon attention and turn those of us whom he meets away from him, breaking the claim that his other attributes have on us. He possesses a stigma, an undesired differentness from what we had anticipated. We and those who do not depart negatively from the particular expectations at issue I shall call the *normals*.

The attitudes we normals have toward a person with a stigma, and the actions we take in regard to him, are well known, since these responses are what benevolent social action is designed to soften and ameliorate. By definition, of course, we believe the person with a stigma is not quite human. On this assumption we exercise varieties of discrimination, through which we effectively, if often unthinkingly, reduce his life chances. We construct a stigma-theory, an ideology to explain his inferiority and account for the danger he represents, sometimes rationalizing an animosity based on other differences, such as those of social class.[2] We use specific stigma terms such as cripple, bastard, moron in our daily discourse as a source of metaphor

* Published 1963, pp. 4–7, 8–9, 121, 122–3, 126–9. Copyright © 1963 by Erving Goffman. Used by permission of Simon and Schuster, Inc.

and imagery, typically without giving thought to the original meaning: We tend to impute a wide range of imperfections on the basis of the original one,[3] and at the same time to impute some desirable but undesired attributes, often of a supernatural cast, such as "sixth sense," or "understanding":[4]

> For some, there may be a hesitancy about touching or steering the blind, while for others, the perceived failure to see may be generalized into a gestalt of disability, so that the individual shouts at the blind as if they were deaf or attempts to lift them as if they were crippled. Those confronting the blind may have a whole range of belief that is anchored in the stereotype. For instance, they may think they are subject to unique judgment, assuming the blinded individual draws on special channels of information unavailable to others.[5]

Further, we may perceive his defensive response to his situation as a direct expression of his defect, and then see both defect and response as just retribution for something he or his parents or his tribe did, and hence a justification of the way we treat him.

Now turn from the normal to the person he is normal against. It seems generally true that members of a social category may strongly support a standard of judgment that they and others agree does not directly apply to them. Thus it is that a businessman may demand womanly behavior from females or ascetic behavior from monks, and not construe himself as someone who ought to realize either of these styles of conduct. The distinction is between realizing a norm and merely supporting it. The issue of stigma does not arise here, but only where there is some expectation on all sides that those in a given category should not only support a particular norm but also realize it.

Also, it seems possible for an individual to fail to live up to what we effectively demand of him, and yet be relatively untouched by this failure; insulated by his alienation, protected by identity beliefs of his own, he feels that he is a full-fledged normal human being, and that we are the ones who are not quite human. He bears a stigma but does not seem to be impressed or repentant about doing so. This possibility is celebrated in exemplary tales about Mennonites, Gypsies, shameless scoundrels, and very orthodox Jews.

In America at present, however, separate systems of honor seem to be on the decline. The stigmatized individual tends to hold the same beliefs about identity that we do; this is a pivotal fact. His deepest feelings about what he is may be his sense of being a "normal person," a human being like anyone else, a person, therefore, who deserves a fair chance and a fair break.[6] (Actually, however phrased, he bases his claims not on what he thinks is due *everyone,* but only everyone of a selected social category into which he unquestionably fits, for example, anyone of his age, sex, profession, and so forth.) Yet he may perceive, usually quite correctly, that whatever others profess, they do not really "accept" him and are not ready to make contact with him on "equal grounds."[7] Further, the standards he has incorporated from the wider society equip him to be intimately alive to what others see as his failing, inevitably causing him, if only for moments, to agree that he does indeed fall short of what he really ought to be. Shame becomes a central possibility, arising from the individual's perception of one of his own attributes as being a defiling thing to possess, and one he can readily see himself as not possessing.

The immediate presence of normals is likely to reinforce this split between self-demands and self, but in fact self-hate and self-derogation can also occur when only he and a mirror are about.

★   ★   ★

The central feature of the stigmatized individual's situation in life can now be stated. It is a question of what is often, if vaguely, called "acceptance." Those who have dealings with him fail to accord him the respect and regard which the uncontaminated aspects of his social identity have led them to anticipate extending, and have led him to anticipate receiving; he echoes this denial by finding that some of his own attributes warrant it.

★   ★   ★

The nature of a "good adjustment" is now apparent. It requires that the stigmatized individual cheerfully and unselfconsciously accept himself as essentially the same as normals, while at the same time he voluntarily withholds himself from those situations in which normals would find it difficult to give lip service to their similar acceptance of him.

Since the good-adjustment line is presented by those who take the standpoint of the wider society, one should ask what the following of it by the stigmatized means to normals. It means that the unfairness and pain of having to carry a stigma will never be presented to them; it means that normals will not have to admit to themselves how limited their tactfulness and tolerance is; and it means that normals can remain relatively uncontaminated by intimate contact with the stigmatized, relatively unthreatened in their identity beliefs. It is from just these meanings, in fact, that the specifications of a good adjustment derive.

★   ★   ★

The general formula is apparent. The stigmatized individual is asked to act so as to imply neither that his burden is heavy nor that bearing it has made him different from us; at the same time he must keep himself at that remove from us which ensures our painlessly being able to confirm this belief about him. Put differently, he is advised to reciprocate naturally with an acceptance of himself and us, an acceptance of him that we have not quite extended him in the first place. A *phantom acceptance* is thus allowed to provide the base for a *phantom normalcy*. So deeply, then, must he be caught up in the attitude to the self that is defined as normal in our society, so thoroughly must he be a part of this definition, that he can perform this self in a faultless manner to an edgy audience that is half-watching him in terms of another show. He can even be led to join with normals in suggesting to the discontented among his own that the slights they sense are imagined slights—which of course is likely at times, because at many social boundaries the markers are designed to be so faint as to allow everyone to proceed as though fully accepted, and this means that it will be realistic to be oriented to minimal signs perhaps not meant.

The irony of these recommendations is not that the stigmatized individual is asked to be patiently for others what they decline to let him be for them, but that this expropriation of his response may well be the best return he can get on his money. If in fact he desires to live as much as possible "like any other person," and be accepted "for what he really is," then in many cases the shrewdest position for him to take is this one which has a false bottom; for in many cases the degree to which normals accept the stigmatized individual can be maximized by his acting with full spontaneity and naturalness as if the conditional acceptance of him, which he is careful not to overreach, is full acceptance. But of course what is a good adjustment for the individual can be an even better one for society. It might be added that the embarrassment of limits is a general feature of social organization; the maintenance of phantom acceptance is what many, to some degree, are being asked to accept. Any mutual adjustment and mutual approval between two individuals can be fundamentally embarrassed if one of the partners accepts in full the offer that the other appears to make; every "positive" relationship is conducted under implied promises of consideration and aid such that the relationship would be injured were these credits actually drawn on.

★   ★   ★

This essay deals with the situation of the stigmatized person and his response to the spot he is in. In order to place the resulting framework in its proper conceptual context, it will be useful to consider from different angles the concept of deviation, this being a bridge which links the study of stigma to the study of the rest of the social world.

It is possible to think of rare and dramatic failings as those most suitable for the analysis here employed. However, it would seem that exotic differentness is most useful merely as a means of making one aware of identity assumptions ordinarily so fully satisfied as to escape one's awareness. It is also possible to think that established minority groups like Negroes and Jews can provide the best objects for this kind of analysis. This could easily lead to imbalance of treatment. Sociologically, the central issue concerning these groups is their place in the social structure; the contingencies these persons encounter in face-to-face interaction is only one part of the problem, and something that cannot itself be fully understood without reference to the history, the political development, and the current policies of the group.

It is also possible to restrict the analysis to those who possess a flaw that uneases almost all their social situations, leading these unfortunates to form a major part of their self-conception reactively, in terms of their response to this plight. This report argues differently. The most fortunate of normals is likely to have his half-hidden failing, and for every little failing there is a social occasion when it will loom large, creating a shameful gap between virtual and actual social identity. Therefore the occasionally precarious and the constantly precarious form a single continuum, their situation in life analyzable by the same framework. (Hence persons with only a minor differentness find they understand the structure of the situation in which the fully stigmatized are placed—often attributing this sympathy to the profundity of their human nature instead of to the isomorphism of human situations. The fully and visibly stigmatized, in turn, must suffer the special indignity of knowing that they wear their situation on their sleeve, that almost anyone will be able to see into the heart of their predicament.) It is implied, then, that it is not to the different that one should look for understanding our differentness, but to the ordinary. The question of social norms is certainly central, but the concern might be less for uncommon deviations from the ordinary than for ordinary deviations from the common.

It can be assumed that a necessary condition for social life is the sharing of a single set of normative expectations by all participants, the norms being sustained in part because of being incorporated. When a rule is broken restorative measures will occur; the damaging is terminated and the damage repaired, whether by control agencies or by the culprit himself.

However, the norms dealt with in this paper concern identity or being, and are therefore of a special kind. Failure or success at maintaining such norms has a very direct effect on the psychological integrity of the individual. At the same time, mere desire to abide by the norm—mere good will—is not enough, for in many cases the individual has no immediate control over his level of sustaining the norm. It is a question of the individual's condition, not his will; it is a question of conformance, not compliance. Only by introducing the assumption that the individual should know and keep his place can a full equivalent in willful action be found for the individual's social condition.

Further, while some of these norms, such as sightedness and literacy, may be commonly sustained with complete adequacy by most persons in the society, there are other norms, such as those associated with physical comeliness, which take the form of ideals and constitute standards against which almost everyone falls short at some stage in his life. And even where widely attained norms are involved, their multiplicity has the effect of disqualifying many persons. For example, in an important sense there is only one complete unblushing male in America: a young, married, white, urban, northern, heterosexual Protestant father of college education, fully employed, of good complexion, weight and height, and a recent record in sports. Every American male tends to look out upon the world from this perspective, this constituting one sense in which one can speak of a common value system in America. Any male who fails to qualify in any of these ways is likely to view himself—during moments at least—as unworthy, incomplete, and inferior; at times he is likely to pass and at times he is likely to find himself being apologetic or aggressive concerning known-about aspects of himself he knows are probably seen as undesirable. The general identity-values of a society may be fully entrenched nowhere, and yet they can cast some kind of shadow on the encounters encountered everywhere in daily living.

Notes

1   In recent history, especially in Britain, low class status functioned as an important tribal stigma, the sins of the parents, or at least their milieu, being visited on the child, should the child rise improperly far above his initial station. The management of class stigma is of course a central theme in the English novel.

2   D. Riesman, "Some Observations Concerning Marginality," *Phylon,* Second Quarter, 1951, 122.

3   In regard to the blind, see E. Henrich and L. Kriegel, eds., *Experiments in Survival* (New York: Association for the Aid of Crippled Children, 1961), pp. 152 and 186; and H. Chevigny, *My Eyes Have a Cold Nose* (New Haven, Conn.: Yale University Press, paperbound, 1962), p. 201.

4   In the words of one blind woman, "I was asked to endorse a perfume, presumably because being sightless my sense of smell was super-discriminating." See T. Keitlen (with N. Lobsenz), *Farewell to Fear* (New York: Avon, 1962), p. 10.

5   A. G. Gowman, *The War Blind in American Social Structure* (New York: American Foundation for the Blind, 1957), p. 198.

6   The notion of "normal human being" may have its source in the medical approach to humanity or in the tendency of large-scale bureaucratic organizations, such as the nation

state, to treat all members in some respects as equal. Whatever its origins, it seems to provide the basic imagery through which laymen currently conceive of themselves. Interestingly, a convention seems to have emerged in popular life-story writing where a questionable person proves his claim to normalcy by citing his acquisition of a spouse and children, and, oddly, by attesting to his spending Christmas and Thanksgiving with them.

7   A criminal's view of this nonacceptance is presented in T. Parker and R. Allerton, *The Courage of His Convictions* (London: Hutchinson & Co., 1962), pp. 110–11.

8

The Recalcitrant Self

From "The Underlife of a Public Institution"*

In every social establishment, there are official expectations as to what the participant owes the establishment. Even in cases where there is no specific task, as in some night-watchman jobs, the organization will require some presence of mind, some awareness of the current situation, and some readiness for unanticipated events; as long as an establishment demands that its participants not sleep on the job, it asks them to be awake to certain matters. And where sleeping is part of the expectation, as in a home or a hotel, then there will be limits on where and when the sleeping is to occur, with whom, and with what bed manners.[1] And behind these claims on the individual, be they great or small, the managers of every establishment will have a widely embracing implicit conception of what the individual's character must be for these claims on him to be appropriate.

Whenever we look at a social establishment, we find a counter to this first theme: we find that participants decline in some way to accept the official view of what they should be putting into and getting out of the organization and, behind this, of what sort of self and world they are to accept for themselves. Where enthusiasm is expected, there will be apathy; where loyalty, there will be disaffection; where attendance, absenteeism; where robustness, some kind of illness; where deeds are to be done, varieties of inactivity. We find a multitude of homely little histories, each in its way a movement of liberty. Whenever worlds are laid on, underlives develop.

II

The study of underlife in restrictive total institutions has some special interest. When existence is cut to the bone, we can learn what people do to flesh out their lives. Stashes, means of transportation, free places, territories,

---

* Originally published in *Asylums*, 1961, pp. 305–20. Copyright © 1961 by Erving Goffman.

supplies for economic and social exchange—these apparently are some of the minimal requirements for building up a life. Ordinarily these arrangements are taken for granted as part of one's primary adjustment; seeing them twisted out of official existence through bargains, wit, force, and cunning, we can see their significance anew. The study of total institutions also suggests that formal organizations have standard places of vulnerability, such as supply rooms, sick bays, kitchens, or scenes of highly technical labor. These are the damp corners where secondary adjustments breed and start to infest the establishment.

The mental hospital represents a peculiar instance of those establishments in which underlife is likely to proliferate. Mental patients are persons who caused the kind of trouble on the outside that led someone physically, if not socially, close to them to take psychiatric action against them. Often this trouble was associated with the "prepatient" having indulged in situational improprieties of some kind, conduct out of place in the setting. It is just such misconduct that conveys a moral rejection of the communities, establishments, and relationships that have a claim to one's attachment.

Stigmatization as mentally ill and involuntary hospitalization are the means by which we answer these offenses against propriety. The individual's persistence in manifesting symptoms after entering the hospital, and his tendency to develop additional symptoms during his initial response to the hospital, can now no longer serve him well as expressions of disaffection. From the patient's point of view, to decline to exchange a word with the staff or with his fellow patients may be ample evidence of rejecting the institution's view of what and who he is; yet higher management may construe this alienative expression as just the sort of symptomatology the institution was established to deal with and as the best kind of evidence that the patient properly belongs where he now finds himself. In short, mental hospitalization outmaneuvers the patient, tending to rob him of the common expressions through which people hold off the embrace of organizations—insolence, silence, *sotto voce* remarks, unco-operativeness, malicious destruction of interior decorations, and so forth; these signs of disaffiliation are now read as signs of their maker's proper affiliation. Under these conditions all adjustments are primary.

Furthermore, there is a vicious-circle process at work. Persons who are lodged on "bad" wards find that very little equipment of any kind is given them—clothes may be taken from them each night, recreational materials may be withheld, and only heavy wooden chairs and benches provided for furniture. Acts of hostility against the institution have to rely on limited, ill-designed devices, such as banging a chair against the floor or striking a sheet of newspaper sharply so as to make an annoying explosive sound. And the more inadequate this equipment is to convey rejection of the hospital, the more the act appears as a psychotic symptom, and the more likely it is that management feels justified in assigning the patient to a bad ward. When a patient finds himself in seclusion, naked and without visible means of expression, he may have to rely on tearing up his mattress, if he can, or writing with feces on the wall—actions management takes to be in keeping with the kind of person who warrants seclusion.

We can also see this circular process at work in the small, illicit, talisman-like possessions that inmates use as symbolic devices for separating themselves from the position they are supposed to be in. What I think is a typical example may be cited from prison literature.

> Prison clothing is anonymous. One's possessions are limited to tooth-brush, comb, upper or lower cot, half the space upon a narrow table, a razor. As in jail, the urge to collect possessions is carried to prepos-terous extents. Rocks, string, knives—anything made by man and forbidden in man's institution—anything,—a red comb, a different kind of toothbrush, a belt—these things are assiduously gathered, jeal-ously hidden or triumphantly displayed.[2]

But when a patient, whose clothes are taken from him each night, fills his pockets with bits of string and rolled up paper, and when he fights to keep these possessions in spite of the consequent inconvenience to those who must regularly go through his pockets, he is usually seen as engaging in symptomatic behavior befitting a very sick patient, not as someone who is attempting to stand apart from the place accorded him.

Official psychiatric doctrine tends to define alienative acts as psychotic ones—this view being reinforced by the circular processes that lead the patient to exhibit alienation in a more and more bizarre form—but the hospital cannot be run according to this doctrine. The hospital cannot decline to demand from its members exactly what other organizations must insist on; psychiatric doctrine is supple enough to do this, but institutions are not. Given the standards of the institution's environing society, there have to be at least the minimum routines connected with feeding, washing, dressing, bedding the patients, and protecting them from physical harm. Given these routines, there have to be inducements and exhortations to get patients to follow them. Demands must be made, and disappointment is shown when a patient does not live up to what is expected of him. Interest in seeing psychiatric "movement" or "improvement" after an initial stay on the wards leads the staff to encourage "proper" conduct and to express disappointment when a patient backslides into "psychosis." The patient is thus re-established as someone whom others are depending on, someone who ought to know enough to act correctly. Some improprieties, especially ones like muteness and apathy that do not obstruct and even ease ward routines, may continue to be perceived naturalistically as symptoms, but on the whole the hospital operates semi-officially on the assumption that the patient ought to act in a manageable way and be respectful of psychiatry, and that he who does will be rewarded by improvement in life conditions and he who doesn't will be punished by a reduction of amenities. Within this semi-official reinstatement of ordinary organizational practices, the patient finds that many of the traditional ways of taking leave of a place without moving from it have retained their validity; secondary adjustments are therefore possible.

III

Of the many different kinds of secondary adjustment, some are of particular interest because they bring into the clear the general theme of involvement and disaffection, characteristic of all these practices.

One of these special types of secondary adjustment is "removal activities" (or "kicks"), namely, undertakings that provide something for the individual to lose himself in, temporarily blotting out all sense of the environment which, and in which, he must abide. In total institutions a useful exemplary case is provided by Robert Stroud, the "Birdman," who, from watching birds out his cell window, through a spectacular career of finagling and make-do, fabricated a laboratory and became a leading ornithological contributor to medical literature, all from within prison. Language courses in prisoner-of-war camps and art courses in prisons can provide the same release.

Central Hospital provided several of these escape worlds for inmates. One, for example, was sports. Some of the baseball players and a few tennis players seemed to become so caught up in their sport, and in the daily record of their efforts in competition, that at least for the summer months this became their overriding interest. In the case of baseball this was further strengthened by the fact that, within the hospital, parole patients could follow national baseball as readily as could many persons on the outside. For some young patients, who never failed to go, when allowed, to a dance held in their service or in the recreation building, it was possible to live for the chance of meeting someone "interesting" or remeeting someone interesting who had already been met—in much the same way that college students are able to survive their studies by looking forward to the new "dates" that may be found in extracurricular activities. The "marriage moratorium" in Central Hospital, effectively freeing a patient from his marital obligations to a non-patient, enhanced this removal activity. For a handful of patients, the semi-annual theatrical production was an extremely effective removal activity: tryouts, rehearsals, costuming, scenery-making, staging, writing and rewriting, performing—all these seemed as successful as on the outside in building a world apart for the participants. Another kick, important to some patients—and a worrisome concern for the hospital chaplains—was the enthusiastic espousal of religion. Still another, for a few patients, was gambling.

Portable ways of getting away were much favored in Central Hospital, paper-back murder mysteries, cards, and even jigsaw puzzles being carried around on one's person. Not only could leave be taken of the ward and grounds be taken leave of through these means, but if one had to wait for an hour or so upon an official, or the serving of a meal, or the opening of the recreation building, the self-implication of this subordination could be dealt with by immediately bringing forth one's own world-making equipment.

Individual means of creating a world were striking. One depressed, suicidal alcoholic, apparently a good bridge player, disdained bridge with almost all other patient players, carrying around his own pocket bridge player and writing away occasionally for a new set of competition hands. Given a supply of his favorite gumdrops and his pocket radio, he could pull himself out of the hospital world at will, surrounding all his senses with pleasantness.

In considering removal activities we can again raise the issue of overcommitment to an establishment. In the hospital laundry, for example, there was a patient worker who had been on the job for several years. He had been given the job of unofficial foreman, and, unlike almost all other patient workers, he threw himself into his work with a capacity, devotion, and seriousness that were evident to many. Of him, the laundry charge attendant said:

> That one there is my special helper. He works harder than all the rest put together. I would be lost without him.

In exchange for his effort, the attendant would bring from home something for this patient to eat almost every day. And yet there was something grotesque in his adjustment, for it was apparent that his deep voyage into the work world had a slightly make-believe character; after all, he was a patient, not a foreman, and he was clearly reminded of this off the job.

Obviously, as some of these illustrations imply, removal activities need not be in themselves illegitimate; it is the function that they come to serve for the inmate that leads us to consider them along with other secondary adjustments. An extreme here, perhaps, is individual psychotherapy in state mental hospitals; this privilege is so rare in these institutions,[3] and the resulting contact with a staff psychiatrist so unique in terms of hospital status structure, that an inmate can to some degree forget where he is as he pursues his psychotherapy. By actually receiving what the institution formally claims to offer, the patient can succeed in getting away from what the establishment actually provides. There is a general implication here. Perhaps every

activity that an establishment obliges or permits its members to participate
in is a potential threat to the organization, for it would seem that there is no
activity in which the individual cannot become overengrossed.

Another property is clearly evident in some undercover practices and
possibly a factor in all of them: I refer to what Freudians sometimes call
"overdetermination." Some illicit activities are pursued with a measure of
spite, malice, glee, and triumph, and at a personal cost, that cannot be
accounted for by the intrinsic pleasure of consuming the product. True, it
is central to closed restrictive institutions that apparently minor satisfactions
can come to be defined as great ones. But even correcting for this re-evalu-
ation, something remains to be explained.

One aspect of the overdetermination of some secondary adjustments is
the sense one gets of a practice being employed *merely* because it is
forbidden.[4] Inmates in Central Hospital who had succeeded in some elaborate evasion of the rules often seemed to seek out a fellow inmate, even one
who could not be entirely trusted, to display before him evidence of the
evasion. A patient back from an overlate foray into the local town's night life
would be full of stories of his exploits the next day; another would call aside
his friends and show them where he had stashed the empty liquor bottle
whose contents he had consumed the night before, or display the condoms
in his wallet. Nor was it surprising to see the limits of safe concealment
tested. I knew an extremely resourceful alcoholic who would smuggle in a
pint of vodka, put some in a paper drinking cup, and sit on the most exposed
part of the lawn he could find, slowly getting drunk; at such times he took
pleasure in offering hospitality to persons of semi-staff status. Similarly, I
knew an attendant who would park his car just outside the patient
canteen—the social hub of the patient universe—and there he and a friendly
patient would discuss the most intimate qualifications of the passing females
while resting a paper cup full of bourbon on the differential covering, just
below the sight line of the crowd, drinking a toast, as it were, to their distance
from the scene around them.

Another aspect of the overdeterminism of some secondary adjustments is
that the very pursuit of them seems to be a source of satisfaction. As previously suggested in regard to courtship contacts, the institution can become
defined as one's opponent in a serious game, the object being to score against
the hospital. Thus I have heard cliques of patients pleasurably discuss the
possibility that evening of "scoring" for coffee, accurately employing this
larger term for a smaller activity. The tendency of prison inmates to smuggle
food and other comforts into the cell of someone suffering solitary confine-
ment may be seen not only as an act of charity but also as a way of sharing
by association the spirit of someone taking a stand against authority. Similarly, the time-consuming elaborate escape planning that patients, prisoners,
and P.O.W. internees engage in can be seen not merely as a way of getting

out but also as a way of giving meaning to being in.

I am suggesting that secondary adjustments are overdetermined, some of them especially so. These practices serve the practitioner in ways other than the most evident ones: whatever else they accomplish these practices seem to demonstrate—to the practitioner if no one else—that he has some self-hood and personal autonomy beyond the grasp of the organization.[5]

IV

If a function of secondary adjustments is to place a barrier between the individual and the social unit in which he is supposed to be participating, we should expect some secondary adjustments to be empty of intrinsic gain and to function solely to express unauthorized distance—a self-preserving "rejection of one's rejectors."[6] This seems to happen with the very common forms of ritual insubordination, for example, griping or bitching, where this behavior is not realistically expected to bring about change. Through direct insolence that does not meet with immediate correction, or remarks passed half out of hearing of authority, or gestures performed behind the back of authority, subordinates express some detachment from the place officially accorded them. An ex-inmate of the penitentiary at Lewisburg provides an illustration:

> On the surface, life here appears to run almost placidly, but one needs to go only a very little beneath the surface to find the whirlpools and eddies of anger and frustration. The muttering of discontent and rebellion goes on constantly: the *sotto voce* sneer whenever we pass an official or a guard, the glare carefully calculated to express contempt without arousing overt retaliation . . .[7]

Brendan Behan provides a British prison illustration:

> The warder shouted at him.
> "Right, sir," he shouted. "Be right along, sir," adding in a lower tone, "You shit-'ouse."[8]

Some of these ways of openly but safely taking a stand outside the authorized one are beautiful, especially when carried out collectively. Again, prisons provide ready examples:

> How to express contempt for authority? The manner of "obeying" orders is one way. . . . Negroes are especially apt at parody, sometimes breaking into a goose-step. They seat themselves at table 10 at a time, snatching off caps simultaneously and precisely.[9]

When the sky pilot got up in the pulpit to give us our weekly pep talk each Sunday he would always make some feeble joke which we always laughed at as loud and as long as possible, although he must have known that we were sending him up. He still used to make some mildly funny remark and every time he did the whole church would be filled with rawcous [sic] laughter, even though only half the audience had heard what had been said.[10]

Some acts of ritual insubordination rely on irony, found in the wider society in the form of gallows gallantry and in institutions in the construction of heavily meaningful mascots. A standard irony in total institutions is giving nicknames to especially threatening or unpleasant aspects of the environment. In concentration camps, turnips were sometimes called "German pineapples,"[11] fatigue drill, "Geography."[12] In mental wards in Mount Sinai Hospital, brain-damage cases held for surgery would call the hospital "Mount Cyanide,"[13] and staff doctors were

> typically misnamed, being referred to by such terms as "lawyer," "white-collar worker," "chief of crew," "one of the presidents," "bartender," "supervisor of insurance" and "credit manager." One of us (E.A.W.) was called by such variations as "Weinberg," "Weingarten," "Weiner" and "Wiseman,". . .[14]

In prison, the punishment block may be called the "tea garden."[15] In Central Hospital, one of the wards containing incontinent patients was sometimes felt to be the punishment ward for attendants, who called it "the rose garden." An ex-mental patient provides another illustration:

> Back in the dayroom Virginia decided that her change of clothing represented Dressing Therapy. D.T. Today was my turn for D.T. This would have been rather amusing if you had had a good stiff drink. Of paraldehyde. The Juniper Cocktail, as we call it, we gay ladies of Juniper Hill. A martini, please, we more sophisticated ones say. And where, nurse, is the olive?[16]

It should be understood, of course, that the threatening world responded to with ironies need not be one sponsored by an alien human authority, but may be one that is self-imposed, or imposed by nature, as when dangerously ill persons joke about their situation.[17]

Beyond irony, however, there is an even more subtle and telling kind of ritual insubordination. There is a special stance that can be taken to alien authority; it combines stiffness, dignity, and coolness in a particular mixture that conveys insufficient insolence to call forth immediate punishment and yet expresses that one is entirely one's own man. Since this communication is made through the way in which the body and face are held, it can be constantly conveyed wherever the inmate finds himself. Illustrations can be found in prison society:

> "Rightness" implies bravery, fearlessness, loyalty to peers, avoidance of exploitation, adamant refusal to concede the superiority of the official value system, and repudiation of the notion that the inmate is of a lower order. It consists principally in the reassertion of one's basic integrity, dignity, and worth in an essentially degrading situation, and the exhibition of these personal qualities regardless of any show of force by the official system.[18]

Similarly, in Central Hospital, in the "tough" punishment wards of maximum security, where inmates had very little more to lose, fine examples could be found of patients not going out of their way to make trouble but by their very posture conveying unconcern and mild contempt for all levels of the staff, combined with utter self-possession.

V

It would be easy to account for the development of secondary adjustments by assuming that the individual possessed an array of needs, native or cultivated, and that when lodged in a milieu that denied these needs the individual simply responded by developing makeshift means of satisfaction. I think this explanation fails to do justice to the importance of these under-cover adaptations for the structure of the self.

The practice of reserving something of oneself from the clutch of an institution is very visible in mental hospitals and prisons, but can be found in more benign and less totalistic institutions, too. I want to argue that this recalcitrance is not an incidental mechanism of defense but rather an essential constituent of the self.

Sociologists have always had a vested interest in pointing to the ways in which the individual is formed by groups, identifies with groups, and wilts away unless he obtains emotional support from groups. But when we closely observe what goes on in a social role, a spate of sociable interaction, a social establishment—or in any other unit of social organization—embracement of the unit is not all that we see. We always find the individual employing methods to keep some distance, some elbow room, between himself and that with which others assume he should be identified. No doubt a state-type mental hospital provides an overly lush soil for the growth of these secondary adjustments, but in fact, like weeds, they spring up in any kind of social organization. If we find, then, that in all situations actually studied the participant has erected defenses against his social bondedness, why should we base our conception of the self upon how the individual would act were conditions "just right"?

The simplest sociological view of the individual and his self is that he is to himself what his place in an organization defines him to be. When pressed, a sociologist modifies this model by granting certain complications: the self may be not yet formed or may exhibit conflicting dedications. Perhaps we should further complicate the construct by elevating these qualifications to a central place, initially defining the individual, for sociological purposes, as a stance-taking entity, a something that takes up a position somewhere between identification with an organization and opposition to it, and is ready at the slightest pressure to regain its balance by shifting its involvement in either direction. It is thus *against something* that the self can emerge. This has been appreciated by students of totalitarianism.

> In short, Ketman means self-realization *against* something. He who practices Ketman suffers because of the obstacles he meets; but if these obstacles were suddenly to be removed, he would find himself in a void which might perhaps prove much more painful. Internal revolt is sometimes essential to spiritual health, and can create a particular form of happiness. What can be said openly is often much less interesting than the emotional magic of defending one's private sanctuary.[19]

I have argued the same case in regard to total institutions. May this not be the situation, however, in free society, too?

Without something to belong to, we have no stable self, and yet total commitment and attachment to any social unit implies a kind of selflessness. Our sense of being a person can come from being drawn into a wider social unit; our sense of selfhood can arise through the little ways in which we resist the pull. Our status is backed by the solid buildings of the world, while our sense of personal identity often resides in the cracks.

Notes

1   When stagecoach travellers in Europe in the fifteenth century might be required to share an inn bed with a stranger, courtesy books laid down codes of proper bed conduct. See Norbert Elias, *Über den Prozess der Zivilisation* (2 vols.; Basel: Verlag Haus Zum Falken, 1934), Vol. II, pp. 219–21, "Über das Verhalten im Schlafraum."

2   Holley Cantine and Dachine Rainer, eds., *Prison Etiquette* (Bearsville, N.Y.: Retort Press, 1950), p. 78. Compare the things that small boys stash in their pockets; some of these items also seem to provide a wedge between the boy and the domestic establishment.

3   Of approximately 7000 patients in Central Hospital, I calculated at the time of the study that about 100 received some kind of individual psychotherapy in any one year.

4   This theme is developed by Albert Cohen in *Delinquent Boys* (Glencoe, Ill.: The Free

Press, 1955).

5   This point is nicely expressed by Dostoevski in his description of life in a Siberian prison camp, *Memoirs from the House of the Dead*, trans. Jessie Coulson (London: Oxford University Press, 1956), p. 17: "There were in the prison many who had been sentenced for smuggling, and there is therefore nothing surprising in the way vodka was brought in in spite of all the guards and inspections. Smuggling, by the way, is by its very nature a rather special crime. Can one imagine, for instance, that with some smugglers money and profit do not stand in the foreground, but play a secondary part? It really is so, however. The smuggler works for love of it, because he has a vocation. He is in some sense a poet. He risks everything, runs into terrible danger, twists and turns, uses his invention, extricates himself; sometimes he seems to act almost by inspiration. It is a passion as strong as that for cards."

6   Lloyd W. McCorkle and Richard Korn, "Resocialization Within Walls," *The Annals*, CCXCIII (1954), p. 88.

7   Alfred Hassler, *Diary of a Self-Made Convict* (Chicago: Regnery, 1954), pp. 70–1. For a military example of bitching, see T. E. Lawrence, *The Mint* (London: Jonathan Cape, 1955), p. 132.

8   Brendan Behan, *Borstal Boy* (London: Hutchinson, 1958), p. 45. Primary school children in American society very early learn how to cross their fingers, mutter contradictions, and grimace covertly—through all of these means expressing a margin of autonomy even while submitting to the teacher's verbal punishment.

9   Cantine and Rainer, op. cit., p. 106.

10   J.F.N. 1797, "Corrective Training," *Encounter*, X [May 1958], pp. 15–16. See also Erving Goffman, *The Presentation of Self in Everyday Life* (New York: Anchor Books, 1959), "derisive collusion," pp. 186–8.

11   Eugen Kogon, *The Theory and Practice of Hell* (New York: Berkley Publishing Corp., n.d.), p. 108.

12   Ibid., p. 103.

13   Edwin Weinstein and Robert Kahn, *Denial of Illness* (Springfield, Ill.: Charles Thomas, 1955), p. 21.

14   Ibid., p. 61. See especially ch. vi, "The Language of Denial."

15   George Dendrickson and Frederick Thomas, *The Truth About Dartmoor* (London: Gollancz, 1954), p. 25.

16   Mary Jane Ward, *The Snake Pit* (New York: New American Library, 1955), p. 65.

17   A useful report on ironies and other devices for dealing with life threat is provided by Renée Fox in *Experiment Perilous* (Glencoe, Ill.: The Free Press, 1959), p. 170 ff.

18   Richard Cloward, "Social Control in the Prison," S.S.R.C. Pamphlet No. 15, p. 40.

19   Czeslaw Milosz, *The Captive Mind* (New York: Vintage Books, 1955), p. 76.

PART III

The Nature of Social Life

9

Social Life as Drama

From *The Presentation of Self in Everyday Life**

Belief in the Part One is Playing

When an individual plays a part he implicitly requests his observers to take seriously the impression that is fostered before them. They are asked to believe that the character they see actually possesses the attributes he appears to possess, that the task he performs will have the consequences that are implicitly claimed for it, and that, in general, matters are what they appear to be. In line with this, there is the popular view that the individual offers his performance and puts on his show "for the benefit of other people." It will be convenient to begin a consideration of performances by turning the question around and looking at the individual's own belief in the impression of reality that he attempts to engender in those among whom he finds himself.

At one extreme, one finds that the performer can be fully taken in by his own act; he can be sincerely convinced that the impression of reality which he stages is the real reality. When his audience is also convinced in this way about the show he puts on—and this seems to be the typical case—then for the moment at least, only the sociologist or the socially disgruntled will have any doubts about the "realness" of what is presented.

At the other extreme, we find that the performer may not be taken in at all by his own routine. This possibility is understandable, since no one is in quite as good an observational position to see through the act as the person who puts it on. Coupled with this, the performer may be moved to guide the conviction of his audience only as a means to other ends, having no ultimate concern in the conception that they have of him or of the situation. When the individual has no belief in his own act and no ultimate concern with the beliefs of his audience, we may call him cynical, reserving the term

* First published 1956; these extracts from the edition of 1959, pp. 17–20, 22–4, 30–3, 34–6, 56–9, 65–6, 70–7. Copyright © 1959 by Erving Goffman. Used by permission of Doubleday, a division of Bantam Doubleday Dell Publishing Group, Inc.

"sincere" for individuals who believe in the impression fostered by their own performance. It should be understood that the cynic, with all his professional disinvolvement, may obtain unprofessional pleasures from his masquerade, experiencing a kind of gleeful spiritual aggression from the fact that he can toy at will with something his audience must take seriously.[1]

It is not assumed, of course, that all cynical performers are interested in deluding their audiences for purposes of what is called "self-interest" or private gain. A cynical individual may delude his audience for what he considers to be their own good, or for the good of the community, etc. For illustrations of this we need not appeal to sadly enlightened showmen such as Marcus Aurelius or Hsun Tzŭ. We know that in service occupations practitioners who may otherwise be sincere are sometimes forced to delude their customers because their customers show such a heartfelt demand for it. Doctors who are led into giving placebos, filling station attendants who resignedly check and recheck tire pressures for anxious women motorists, shoe clerks who sell a shoe that fits but tell the customer it is the size she wants to hear—these are cynical performers whose audiences will not allow them to be sincere. Similarly, it seems that sympathetic patients in mental wards will sometimes feign bizarre symptoms so that student nurses will not be subjected to a disappointingly sane performance. So also, when inferiors extend their most lavish reception for visiting superiors, the selfish desire to win favor may not be the chief motive; the inferior may be tactfully attempting to put the superior at ease by simulating the kind of world the superior is thought to take for granted.

I have suggested two extremes: an individual may be taken in by his own act or be cynical about it. These extremes are something a little more than just the ends of a continuum. Each provides the individual with a position which has its own particular securities and defenses, so there will be a tendency for those who have travelled close to one of these poles to complete the voyage. Starting with lack of inward belief in one's role, the individual may follow the natural movement described by Park:

> It is probably no mere historical accident that the word person, in its first meaning, is a mask. It is rather a recognition of the fact that everyone is always and everywhere, more or less consciously, playing a role . . . It is in these roles that we know each other; it is in these roles that we know ourselves.[2]

In a sense, and in so far as this mask represents the conception we have formed of ourselves—the role we are striving to live up to—this mask is our truer self, the self we would like to be. In the end, our conception of our role becomes second nature and an integral part of our personality. We come into the world as individuals, achieve character, and become persons.[3]

★   ★   ★

Front

I have been using the term "performance" to refer to all the activity of an individual which occurs during a period marked by his continuous presence before a particular set of observers and which has some influence on the observers. It will be convenient to label as "front" that part of the individual's performance which regularly functions in a general and fixed fashion to define the situation for those who observe the performance. Front, then, is the expressive equipment of a standard kind intentionally or unwittingly employed by the individual during his performance. For preliminary purposes, it will be convenient to distinguish and label what seem to be the standard parts of front.

First, there is the "setting," involving furniture, décor, physical layout, and other background items which supply the scenery and stage props for the spate of human action played out before, within, or upon it. A setting tends to stay put, geographically speaking, so that those who would use a particular setting as part of their performance cannot begin their act until they have brought themselves to the appropriate place and must terminate their performance when they leave it. It is only in exceptional circumstances that the setting follows along with the performers; we see this in the funeral cortège, the civic parade, and the dream-like processions that kings and queens are made of. In the main, these exceptions seem to offer some kind of extra protection for performers who are, or who have momentarily become, highly sacred. These worthies are to be distinguished, of course, from quite profane performers of the peddler class who move their place of work between performances, often being forced to do so. In the matter of having one fixed place for one's setting, a ruler may be too sacred, a peddler too profane.

In thinking about the scenic aspects of front, we tend to think of the living room in a particular house and the small number of performers who can thoroughly identify themselves with it. We have given insufficient attention to assemblages of sign-equipment which large numbers of performers can call their own for short periods of time. It is characteristic of Western European countries, and no doubt a source of stability for them, that a large number of luxurious settings are available for hire to anyone of the right kind who can afford them. One illustration of this may be cited from a study of the higher civil servant in Britain:

The question how far men who rise to the top in the Civil Service take on the "tone" or "color" of a class other than that to which they belong by birth is delicate and difficult. The only definite information bearing on the question is the figures relating to the membership of the great London clubs. More than three-quarters of our high administrative officials belong to one or more clubs of high status and considerable luxury, where the entrance fee might be twenty guineas or more, and the annual subscription from twelve to twenty guineas. These institutions are of the upper class (not even of the upper-middle) in their premises, their equipment, the style of living practiced there, their whole atmosphere. Though many of the members would not be described as wealthy, only a wealthy man would unaided provide for himself and his family space, food and drink, service, and other amenities of life to the same standard as he will find at the Union, the Travellers', or the Reform.[4]

Another example can be found in the recent development of the medical profession where we find that it is increasingly important for a doctor to have access to the elaborate scientific stage provided by large hospitals, so that fewer and fewer doctors are able to feel that their setting is a place that they can lock up at night.[5]

If we take the term "setting" to refer to the scenic parts of expressive equipment, one may take the term "personal front" to refer to the other items of expressive equipment, the items that we most intimately identify with the performer himself and that we naturally expect will follow the performer wherever he goes. As part of personal front we may include: insignia of office or rank; clothing; sex, age, and racial characteristics; size and looks; posture; speech patterns; facial expressions; bodily gestures; and the like. Some of these vehicles for conveying signs, such as racial characteristics, are relatively fixed and over a span of time do not vary for the individual from one situation to another. On the other hand, some of these sign vehicles are relatively mobile or transitory, such as facial expression, and can vary during a performance from one moment to the next.

★   ★   ★

Dramatic Realization

While in the presence of others, the individual typically infuses his activity with signs which dramatically highlight and portray confirmatory facts that might otherwise remain unapparent or obscure. For if the individual's activity is to become significant to others, he must mobilize his activity so that it will express *during the interaction* what he wishes to convey. In fact, the performer may be required not only to express his claimed capacities during the interaction but also to do so during a split second in the interaction. Thus, if a baseball umpire is to give the impression that he is sure of his judgment, he must forgo the moment of thought which might make him sure of his judgment; he must give an instantaneous decision so that the audience will be sure that he is sure of his judgment.[6]

It may be noted that in the case of some statuses dramatization presents no problem, since some of the acts which are instrumentally essential for the completion of the core task of the status are at the same time wonderfully adapted, from the point of view of communication, as means of vividly conveying the qualities and attributes claimed by the performer. The roles of prizefighters, surgeons, violinists, and policemen are cases in point. These activities allow for so much dramatic self-expression that exemplary practitioners—whether real or fictional—become famous and are given a special place in the commercially organized fantasies of the nation.

In many cases, however, dramatization of one's work does constitute a problem. An illustration of this may be cited from a hospital study where the medical nursing staff is shown to have a problem that the surgical nursing staff does not have:

The things which a nurse does for post-operative patients on the surgical floor are frequently of recognizable importance, even to patients who are strangers to hospital activities. For example, the patient sees his nurse changing bandages, swinging orthopedic frames into place, and can realize that these are purposeful activities. Even if she cannot be at his side, he can respect her purposeful activities.

Medical nursing is also highly skilled work. . . . The physician's diagnosis must rest upon careful observation of symptoms over time where the surgeon's are in larger part dependent on visible things. The lack of visibility creates problems on the medical. A patient will see his nurse stop at the next bed and chat for a moment or two with the patient there. He doesn't know that she is observing the shallowness of the breathing and color and tone of the skin. He thinks she is just visiting. So, alas, does his family who may thereupon decide that these nurses aren't very impressive. If the nurse spends more time at the next bed than at his own, the patient may feel slighted. . . . The nurses are "wasting time" unless they are darting about doing some visible thing such as administering hypodermics.[7]

Similarly, the proprietor of a service establishment may find it difficult to dramatize what is actually being done for clients because the clients cannot "see" the overhead costs of the service rendered them. Undertakers must therefore charge a great deal for their highly visible product—a coffin that has been transformed into a casket—because many of the other costs of conducting a funeral are ones that cannot be readily dramatized.[8] Merchants, too, find that they must charge high prices for things that look intrinsically expensive in order to compensate the establishment for expensive things like insurance, slack periods, etc., that never appear before the customers' eyes.

The problem of dramatizing one's work involves more than merely making invisible costs visible. The work that must be done by those who fill certain statuses is often so poorly designed as an expression of a desired meaning, that if the incumbent would dramatize the character of his role, he must divert an appreciable amount of his energy to do so. And this activity diverted to communication will often require different attributes from the ones which are being dramatized. Thus to furnish a house so that it will express simple quiet dignity, the householder may have to race to auction sales, haggle with antique dealers, and doggedly canvass all the local shops for proper wallpaper and curtain materials. To give a radio talk that will sound genuinely informal, spontaneous, and relaxed, the speaker may have to design his script with painstaking care, testing one phrase after another, in order to follow the content, language, rhythm, and pace of everyday talk.[9] Similarly, a *Vogue* model, by her clothing, stance, and facial expression, is able expressively to portray a cultivated understanding of the book she poses in her hand; but those who trouble to express themselves so appropriately will have very little time left over for reading. As Sartre suggested: "The attentive pupil who wishes to *be* attentive, his eyes riveted on the teacher, his ears open wide, so exhausts himself in playing the attentive role that he ends up by no longer hearing anything."[10] And so individuals often find themselves with the dilemma of expression *versus* action. Those who have the time and talent to perform a task well may not, because of this, have the time or talent to make it apparent that they are performing well. It may be said that some organizations resolve this dilemma by officially delegating the dramatic function to a specialist who will spend his time expressing the meaning of the task and spend no time actually doing it.

★   ★   ★

Idealization

It was suggested earlier that a performance of a routine presents through its front some rather abstract claims upon the audience, claims that are likely to be presented to them during the performance of other routines. This constitutes one way in which a performance is "socialized," molded, and modified to fit into the understanding and expectations of the society in which it is presented. I want to consider here another important aspect of this socialization process—the tendency for performers to offer their observers an impression that is idealized in several different ways.

The notion that a performance presents an idealized view of the situation is, of course, quite common. Cooley's view may be taken as an illustration:

> If we never tried to seem a little better than we are, how could we improve or "train ourselves from the outside inward?" And the same impulse to show the world a better or idealized aspect of ourselves finds an organized expression in the various professions and classes, each of which has to some extent a cant or pose, which its members assume unconsciously, for the most part, but which has the effect of a conspiracy to work upon the credulity of the rest of the world. There is a cant not only of theology and of philanthropy, but also of law, medicine, teaching, even of science—perhaps especially of science, just now, since the more a particular kind of merit is recognized and admired, the more it is likely to be assumed by the unworthy.[11]

Thus, when the individual presents himself before others, his performance will tend to incorporate and exemplify the officially accredited values of the society, more so, in fact, than does his behavior as a whole.

To the degree that a performance highlights the common official values of the society in which it occurs, we may look upon it, in the manner of Durkheim and Radcliffe-Brown, as a ceremony—as an expressive rejuvenation and reaffirmation of the moral values of the community. Furthermore, in so far as the expressive bias of performances comes to be accepted as reality, then that which is accepted at the moment as reality will have some of the characteristics of a celebration. To stay in one's room away from the place where the party is given, or away from where the practitioner attends his client, is to stay away from where reality is being performed. The world, in truth, is a wedding.

* * *

The expressive coherence that is required in performances points out a crucial discrepancy between our all-too-human selves and our socialized selves. As human beings we are presumably creatures of variable impulse with moods and energies that change from one moment to the next. As characters put on for an audience, however, we must not be subject to ups and downs. As Durkheim suggested, we do not allow our higher social activity "to follow in the trail of our bodily states, as our sensations and our general bodily consciousness do."[12] A certain bureaucratization of the spirit is expected so that we can be relied upon to give a perfectly homogeneous performance at every appointed time. As Santayana suggests, the socialization process not only transfigures, it fixes:

> But whether the visage we assume be a joyful or a sad one, in adopting and emphasizing it we define our sovereign temper. Henceforth, so long as we continue under the spell of this self-knowledge, we do not merely live but act; we compose and play our chosen character, we wear the buskin of deliberation, we defend and idealize our passions, we encourage ourselves eloquently to be what we are, devoted or scornful or careless or austere; we soliloquize (before an imaginary audience) and we wrap ourselves gracefully in the mantle of our inalienable part. So draped, we solicit applause and expect to die amid a universal hush. We profess to live up to the fine sentiments we have uttered, as we try to believe in the religion we profess. The greater our difficulties the greater our zeal. Under our published principles and plighted language we must assiduously hide all the inequalities of our moods and conduct, and this without hypocrisy, since our deliberate character is more truly ourself than is the flux of our involuntary dreams. The portrait we paint in this way and exhibit as our true person may well be in the grand manner, with column and curtain and distant landscape and finger pointing to the terrestrial globe or to the Yorick-skull of philosophy; but if this style is native to us and our art is vital, the more it transmutes its model the deeper and truer art it will be. The severe bust of an archaic sculpture, scarcely humanizing the block, will express a spirit far more justly than the man's dull morning looks or casual grimaces. Everyone who is sure of his mind, or proud of his office, or anxious about his duty assumes a tragic mask. He deputes it to be himself and transfers to it almost all his vanity. While still alive and subject, like all existing things, to the undermining flux of his own substance, he has crystallized his soul into an idea, and more in pride than in sorrow he has offered up his life on the altar of the Muses. Self-knowledge, like any art or science, renders its subject-matter in a new medium, the medium of ideas, in which it loses its old dimensions and its old place. Our animal habits are transmuted by conscience into loyalties and duties, and we become "persons" or masks.[13]

Through social discipline, then, a mask of manner can be held in place from within. But, as Simone de Beauvoir suggests, we are helped in keeping this pose by clamps that are tightened directly on the body, some hidden, some showing:

Even if each woman dresses in conformity with her status, a game is still being played: artifice, like art, belongs to the realm of the imaginary. It is not only that girdle, brassiere, hair-dye, make-up disguise body and face; but that the least sophisticated of women, once she is "dressed," does not present *herself* to observation: she is, like the picture or the statue, or the actor on the stage, an agent through whom is suggested someone not there; that is, the character she represents, but is not. It is this identification with something unreal, fixed, perfect as the hero of a novel, as a portrait or a bust, that gratifies her; she strives to identify herself with this figure and thus to seem to herself to be stabilized, justified in her splendour.[14]

Misrepresentation

It was suggested earlier that an audience is able to orient itself in a situation by accepting performed cues on faith, treating these signs as evidence of something greater than or different from the sign-vehicles themselves. If this tendency of the audience to accept signs places the performer in a position to be misunderstood and makes it necessary for him to exercise expressive care regarding everything he does when before the audience, so also this sign-accepting tendency puts the audience in a position to be duped and misled, for there are few signs that cannot be used to attest to the presence of something that is not really there. And it is plain that many performers have ample capacity and motive to misrepresent the facts; only shame, guilt, or fear prevent them from doing so.

As members of an audience it is natural for us to feel that the impression the performer seeks to give may be true or false, genuine or spurious, valid or "phony." So common is this doubt that, as suggested we often give special attention to features of the performance that cannot be readily manipulated, thus enabling ourselves to judge the reliability of the more misrepresentable cues in the performance. (Scientific police work and projective testing are extreme examples of the application of this tendency.) And if we grudgingly allow certain symbols of status to establish a performer's right to a given treatment, we are always ready to pounce on chinks in his symbolic armor in order to discredit his pretensions.

When we think of those who present a false front or "only" a front, of those who dissemble, deceive, and defraud, we think of a discrepancy between fostered appearances and reality. We also think of the precarious position in which these performers place themselves, for at any moment in their performance an event may occur to catch them out and baldly contradict what they have openly avowed, bringing them immediate humiliation and sometimes permanent loss of reputation. We often feel that it is just these terrible eventualities, which arise from being caught out *flagrante delicto* in a patent act of misrepresentation, that an honest performer is able to avoid. This common-sense view has limited analytical utility.

Sometimes when we ask whether a fostered impression is true or false we really mean to ask whether or not the performer is authorized to give the performance in question, and are not primarily concerned with the actual performance itself. When we discover that someone with whom we have dealings is an impostor and out-and-out fraud, we are discovering that he did not have the right to play the part he played, that he was not an accredited incumbent of the relevant status. We assume that the impostor's performance, in addition to the fact that it misrepresents him, will be at fault in other ways, but often his masquerade is discovered before we can detect any other difference between the false performance and the legitimate one which it simulates. Paradoxically, the more closely the impostor's performance approximates to the real thing, the more intensely we may be threatened, for a competent performance by someone who proves to be an impostor may weaken in our minds the moral connection between legitimate authorization to play a part and the capacity to play it. (Skilled mimics, who admit all along that their intentions are unserious, seem to provide one way in which we can "work through" some of these anxieties.)

★　★　★

While we could retain the common-sense notion that fostered appearances can be discredited by a discrepant reality, there is often no reason for claiming that the facts discrepant with the fostered impression are any more the real reality than is the fostered reality they embarrass. A cynical view of everyday performances can be as one-sided as the one that is sponsored by the performer. For many sociological issues it may not even be necessary to decide which is the more real, the fostered impression or the one the performer attempts to prevent the audience from receiving. The crucial sociological consideration, for this report at least, is merely that impressions fostered in everyday performances are subject to disruption. We will want to know what kind of impression of reality can shatter the fostered impression of reality, and what reality really is can be left to other students. We will want to ask, "What are the ways in which a given impression can be discredited?" and this is not quite the same as asking, "What are the ways in which the given impression is false?"

We come back, then, to a realization that while the performance offered by impostors and liars is quite flagrantly false and differs in this respect from ordinary performances, both are similar in the care their performers must exert in order to maintain the impression that is fostered. Thus, for example, we know that the formal code of British civil servants[15] and of American baseball umpires[16] obliges them not only to desist from making improper "deals" but also to desist from innocent action which might possibly give the (wrong) impression that they are making deals. Whether an honest performer wishes to convey the truth or whether a dishonest performer wishes to convey a falsehood, both must take care to enliven their performances with appropriate expressions, exclude from their performances expressions that might discredit the impression being fostered, and take care lest the audience impute unintended meanings. Because of these shared dramatic contingencies, we can profitable study performances that are quite false in order to learn about ones that are quite honest.

★   ★   ★

Reality and Contrivance

In our own Anglo-American culture there seems to be two common-sense models according to which we formulate our conceptions of behavior: the real, sincere, or honest performance; and the false one that thorough fabricators assemble for us, whether meant to be taken unseriously, as in the work of stage actors, or seriously, as in the work of confidence men. We tend to see real performances as something not purposely put together at all, being an unintentional product of the individual's unselfconscious response to the facts in his situation. And contrived performances we tend to see as something painstakingly pasted together, one false item on another, since there is no reality to which the items of behavior could be a direct response. It will be necessary to see now that these dichotomous conceptions are by way of being the ideology of honest performers, providing strength to the show they put on, but a poor analysis of it.

First, let it be said that there are many individuals who sincerely believe that the definition of the situation they habitually project is the real reality. In this report I do not mean to question their proportion in the population but rather the structural relation of their sincerity to the performances they offer. If a performance is to come off, the witnesses by and large must be able to believe that the performers are sincere. This is the structural place of sincerity in the drama of events. Performers may be sincere—or be insincere but sincerely convinced of their own sincerity—but this kind of affection for one's part is not necessary for its convincing performance. There are not many French cooks who are really Russian spies, and perhaps there are not many women who play the part of wife to one man and mistress to another, but these duplicities do occur, often being sustained successfully for long periods of time. This suggests that while persons usually are what they appear to be, such appearances could still have been managed. There is, then, a statistical relation between appearances and reality, not an intrinsic or necessary one. In fact, given the unanticipated threats that play upon a performance, and given the need (later to be discussed) to maintain solidarity with one's fellow performers and some distance from the witnesses, we find that a rigid incapacity to depart from one's inward view of reality may at times endanger one's performance. Some performances are carried off successfully with complete dishonesty, others with complete honesty; but for performances in general neither of these extremes is essential and neither, perhaps, is dramaturgically advisable.

The implication here is that an honest, sincere, serious performance is less firmly connected with the solid world than one might first assume. And this implication will be strengthened if we look again at the distance usually placed between quite honest performances and quite contrived ones. In this connection take, for example, the remarkable phenomenon of stage acting. It does take deep skill, long training, and psychological capacity to become a good stage actor. But this fact should not blind us to another one: that almost anyone can quickly learn a script well enough to give a charitable audience some sense of realness in what is being contrived before them. And it seems this is so because ordinary social intercourse is itself put together as a scene is put together, by the exchange of dramatically inflated actions, counteractions, and terminating replies. Scripts even in the hands of unpracticed players can come to life because life itself is a dramatically enacted thing. All the world is not, of course, a stage, but the crucial ways in which it isn't are not easy to specify.

The recent use of "psychodrama" as a therapeutic technique illustrates a further point in this regard. In these psychiatrically staged scenes patients not only act out parts with some effectiveness, but employ no script in doing so. Their own past is available to them in a form which allows them to stage a recapitulation of it. Apparently a part once played honestly and in earnest leaves the performer in a position to contrive a showing of it later. Further, the parts that significant others played to him in the past also seem to be available, allowing him to switch from being the person that he was to being the persons that others were for him. This capacity to switch enacted roles when obliged to do so could have been predicted; everyone apparently can do it. For in learning to perform our parts in real life we guide our own productions by not too consciously maintaining an incipient familiarity with the routine of those to whom we will address ourselves. And when we come to be able properly to manage a real routine we are able to do this in part because of "anticipatory socialization,"[17] having already been schooled in the reality that is just coming to be real for us.

Notes

1 Perhaps the real crime of the confidence man is not that he takes money from his victims but that he robs all of us of the belief that middle-class manners and appearance can be sustained only by middle class people. A disabused professional can be cynically hostile to the service relation his clients expect him to extend to them; the confidence man is in a position to hold the whole "legit" world in this contempt.

2 Robert Ezra Park, *Race and Culture* (Glencoe, Ill.: The Free Press, 1950), p. 249.

3 Ibid., p. 250.

4 H. E. Dale, *The Higher Civil Service of Great Britain* (Oxford: Oxford University Press, 1941), p. 50.

5 David Solomon, "Career Contingencies of Chicago Physicians" (unpublished Ph.D., dissertation, Department of Sociology, University of Chicago, 1952), p. 74.

6 See Babe Pinelli, as told to Joe King, *Mr. Ump* (Philadelphia: Westminster Press, 1953), p. 75.

7 Edith Lentz, "A Comparison of Medical and Surgical Floors" (Mimeo: New York State School of Industrial and Labor Relations. Cornell University, 1954), pp. 2–3.

8 Material on the burial business used throughout this report is taken from Robert W. Habenstein, "The American Funeral Director" (unpublished Ph.D. dissertation, Department of Sociology, University of Chicago, 1954). I owe much to Mr. Habenstein's analysis of a funeral as a performance.

9 John Hilton, "Calculated Spontaneity," *Oxford Book of English Talk* (Oxford: Clarendon Press, 1953), pp. 399–404.

10 Jean-Paul Sartre, *Being and Nothingness* (London: Methuen, 1957), p. 60.

11 Charles H. Cooley, *Human Nature and the Social Order* (New York: Scribner's, 1922), pp. 352–3.

12 Emile Durkheim, *The Elementary Forms of the Religious Life,* trans. J. W. Swain (London: Allen & Unwin, 1926), p. 272.

13 George Santayana, *Soliloquies in England and later Soliloquies* (London: Constable, 1922), pp. 133–4.

14 Simone de Beauvoir, *The Second Sex,* trans. H. M. Parshley (New York: Knopf, 1953), p. 533.

15 Dale, op. cit., p. 103.

16 Pinelli, op. cit., p. 100.

17 See R. K. Merton, *Social Theory and Social Structure* (Glencoe, Ill.: The Free Press, revised and enlarged edition, 1957), p. 265 ff.

10

Social Life as Ritual

From "On Face-work: An Analysis of Ritual Elements in Social Interaction"*

The Nature of the Ritual Order

The ritual order seems to be organized basically on accommodative lines, so that the imagery used in thinking about other types of social order is not quite suitable for it. For the other types of social order a kind of schoolboy model seems to be employed: if a person wishes to sustain a particular image of himself and trust his feelings to it, he must work hard for the credits that will buy this self-enhancement for him; should he try to obtain ends by improper means, by cheating or theft, he will be punished, disqualified from the race, or at least made to start all over again from the beginning. This is the imagery of a hard, dull game. In fact, society and the individual join in one that is easier on both of them, yet one that has dangers of its own.

Whatever his position in society, the person insulates himself by blindnesses, half-truths, illusions, and rationalizations. He makes an "adjustment" by convincing himself, with the tactful support of his intimate circle, that he is what he wants to be and that he would not do to gain his ends what the others have done to gain theirs. And as for society, if the person is willing to be subject to informal social control—if he is willing to find out from hints and glances and tactful cues what his place is, and keep it—then there will be no objection to his furnishing this place at his own discretion, with all the comfort, elegance, and nobility that his wit can muster for him. To protect this shelter he does not have to work hard, or join a group, or compete with anybody; he need only be careful about the expressed judgments he places himself in a position to witness. Some situations and acts and persons will have to be avoided; others, less threatening, must not be pressed too far. Social life is an uncluttered, orderly thing

* First published 1955; this extract from *Interaction Ritual: Essays on Face-to-Face Behavior*, 1967, pp. 42–5. Copyright © 1967 by Erving Goffman. Reprinted by permission of Pantheon Books, a division of Random House, Inc.

because the person voluntarily stays away from the places and topics and times where he is not wanted and where he might be disparaged for going. He cooperates to save his face, finding that there is much to be gained from venturing nothing.

Facts are of the schoolboy's world—they can be altered by diligent effort but they cannot be avoided. But what the person protects and defends and invests his feelings in is an idea about himself, and ideas are vulnerable not to facts and things but to communications. Communications belong to a less punitive scheme than do facts, for communications can be by-passed, withdrawn from, disbelieved, conveniently misunderstood, and tactfully conveyed. And even should the person misbehave and break the truce he has made with society, punishment need not be the consequence. If the offense is one that the offended persons can let go by without losing too much face, then they are likely to act forbearantly, telling themselves that they will get even with the offender in another way at another time, even though such an occasion may never arise and might not be exploited if it did. If the offense is great, the offended persons may withdraw from the encounter, or from future similar ones, allowing their withdrawal to be reinforced by the awe they may feel toward someone who breaks the ritual code. Or they may have the offender withdrawn, so that no further communication can occur. But since the offender can salvage a good deal of face from such operations, withdrawal is often not so much an informal punishment for an offense as it is merely a means of terminating it. Perhaps the main principle of the ritual order is not justice but face, and what any offender receives is not what he deserves but what will sustain for the moment the line to which he has committed himself, and through this the line to which he has committed the interaction.

Throughout this paper it has been implied that underneath their differences in culture, people everywhere are the same. If persons have a universal human nature, they themselves are not to be looked to for an explanation of it. One must look rather to the fact that societies everywhere, if they are to be societies, must mobilize their members as self-regulating participants in social encounters. One way of mobilizing the individual for this purpose is through ritual; he is taught to be perceptive, to have feelings attached to self and a self expressed through face, to have pride, honor, and dignity, to have considerateness, to have tact and a certain amount of poise. These are some of the elements of behavior which must be built into the person if practical use is to be made of him as an interactant, and it is these elements that are referred to in part when one speaks of universal human nature.

Universal human nature is not a very human thing. By acquiring it, the person becomes a kind of construct, built up not from inner psychic propensities but from moral rules that are impressed upon him from without. These rules, when followed, determine the evaluation he will make of himself and of his fellow-participants in the encounter, the distribution of his feelings, and the kinds of practices he will employ to maintain a specified and obligatory kind of ritual equilibrium. The general capacity to be bound by moral rules may well belong to the individual, but the particular set of rules which transforms him into a human being derives from requirements established in the ritual organization of social encounters. And if a particular person or group or society seems to have a unique character all its own, it is because its standard set of human-nature elements is pitched and combined in a particular way. Instead of much pride, there may be little. Instead of abiding by the rules, there may be much effort to break them safely. But if an encounter or undertaking is to be sustained as a viable system of interaction organized on ritual principles, then these variations must be held within certain bounds and nicely counterbalanced by corresponding modifications in some of the other rules and understandings. Similarly, the human nature of a particular set of persons may be specially designed for the special kind of undertakings in which they participate, but still each of these persons must have within him something of the balance of characteristics required of a usable participant in any ritually organized system of social activity.

From "The Structure and Function of Situational Proprieties"*

I have suggested that the behavior of an individual while in a situation is guided by social values or norms concerning involvement. These rulings apply to the intensity of his involvements, their distribution among possible main and side activities, and, importantly, their tendency to bring him into an engagement with all, some, or none present. There will be then a patterned distribution or *allocation* of the individual's involvement. By taking the point of view of the situation as a whole, we can link the involvement allocation of each participant to that maintained by each of the other participants, piecing together in this way a pattern than can be described as the *structure of involvement in the situation.* (And just as we speak of *actual* allocations and structures of involvement, so we can consider matters from the normative point of view and speak of *prescribed* allocations and structures of involvement.) Since the shape and distribution of involvement nicely enfolds an aspect of everything that goes on within a situation, we can perhaps speak here of the structure of the situation. In any case, if we want to describe conduct on a back ward, or in a street market, a bridge game, an investiture, or a revivalistic church service, it would seem reasonable to employ the structure of involvement in these situations as one frame of reference.

Now let us briefly review the kinds of situational proprieties that have been described and the social functions that appear to be performed by them.

Rules about access to a bounded region, and the regard that is to be shown its boundaries, are patently rules of respect for the gathering itself. Regulations against external preoccupation, "occult" involvements, and certain forms of "away" ensure that the individual will not give himself up to matters that fall outside of the situation. Regulations against un-occasioned main involvements or overtaxing side involvements (especially when either of these represents an auto-involvement) seem to ensure that the individual will not become embroiled divisively in matters that incorporate only himself; regulations against intense mutual-involvement provide the same assurances about the conduct of a subset of those present. In short, interests that are larger or smaller than the ones sustainable by everyone in the gathering as a whole are curtailed; limits are put on those kinds of emigration of the self which can occur without leaving one's physical position. Being thus constrained to limit his involvements outside the situation as well as divisive ones within the situation, the individual perforce demonstrates that something of himself has been reserved for what remains, namely, the little system of regulated social life that is jointly and exclusively maintained by all those in the situation as a whole—the situation being that entity neatly matching the area within which the individual's regulation of involvement is perceptible. However, we know that the gathering and the joint life it currently sustains are merely an expression, a visible phase, of the social occasion within which the situation occurs. To engage in situational impropriety, then, is to draw improperly on what one owes the social occasion.

Similar implications emerge when we turn from those constraints that play upon choice of object of involvement to those that pertain to the way in which the individual handles himself. By sustaining a publicly oriented composition of his face and a suitable organization of the more material aspects of his personal appearance, the individual shows himself a person ready for social interaction in the situation. By inhibiting creature releases and keeping a check upon intense involvement, he ensures that he will be ready for any event that occurs within the situation, and that he is respectful of these possibilities. By keeping himself from going too far into a situated task, he is able to remain in readiness near the surface of the situation. Through all of these means, the individual shows that he is "in play" in the situation, alive to the gathering it contains, oriented in it, and ready and open for whatever interaction it may bring.

A similar picture presents itself when we look at some of the traffic regulations regarding accessible engagements, especially engagements during social occasions such as parties. Prohibitions against improper involvement with others are prohibitions against taking joint leave of the gathering and the encompassing social occasion. Often prohibitions regarding disloyalty to one's encounter are also prohibitions about intruding upon bystanders—persons presumably maintaining an appropriate regard for the social occasion. Rules obliging one to give oneself up to occasioned mutual-engagements, and rules against excluding deferential newcomers, are rules assuring that the occasion as a whole will provide the basis of involvement. By maintaining accessibility to all those present, one shows that the gathering is significant enough in itself to ensure that any participant, merely by virtue of his participation, has a right to obtain attention and an obligation to give attention to any other participant. Loyalty, damping, spacing, drift—these are all issues basic to the organization of both accessible engagements and the setting of bystanders in which they occur. These issues are difficult even to describe unless reference is made to their function as supports for the gathering as a whole and, behind this, the social occasion.

The constraints that apply to objects of involvement, to modes of managing one's involvements, and (through these) to the management of accessible engagements, seem together to provide evidence of the weight and reality of the "situation." Indeed, one might be inclined to summarize the whole matter by saying that the individual is obliged to demonstrate involvement *in* a situation through the modulation of his involvements *within* the situation. But this would be a loose way of talking. First, that which the individual owes is conveyed through appropriate modulation of situated involvements. What is thereby conveyed, however, is not "involvement," but rather a kind of respect and regard for that to which attachment and belongingness are owed. At the heart of it is a kind of concern that shows one to be a part of the thing for which one is concerned. Second, a situation, as defined in this study, is merely an environment of communication possibilities, and not the sort of thing to which one can become attached. The little society involved is that of the gathering in the situation, and the little social system found therein is made up from conduct performed in accordance with the norms of situational propriety. Finally, what is owed the gathering is owed the social occasion in which it occurs, the joint social life sustained by the gathering being an embodiment of the occasion itself.

Situational proprieties then, give body to the joint social life sustained by a gathering, and transform the gathering itself from a mere aggregate of persons present into something akin to a little social group, a social reality in its own right. Behind this social function we can see still further ones.

When a situation comes into being, mutual accessibility of body signs is not the only contingency faced by those who are present. As already suggested, each person becomes a potential victim or aggressor in the potential occurrence of violent interpersonal actions, such as physical or sexual assault, blocking of the way, and so forth. Further, each person present is in a position to accost or be accosted by the others for the purpose of initiating a state of talk—a joint conversational engagement. And this, too, has its own dangers, for when persons are joined in this way they can command and plead with each other, insult or compliment each other, inform and misinform each other, or be seen (by others) as being on close terms, and the like. Further, when an engagement is sustained in the presence of bystanders, the participants open themselves up to being listened in on and interfered with, just as the bystanders become vulnerable to undesired distractions.

Although these various dangers of being in the presence of others are perhaps not frequently realized, especially in middle-class society, the possibility of their occurrence is always there. And it is through body signs that persons present signify to each other that they can be trusted not to exploit these threatening possibilities. Only when these signs are received may the individual feel secure enough to forget about defending himself, secure enough to give himself up to the merely-situated aspects of his involvements. Aside, then, from the disrespect an individual shows to a gathering by conducting himself improperly, such improprieties can also cause the others present to fear for their physical and social inviolability, whether rightly or not.

And here, incidentally, is one reason for arguing that social situations and the gatherings occurring therein are worth studying, even apart from the social occasion that incorporates them. Ordinarily, situations are thought to be so closely enmeshed in a particular on-going institutional setting, and these settings to be so very different one from another, that excision of situations and their gatherings for separate study might seem questionable. However, it is only in situations that individuals can be physically assaulted, accosted by requests for talk, or drawn away from conversations and other involvements by the antics of bystanders. It is in situations that these accessibilities will have to be face and dealt with. And in facing these accessibilities and dealing with them, a common and distinctive character is given to the social life sustained in situations, regardless of the uniqueness of the larger span of social life in which each gathering is embedded and of which each is an expression.

From "Supportive Interchanges"*

Ritual is a perfunctory, conventionalized act through which an individual portrays his respect and regard for some object of ultimate value to that object of ultimate value or to its stand-in.[1]

* Originally published in *Relations in Public: Mircrostudies of the Public Order*, 1971, pp. 62–9. Copyright © 1971 by Erving Goffman. Reprinted by permission of Basic Books, a division of Harper Collins Publishers, Inc.

In his famous analysis of religion, Durkheim divided ritual into two classes: positive and negative.[2] The negative kind involves interdictions, avoidance, staying away. It is what we consider when we look at the preserves of the self and the right to be let alone. Positive ritual consists of the ways in which homage can be paid through offerings of various kinds, these involving the doer coming close in some way to the recipient. The standard argument is that these positive rites affirm and support the social relationship between doer and recipient. Improper performance of positive rites is a slight; of negative rites, a violation.

In contemporary society rituals performed to stand-ins for supernatural entities are everywhere in decay, as are extensive ceremonial agendas involving long strings of obligatory rites. What remains are brief rituals one individual performs for and to another, attesting to civility and good will on the performer's part and to the recipient's possession of a small patrimony of sacredness. What remains, in brief, are interpersonal rituals. These little pieties are a mean version of what anthropologists would look for in their paradise. But they are worth examining. Only our secular view of society prevents us from appreciating the ubiquitousness and strategy of their location, and, in turn, their role in social organization.

Interpersonal ritual in our secular society has a special bearing on Durkheim's distinction between positive and negative rites.

First, as Durkheim could not have expected, current work on territoriality and personal preserves allows us to describe negative rites in very close detail, and not as an occasional restriction, but as a central organizational device of public order.

Second, interpersonal rituals have a dialogistic character, and this differently impinges on positive and negative rites. When a ritual offering occurs, when, that is, one individual provides a sign of involvement in and connectedness to another, it behooves the recipient to show that the message has been received, that its import has been appreciated, that the affirmed relationship actually exists as the performer implies, that the performer himself has worth as a person, and finally, that the recipient has an appreciative, grateful nature. Prestation (to use Mauss'[3] favorite term) thus leads to counter-prestation, and when we focus on minor rituals performed between persons who are present to each other, the giving statement tends to be followed immediately by a show of gratitude. Both moves taken together form a little ceremony—a "supportive interchange." Negative ritual leads to dialogue, too, but less directly and through a different route. Ordinary circumspections ordinarily call for no responding comment. When exemplary delicacy is exhibited, signs of gratitude may be returned, although there is a natural limitation here since these displays undercut the very privacy which the initial maintenance of distance ensured. More important, when an infraction occurs, then a dialogue is indicated, the offender having to provide remedial accounts and assurances and the offended a sign that these have been received and are sufficient; in brief, a "remedial interchange" occurs. I might add in passing that these two basic interchanges, the supportive and the remedial, are among the most conventionalized and perfunctory doings we engage in and traditionally have been treated by students of modern society as part of the dust of social activity, empty and trivial. And yet, as we shall see, almost all brief encounters between individuals consist precisely and entirely of one or the other of these two interchanges. In brief, whenever one individual rubs up against another, he is likely to say hello or excuse me. Surely it is time to examine "Hello" or "Excuse me," or their equivalent. Moreover, as we also shall see, conversational encounters of the more extended kind are typically opened and closed by these devices, if not built up in terms of them. Surely, then, in spite of the bad name that etiquette has given to etiquette, it is time to study these performances.

Finally, it is to be noted that when negative and positive rites are examined, it is often found that although one social relationship requires keeping away from a particular personal preserve, another relation will license and even oblige its penetration. All of these penetrative acts through which some persons are shown support are acts, which, if performed to other persons, would violate them. (It is also true, if less generally, that ritually cautious acts that show proper respect in a distant relation can affront a recipient when exhibited for his benefit by someone to whom he is closely related.) Thus very ritual idiom seems to make a double use of behavioral arrangements, as Durkheim, of course, suggested:

> Perhaps some will be surprised that so sacred a food may be eaten by ordinary profane persons. But in the first place, there is no positive cult which does not face this contradiction. Every sacred being is removed from profane touch by this very character with which it is endowed; but, on the other hand, they would serve for nothing and have no reason whatsoever for their existence if they could not come in contact with these same worshippers who, on another ground, must remain respectfully distant from them. At bottom, there is no positive rite which does not constitute a veritable sacrilege, for a man cannot hold commerce with the sacred beings without crossing the barrier which should ordinarily keep them separate.[4]

This essay will be concerned with positive interpersonal ritual, that is, with supportive acts, not avoidant ones. These positive rites are apparently more important for relations between persons who know each other ("personal" relationships, broadly defined) than for anonymous ones. As suggested, these acts have been surprisingly little studied—certainly hardly at all in our

Western society, in spite of the fact that it would be hard to imagine a more obvious contemporary application of the analysis recommended by Durkheim and Radcliffe-Brown.

One approach to the study of supportive ritual is to bring together phenomenally different acts that seem to have some sort of formal feature in common, some sort of shared interpersonal theme. One example might be cited: the ritualization of identifactory sympathy. The needs, desires, conditions, experiences, in short, the situation of one individual, when seen from his own point of view, provides a second individual with directions for formulating ritual gestures of concern. Here we find the indulgences and solicitousness that hosts provide by way of food, drink, comfort, and lodging; here "grooming talk,"[5] as when inquiries are made into another's health, his experience on a recent trip, his feelings about a recent movie, the outcome of his fateful business; here the neighborly act of lending various possessions and providing minor services. And here, incidentally, are positive rites performed between the anonymously related, as when, upon request, an individual gives direction, the time, a match, or some other "free good" to a stranger.[6] Note, the breadth of disinterested concern displayed through these various acts of identificatory sympathy is similar to what a parent exhibits in regard to a child, but the similarity stops there. Courtesies are involved, not substantive care; small offerings are received as though they were large, and large ones, when made, are often made with the expectation that they will be declined.

Other themes suggest themselves. For example, there are those ritual offerings associated with the tactful avoidance of open exclusion, a means of avoiding openly denying the worth of others. Examples are: the practice of "courtesy" introductions, whereby Harry, when with Mary, introduces her to Dick, who happens to pass their way; the nicety of extending to all those in one's conversational circle an offer to minor comforts and consumables one is about to enjoy oneself; the practice of lightly proffering to all persons in hearing an invitation extended to one.

A second approach to the study of supportive ritual is to try to isolate specialized functions, the assumption being that although all of these rites serve to support social relationships, this can be done at different junctures and in different ways, and these differences provide a means of distinguishing classes of these rituals.[7] One illustration is provided.

There are "rituals of ratification" performed for and to an individual who has altered his status in some way—his relationships, appearance, rank, certification, in short, his prospects and direction in life. Ratificatory rituals express that the performer is alive to the situation of the one who has sustained change, that he will continue his relationship to him, that support will be maintained, that in fact things are what they were in spite of the acknowledged change. In brief, there are "reassurance displays."

Considerable range is shown here. There are the congratulations at marriage, the careful commiserations at divorce, the doleful condolences at deaths; at the other extreme is the ribbing and joking that results when a youth appears among his friends wearing his skiing accident in a cast or when he newly acquires a driver's license.

Ratificatory rituals also present another side. The individual can take many steps that represent self-determined claims to altered and desired status, and when he does, ratificatory rituals may be provided him, not so much to establish a link between the new and the old as to confirm that the new presentation of self is accepted and approved; and this support is the more owed the more the claim is doubtful. Again, a wide range of matters is involved. Marriage congratulations to those who have acquired unattractive spouses are often weighted with this kind of tact, as are the joking remarks made to a male who newly affects a beard. Of special interest, I think, are what the latter illustrates, namely, little strokings call forth by minor, doubtful claims. An example can be cited from a report by a woman who passed as a high school student to relearn about adolescent life, the scene being a shopping expedition by the poseur and a newly acquired girl friend:

> I bought the shoes and made Gretel's day. "Oh, I'm so happy for you," she said. "I know just what you'll go through tomorrow when everybody sees them. Everybody'll say, 'Oh, they're *cute.*' Just you wait. You'll have such fun."
>
> I am obliged to elaborate here. You see, "everybody" knew I was going shoe-hunting because I had said so at lunch. When Gretel got home she would telephone the report on our trip, thereby alerting all eyes to my feet. When I would arrive in school in the morning, if the new shoes were found on me, appropriate comments would be made. Thus did it happen the next morning—and all day long—that everybody did indeed examine my shoes and say, "Oh, they're cute." They also said, "Oh, let's *see* them. Oh, how tough." One girl told me that she loved my shoes without looking at them. She knew just from hearing about them that she loved them.[8]

Occasions for ratificatory rituals are everywhere even humbler. In a conversation, let a participant whom others would rather see silent make a statement, and he will have expressed the belief that he has a full right to talk and is worth listening to, thereby obliging his listeners to give a sign, however begrudging and however mean, that he is qualified to speak. (The complete withholding of these ritual supports is often inclined to but rarely achieved, and understandably. Without such mercies, conversation would want of its fundamental basis of organisation—the ritual interchange—and everywhere unsatisfactory persons would be left to bleed to death from the conversational savageries performed on them.)

It is worth noting that when the situation of one party to a relationship changes, the other party may not be in a position to know it. In such cases the person who is in line to receive ratificatory regard will sometimes provide the information necessary so that the other will see what by way of ritual needs to be done. He "fills in" the other so that the relationship can be updated, and incidentally gives the appearance of inviting compliments or condolences.

An examination of the conduct of individuals who have experienced a sharp change in their social personage throws light on the relativity of "contactability." The greater the change in the self of a person, the further he can be physically from those whom he yet defines as close enough for the telling. And often a careful order of telling will be required, with those "closest" being told first, and so on, so that the flow of information and ratification rituals nicely reflects the relational structure of the individual's social world.[9] Note that in case of deep change, all an individual's close others may have to be allowed to reconfirm their relationship to him before he is able to reestablish some degree of ritual ease. He will have to check his network out, often by engineering contacts that can be given a less delicate apparent purpose.

From "Remedial Interchanges"*

In order to understand remedial work, I think it is useful to assume that the actor and those who witness him can imagine (and have some agreement regarding) one or more "worst possible readings," that is, interpretations of the act that maximize either its offensiveness to others or its defaming implications for the actor himself. This ugliest imaginable significance I shall call the "virtual offense." This name is selected because the remedial activity that follows a possibly offensive act very often can be understood best by assuming that the actor has these worst possible readings in mind as that which he must respond to and manage. Note that the virtual offense has largely a cautionary effect, detailing what everyone concerned must be careful to avoid confirming. It should be added that to speak of a virtual offense requires speaking of a "virtual offender," the individual most likely to be perceived as the party at fault, and a "virtual claimant," the individual who is the most obvious choice for he whose claims have been infringed.

The function of remedial work is to change the meaning that otherwise might be given to an act, transforming what could be seen as offensive into what can be seen as acceptable. This change seems to be accomplished, in our Western society at least, by striking in some way at the moral responsibility otherwise imputed to the offender; and this in turn seems to be accomplished by three main devices: accounts, apologies, and requests.

1. *Accounts:* The nature of accounts has been considered somewhat by students of law in connection with the issue of defenses, pleas, the mitigation of offenses, and the defeasibility of claims. Law, then, provides the beginning of an analysis; its weakness for us is its concern with arguments of an extended verbal kind made considerably after the event and in regard to relatively minor offenses.[10]

First, the offender can introduce a "traverse" or "joinder," arguing that the act he is accused of committing did not in fact occur. Or he can grant the occurrence of the offensive act but argue that he himself had nothing to do with its happening, that, indeed, the wrong person has been accused.

Second, there are acts that the individual admits to doing, admits to foreseeing the adverse consequences of (or agrees that although he didn't foresee the consequences he would have proceeded even if he had), but claims that the circumstances were such as to make the act radically different from what it appears to have been, and that, in fact, he is not really at fault at all. To throw someone to the ground, thereby injuring him, in order to prevent him from stepping on one's clean floor is an offense; to do the same act in order to prevent him from being hit by a sniper's bullet is, in fact, not to do the same act. In the latter case "higher" considerations alter the meaning of the deed. Similarly, there are killings that are claimed to be not murders but acts of self-defense. Indeed, there are many circumstances in which the individual can attempt to redefine what he is accused of doing by shifting some or all of the responsibility for the offense to his accusers, a process described as "counter-denunciation," albeit one whose consequences can hardly be remedial unless the sympathy of a third party is at issue.[11] Note, here again we see that there is no act whose meaning is independent of reasons understood for its occurrence; and there seems to be no act for which radically different reasons cannot be provided, and hence radically different meanings. That the individual routinely imputes intent while forming a perception of the act and then typically finds no reason to change his view should not blind us to the fact that the perception is dependent on an assessment of intent and is necessarily subject to reappraisal, for there is no such assessment that is immune to the possibility that it might have to be altered.

Third, the putative offender can agree that the act occurred and that he did it but present the mitigation that he was ignorant and unforeseeing, excusably so, and could not reasonably be asked to have acted so as to forestall it. He can claim that his was an involuntary motor act whose occurrence he did nothing to facilitate, as when one stranger pushed him into another stranger who was thereby injured. Or he can claim that although his act was self-controlled, its dire outcome in this case was not something he could be expected to foresee or take precautions against, but that certainly he would not have so acted had he known what was to happen.[12] Here is the case of the truck driver who runs over someone who has left a note testifying that this is how he planned to die. Here, too, the individuals whose gossiping becomes destructive because no one participating could be expected to anticipate that the subject might be in the next booth overhearing. And here to be included, too, is the plea more typically heard outside of court but also, in fact, employed in regard to very serious crimes; the argument of unseriousness. In brief, the offender can claim that all along he has been acting unseriously, for a joke, and that certainly had he known of the unhappy consequences that were to result, he would have refrained from his playfulness.

Fourth, there are pleas that claim reduced responsibility by virtue of reduced competence, the understanding often being that although the actor is guilty of something, it is guilt for being incompetent and not guilt for the specific deed resulting therefrom. Here are claims of mitigation based on sleepiness, drunkenness, youthfulness, senility, druggedness, passion, lack of training, subordination to the will of superiors, mental deficiency, and so forth. Reduced states of competency vary, of course, in terms of their power to excuse: sleepwalking can absolve the individual totally; drunkenness, on occasion, can increase the fault instead of diminishing it. Here, too, the context must be considered. To fail to arrive in time for tea is excusable on the grounds that one was geographically unsure of the neighborhood and drove in the wrong direction; an ambulance driver, on the other hand, cannot offer this kind of incompetence in explaining why it was that he failed to pick up a dangerously ill person until forty minutes after the call was placed, this being twenty minutes eternally too late.

Finally, the weakest of pleas, he can admit that he was fully competent at the time to appreciate the consequence of his act, that he was easily able to desist from performing it, that he would have desisted had he known what was to occur, but that he was indefensibly unmindful or ignorant of what was to happen.

Note, the more an actor can argue mitigating circumstances successfully, the more he can establish that the act is not to be taken as an expression of his moral character; contrarily, the more he is held responsible for his act, the more fully it will define him for others.

When individuals speak of a "good" account for an act, they seem to mean an account that succeeds in restructuring the initial response of the offended and appreciably reducing the fault of the actor—at least among the fair-minded. And a "bad" account is one that fails to perform this service. The goodness or badness of an account must, of course, be distinguished from its trueness or falseness. True accounts are often good, but false accounts are sometimes better.

As suggested, the possibility of introducing a false, good account adds flexibility, making it feasible to bypass rules or break them with impunity provided only that proper wit is applied. However, this flexibility is reduced somewhat by the fact that good accounts acquire a bad name, being exactly what quick-witted offenders would come up with were they to offer false ones.

In common usage, the terms for accounts—explanations, excuses, pretexts—tend to be used interchangeably, although some differentiation can be detected.[13] An explanation can be defined as an account that attempts to exonerate the offender fully by providing details concerning what it was he was actually about, this being offered after the virtual offense but before blame has been imputed openly. An excuse is an account provided in response to an overt or implied accusation but presented as only partially diminishing the blame. A pretext is an excuse provided before or during the questionable act.

2. *Apologies:* Although accounts have been treated at considerable length in the literature, especially, as suggested, in the legal literature, apologies have not; yet they are quite central. An apology is a gesture through which an individual splits himself into two parts, the part that is guilty of an offense and the part that dissociates itself from the delict and affirms a belief in the offended rule.

In its fullest form, the apology has several elements: expression of embarrassment and chagrin; clarification that one knows what conduct had been expected and sympathizes with the application of negative sanction; verbal rejection, repudiation, and disavowal of the wrong way of behaving along with vilification of the self that so behaved; espousal of the right way and an avowal henceforth to pursue that course; performance of penance and the volunteering of restitution.

Note that the offender's willingness to initiate and perform his own castigation has certain unapparent values. Were others to do to him what he is willing to do to himself, he might be obliged to feel affronted and to engage in retaliatory action to sustain his moral worth and autonomy. And he can overstate or overplay the case against himself, thereby giving to the others the task of cutting the self-derogation short—this latter, in turn, being a function that is safer to lodge with the offended since they are not likely to abuse it, whereas he, the offender, might.

As suggested, apologies represent a splitting of the self into a blameworthy part and a part that stands back and sympathizes with the blame giving, and, by implication, is worthy of being brought back into the fold. This splitting is but one instance, and often a fairly crude one, of a much more general phenomenon—the tendency for individuals when in the immediate presence of others to project somehow a self that then is cast off or withdrawn from. In the case of apologies, there is usually an admission that the offense was a serious or real act. This provides a contrast to another type of splitting, one that supports an account, not an apology, in which the actor projects the offensive act as something not to be taken literally, that is, seriously, or after the act claims that he was not acting seriously.

3. Two principal forms of remedial work have been considered; accounts and apologies. Although both may occur, as we shall see, before the virtual offense has taken place, they characteristically are seen as occurring after the event. The third main form of ritual work consists of requests; these typically occur before the questionable event or, at the latest, during its initial phases.

A request consists of asking license of a potentially offended person to engage in what could be considered a violation of his rights. The actor shows that he is fully alive to the possible offensiveness of his proposed act and begs sufferance. At the same time he exposes himself to denial and rejection. The recipient of the request thus clearly is presented with the possibility of making an offer, one that would allow the suppliant's needs. An offer, in short, is stimulated. The value to the potential offender of doing this is based, of course, upon the character of offers.

An offer is not a remedial ritual but a supportive one, albeit of a special kind. Although most supportive acts entail some penetration of the recipient's preserves (and can be thought presumptuous for this reason), offers very often involve penetration of the *maker's* preserves, the recipient's territoriality being less at issue. The fact that offers are possible reflects a basic organizational principle in social life. The assumption is that when a violation is invited by he who ordinarily would be its victim, it ceases to be a violation and becomes instead a gesture of regard performed by this person. A single act thus can have related but different symbolic meanings, and behavioral arrangements can be given double use, once as part of "positive" supportive rites and once as part of "negative" avoidant ones. Note, in presenting a request, the actor gives up his autonomy in regard to deciding the matter; the recipient of the request, in granting the request, retains his, it being assumed that he alone was the one to decide the matter.

The value of transforming a virtual violation into a request is recognized so broadly in our society, that a whole style is available whereby, for example, all compellings are clothed, howsoever lightly, as requests. (A nice example is the personal search technique employed in precinct stations. Routinely in American practice, the police *ask* the subject to empty purse and pockets instead of doing this themselves.[14] In this way the prisoner can be given a slight sense of autonomy and self-determination the law presumably guarantees him, and the slight mollification of him this produces be used in managing him.) For every territory of the self, then, there will be a means of requesting permission to intrude. Moreover, there are countless dodges whereby an importuner seeks permission in advance for violation that has not yet been specified, as in the questions, "Can I ask you something personal?" or "Will you lend me something?"

It has been suggested that there are three basic types of remedial work: accounts, apologies, and requests. A common practice among students is to consider these remedial acts as part of "distributive justice," a sort of payment or compensation for harm done, the greater the harm the greater the recompense. And of course there is some evidence supporting this actuarial approach. For example, often a brief apology is given for a minor offense and a protracted apology for something bigger. But in fact when corrective behavior is examined closely, it is found that apparently there are two different, independently occurring processes involved. One is ritualistic, whereby the virtual offender portrays his current relationship to rules, which his actions appear to have broken, and to persons present whose territories should have been protected by these rules. The second is restitutive, whereby an offended party receives some compensation, especially of a material kind, for what has been done to him and by implication, to the rules that otherwise would have protected him.

It is apparent that there is great variation from case to case regarding the weight that is given these two processes. An individual whose vault has been robbed may be little concerned to obtain an expression of remorse from robbers if they have already disposed of the money. He can find their change of heart of little consequence, much preferring to deal with unrepentant criminals who have been caught with the loot still in hand. There are other offenses in which the party offended is concerned principally with the principle of the thing and not with compensation.

The behavior of the offender will also illustrate this split between substantive relations and ritual ones. Thus, when an individual commits crimes deemed to be quite heinous, crimes for which his life is small compensation, he still may feel strongly obliged to ritually disavow his previous self and show that the person he now is sees his offenses from the perspective of a moral-minded man. No matter what is done to the individual by way of punishment for crime, he is likely to have a moment free before the punishment is inflicted to proclaim identity with the powers whose ire is about to be visited upon him and to express separateness from the self upon whom the justice will fall.[15] No matter what a person has done, he can express a change of heart at any moment, and although this may not soften appreciably what is done to him, he must either be disbelieved or be allowed to create something of a new self for himself on the spot. The position can be taken that this sort of redemption is but one expression of the "splitting" character of the self during interaction, that is, the general capacity of an individual to handle himself by stepping back from what he seems to have become in order to take up alignment involving distance from this person; and that, in turn, this capacity results from the inevitable interactional fact that that which comments on what has happened cannot be what has happened. I here attempt to derive a property of interactants from interaction. My claim is that the individual is constituted so that he can split himself in two, the better to allow one part to join the other members of an encounter in any attitude whatsoever to his other part.[16]

A further illustration of the difference between ritual concerns and substantive ones comes from occasions of accident in which the carelessness of one individual is seen as causing injury or death to another. Here there may be no way at all to compensate the offended, and no punishment may be prescribed. All that the offended can do is say he is sorry. And this expression itself may be *relatively* little open to gradation. The fact—at least in our society—is that a very limited set of ritual enactments are available for contrite offenders. Whether one runs over another's sentence, time, dog, or body, one is more or less reduced to saying some variant of "I'm sorry." The variation in degree of anguish expressed by the apologizer seems a poor reflection of the variation in loss possible to the offended. In any case, while the original infraction may be quite substantive in its consequence, the remedial work, however vociferous, is in these cases still largely expressive. And there is a logic in this. After an offense has occurred, the job of the offender is to show that it was not a fair expression of his attitude, or, when it evidently was, to show that he has changed his attitude to the rule that was violated. In the latter case, his job is to show that whatever happened before, he now has a right relationship—a pious attitude—to the rule in question, *and this is a matter of indicating a relationship, not compensating a loss.*[17]

Just as a right relation to the rules must be established in matters so monumental that this seems hopeless, so, too, a right relationship must be established no matter how minute the issue is. This is but another way of saying that regardless of the substantive character of the offense, much the same sort of ritual work must be done. As suggested, a single ritual idiom of remedial moves must be called on whether a toe has been accidentally stepped on or a destroyer accidentally sunk. It therefore follows that in occasions of face-to-face interaction in which many minor, potential delicts arise, ritual performances will be very frequent; and frequent they are, no matter how perfunctory.

Notes

1   The term "ritualization" is widely used in ethology (following initial work by Julian Huxley) in a derivative sense to refer to a physically adaptive behavior pattern that has become removed somewhat from its original function, rigidified as to form, and given

weight as a signal or "releaser" to conspecifics. See, for example, A. D. Best, "The Concept of Ritualization," in W. H. Thorpe and O. L. Zangwill, eds., *Current Problems in Animal Behaviour* (Cambridge: Cambridge University Press, 1961), pp. 102–24. A very useful volume is *A Discussion of Ritualization of Behaviour in Animals and Man*, Philosophical Transactions of the Royal Society of London, series B, Biological Sciences, vol. 251, no. 772 (London: December 1966), pp. 247–526.

2   Emile Durkheim, *Elementary Forms of the Religious Life*, Joseph Ward Swain, trans. (New York: The Macmillan Co., 1926: Allen and Unwin).

3   Marcel Mauss, *The Gift*, Ian Cunnison, trans. (London: Cohen and West, 1954).

4   Durkheim, op. cit., p. 338.

5   Discussed in Desmond Morris, *The Naked Ape* (London: Jonathan Cape, 1967; New York: McGraw-Hill Book Co., 1967), pp. 204–6. The phrase is attributed to J. A. R. A. M. Van Hoof.

6   It is interesting that in middle-class Anglo-American society it is often less incursive to ask a stranger for a free good than it is to initiate the offering of one. One reason is that an individual's needs are typically more apparent to him than to others; indeed, when circumstances make it very clear what an individual's need is, help may be volunteered by a stranger, providing the need can be satisfied at little cost to the satisfier. Another reason is that to make a request or accept an offer is to show a need over whose containment or satisfaction one does not have complete self-control; one thereby is subject to a limitation on self-determination and autonomy. When an individual is among strangers, he is usually sustained in the right to decide for himself when he will accept such a limit, this power preserving some of his autonomy in the face even of his losing most of it. Of course, to beg for anything more than a free good is to trade one's autonomy for what can be gotten thereby. The current hippie practice of panhandling is a nice send-up of this whole ritual code.

7   Here the ethological and the social anthropological approaches employ much the same model and are subject to much the same criticisms. Indeed, to class a handshake as a "mutual appeasement gesture," and to let it go at that, is something both schools could do and could have the same reasons to be leery about doing.

8   Lyn Tornabene, *I Passed as a Teenager* (New York; Lancer Books, 1968), p. 144.

9   A useful treatment of this theme may be found in David Sudnow, *Passing On* (Englewood Cliffs, New Jersey: Prentice-Hall, Inc., 1967), ch 5. "On Bad News." pp. 117–52.

10 See John Austin, "A Plea for Excuses," in his *Philosophical Papers* (Oxford: Oxford University Press, 1961), chapter, 6, pp. 123–52; H. L. A. Hart, "The Ascription of Responsibility and Rights," chapter 8 in A. G. N. Flew, ed., *Logic and Language* (First Series; Oxford: Basil Blackwell, 1955), pp. 145–66; see also Marvin B. Scott and Stanford M. Lyman, "Accounts," *American Sociological Review*, XXII (February 1968): 46–62.

11 Case study examples are provided in the useful monograph by Robert M. Emerson, *Judging Delinquents* (Chicago: Aldine Publishing Co., 1969), esp. pp. 155–66.

12 The law, of course, is much concerned with the difference between the foreseen and unforeseen, and, within the latter, the difference between the excusably and inexcusably unforeseen. Criminal liability tends to attach only if it can be shown that the offender in some way or other did anticipate the adverse consequences of his act; civil liability, a much broader possibility, applies if it can be shown that the offender either foresaw what was to happen or was inexcusably ignorant and unthinking, that is, unwitting in the way a reasonable man would not be—and there are even some grounds on which "strict liability" can be pressed in civil action, warranted ignorance not being a defense.

13 A treatment of these differences is suggested in Scott and Lyman, op. cit.

14 See, for example, Donald M. McIntyre and Nicholas D. Chabraja, "The Intensive Search of a Suspect's Body and Clothing," *Journal of Criminal Law, Criminology and Police*

Science, LVIII, no. 1 (1967): 18–26. It might be added that whenever an individual's body is to be managed, there is very likely to be some juncture where he is accorded the courtesy of performing the other's will on his own, if for no other reason than the fact that the body is hard to manage nicely without cooperation. Thus, for example, in the early days of drop hanging, the victim apparently was allowed to govern the moment of his own demise by being put in charge of the signal (a handkerchief) for the drop. See Justin Atholl, *Shadow of the Gallows* (London: John Long, 1954), p. 48. Today, apparently, persons being gassed are allowed to signal for the pellet and are encouraged to breathe deeply on their own. Last requests, of course, can be similarly understood; the self-determinism is somewhat displaced in time and content but still attests to the fact that the person going to his death is someone whose will and competency are being respected. How clever, if not obscene, are the workings of society that occasions of ultimate coercion can be used to affirm ritually the respectfulness of the coercers and the free will of the coerced.

15 A nice example is provided by Albert DeSalvo's testimony regarding himself during the court hearing to determine his competency in connection with the crimes he committed as the "Boston Strangler." Even after strangling a fair number of defenseless women, some very unpleasantly, and terrorizing a city, he still could find a little spot to stand upon in court as he cut himself off from himself. After all, no natural man could have been so beastly, and so there must have been deep-seated psychological reasons for his misbehavior and some value to the world in his helping to find out what they were. See Gerald Frank, *The Boston Strangler* (New York: The New American Library, 1966; London: Jonathan Cape, 1967), especially pp. 361–3.

16 Christian theology has been much concerned with this same divine splitting, but its derivation of this duality is not fully convincing.

17 The best discussion of these issues is still, I think, the very fine section on ritual in Talcott Parsons, *Structure of Social Action* (New York: McGraw-Hill, Inc., 1937; London: Allen and Unwin, 1949 new edn., 1968), pp. 429–41. I might add that a caution is implied for students who would apply an exchange perspective to all areas of social life.

11

Social Life as Game

From "Fun in Games"*

Bases of Fun

In this paper, we have come by stages to focus on the question of euphoria in encounters, arguing that euphoria arises when persons can spontaneously maintain the authorized transformation rules. We assume that participants will judge past encounters according to whether they were or were not easy to be in and will be much concerned to maximize euphoria, through, for example, integrative acts, topic selection, and avoidance of encounters likely to be dysphoric.

But of course this tells us only in a very general way what people do to ensure easeful interaction, for in pointing to the requirement that spontaneous involvement must coincide with obligatory involvement, we are merely pushing the problem back one step. We still must go on to consider what will produce this congruence for any given encounter.

In concluding this paper, then, I would like to take a speculative look at some of the conditions, once removed, that seem to ensure easeful interaction. Again, there seems to be no better starting point than what I labeled gaming encounters. Not only are games selected and discarded on the basis of their ensuring euphoric interaction, but, to ensure engrossment, they are also sometimes modified in a manner provided for within their rules, thus giving us a delicate tracer of what is needed to ensure euphoria. Instead of having to generate an allocation of spontaneous involvement that coincides with the transformation rules, it is possible to modify the transformation rules to fit the distribution and possibilities of spontaneous involvement. The practices of "balancing" teams, handicapping, limiting participation to skill classes, or adjusting the betting limits, all introduce sufficient malleability into the materials of the game to allow the game to be molded and fashioned into a shape best suited to hold the participants entranced. We

* Originally published in *Encounters: Two Studies in the Sociology of Interaction* by Erving Goffman, 1961, pp. 66–81. Copyright © 1961. All rights reserved. Reprinted/adapted by permission of Allyn & Bacon.

can at last return, therefore, to our original theme: fun in games.

There is a common-sense view that games are fun to play when the outcome or pay-off has a good chance of remaining unsettled until the end of play (even though it is also necessary that play come to a final settlement within a reasonable period of time). The practices of balancing teams and of handicapping unmatched ones, and the practice of judiciously interposing a randomizing element, "pure luck" (especially to the degree that perfect matching or handicapping is not possible), all work to ensure that a prior knowledge of the attributes of the players will not render the outcome a foregone conclusion. On similar grounds, should the final score come to be predictable, as often happens near the end of the play, concession by the loser is likely, terminating the action in the interests of both the play and the gaming encounter.

To speak of the outcome as problematic, however, is, in effect, to say that one must look to the play itself in order to discover how things will turn out. The developing line built up by the alternating, interlocking moves of the players can thus maintain sole claim upon the attention of the participants, thereby facilitating the game's power to constitute the current reality of its players and to engross them. We can thus understand one of the social reasons why cheaters are resented; by locating the power of determining the outcome of the play in the arrangements made by one player, cheating, like mismatching, destroys the reality-generating power of the game.[1] (Of course, whereas the mismatching of teams prevents a play world from developing, the discovery that someone is cheating punctures and deflates a world that has already developed.)

But this analysis is surely not enough. In games of pure chance, such as flipping coins, there would never be a problem of balancing sides, yet, unless such other factors as money bets are carefully added, mere uncertainty of outcome is not enough to engross the players.

Another possibility is that games give the players an opportunity to exhibit attributes valued in the wider social world, such as dexterity, strength, knowledge, intelligence, courage, and self-control. Externally relevant attributes thus obtain official expression within the milieu of an encounter. These attributes could even be earned within the encounter, to be claimed later outside it.

Again, this alone is not enough, for mismatched teams allow the better player to exhibit all kinds of capacities. He, at least, should be satisfied. Still, we know that, whatever his actual feelings, he is not likely to admit to getting much satisfaction out of this kind of gaming and is, in fact, quite likely to find himself bored and unengrossed in the play.

But if we combine our two principles—problematic outcome and sanctioned display—we may have something more valid. A successful game would then be one which, first, had a problematic outcome and then, within these limits, allowed for a maximum possible display of externally relevant attributes.

This dual theme makes some sense. A good player who is unopposed in displaying his powers may give the impression of too openly making claims; he would be acting contrary to the rules of irrelevance which require him to forego attending to many of his externally relevant social attributes. But as long as his efforts are called forth in the heat of close competition, they are called forth by the interaction itself and not merely for show. Uncertainty of outcome gives the player a shield behind which he can work into the inter-action attributes that would threaten the membrane surrounding the encounter if openly introduced.

How far can we generalize this explanation? First we must see that this conception of a dual principle leads us back to a consideration of betting games and the efforts of those around a table to locate a euphoria function. If the participants perceive that the betting is very low relative to their financial capacities, then interest in money itself cannot penetrate the encounter and enliven it. Interest in the game may flag; participants may fail to "take it seriously." On the other hand, if the players feel that the betting is high in relation to their income and resources, then interest may be strangled, a participant in a play flooding out of the gaming encounter into an anxious private concern for his general economic welfare.[2] A player in these circumstances is forced to take the game "too seriously."

When players at the beginning of play give thought to an appropriate scale of stakes, they are seeking for that kind of screen behind which an interest in money can seep into the game. This is one reason for restricting the game to persons who, it is felt, can afford to lose roughly the same amount. We can similarly understand the tendency for the level of bets to be raised part way through the gaming, since by then the game itself has had a chance to grasp the players and inure them against what they previously considered too worrisome a loss.

We also see that the notion of taking a game too seriously or not seriously enough does not quite fit our notions of the contrast between recreational "unserious" activity and workaday "serious" activity. The issue apparently is not whether the activity belongs to the recreational sphere or the work sphere, but whether external pulls upon one's interest can be selectively held in check so that one can become absorbed in the encounter as a world in itself. The problem of too-serious or not-serious-enough arises in gaming encounters not because a game is involved but because an encounter is involved.

Financial status is not the only fundamental aspect of a person's life which can enter through the membrane of an encounter and enliven or spoil the proceedings. Physical safety, for example, seems to be another. In children's play activities, risk to the physical integrity of the body is often introduced, again on a carefully graded not-too-much-not-too-little basis. For example, slides must be steep enough to be a challenge, yet not so steep as to make an accident too likely: a little more risk than can be easily handled seems to do the trick. (Adult sports such as skiing seem to be based on the same principle—a means of creating tension in regard to physical safety is here integrated into the play activity, giving rise to merriment.)[3] All of this has been stated by Fritz Redl in his discussion of the "ego-supporting" functions of successful games:

> I would like to list a few of the things that must happen for a "game" to "break down." It breaks down if it is not fun any more; that means if certain gratification guarantees, for the sake of which individuals were lured into it, stop being gratifying. There are many reasons why that may happen. It breaks down, too, if it is not safe any more, that is, when the risks or the dangers an individual exposes himself to in the game outweigh whatever gratification he may derive from it. By safe, I mean internally and externally. The actual risks and the physical strain or the fear of hurt may become too great or the fear of one's own passivity may become too great. This is why, by choice, children sometimes do not allow themselves to play certain games, because they are afraid of their own excitation or they know that the danger of loss of self-control in this activity is so seductive and so great that they would rather not play. In fact, some of the mechanisms of games seem to be built to guarantee gratification, but they also guarantee security against one's own superego pressures or against the outside dangers. Again, a game breaks down when the "as if" character cannot be maintained, or when the reality proximity is too great, and this may vary from game to game. There are some games that stop being fun when they get too fantastic and there is not enough similarity to a real competitive situation; there are other games which stop being fun the other way around. If one comes too close to reality, then the activity may lose its game character, as do some games that are too far from reality. Where is too far away or too close? This is the question for which I do not know the answer.[4]

It is possible to go on and see in games a means of infusing or integrating into gaming encounters many different socially significant externally based matters. This seems to be one reason why different cultural milieux favor different kinds of games, and some historical changes in the equipment of a game appear to respond to social changes in the milieu in which the game is played.[5] And apart from the equipment itself, there is the issue of the wider social position of the contending players. Thus, for example, the clash of football teams on a playing field can provide a means by which the antagonism between the two groups represented by the teams may be allowed to enter an encounter in a controlled manner and to be given expression.[6] We can then predict that, at least as far as spectators are concerned, two teams drawn from the same social grouping may produce a conflict that falls flat, and two teams drawn from groupings openly opposed to each other may provide incidents during which so much externally based hostility flows into the mutual activity of the sporting encounter as to burst the membrane surrounding it, leading to riots, fights, and other signs of a breakdown in order. All this is suggested by Max Gluckman in his discussion of British football, where he attempts to explain why league teams can represent different schools, towns, and regions, but with much more difficulty different religious groupings and different social classes:

> A similar situation might be found in school matches. We know that the unity and internal loyalty of schools is largely built up by formalized competition in games with other schools—and I should expect this system to work well as long as each school mainly played other schools of the same type as itself. What would happen if public schools became involved in contests with secondary modern schools? Would the whole national background of divergence in opportunity, prospects, and privilege, embitter the game till they ceased to serve their purpose of friendly rivalry? Is it only because Oxford and Cambridge can produce better teams than the provincial universities that they confine their rivalry in the main to contests between themselves?[7]

The social differences, then, between the two supporting audiences for the teams must be of the kind that can be tapped without breaking the barrel. It may be, however, that the same can be said about any major externally based experience common to members of an audience. A stage play that does not touch on issues relevant to the audience is likely to fall flat, and yet staged materials can be pressed to a point where they insufficiently disguise the realities on which they dwell, causing the audience to be moved too much. Thus, realistic plays put on for unsophisticated audiences are felt by some to be in bad taste, to "go too far," or to "come too close to home"—as was the feeling, so I was informed, when *Riders to the Sea* was staged for a Shetland audience. What has been called "symbolic distance" must be assured. A membrane must be maintained that will control the flow of externally relevant sentiments into the interaction. Interestingly enough, the same effect can be seen in the judgment adult audiences make in watching their children use sacred materials for purposes of play, as Caillois points out in discussing the fact that games are not merely current residues of past realities:

These remarks are no less valid for the sacred than for the profane. The katcinas are semidivinities, the principal objects of worship among the Pueblo Indians of New Mexico; this does not prevent the same adults who worship them and incarnate them in their masked dances from making dolls resembling them for the amusement of their sons. Similarly, in Catholic countries, children currently play at going to Mass, at being confirmed, at marriage and funerals. Parents permit this at least as long as the imitation remains a respectful one. In black Africa the children make masks and rhombs in the same way and are punished for the same reasons, if the imitation goes too far and becomes too much of a parody or a sacrilege.[8]

It seems, then, that in games and similar activities disguises must be provided which check, but do not stop, the flow of socially significant matters into the encounter. All this goes beyond my earlier statement that the material character of game equipment is not relevant. The game-relevant meanings of the various pieces of the game equipment are in themselves a useful disguise, for behind these meanings the sentimental, material, and esthetic value of the pieces can steal into interaction, infusing it with tones of meaning that have nothing to do with the logic of the game but something to do with the pleasure of the gaming encounter; the traditional concern in Japan about the quality of equipment used to play *Go* is an extreme example. In this way, too, perhaps, the conversation and cuisine in a restaurant can, if good enough, not only blot out a humble setting, but also, in elegant establishments, allow us a deepened identification with the cost of the *décor,* the command in the service, and the social status of groups at the other tables—an identification we would not allow ourselves were the process not disguised. And it seems that the malleability of game arrangements—choice of games, sides, handicaps, bets—allows for the fabrication of exactly the right amount of disguise.

But here we have a theme that echoes the doctrine that has been built around projective testing, namely, that the ambiguity and malleability of test material allows subjects to structure it according to their own propensity, to express quite personal "loaded" themes because the materials are sufficiently removed from reality to allow the subject to avoid seeing what he is doing with them. A discontinuity with the world is achieved even while a connection with it is established. Of course, these tests are usually directed to one subject and his world, as opposed to an encounter with many individuals in it, but the presence of the tester focusing his attention on the subject's response does in a way supply the conditions of a two-person encounter.

A glance at the literature on projective devices encourages us to continue along this tack. Take for example the beautiful work of Erikson on play

therapy published in 1937.[9] He describes children who cannot bring themselves to talk about their troubles—in fact, may even be too young to do so.
The affect attached to the suppressed and repressed materials would rupture
any membrane around any mutual or individual activity that alluded to this
material. In some cases these constraints block any verbal communication.
But by allowing the child to construct play configurations out of doll-like
objects that are somewhat removed from the reality projected on them, the
child feels some relief, some ease; and he does so through the process of
infusing his painful concerns into the local situation in a safely transformed
manner.

Once the special relevance of projective testing is granted, we need not be
bound by formal test materials, but can include any situation where an individual can permit himself to interact by virtue of a disguise, in fact,
transformation rules that he is allowed to create. Fromm-Reichmann
provides an example:

> Perhaps my interest began with the young catatonic woman who broke
> through a period of completely blocked communication and obvious
> anxiety by responding when I asked her a question about her feeling
> miserable: She raised her hand with her thumb lifted, the other four
> fingers bent toward her palm, so that I could see only the thumb,
> isolated from the four hidden fingers. I interpreted the signal with,
> "That lonely?" in a sympathetic tone of voice. At this, her facial expres-
> sion loosened up as though in great relief and gratitude, and her fingers
> opened. Then she began to tell me about herself by means of her
> fingers, and she asked me by gestures to respond in kind. We continued
> with this finger conversation for one or two weeks, and as we did so,
> her anxious tension began to decrease and she began to break through
> her noncommunicative isolation; and subsequently she emerged alto-
> gether from her loneliness.[10]

In both these cases what we see is an individual himself determining the kind
of veil that will be drawn over his feelings while in communication with
another. The system of etiquette and reserve that members of every group
employ in social intercourse would seem to function in the same way, but
in this case the disguise is socially standardized; it is applied by the individual
but not tailored by himself to his own particular needs.

In psychotherapeutic intervention with greatly withdrawn patients, the
therapist may have to agree to the patient's using a very heavy disguise, but
in psychotherapy with "neurotics," we may see something of the opposite
extreme. In the psychoanalytical doctrine of transference and the psychoanalytical rule of free association, we meet the notion that a membrane can
be established that is so diaphanous and yet so tough that any externally

related feeling on the part of the patient can be activated and infused into the encounter without destroying the doctor-patient encounter. This is facilitated, of course, by the professional arrangement that separates the analytical couch from home life and home authorities.[11] The extension of this tell-all doctrine to group psychotherapy merely moves matters more in the direction of the kind of encounter considered in this paper.

This view of the function of disguise allows us to consider the phenomenon of "subversive ironies." One of the most appealing ways in which situations are "made" can be found in times and places of stress where matters that are extremely difficult to bear and typically excluded by the official transformation rules are introduced lightly and ironically. The classic case is "gallows humor." In concentration camps, for example, turnips were sometimes called "German pineapples,"[12] fatigue drill, "geography."[13] In a mental hospital, a patient may express to other patients his feelings about the place by referring to the medical and surgical building with conscious irony as the "hospital," thereby establishing the rest of the institution as a different kind of place.[14] In general, these subversive ironies would seem to "come off" when they open the way for some expression of feeling that is generated in the institutional situation at large but disguise what is being expressed sufficiently to ensure the orderliness of the particular encounter.

Within the same perspective, we can consider the functions of indirection in informal social control. For example, when a member of a work group begins to threaten informal work quotas by producing too much, we can follow the actions of his fellow workers who, perhaps unwilling to express directly their resentment and their desire for control, may employ a game of "binging" or "piling" through which the non-conformist is brought back into line under the guise of being the butt of a joke.[15]

Whatever the interaction, then, there is this dual theme: the wider world must be introduced, but in a controlled and disguised manner. Individuals can deal with one another face to face because they are ready to abide by rules of irrelevance, but the rules seem to exist to let something difficult be quietly expressed as much as to exclude it entirely from the scene. Given the dangers of expression, a disguise may function not so much as a way of concealing something as a way of revealing as much of it as can be tolerated in an encounter. We fence our encounters in with gates; the very means by which we hold off a part of reality can be the means by which we can bear introducing it.

As a final step, I would like to trace the same dual theme in sociability, in occasions such as parties, which form a structured setting for many comings-together during an evening.

It can be argued that informal social participation is an ultimate validation of relationships of intimacy and equality with those with whom one shares this activity.[16] A party, then, is by way of being a status blood bath, a leveling

up and leveling down of all present, a mutual contamination and sacralization. Concretely phrased, a party is an opportunity to engage in encounters
that will widen one's social horizons through, for example, sexual bond-
formation, informality with those of high rank, or extending one's invitation
circle. Where boundaries have already been tentatively widened, parties can
function to confirm and consolidate work begun elsewhere.

Thus defined, a party presents us with a double set of requirements and,
behind these, another illustration of our double theme. On one hand, we
can look to the common rationalizations and causes of social endogamy, the
rule that only equals be invited to a sociable gathering. When we ask persons
about their exclusiveness, they tend to claim that they would not have
"anything in common" with those not invited and that mixing different
classes of persons makes everyone "uncomfortable." Presumably, what they
mean here is that officially irrelevant attributes would obtrude upon the
occasion, destroying the identities upon which the sociability was organized
and killing spontaneous involvement in the recreation at hand.

But precisely the opposite concern will be felt, too. Often, sociable conversations and games fail not because the participants are insufficiently close
socially but because they are not far enough apart. A feeling of boredom,
that nothing is likely to happen, can arise when the same persons spend all
their sociable moments together. Social horizons cannot be extended. One
hears the phrases: "The same old people," "the same old thing, let's not go."
The speakers, in fact, usually go, but not hopefully.

So we find that the euphoria function for a sociable occasion resides somewhere between little social difference and much social difference. A
dissolution of some externally based social distance must be achieved, a
penetration of ego-boundaries, but not to an extent that renders the participants fearful, threatened, or self-consciously concerned with what is
happening socially. Too much potential loss and gain must be guarded
against, as well as too little.

Too much or too little of this "working through" will force participants to
look directly at the kind of work that parties are expected to do and at the
impulses that cause persons to attend or stay away—impulses that ought to
be concealed in what is done at parties even while providing the energy for
doing it. Sociologically speaking, a very decorous party, as well as an indeco-
rous one, can become obscene, exposing desires out of the context in which
they can be clothed by locally realized events.

From this, it follows, of course, that what is a successful and happy occasion for one participant may not be such for another. Further, it follows
that if the many are to be pleased, then the few may have to sacrifice themselves to the occasion, allowing their bodies to be cast into the blend to make
the bell sound sweet. Perhaps they rely at such times on other kinds of
pleasures.

Conclusions

I have argued in this paper that any social encounter, any focused gathering, is to be understood, in the first instance, in terms of the functioning of the "membrane" that encloses it, cutting it off from a field of properties that could be given weight. There is a set of transformation rules that officially lays down what sorts of properties are to be given what kind of influence in the allocation of locally realized resources. If a participant can become spontaneously involved in the focus of attention prescribed by these transformation rules, he will feel natural, at ease, sure about the reality in which he and the others are sustained. An encounter provides a world for its participants, but the character and stability of this world is intimately related to its selective relationship to the wider one. The naturalistic study of encounters, then, is more closely tied to studies of social structure on one hand, and more separate from them, than one might at first imagine.

I have attempted to show the effects of standard socio-economic attributes on the workings of an encounter. In this, a course has been followed that is customary in sociological analysis, but one important difference must be noted. Empirically, the effect of externally based social attributes on social encounters is very great. But the analysis and theory of this effect must give equal weight to matters such as noise, fatigue, or facial disfigurations. The race-group status of one participant in a focused gathering can have something of the same effect as the harelip of another; the route through which socio-economic factors enter an encounter is one that is equally open to a strange and undignified set of vehicles.

As far as gaming encounters and other focused gatherings are concerned, the most serious thing to consider is the fun in them. Something in which the individual can become unselfconsciously engrossed is something that can become real to him. Events that occur in his immediate physical presence are ones in which he can become easily engrossed. *Joint* engrossment in something with others reinforces the reality carved out by the individual's attention, even while subjecting this entrancement to the destructive distractions that the others are now in a position to cause.

The process of mutually sustaining a definition of the situation in face-to-face interaction is socially organized through rules of relevance and irrelevance. These rules for the management of engrossment appear to be an insubstantial element of social life, a matter of courtesy, manners, and etiquette. But it is to these flimsy rules, and not to the unshaking character of the external world, that we owe our unshaking sense of realities. to be at ease in a situation is to be properly subject to these rules, entranced by the meanings they generate and stabilize; to be ill at ease means that one is ungrasped by immediate reality and that one loosens the grasp that others have of it. To be awkward or unkempt, to talk or move wrongly, is to be a dangerous giant, a destroyer of worlds. As every psychotic and comic ought to know, any accurately improper move can poke through the thin sleeve of immediate reality.

From "Where the Action Is"*

And now we begin to see character for what it is. On the one hand, it refers to what is essential and unchanging about the individual—what is *characteristic* of him. On the other, it refers to attributes that can be generated and destroyed during fateful moments. In this latter view the individual can act so as to determine the traits that will thereafter be his; he can act so as to create and establish what is to be imputed to him. Every time a moment occurs, its participants will therefore find themselves with another little chance to make something of themselves.

Thus a paradox. Character is both unchanging and changeable. And yet that is how we conceive of it.

It should be no less clear that our illogic in this matter has its social value. Social organization everywhere has the problem of morale and continuity. Individuals must come to all their little situations with some enthusiasm and concern, for it is largely through such moments that social life occurs, and if a fresh effort were not put into each of them, society would surely suffer. The possibility of effecting reputation is the spur. And yet, if society is to persist, the same pattern must be sustained from one actual social occasion to the next. Here the need is for rules and conventionality. Individuals must define themselves in terms of properties already accepted as theirs, and act reliably in terms of them.

To satisfy the fundamental requirements of morale and continuity, we are encouraged in a fundamental illusion. It is our character. A something entirely our own that does not change, but is none the less precarious and mutable. Possibilities regarding character encourage us to renew our efforts at every moment of society's activity we approach, especially its social ones; and it is precisely through these renewals that the old routines can be sustained. We are allowed to think there is something to be won in the moments that we face so that society can face moments and defeat them.

Character Contests

Starting with the notion of fateful occupational duties, we can view action as a kind of self-oriented evocation in ritualized form of the moral scene

---

*Originally published in *Interaction Ritual: Essays on Face-to-face Behavior,* 1967, pp. 238–40. Copyright © 1967 by Erving Goffman. Reprinted by permission of Pantheon Books, a division of Random House Inc.

arising when such duties are exercised. Action consists of chancy tasks undertaken for "their own sake." Excitement and character display, the by-products of practical gambles, of serious fateful scenes, become in the case of action the tacit purpose of the whole show. However, neither fateful duties nor action tell us very much about the mutual implications that can occur when one person's display of character directly bears upon another's, nor do we learn about the framework of understanding we possess for dealing with such occurrences. For this we must turn to interpersonal action.

During occasions of this kind of action, not only will character be at stake, mutual fatefulness will prevail in this regard. Each person will be at least incidentally concerned with establishing evidence of strong character, and conditions will be such as to allow this only at the expense of the character of the other participants. The very field that the one uses to express character may be the other's character expression. And at times the primary properties at play may themselves be openly made a convenience, pointedly serving merely as an occasion for doing battle by and for character. A *character contest* results; a special kind of moral game.

From *Strategic Interaction**

In this paper I want to explore one general human capacity in terms of the conceptions we have of its physical and social limits: the individual's capacity to acquire, reveal and conceal information. The perspective here is that of an organizationally committed observer who needs information from another person. I will draw upon the popular literature on intelligence and espionage for illustration, for no party seems more concerned than an intelligence organization about the capacity we will consider, and more likely to bring assumptions to the surface for us. Special attention will be given to occasions when the informing individual is in the immediate presence of the party collecting the information.

★   ★   ★

It is certainly the case that nations at war (and is likely the case that industrial organizations at peace) have been wonderfully served by effective spies; Sorge and Cicero are only two examples. But just as certainly, the overall value of intelligence organizations of the national kind can be questioned.[17]

The more needful an organization is of acquiring or guarding a piece of information, the more it must suspect the employee associated with it, for that is just the time when the opponent will make the greatest effort to get

* Published 1969, pp. 4, 77–81, 100–1, 136–7. Reprinted by permission of the University of Pennsylvania Press.

to him. Officers in the home establishment can be subverted through ideology, blackmail, bribery, and carelessness. One's agents in enemy lands are even more vulnerable. They can easily be caught without this being known, and bribed with their lives into working for the other side. (Even if this requires that they not be trusted out of the sight of their new masters, they can still be used, since a considerable amount of a wartime agent's work consists in receiving and sending messages and arranging to receive agents and supplies.)

For an intelligence organization, rationalization in the conventional sense generates special vulnerabilities, and growth special weaknesses. Hierarchical organization means that one man "in place" near the top can render the whole establishment vulnerable. In the field, lateral expansion through links means that one caught spy can lead to the sequential entrapment of a whole network.[18] In both cases, the damage that can be done by a disloyal member is multiplied. The usual answer is compartmental insulation and minimization of channels of communication. But these devices, in turn, reduce coordination of action and dangerously impede corroboration of information.

Behind the instability of intelligence organization, I think we can find two fundamental facts. First, much of the work of the organization ultimately depends on guarding information the other side is seeking. (This is directly true of the security branch and indirectly true for the espionage branch, the latter simply because agents can't uncover other organizations' secrets without maintaining secrecy concerning their attempts.) And among all the things of this world, information is the hardest to guard, since it can be stolen without removing it. Second, in working with information, individuals must be employed, and of all the capacities that an individual has, that of being a caretaker of information is one that seems to render him most vulnerable. Hence intelligence work and intelligence workers provide much material on the playing of expression games. It is here we can see most clearly the contingencies a member creates as a source and manager of information. And it is here we can most easily learn about the beliefs which prevail concerning the moral and practical limits of this capacity.

A final point. It is plain that the experience of intelligence agents—more so the popular recountings of the supposed experiences of intelligence agents—might provide an overly colorful source of data on which to base an analysis of expression games. Nonetheless, I think there is some warrant for using this literature. Intelligence agents, especially from the larger countries, have considerable resources at their disposal, a certain amount of specialized training, a government's secret blessing to commit mayhem, and stakes that are very high. In these respects agents are unlike ordinary mortals. But along with everyone else, they must make their peace with one massive contingency: the player's chief weapon and chief vulnerability is himself. Getting oneself through an international incident involves contingencies and capacities that have a bearing on the games that go on in local neighborhoods. For example, the very great Russian spy, Sorge, after having maneuvered himself into the position of unofficial secretary to the German military attaché in Tokyo, found it necessary to photograph documents in Embassy rooms in which he could easily have been surprised at work.[19] Being caught once in such an act in such a place would have rather dramatically altered his working identity. Yet he was able coolly to proceed with his work and his risk-taking. What is special here is the place, the equipment, and the consequences of discovery. But these are special only in degree. At the center is a man having to engage in a complex technical act over a brief period of available time under conditions where the chances of discovery by others, with consequent exposure and discrediting, are considerable; and he must execute his technical task without allowing thoughts of his situation to reduce his effective speed—for this would only increase time, risk, and fear, which, in turn, could lead to still further incapacity. We all must face moments of this kind, albeit much less extreme in every regard, and it is the sharing of this core contingency that makes the stories of agents relevant. Similarly, to hide bulky transmitter and receiver parts in a rucksack while ostensibly going on a hike,[20] or to regularly meet with a member of one's spy ring in his own house under cover of giving painting lessons to his daughter,[21] or to pass a vital message to a confederate during the act of shaking hands with a member of another embassy at a cocktail party, is to engage in spectacular concealment; but there is no one who does not have to orient his body's covering as a means of concealing something, or who has not used ordinary arrangements of social contact as a front behind which to engage in questionable dealings, or who has not fabricated a "good" reason for actions that spring from a concealed intent. It is an unusual feat, even in espionage, for a man to move "into place" and stay in play for fourteen years, establishing a social reputation as a watch repair proprietor so that he could make his move when needed, as indeed "Albert Oertal" did;[22] but there is no one who has not gone somewhere for reasons he did not want to avow and protected himself by providing "good" reasons for his visit. It is mainly wanted criminals, spies, and secret police who must extendedly present themselves in a false personal and/or social identity to those who think they know them well; but there can hardly be a person who has never been concerned about giving his social or personal identities away, whether through lack of emotional and intellectual self-control, or the failure to inhibit expression, or the acknowledgment of a social relationship he was not supposed to have, or the demonstration of incongruous social practices.

And note, just as we are like them in significant ways, so they are like us. In the little service contacts we have in stores and offices, occasions are always arising when we must ask for advice and then determine how to read the advice by trying to analyze the sincerity of the server's manner. When we come into contact with the person who employs us, a similar task arises; he has reason to almost cover his actual assessment with an equable, supporting air, and we have reason to try to read his for what he "really" thinks. The same is true in the warmer circles of social life. Surely every adult who has had a friend or spouse has had occasion to doubt expression of relationship and then to doubt the doubt even while giving the other reasons to suspect that something is being doubted. These, then, are the occasions for our expression games, but a nation's gamesmen play here too. He who manages the affairs of state has to make fateful decisions on the basis of the appearances of good faith of those with whom he negotiates; similarly, an intelligence officer is dependent on being able to appraise correctly the show of loyalty displayed by his agents.

In every social situation we can find a sense in which one participant will be an observer with something to gain from assessing expressions, and another will be a subject with something to gain from manipulating this process. A single structure of contingencies can be found in this regard which renders agents a little like us all and all of us a little like agents.

★   ★   ★

Now it is possible to review the defining conditions for *strategic interaction*.[23] Two or more parties must find themselves in a well-structured situation of mutual impingement where each party must make a move and where every possible move carries fateful implications for all of the parties. In this situation, each player must influence his own decisions by his knowing that the other players are likely to try to dope out his decision in advance, and may even appreciate that he knows this is likely. Courses of action or moves will then be made in the light of one's thoughts about the others' thoughts about oneself. An exchange of moves made on the basis of this kind of orientation to self and others can be called strategic interaction. One part of strategic interaction consists of concrete courses of action taken in the real world that constrains the parties; the other part, which has no more intrinsic relation to communication than the first, consists of a special kind of decision-making—decisions made by directly orienting oneself to the other parties and giving weight to their situation as they would seem to see it, including their giving weight to one's own. The special possibilities that result from this mutually assessed mutual assessment, as these effect the fate of the parties, provide reason and grounds for employing the special perspective of strategic interaction.

★   ★   ★

It should be noted that strategic interaction is, of course close to Meadian social psychology and to what has come to be called "symbolic interaction"—since nowhere more than in game analysis does one see the actor as putting himself in the place of the other and seeing things, temporarily at least, from his point of view. Yet it is quite doubtful that there are significant historical connections between the two types of analysis. In any case, strategic interaction appears to advance the symbolic interactionist approach in two ways. First, the strategic approach, by insisting on *full* interdependence of outcomes, on mutual awareness of this fact, and on the capacity to make use of this knowledge, provides a natural means for excluding from consideration merely any kind of interdependence. This is important, for if all interdependence is included in the study of interaction, hardly anything distinctive can remain. Second, following the crucial work of Schelling, strategic interaction addresses itself directly to the dynamics of interdependence involving mutual awareness; it seeks out basic moves and inquires into natural stopping points in the potentially infinite cycle of two players taking into consideration their consideration of each other's consideration, and so forth.

Now the main analytical argument. The framework of strategic interaction is quite formal; no limit is placed on its application, including the type of payoff involved, as long as the participants are locked in what they perceive as mutual fatefulness and are obliged to take some one of the available, highly structured courses of action. Because of this inclusion of any kind of payoff, the game approach has an easy application to almost everything that is considered under the ill-defined rubric "interaction." Furthermore, howsoever interaction is defined, the actors involved must be accorded some attributes and given some internal structure and design, and here the propensities of a gamesman will have a place. The strategic approach will therefore always apply in some way; it is important to be clear, then, about the limits of this application.

Notes

1   Harvey Sacks has suggested to me that game etiquette may oblige those who discover a cheater to warn him secretly so that he is enabled to desist or withdraw without totally breaking up the play. Presumably, an open accusation of cheating would be even more destructive of the play than the knowledge on the part of some of the players that cheating is occurring. That which is threatened by cheating is that which determines the form that control of cheating can take.

2   It is interesting that in daily life when individuals personally convey or receive what is for them large amounts of money they often make a little joke about money matters. Presumably, the integrity of the exchange encounter is threatened by concern about the funds, and the joke is an effort to assimilate this source of distraction to the interaction in progress, thereby (hopefully) reducing tension. In any case, to demonstrate that the

money is not being treated "seriously" is presumably to imply that the encounter itself is the important thing.

3   Roger Caillois, "Unity of Play: Diversity of Games," *Diogenes,* No. 19 (1957), p. 107, speaks here of "games based on the pursuit of vertigo." He says, "The question is less one of overcoming fear than of voluptuously experiencing fear, a shudder, a state of stupor that momentarily causes one to lose self-control." See also his *Les Jeux et les Hommes* (Paris: Gallimard, 1958), pp. 45–51, where he elaborates his discussion of games based on *"ilinx."*

4   Fritz Redl, discussing Gregory Bateson's "The Message 'This is Play,'" in Bertram Schaffner, ed., *Group Processes,* Transactions of the Second (1955) Conference (New York: The Josiah Macy, Jr. Foundation, 1956), pp. 212–13. See also Redl's "The Impact of Game-Ingredients on Children's Play Behavior," in Bertram Schaffner, ed., *Group Processes,* Transactions of the Fourth (1957) Conference (New York: The Josiah Macy, Jr. Foundation, 1959), pp. 33–81.

5   See, for example, K. M. Colby's treatment of the changing character of chessmen in "Gentlemen, The Queen!" *Psychoanalytic Review,* 40 (1953), pp. 144–8.

6   In this connection, see the functional interpretation of North Andamanese peace-making ceremonies in A. R. Radcliffe-Brown, *The Andaman Islanders* (Glencoe, Ill.: The Free Press, 1948), pp. 134–5, 238 ff.

7   Max Gluckman, "How Foreign Are You?," *The Listener,* Jan. 15, 1959, p. 102. Of course, the Olympic games bring teams of different nationalities against each other, but the heavy institutionalization of these competitions seems to be exactly what is needed to strengthen the membrane within which these games are played; and, in spite of the dire implication, opposing Olympic teams do occasionally fight. P. R. Reid (*Escape from Colditz,* New York: Berkley Publishing Corp., 1952, p. 64), suggests a similar argument in his discussion of the wall games played by British prisoners of war at Colditz:

> The Poles, and later the French when they arrived, were always interested spectators. Although we had no monopoly of the courtyard, they naturally took to their rooms and watched the game from the windows. They eventually put up sides against the British and games were played against them, but these were not a success. Tempers were lost and the score became a matter of importance, which it never did in an "all-British" game.

See also George Orwell, "The Sporting Spirit," in *Shooting an Elephant* (New York: Harcourt, Brace, 1950), pp. 151–5.

8   Caillois, "Unity of Play," p. 97.

9   Erik Homburger [Erikson], "Configurations in Play—Clinical Notes," *The Psychoanalytic Quarterly,* 6 (1937), pp. 139–214.

10   Frieda Fromm-Reichmann, "Loneliness," *Psychiatry,* 22 (1959), p. 1.

11   See Melanie Klein, "The Psycho-Analytic Play Technique: its history and significance," in Klein, et al., *New Directions in Psycho-Analysis* (London: Tavistock, 1955), p. 6:

> More important still, I found that the transference situation—the backbone of the psycho-analytic procedure—can only be established and maintained if the patient is able to feel that the consulting-room or the play-room, indeed the whole analysis, is something separate from his ordinary home life. For only under such conditions can he overcome his resistances against experiencing and expressing thoughts, feelings, and desires, which are incompatible with convention, and in the case of children felt to be in contrast to much of what they have been taught.
>
> Perhaps, then, an ocean voyage is fun not because it cuts us off from ordinary life but because in being apparently cut off from ordinary life, we can afford to experience certain aspects of it.

12	Eugen Kogon, *The Theory and Practice of Hell* (New York: Berkley Publishing Corp., n.d.), p. 108.

13	Ibid., p. 103.

14	Writer's study of a mental hospital. A systematic treatment of patient joking in mental hospitals can be found in Rose Coser, "Some Social Functions of Laughter," *Human Relations,* 12 (1959), pp. 171–82. Somewhat similar practices are reported at length in a study of brain-damage cases held for surgery in a medical hospital: Edwin Weinstein and Robert Kahn, *Denial of Illness* (Springfield: Charles Thomas, 1955), chapter 16, "The Language of Denial."

15	See F. J. Roethlisberger and W. J. Dickson, *Management and the Worker* (Cambridge: Harvard University Press, 1950), p. 420, and the interesting paper by Lloyd Street, "Game Forms in the Factory Group," *Berkeley Publications in Society and Institutions,* 4 (1958), esp. pp. 48–50:

Piling consisted of passing to the "speed artist" or "ratebuster" a greater number of units than he could possibly assemble. The rules of the game were to embarrass and ridicule the fast worker without hurting any of the members of the line. Typically it was necessary to pile the "ratebuster" but once or twice in order to bring him into line with the production norms. (p. 48).

16	This view of sociability derives from W. L. Warner. He seems to have been the first American sociologist to have appreciated and studied this structural role of informal social life. For a recent treatment of sociability that deals with many of the themes discussed in this paper, see D. Riesman, R. J. Potter, and J. Watson, "Sociability, Permissiveness, and Equality," *Psychiatry,* 23 (1960), pp. 323–40.

17	Here see H. Wilensky, *Organizational Intelligence* (New York: Basic Books, 1967).

18	The classic case here was the breaking of the British code and security signal for Dutch agents in 1941 by the Germans and the eventual establishment of 17 false radio links with Britain along with the capture of all agents sent during a three-year period. See E. Cookridge, *Inside S.O.E.* (London: Arthur Barker, 1966), pp. 390ff.; also H Giskes, *London Calling North Pole* (London: Kimber, 1953).

19	F. Deakin and G. Storry, *The Case of Richard Sorge* (New York: Harper & Row, 1966), p. 181.

20	Ibid., p. 207.

21	Ibid., p. 215.

22	A version can be found in K. Singer, *Spies Who Changed History* (New York: Ace Books, 1960), pp. 140–7.

23	The label is mine; the notion that there may here be an intelligible area in its own right I take from T. C. Schelling.

24	A phrase first used in this connection by Herbert Blumer in "Social Psychology," ch. 4, in E. Schmidt, *Man and Society* (New York: Prentice-Hall, 1937), p. 153. Blumer also provides an excellent current statement in "Society as Symbolic Interaction," ch. 9, in A. Rose, *Human Behavior and Social Processes* (Boston: Houghton Mifflin, 1962), pp. 179–92.

PART IV

Frames and the Organization of Experience

12

Frame Analysis

From *Frame Analysis: An Essay on the Organization of Experience**

There is a venerable tradition in philosophy that argues that what the reader assumes to be real is but a shadow, and that by attending to what the writer says about perception, thought, the brain, language, culture, a new methodology, or novel social forces, the veil can be lifted. That sort of line, of course, gives as much a role to the writer and his writings as is possible to imagine and for that reason is pathetic. (What can better push a book than the claim that it will change what the reader thinks is going on?) A current example of this tradition can be found in some of the doctrines of social psychology and the W. I. Thomas dictum: "If men define situations as real, they are real in their consequences." This statement is true as it reads but false as it is taken. Defining situations as real certainly has consequences, but these may contribute very marginally to the events in progress; in some cases only a slight embarrassment flits across the scene in mild concern for those who tried to define the situation wrongly. All the world is not a stage—certainly the theater isn't entirely. (Whether you organize a theater or an aircraft factory, you need to find places for cars to park and coats to be checked, and these had better be real places, which, incidentally, had better carry real insurance against theft.) Presumably, a "definition of the situation" is almost always to be found, but those who are in the situation ordinarily do not *create* this definition, even though their society often can be said to do so; ordinarily, all they do is to assess correctly what the situation ought to be for them and then act accordingly. True, we personally negotiate aspects of all the arrangements under which we live, but often once these are negotiated, we continue on mechanically as though the matter had always been settled. So, too, there are occasions when we must wait until things are almost over before discovering what has been occurring and occasions of our own activity when we can considerably put off deciding what to claim we have been doing. But surely these are not the only principles of organization. Social life is dubious enough and ludicrous enough without having to wish it further into unreality.

Within the terms, then, of the bad name that the analysis of social reality has, this book presents another analysis of social reality. I try to follow a tradition established by William James in his famous chapter "The Perception of Reality,"[1] first published as an article in *Mind* in 1869. Instead of asking what reality is, he gave matters a subversive phenomenological twist, italicizing the following question: *Under what circumstances do we think things are real?* The important thing about reality, he implied, is our sense of its realness in contrast to our feeling that some things lack this quality. One can then ask under what conditions such a feeling is generated, and this question speaks to a small, manageable problem having to do with the camera and not what it is the camera takes pictures of.

In his answer, James stressed the factors of selective attention, intimate involvement, and noncontradiction by what is otherwise known. More important, he made a stab at differentiating the several different "worlds" that our attention and interest can make real for us, the possible subuniverses, the "orders of existence" (to use Aron Gurwitsch's phrase), in each of which an object of a given kind can have its proper being: the world of the senses, the world of scientific objects, the world of abstract philosophical truths, the worlds of myth and supernatural beliefs, the madman's world, etc. Each of these subworlds, according to James, has "its own special and separate style of existence,"[2] and "each world, *whilst it is attended to*, is real after its own fashion; only the reality lapses with the attention."[3] Then, after taking this radical stand, James copped out; he allowed that the world of the senses has a special status, being the one we judge to be the realest reality, the one that retains our liveliest belief, the one before which the other worlds must give way.[4] James in all this agreed with Husserl's teacher, Brentano, and implied, as phenomenology came to do, the need to distinguish between the content of a current perception and the reality status we give to what is thus enclosed or bracketed within perception.[5]

James' crucial device, of course, was a rather scandalous play on the word "world" (or "reality"). What he meant was not *the* world but a particular person's current world—and, in fact, as will be argued, not even that. There was no good reason to use such billowy words. James opened a door; it let in wind as well as light.

In 1945 Alfred Schutz took up James' theme again in a paper called "On Multiple Realities."[6] His argument followed James' surprisingly closely, but more attention was given to the possibility of uncovering the conditions that must be fulfilled if we are to generate one realm of "reality," one "finite province of meaning," as opposed to another. Schutz added the notion, interesting but not entirely convincing, that we experience a special kind of "shock" when suddenly thrust from one "world," say, that of dreams, to another, such as that of the theater:

There are as many innumerable kinds of different shock experiences as there are different finite provinces of meaning upon which I may bestow the accent of reality. Some instances are: the shock of falling asleep as the leap into the world of dreams; the inner transformation we endure if the curtain in the theater rises as the transition into the world of the stageplay; the radical change in our attitude if, before a painting, we permit our visual field to be limited by what is within the frame as the passage into the pictorial world; our quandary, relaxing into laughter, if, in listening to a joke, we are for a short time ready to accept the fictitious world of the jest as a reality in relation to which the world of our daily life takes on the character of foolishness; the child's turning toward his toy as the transition into the play-world; and so on. But also the religious experiences in all their varieties—for instance, Kierkegaard's experience of the "instant" as the leap into the religious sphere—are examples of such a shock, as well as the decision of the scientist to replace all passionate participation in the affairs of "this world" by a disinterested contemplative attitude.[7]

And although, like James, he assumed that one realm—the "working world"—had a preferential status, he was apparently more reserved than James about its objective character:

We speak of provinces of *meaning* and not of subuniverses because it is the meaning of our experience and not the ontological structure of the objects which constitute reality,[8]

attributing its priority to ourselves, not the world:

For we will find that the world of everyday life, the common-sense world, has a paramount position among the various provinces of reality, since only within it does communication with our fellow-men become possible. But the common-sense world is from the outset a sociocultural world, and the many questions connected with the inter-subjectivity of the symbolic relations originate within it, are determined by it, and find their solution within it.[9]

and to the fact that our bodies always participate in the everyday world whatever our interest at the time, this participation implying a capacity to affect and be affected by the everyday world.[10] So instead of saying of a subuniverse that it is generated in accordance with certain structural principles, one says it has a certain "cognitive style."

Schutz's paper (and Schutz in general) was brought to the attention of ethnographic sociologists by Harold Garfinkel, who further extended the argument about multiple realities by going on (at least in his early comments) to look for rules which, when followed, allow us to generate a "world" of a given kind. Presumably a machine designed according to the proper specifications could grind out the reality of our choice. The conceptual attraction here is obvious. A game such as chess generates a habitable universe for those who can follow it, a plane of being, a cast of characters with a seemingly unlimited number of different situations and acts through which to realize their natures and destinies. Yet much of this is reducible to a small set of interdependent rules and practices. If the meaningfulness of everyday activity is similarly dependent on a closed, finite set of rules, then explication of them would give one a powerful means of analyzing social life. For example, one could then see (following Garfinkel) that the significance of certain deviant acts is that they undermine the intelligibility of everything else we had thought was going on around us, including all next acts, thus generating diffuse disorder. To uncover the informing, constitutive rules of everyday behavior would be to perform the sociologist's alchemy—the transmutation of any patch of ordinary social activity into an illuminating publication. It might be added that although James and Schutz are convincing in arguing that something like the "world" of dreams is differently organized from the world of everyday experience, they are quite unconvincing in providing any kind of account as to how many different "worlds" there are and whether everyday, wide-awake life can actually be seen as but one rule-produced plane of being, if so seen at all. Nor has there been much success in describing constitutive rules of everyday activity.[11] One is faced with the embarrassing methodological fact that the announcement of constitutive rules seems an open-ended game that any number can play forever. Players usually come up with five or ten rules (as I will), but there are no grounds for thinking that a thousand additional assumptions might not be listed by others. Moreover, these students neglect to make clear that what they are often concerned with is not an individual's sense of what is real, but rather what it is he can get caught up in, engrossed in, carried away by; and this can be something he can claim is really going on and yet claim is not real. One is left, then, with the structural similarity between everyday life—neglecting for a moment the possibility that no satisfactory catalog might be possible of what to include therein—and the various "worlds" of make-believe but no way of knowing how this relationship should modify our view of everyday life.

Interest in the James–Schutz line of thought has become active recently among persons whose initial stimulus came from sources not much connected historically with the phenomenological tradition: The work of those who created what has come to be called "the theater of the absurd," most fully exhibited in the analytical dramas of Luigi Pirandello. The very useful paper by Gregory Bateson, "A Theory of Play and Phantasy,"[12] in which he directly raised the question of unseriousness and seriousness, allowing us to see what a startling thing experience is, such that a bit of serious activity can be used as a model for putting together unserious versions of the same activity, and that, on occasion, we may not know whether it is play or the real thing that is occurring. (Bateson introduced his own version of the notion of "bracketing," a usable one, and also the argument that individuals can intentionally produce framing confusion in those with whom they are dealing; it is in Bateson's paper that the term "frame" was proposed in roughly the sense in which I want to employ it.)[13] The work of John Austin, who, following Wittgenstein,[14] suggested again that what we mean by "really happening" is complicated, and that although an individual may dream unrealities, it is still proper to say of him on that occasion that he is really dreaming.[15] (I have also drawn on the work of a student of Austin, D. S. Schwayder, and his fine book, *The Stratification of Behavior.*)[16] The efforts of those who study (or at least publish on) fraud, deceit, misidentification, and other "optical" effects, and the work of those who study "strategic interaction," including the way in which concealing and revealing bear upon definitions of the situation. The useful paper by Barney Glaser and Anselm Strauss, "Awareness Contexts and Social Interaction."[17] Finally, the modern effort in linguistically oriented disciplines to employ the notion of a "code" as a device which informs and patterns all events that fall within the boundaries of its application.

I have borrowed extensively from all these sources, claiming really only the bringing of them together. My perspective is situational, meaning here a concern for what one individual can be alive to at a particular moment, this often involving a few other particular individuals and not necessarily restricted to the mutually monitored arena of a face-to-face gathering. I assume that when individuals attend to any current situation, they face the question: "What is it that's going on here?" Whether asked explicitly, as in times of confusion and doubt, or tacitly, during occasions of usual certitude, the question is put and the answer to it is presumed by the way the individuals then proceed to get on with the affairs at hand. Starting, then, with that question, this volume attempts to limn out a framework that could be appealed to for the answer.

Let me say at once that the question "What is it that's going on here?" is considerably suspect. Any event can be described in terms of a focus that includes a wide swath or a narrow one and—as a related but not identical matter—in terms of a focus that is close-up or distant. And no one has a theory as to what particular span and level will come to be the ones employed. To begin with, I must be allowed to proceed by picking my span and level arbitrarily, without special justification.[18]

A similar issue is found in connection with perspective. When participant roles in an activity are differentiated—a common circumstance—the view that one person has of what is going on is likely to be quite different from that of another. There is a sense in which what is play for the golfer is work for the caddy. Different interests will—in Schutz's phrasing—generate different motivational relevancies. (Moreover, variability is complicated here by the fact that those who bring different perspectives to the "same" events are likely to employ different spans and levels of focus.) Of course, in many cases some of those who are committed to differing points of view and focus may still be willing to acknowledge that theirs is not the official or "real" one. Caddies work at golf, as do instructors, but both appreciate that their job is special, since it has to do with servicing persons engaged in play. In any case, again I will initially assume the right to pick my point of view, my motivational relevancies, only limiting this choice of perspective to one that participants would easily recognize to be valid.

Further, it is obvious that in most "situations" many different things are happening simultaneously—things that are likely to have begun at different moments and may terminate dissynchronously.[19] To ask the question "What is *it* that's going on here?" biases matters in the direction of unitary exposition and simplicity. This bias, too, I must be temporarily allowed.

So, too, to speak of the "current" situation (just as to speak of something going on "here") is to allow reader and writer to continue along easily in their impression that they clearly know and agree on what they are thinking about. The amount of time covered by "current" (just as the amount of space covered by "here") obviously can vary greatly from one occasion to the next and from one participant to another; and the fact that participants seem to have no trouble in quickly coming to the same apparent understanding in this matter does not deny the intellectual importance of our trying to find out what this apparent consensus consists of and how it is established. To speak of something happening before the eyes of observers is to be on firmer ground than usual in the social sciences; but the ground is still shaky, and the crucial question of how a seeming agreement was reached concerning the identity of the "something" and the inclusiveness of "before the eyes" still remains.

Finally, it is plain that retrospective characterization of the "same" event or social occasion may differ very widely, that an individual's role in an undertaking can provide him with a distinctive evaluative assessment of what sort of an instance of the type the particular undertaking was. In that sense it has been argued, for example, that opposing rooters at a football game do not experience the "same" game,[20] and that what makes a party a good one for a participant who is made much of is just what makes it a bad one for a participant who thereby is made little of.

All of which suggests that one should even be uneasy about the easy way in which it is assumed that participants in an activity can be terminologically identified and referred to without issue. For surely, a "couple" kissing can also be a "man" greeting his "wife" or "John" being careful with "Mary's" makeup.

I only want to claim that although these questions are very important, they are not the only ones, and that their treatment is not necessarily required before one can proceed. So here, too, I will let sleeping sentences lie.

My aim is to try to isolate some of the basic frameworks of understanding available in our society for making sense out of events and to analyze the special vulnerabilities to which these frames of reference are subject. I start with the fact that from an individual's particular point of view, while one thing may momentarily appear to be what is really going on, in fact what is actually happening is plainly a joke, or a dream, or an accident, or a mistake, or a misunderstanding, or a deception, or a theatrical performance, and so forth. And attention will be directed to what it is about our sense of what is going on that makes it so vulnerable to the need for these various rereadings.

Elementary terms required by the subject matter to be dealt with are provided first. My treatment of these initial terms is abstract, and I am afraid the formulations provided are crude indeed by the standards of modern philosophy. The reader must initially bestow the benefit of mere doubt in order for us both to get to matters that (I feel) are less dubious.

The term "strip" will be used to refer to any arbitrary slice or cut from the stream of ongoing activity, including here sequences of happenings, real or fictive, as seen from the perspective of those subjectively involved in sustaining an interest in them. A strip is not meant to reflect a natural division made by the subjects of inquiry or an analytical division made by students who inquire; it will be used only to refer to any raw batch of occurrences (of whatever status in reality) that one wants to draw attention to as a starting point for analysis.

And of course much use will be made of Bateson's use of the term "frame." I assume that definitions of a situation are built up in accordance with principles of organization which govern events—at least social ones—and our subjective involvement in them; frame is the word I use to refer to such of these basic elements as I am able to identify. That is my definition of frame. My phrase "frame analysis" is a slogan to refer to the examination in these terms of the organization of experience.

In dealing with conventional topics, it is usually practical to develop concepts and themes in some sort of logical sequence: nothing coming earlier depends on something coming later, and, hopefully, terms developed at any one point are actually used in what comes thereafter. Often the complaint of the writer is that linear presentation constrains what is actually a circular affair, ideally requiring simultaneous introduction of terms, and the complaint of the reader is that concepts elaborately defined are not much used beyond the point at which the fuss is made about their meaning. In the analysis of frames, linear presentation is no great embarrassment. Nor is the defining of terms not used thereafter. The problem, in fact, is that once a term is introduced (this occurring at the point at which it is first needed), it begins to have too much bearing, not merely applying to what comes later, but reapplying in each chapter to what it has already applied to. Thus each succeeding section of the study becomes more entangled, until a step can hardly be made because of what must be carried along with it. The process closely follows the horrors of repetition songs, as if—in the case of frame analysis—what Old MacDonald had on his farm were partridge and juniper trees.

Discussions about frame inevitably lead to questions concerning the status of the discussion itself, because here terms applying to what is analyzed ought to apply to the analysis also. I proceed on the commonsense assumption that ordinary language and ordinary writing practices are sufficiently flexible to allow anything that one wants to express to get expressed. Here I follow Carnap's position:

> The sentences, definitions, and rules of the syntax of a language are concerned with the forms of that language. But, now, how are these sentences, definitions, and rules themselves to be correctly expressed? Is a kind of super-language necessary for the purpose? And, again, a third language to explain the syntax of this super-language, and so on to infinity? Or is it possible to formulate the syntax of a language within that language itself? The obvious fear will arise that in the latter case, owing to certain reflexive definitions, contradictions of a nature seemingly similar to those which are familiar both in Cantor's theory of transfinite aggregates and in the pre-Russellian logic might make their appearance. But we shall see later that without any danger of contradictions or antinomies emerging it is possible to express the syntax of a language in that language itself, to an extent which is conditioned by the wealth of means of expression of the language in question.[21]

Thus, even if one took as one's task the examination of the use made in the humanities and the less robust sciences of "examples," "illustrations," and "cases in point," the object being to uncover the folk theories of evidence which underlie resort to these devices, it would still be the case that examples and illustrations would probably have to be used, and they probably could be without entirely vitiating the analysis.

In turning to the issue of reflexivity and in arguing that ordinary language is an adequate resource for discussing it, I do not mean that these particular linguistic matters should block all other concerns. Methodological self-consciousness that is full, immediate, and persistent sets aside all study and analysis except that of the reflexive problem itself, thereby displacing fields of inquiry instead of contributing to them. Thus, I will throughout use quotation marks to suggest a special sense of the word so marked and not concern myself systematically with the fact that this device is routinely used in a variety of quite different ways,[22] that these seem to bear closely on the question of frame, and that I must assume that the context of use will automatically lead my readers and me to have the same understanding, although neither I nor they might be able to explicate the matter further. So, too, with the warning and the lead that ordinary language philosophers have given us. I know that the crucial term "real" may have been permanently Wittgensteined into a blur of slightly different uses, but proceed on the assumption that carefulness can gradually bring us to an understanding of basic themes informing diversity, a diversity which carefulness itself initially establishes, and that what is taken for granted concerning the meaning of this word can safely so be done until it is convenient to attend to what one has been doing.

A further caveat. There are lots of good grounds for doubting the kind of analysis about to be presented. I would do so myself if it weren't my own. It is too bookish, too general, too removed from fieldwork to have a good chance of being anything more than another mentalistic adumbration. And, as will be noted throughout, there are certainly things that cannot be nicely dealt with in the arguments that follow. (I coin a series of terms—some "basic"; but writers have been doing that to not much avail for years.) Nonetheless, some of the things in this world seem to urge the analysis I am here attempting, and the compulsion is strong to try to outline the framework that will perform this job, even if this means some other tasks get handled badly.

Another disclaimer. This book is about the organization of experience—something that an individual actor can take into his mind—and not the organization of society. I make no claim whatsoever to be talking about the core matters of sociology—social organization and social structure. Those matters have been and can continue to be quite nicely studied without reference to frame at all. I am not addressing the structure of social life but the structure of experience individuals have at any moment of their social lives. I personally hold society to be first in every way and any individual's current involvements to be second; this report deals only with matters that are second. This book will have weaknesses enough in the areas it claims to deal with; there is no need to find limitations in regard to what it does not set about to cover. Of course, it can be argued that to focus on the nature of personal experiencing—with the implication this can have for giving equally serious consideration to all matters that might momentarily concern the individual—is itself a standpoint with marked political implications, and that these are conservative ones. The analysis developed does not catch at the differences between the advantaged and disadvantaged classes and can be said to direct attention away from such matters. I think that is true. I can only suggest that he who would combat false consciousness and awaken people to their true interests has much to do, because the sleep is very deep. And I do not intend here to provide a lullaby but merely to sneak in and watch the way the people snore.

★   ★   ★

It has been argued that a strip of activity will be perceived by its participants in terms of the rules or premises of a primary framework, whether social or natural, and that activity so perceived provides the model for two basic kinds of transformation—keying and fabrication. It has also been argued that these frameworks are not merely a matter of mind but correspond in some sense to the way in which an aspect of the activity itself is organized—especially activity directly involving social agents. Organizational premises are involved, and these are something cognition somehow arrives at, not something cognition creates or generates. Given their understanding of what it is that is going on, individuals fit their actions to this understanding and ordinarily find that the ongoing world supports this fitting. These organizational premises—sustained both in the mind and in activity—I call the frame of the activity.

It was also suggested that activity interpreted by the application of particular rules and inducing fitting actions from the interpreter, activity, in short, that organizes matter for the interpreter, itself is located in a physical, biological, and social world. Fanciful words can speak about make-believe places, but these words can only be spoken *in* the real world. Even so with dreaming. When Coleridge dreamed his "Kubla Khan," he dreamed it *in* an undreaming world: he had to begin and terminate his dreaming in the "natural" flow of time; he had to use up a bed, a good portion of the night, and apparently some supplies of a medicinal kind in order to be carried away into his dream; and a sufficient control of the environment was assumed, pertaining to air, temperature, and noise level so that he could go on dreaming. (Think what has to be organized materially and correctly so that an astronaut in flight will be able to dream.) It is this intermeshing of framed activity in the everyday unstaged world that I want to consider in this chapter.

The relation of the frame to the environing world in which the framing occurs is complex. An illustration. Two men sit down at a game-equipped table and decide whether to play chess or checkers. In terms of the game-generated realm in which they will soon be lodged, the difference between chess and checkers is considerable; quite different dramas will unfold involving quite different game-generated characters. But should a stranger or employer or a janitor or policeman approach the two players, it will usually be quite sufficient to know that the men are playing a board game. The gearing of the game into the immediately surrounding workaday world is largely in terms of this relatively abstract categorization, for what are involved are such matters as the electric light, the room space, the time needed, the right of others to openly watch and under certain circumstances to interrupt the men and ask them to postpone the game or shift its physical location, the right of the players to phone their wives to say they will be delayed because of a game to finish. These and a host of other detailed ways in which what is going on must find a place in the rest of the ongoing world are relatively independent of *which* game is being played. By and large it is the mode of transformation, not what is thus transformed, that is geared into the world. And yet, of course, this independence is not complete. There are implications in the difference between chess and checkers that bear upon the world external to the playing of these games. For example, in America those seen playing chess tend to be regarded as possibly cultivated, an identification not secured by those seen playing checkers. Also, if but one set of each of the games is available, then the players who elect to play one of the games can force a next pair to play the other. And, of course, the players must come to whichever game they decide to play with prior knowledge of it. (They must enter also with a desire to play and a willingness to play each other, but these psychological prerequisites do not much differentiate between chess and checkers.) It should be repeated: a similar argument can be advanced in regard to any self-absorbing, fanciful activity.[23] A cup can be filled from any realm, but the handle belongs to the realm that qualifies as reality.

Observe that any discussion of the gearing of the playing of a game into its surround—any discussion of the rim of this frame—leads to apparent paradox. The understanding that players and nonplayers have of where the claims of the ongoing world leave off and where the claims of play take over is part of what the players bring to their playing from the outside world, and yet is a necessary constituent of play. The very points at which the internal activity leaves off and the external activity takes over—the rim of the frame itself—become generalized by the individual and taken into his framework of interpretation, thus becoming, recursively, an additional part of the frame. In general, then, the assumptions that cut an activity off from the external surround also mark the ways in which this activity is inevitably bound to the surrounding world.

This paradoxical issue is a harsh fact of life for those who we might think had other business. When two individuals come together to engage in one tossing of a coin, we might be brought to admit that enough light will have to be available to allow the gamblers to read the fall. But there is no need to think we might have to supply the gamblers with a snack and a bathroom. When the game is longer lasting, these latter services might have to be laid on, for wherever one's person goes, so, after a certain while, goes the role-irrelevant need for basic caterings. And the material equipment may come to require refurbishment. (Thus, in casinos, arrangements must be made to replace worn cards and to wash dirty chips.) But note that very often the services required by men and equipment—whatever the realm of activity sustained by what is thus kept in working order—are institutionally available, part of the fixed social plant. Indeed, the players and equipment used in quite different activities can employ the same service in a close interweaving of use. All this routine servicing allows individuals to take the matter for granted and to forget about the conditions that are being quietly satisfied. But there is a special set of activities calculated to remind us of the anchoring of our doings, namely, ones which draw us away for an extended time from socially institutionalized provisioning. Family camping trips, mountaineering expeditions, and armies in the field provide examples. Here the institutional plant must be carried along; logistics acquires a name and becomes a conscious problem, as much a part of the plans as the story line.[24]

The question of how a framed activity is embedded in ongoing reality appears to be closely tied to two others, namely, how an activity can be keyed and (especially) how it can be fabricated. William James himself gives us reason to inquire along these lines.

When James asked, "Under what circumstances do we think things real?" he assumed that somehow reality in itself was not enough and, instead, principles of convincingness were what really counted. (His answer, no doubt inadequate, does raise the question as to how it is that the world is tied together for us.) Now it might be thought that these principles could be fulfilled at times when what seemed to be going on was not in fact going on, and this is no doubt true. Immediately, then, a basic dilemma is produced. Whatever it is that generates sureness is precisely what will be employed by those who want to mislead us. For surely, although some evidence will be much more difficult than other evidence to fake, and therefore will be of special use as a test of what is really going on, the more it is relied upon for this reason the more reason there is to make the effort to fake it. In any case, it turns out that the study of how to uncover deception is also by and large the study of how to build up fabrications. The way in which strips of activity are geared into the world and the way in which deceptions can be fabricated turn out, paradoxically, to be much the same. In consequence one can learn how our sense of ordinary reality is produced by examining something that is easier to become conscious of, namely, how reality is mimicked and/or how it is faked.

★   ★   ★

1.   This study began with the observation that we (and a considerable

number of theys) have the capacity and inclination to use concrete, actual activity—activity that is meaningful in its own right—as a model upon which to work transformations for fun, deception, experiment, rehearsal, dream, fantasy, ritual, demonstration, analysis, and charity. These lively shadows of events are geared into the ongoing world but not in quite the close way that is true of ordinary, literal activity.

Here, then, is a warrant for taking ordinary activity seriously, a portion of the paramount reality. For even as it is shown that we can become engrossed in fictive planes of being, giving to each in its turn the accent of reality, so it can be shown that the resulting experiences are derivative and insecure when placed up against the real thing. James and even Schutz can be read in this way. But if that is comfort, it comes too easy.

First, we often use "real" simply as a contrast term. When we decide that something is unreal, the reality it isn't need not itself be very real, indeed, can just as well be a dramatization of events as the events themselves—or a rehearsal of the dramatization, or a painting of the rehearsal, or a reproduction of the painting. Any of these latter can serve as the original of which something is a mere mock-up, leading one to think that what is sovereign is relationship, not substance. (A valuable watercolor stored—for safe-keeping—in a portfolio of reproduced masters is, in that context, a fake reproduction.)

Second, any more or less protracted strip of everyday, literal activity seen as such by all its participants is likely to contain differently framed episodes, these having different realm statuses. A man finishes giving instructions to his postman, greets a passing couple, gets into his car, and drives off. Certainly this strip is the sort of thing that writers from James on have had in mind as everyday reality. But plainly, the traffic system is a relatively narrow role domain, impersonal yet closely geared into the ongoing world; greetings are part of the ritual order in which the individual can figure as a representative of himself, a realm of action that is geared into the world but in a special and restricted way. Instruction giving belongs to the realm of occupational roles, but it is unlikely that the exchange will have occurred without a bordering of small talk cast in still another domain. The physical competence exhibited in giving over and receiving a letter (or opening and closing a car door) pertains to still another order, the bodily management of physical objects close at hand. Moreover, once our man goes on his way, driving can become routine, and his mind is likely to leave the road and dart for moments into fantasy. Suddenly finding himself in a tight spot, he may simultaneously engage in physically adroit evasion *and* prayer, melding the "rational" and the "irrational" as smoothly as any primitive and as characteristically. (Note that all these differently framed activities could be subsumed under the term "role"—for example, the role of suburbanite—but that would provide a hopelessly gross conceptualization for our purposes.)

Of course, this entire stratified strip of overlapped framings could certainly be transformed as a whole for presentation on the screen, and it would there be systematically different by one lamination, giving to the whole a different realm status from the original. But what the cinematic version would be a copy of, that is, an unreal instance of, would itself be something that was not homogeneous with respect to reality, itself something shot through with various framings and their various realms.

And by the same argument, a movie showing could itself be seen as part of the ordinary working world. It is easily possible to imagine the circumstances in which an individual attended the movies and became involved in its offering as one phase of an evening's outing—a round that might include eating, talking, and other actualities. Granting this, one can imagine the circumstances in which the moviegoer might compare the reality of the evening's round with watching a TV drama in which such an evening was depicted. Contrariwise, in court, establishing an alibi, our individual could avow that he really had gone to the movies on a particular evening in question, and that doing so was for him an ordinary, uneventful, everyday thing to do, when, in fact, he had really been doing something else.

2.   But there are deeper issues. In arguing that everyday activity provides an original against which copies of various kinds can be struck, the assumption was that the model was something that could be actual and, when it was, would be more closely enmeshed in the ongoing world than anything modeled after it. However, in many cases, what the individual does in serious life, he does in relationship to cultural standards established for the doing and for the social role that is built up out of such doings. Some of these standards are addressed to the maximally approved, some to the maximally disapproved. The associated lore itself draws from the moral traditions of the community as found in folk tales, characters in novels, advertisements, myth, movie stars and their famous roles, the Bible, and other sources of exemplary representation. So everyday life, real enough in itself, often seems to be a laminated adumbration of a pattern or model that is itself a typification of quite uncertain realm status.[25] (A famous face who models a famous-name dress provides in her movements a keying, a mock-up, of an everyday person walking about in everyday dress, something, in short, modeled *after* actual wearings; but obviously she is also a model *for* everyday appearance-while-dressed, which appearance is, as it were, always a bridesmaid but never a bride.) Life may not be an imitation of art, but ordinary conduct, in a sense, is an imitation of the proprieties, a gesture at the exemplary forms, and the primal realization of these ideals belong more to make-believe than to reality.

Moreover, what people understand to be the organization of their experience, they buttress, and perforce, self-fulfillingly. They develop a corpus of cautionary tales, games, riddles, experiments, newsy stories, and other scenarios which elegantly confirm a frame-relevant view of the workings of the world. (The young especially are caused to dwell on these manufactured clarities, and it comes to pass that they will later have a natural way to figure the scenes around them.) And the human nature that fits with this view of viewing does so in part because its possessors have learned to comport themselves so as to render this analysis true of them. Indeed, in countless ways and ceaselessly, social life takes up and freezes into itself the understandings we have of it. (And since my analysis of frames admittedly merges with the one that subjects themselves employ, mine, in that degree, must function as another supportive fantasy.)

In looking at strips of everyday, actual doings involving flesh-and-blood individuals in face-to-face dealings with one another, it is tempting and easy to draw a clear contrast to copies presented in fictive realms of being. The copies can be seen as mere transformations of an original, and everything uncovered about the organization of fictive scenes can be seen to apply only to copies, not to the actual world. Frame analysis would then become the study of everything but ordinary behavior.

However, although this approach might be the most congenial, it is not the most profitable. For actual activity is not merely to be contrasted with something obviously unreal, such as dreams, but also to sports, games, ritual, experimentation, practicing, and other arrangements, including deception, and these activities are not all that fanciful. Furthermore, each of these alternatives to the everyday is different from the others in a different way. Also, of course, everyday activity itself contains quickly changing frames, many of which generate events which depart considerably from anything that might be called literal. Finally, the variables and elements of organization found in nonliteral realms of being, albeit manifest and utilized in distinctive ways in each of these realms, are also found in the organization of actual experience, again in a version distinctive to it.

Notes

1   William James, *Principles of Psychology*, vol. 2 (New York: Dover Publications, 1950), chapter 21, pp. 283–324. Here, as throughout, italics in quoted materials are as in the original.
2   Ibid., p. 291.
3   Ibid., p. 293
4   James' interest in the varieties-of-worlds problem was not fleeting. In his *Varieties of Religious Experience* (New York: Longmans, Green & Co., 1902) he approached the same question but through a different route.
5   "But who does not see that in a disbelieved or doubted or interrogative or conditional proposition, the ideas are combined in the same identical way in which they are in a proposition which is solidly believed" (James, *Principles of Psychology*, 2:286). Aron

Gurwitsch in his *The Field of Consciousness* (Pittsburgh: Duquesne University Press, 1964) makes a similar comment in a discussion of Husserl:

> Among such characters we mentioned those concerning modes of presentation, as when a thing is one time perceived, another time remembered or merely imagined, or when a certain state of affairs (the identical matter of a proposition) is asserted or denied, doubted, questioned, or deemed probable. [p. 327]

6   First appearing in *Philosophy and Phenomenological Research*, V (1945): 533–76; reprinted in his *Collected Papers*, 3 vols. (The Hague: Martinus Nijhoff, 1962), 1:207–59.) A later version is "The Stratification of the Life-World," in Alfred Schutz and Thomas Luckmann, *The Structures of the Life-World*, trans. Richard M. Zaner and H. Tristram Engelhardt, Jr. (Evanston, Ill.: Northwestern University Press, 1973), pp. 21–98. An influential treatment of Schutz's ideas is Peter L. Berger and Thomas Luckmann, *The Social Construction of Reality* (Garden City, N.Y.: Doubleday & Company, Anchor Books, 1966).

7   Schutz, *Collected Papers*, 1:231.

8   Ibid., p. 230. See also Alfred Schutz, *Reflections on the Problem of Relevance*, ed. Richard M. Zaner (New Haven, Conn.: Yale University Press, 1970), p. 125.

9   From "Symbol, Reality, and Society," Schutz, *Collected Papers*, 1:294.

10 Ibid., p. 342.

11 Schutz's various pronouncements seem to have hypnotized some students into treating them as definitive rather than suggestive. His version of the "cognitive style" of everyday life he states as follows:

1. a specific tension of consciousness, namely, wide-awakeness, originating in full attention to life;

2   a specific *epoché*, namely suspension of doubt;

3   a prevalent form of spontaneity, namely working (a meaningful spontaneity based upon a project and characterized by the intention of bringing about the projected state of affairs by bodily movements gearing into the outer world);

4   a specific form of experiencing one's self (the working self as the total self);

5   a specific form of sociality (the common intersubjective world of communication and social action);

6   a specific time-perspective (the standard time originating in an interaction between *durée* and cosmic time as the universal temporal structure of the intersubjective world).

> These are at least some of the features of the cognitive style belonging to this particular province of meaning. As long as our experiences of this world—the valid as well as the invalidated ones—partake of this style we may consider this province of meaning as real, we may bestow upon it the accent of reality. [Ibid., pp. 230–1.]

12 *Psychiatric Research Reports* 2, American Psychiatric Association (December 1955), pp. 39–51. Now reprinted in his *Steps to an Ecology of Mind* (New York: Ballantine Books, 1972), pp. 177–93. A useful exegesis is William F. Fry, Jr., *Sweet Madness: A Study of Humor* (Palo Alto, Calif.: Pacific Books, 1968).

13 Edward T. Cone, in the first chapter of his *Musical Form and Musical Performance* (New York: W. W. Norton & Company, 1968), quite explicitly uses the term "frame" in much the same way that Bateson does and suggests some of the same lines of inquiry, but I think quite independently.

14 See, for example, Ludwig Wittgenstein, *Philosophical Investigations*, trans. G. E. M. Anscombe (Oxford: Basil Blackwell, 1958), pt. 2, sec. 7.

15 See, for example, chapter 7 in his *Sense and Sensibilia* (Oxford: Oxford University Press, 1962).

16 London: Routledge & Kegan Paul, 1965.

17 *American Sociological Review*, XXIX (1964): 669–79.

18 See the discussion by Emanuel A. Schegloff, "Notes on a Conversational Practice: Formulating Place," in David Sudnow, ed., *Studies in Social Interaction* (New York: The Free Press, 1972), pp. 75–119. There is a standard criticism of "role" as a concept which presents the same argument.

19 Nicely described by Roger G. Barker and Herbert F. Wright, *Midwest and Its Children* (Evanston, Ill.: Row, Peterson & Company, 1964), chapter 7, "Dividing the Behavior Stream," pp. 225–73.

20 Presented perhaps overstrongly in a well-known early paper by Albert H. Hastorf and Hadley Cantril, "They Saw A Game: A Case Study," *Journal of Abnormal and Social Psychology*, XLIX (1954): 129–234.

21 Rudolf Carnap, *The Logical Syntax of Language*, trans. Amethe Smeaton (London: Kegan Paul, Trench, Trubner & Co., 1937), p. 3.

22 I. A. Richards, for example, has a version in his *How to Read a Page* (New York: W. W. Norton & Company, 1942):

> We all recognize—more or less unsystematically—that quotation marks serve varied purposes:
>
> 1. Sometimes they show merely that we are quoting and where our quotation begins and ends.
> 2. Sometimes they imply that the word or words within them are in some way open to question and are only to be taken in some special sense with reference to some special definition.
> 3. Sometimes they suggest further that what is quoted is nonsense or that there is really no such thing as the thing they profess to name.
> 4. Sometimes they suggest that the words are improperly used. The quotation marks are equivalent to *the so-called.*
> 5. Sometimes they only indicate that we are talking of the words as distinguished from their meanings. "Is" and "at" are shorter than "above." "Chien" means what "dog" means, and so forth.
>
> There are many other uses . . . [p. 66]

23 Simmel presents the case for works of art in "The Handle," in Georg Simmel et al., *Essays on Sociology, Philosophy and Aesthetics*, ed. Kurt H. Wolff (New York: Harper & Row, 1965):

> Modern theories of art strongly emphasize that the essential task of painting and sculpture is the depiction of the spatial organization of things. Assenting readily to this, one may then easily fail to recognize that space within a painting is a structure altogether different from the real space we experience. Within actual space an object can be touched, whereas in a painting it can only be looked at; each portion of real space is experienced as part of an infinite expanse, but the space of a picture is experienced as a self-enclosed world; the real object interacts with everything that surges past or hovers around it, but the content of a work of art cuts off these threads, fusing only its own elements into a self-sufficient unity. Hence, the work of art leads its life beyond reality. To be sure, the work of art draws its content from reality; but from visions of reality it builds a sovereign realm. While the canvas and the pigment on it are parts of reality, the work of art constructed out of them exists in an ideal space which can no more come in contact with actual space than tones can touch smells. [p. 267]

24 War games introduce a special twist. Since logistics is a major part of a military undertaking, the *practicing* of such a doing must include attention to supplies, medical treatment, communication channels, and all the other paraphernalia of a community. But since those engaging in the exercise will in fact be cut off somewhat from institutional services, it follows that real supplies, medical facilities, communication channels, and so

forth will have to be assured, and, moreover, carefully kept from getting mixed up with the practice versions. Observe that the more the circumstances of the exercise give weight to logistics and the need to practice at it, the greater are likely to be the real logistics requirements.

25   See Alfred Schutz, "Symbol, Reality and Society," *Collected Papers*, vol. 1 (The Hague: Martinus Nijhoff, 1962), p. 328.

13

Frame Analysis of Talk

From "Felicity's Condition"*

A *presupposition* (or assumption, or implication, or background expectation) can be defined very broadly as a state of affairs we take for granted in pursuing a course of action. We can perform these acts of faith without "doing" anything. And even appreciation figures variably. We may never come to be aware of something our action presupposes; having once been aware, we may no longer be; having not been aware, we may come to be; being aware, we may try to conceal this fact from others or to allude to it indirectly. Yet, according to one reading of the term, if we explicitly attest to a condition of our action we cease to *presuppose* it, although this ceasing does not lessen our dependency on it.

By this broad definition, in planning at night to leave at dawn, we would be presupposing the sun will come up. We do and it will. So what? We also presuppose that an earthquake will not occur before morning and drop us forever through a fault, and there is an infinitude of other possibilities. Clearly, almost all of what we presuppose is footless to any but those who discuss presuppositions and want to make the point that there are presuppositions of concern to no one. So it behooves the student not merely to uncover presuppositions but also to present reasons for doing so, and not merely the reason just cited. Opportunity abounds. An imaginative analyst ought to be able to show the significance of presuppositions that no one else had ever thought would signify,[1] and certainly every quirk and crisis in social life generates sudden insight in this connection, spreading appreciation that what had been unthinkingly taken for granted should have been given thought. For indeed, we are as unthinking about many of the political and economic conditions of our lives as we are about the sun coming up.

Plainly there are unstated grounds of our action that particular others do not require for their understanding of it and their further response (if any) to it. The contrast is with "social presuppositions," these incorporating a double theme, namely, our tacitly taking something for granted (whether aware of having done so or not), and also unabashedly, even unthinkingly,

* Originally published in *American Journal of Sociology* 89 (1), pp. 1–3, 25–51. Reproduced by permission of the University of Chicago Press. © 1983 by The University of Chicago.

counting on others involved in the action doing likewise, at least enough so they can easily interpret and understand our action accordingly.[2]

Of social presuppositions I propose to deal with only one sort, those involving language use. After all, more perhaps than any other class of actions, writing or saying makes sense only if the actor intends a meeting of the minds—if only enough to inform self-interestedly. Indeed, almost always in using language we take for granted that what we want to get across will get across (along with the message—true or not—that this is the avowed and controlling purpose of our action). Further, if we could not rely on our listeners grasping the point without extended elaboration, we could hardly afford the time to say anything; similarly, if they could not depend on our taking into consideration what they already know, they could hardly afford the time to listen.

The purpose of this paper, then, will be to consider social presuppositions in language use, particularly speech, not writing. Surely a classical socio-logical theme. And just as surely I must presuppose, as every student of presuppositions has done and does, the rule that accounts for how I decide which social presuppositions are worth discovering. For as with background expectations in general, there are countless social presuppositions in speech that do not have even academic interest. And the presuppositions that ought to be of interest, themselves involve embarrassment; after all, it should be apparent that spoken (and written) discourse, in context, has the capacity to presuppose anything in the world (including bits of the universe beyond), the sorting of which might well seem to be a hapless, immodest undertaking.

So there are problems. One can take encouragement from the fact that a wide range of social presuppositions in discourse appear to be systematically represented through the ways in which we select, order, and prosodically time and intone our words, thus providing a record that is engagingly objec-tive and sensitive—a workable tracing (indeed, machine-preservable) of practices that could otherwise be rendered only by impressionistic analysis. So one can try to work backward from the verbal consequences of presup-positions to what is presupposed, allowing the direction of analysis to constrain what one examines.

★   ★   ★

So far I have focused on the issue of cognitive presuppositions as reflected in the syntax and prosody of utterances. But I hope it has become clear that another phrasing would have been possible, one that directly addresses the quite fundamental issue which so far linguists have not been able to resolve, though not for want of trying: namely, how, in a systematic way, to get from what an individual says to what that individual means.

One attempt to solve the problem was initiated by John Austin as an implication of his notion of "performative utterance," or "performative," namely, an utterance that does something. The tack was to consider the condition which would render such performance null and void, that is, "infelicitous." The assumption is that the effective execution of a performative would have to satisfy a list of "felicity conditions."[3] Austin (1965, pp. 14–15) lists six—a rather modest number to which to reduce the subject matter of those who study face-to-face interaction. Later John Searle (1969) refined Austin's effort to classify types of performatives (now called speech acts) and made an effort to explicate the felicity conditions (now partly covered by the term "sincerity conditions") presupposed by some of them. This line of work has merged with an analysis initiated by Paul Grice (1975), who recommends four maxims cooperative speakers must be guided by if their utterances are to be maximally usable by recipients.[4]

The short list of Austin–Searle conditions for the felicitous performance of a speech act and the shorter list of Gricean maxims are presented as culture and context free; they (along with the rest of "speech act theory") have had a vast impact on sociolinguistics. As an analysis of speech in context, the whole approach might strike the sociologist as somewhat optimistic, if not silly. However, there is an important element in this scholastic foray into microanalysis which provides some useful suggestions as to the way the mind works in conversational analysis. For it is assumed that felicity conditions (broadly concerned) and conversational maxims will constantly be breached, causing the hearer to reread the utterance as an expression of unseriousness, sarcasm, understatement, rhetorical question, and the like. These "keyings" provide something like a systematic convention-based means for shifting from what is more or less literally said to what is meant, a presupposed interpretive repertoire that introduces much flexibility in the presuppositional bases of reference and inference. Now, although felicity conditions and conversational maxims may provide us with an inadequate means for determining when an individual is serious or cooperating as an interactant, the patent breaching of one or more of these rules may provide us with a culturally recognized signal that something unserious, skittish, or fey is intended.

In this paper I will be concerned with a further point, namely, what happens when these rereading rules, these presuppositions about presuppositions, are *themselves* breached. For when the "literal" (or, in Austin's terms, "locutionary") content of an utterance makes no sense in the context, *and* neither do conventional keyings, then a drastic interpretation must be made: namely, that the speaker is temporarily incompetent, or, if there is no corroborating evidence for that, that she or he is deranged.

Take, for example, anaphora. Its use is not only a right but also, betimes, an obligation. Speaker's failure to exploit available means for succinctness can lead hearer, and be meant to lead hearer, to look for an indirectly expressed intent, namely, that the speaker is being unserious, emphatic, sarcastic, ironic, distancing, overly polite, and the like. So, too, when hearer seems to fail to catch the speaker's obvious intent and responds as though the speaker's words were being taken literally; this also must be read as anger, joking, teasing, and so forth. However, when these "normal" ways of saying one thing and intending another, or acting as though speaker has been misunderstood, do not plausibly account for what is in the mind of the individual in question, then a second interpretive step must be taken, and another order of explanation must be sought. To wit: that the individual is temporarily incompetent owing, for example, to tiredness, preoccupation, inebriation, or narcosis. Or, if not this, then unhappily that he or she is strange, odd, peculiar, in a word, nutty. Either their mind is fully and fixedly not where it should be or they presume the other's is where it is not reasonable to expect it to be, or both. Each utterance presupposes, and contributes to the presuppositions of, a jointly inhabitable mental world, and even though such worlds last only as long as there is a warrant for a common focus of cognitive attention, one should not think one can go around failing to sustain them.

As with anaphora, so, too, with topicality. In many states of talk, an abrupt change in topic is to be read as a pointed thing, done to convey something about speaker's relation to prior topic that cannot easily be put into words without, for example, giving offense or making disclosures. Should such readings of breaches not be available in the circumstances, hearer can only surmise that speaker is temporarily not himself, or, failing that, that something is profoundly defective in his relation to what has been jointly entered into.

Perhaps a qualification should be added here. As suggested, in conversation persons are not obliged to adhere to the topic (even versions unanticipated by the initiator), providing they give a little prefatory excuse for failing to do so. So in some conversations, topic is more often evaded than sustained. But note that there are two senses in which mere excuses are not really mere. First, an excuse provides a warning that a topic change is about to occur and so warns the hearer that something outside the current focus is about to be placed in attention, and that a memory search may now be required in order to make sense of what the upcoming remarks will prove to deal with. Thus, "alerts" and "disjunct markers." Second, when speakers show they are concerned about norms with respect to topicality or relevance albeit not sustaining them on this occasion, their demonstration does indeed accomplish what appropriately relevant behavior would do, namely, give evidence that they are properly alive to the current situation.[5]

All of which leads me to hazard a definition of the felicity condition behind all other felicity conditions, namely, *Felicity's Condition:* to wit, any arrangement which leads us to judge an individual's verbal acts to be not a manifestation of strangeness. Behind Felicity's Condition is our sense of what it is to be sane. Well, of course, that has been argued for some years now. What is new (as opposed to given) is that syntactic and pragmatic analyses are to be seen as describing in empirical detail how we are obliged to display that we are sane during spoken interaction, whether through the management of our own words or the display of our understanding of the words of others.

I have so far considered the bearing of some linguistic analysis on the question of what we take for granted when we talk to one another, and I have not been fastidious in pointing out the normative presuppositions of some of this work. It is time now to reverse directions and consider what sociological analysis can contribute to linguistic formulations.

Given Marsha and John lodged in face-to-face talk, the argument has been that their cumulative discourse to that point, their jointly perceivable surroundings, and the knowledge each knows or assumes the other has brought to the encounter, can all provide understandings that are presupposed in the phrasing of a next utterance and without which the relevant meaning of the utterance might not be easily discoverable. These understandings can readily be seen as essentially *cognitive* in character, the only normative feature being the obligation to speak in an understandable way. However, if for a moment we think of these three sources of presupposition not so much as a resource to use in speaking laconically but as bases of constraint in formulating utterances, then it becomes reasonable to consider another factor: the moral norms of considerateness which bind individuals qua interactants. Delicacy, courtesy, modesty, politeness—these are the sort of attributes that are involved.

Take, for example, referential tact. Speaker is obliged not only to be alive to what is in his hearer's head—alive enough to find a phrasing that is succinct yet sufficiently detailed—but also to find a phrasing that is inoffensive and not indelicate in the circumstances. Meeting John on the street, his friend has the right (indeed, often the obligation) to ask him how his wife Marsha is and to use her first name as a fully specifying designation; John will know which Marsha his friend is referring to and will have a ready answer. Meeting John on the street just after John (it is known) has broken up with Marsha, his friend omits the nicety, and not because John would not know who was being spoken of. (However, now asking after Marsha can be in order if the phrasing carefully distinguishes the concern from the perfunctory kind, somewhat as it might were John and Marsha still a couple but she had just spent her first week in prison.) Our saying something that is considered to be salacious, intrusive, ill-timed, impertinent, or importuning is not to presume wrongly on what the other can easily bring to mind, but to presume in quite another sense, namely, to raise questions that the recipient might want to avoid considering with the likes of us. Thus, to say that there is a set of persons that John and Marsha *can* effectively specify to each other for the first time in a conversation by means of first name does not tell us whether they are free to do so. One would also have to know whether John and Marsha are in such a social relation to each other and to the mentioned party that this use of a familiar form of reference is thought to be appropriate between them. John, speaking to his and Marsha's seven-year-old, asks the child where mummy is, not where Marsha is, although the child will know perfectly well who is being referred to by that proper name when, for example, she hears her father use it in talk to an adult family friend. This reference practice, then, is based not merely on what has been referred to in the talk, can be pointed to, or imported informationally; it is also based on the verbal license and constraint normatively binding the two participants. (Observe, although these constraints specifically condition speech, neither a syntactician nor a phonologist would have much to say about them.)

John can, of course, *refer* to these niceties using laconic expressions to so do, but then he would be taking for granted Marsha's knowing what he was talking about, and this is quite a different kind of assumption than that of his presupposing that Marsha will have (and exercise) these politeness norms in the uptake of his remarks. To presuppose another's understanding is not to presuppose another's capacity and disposition for considerateness in talk.

Now it should be seen that one's cognitive presuppositions about the interactional capacities of others present can become closely mingled with politeness understandings, so much so that on occasion the distinction may not be easily or even profitably made. For example, when John speaks to Marsha he cognitively presupposes that she can understand and speak the language he uses (much as he does that transmission conditions will allow her to do so effectively), but he also presupposes that she will be reasonable enough to put her language capacity at the disposal of the exchange he has initiated. And there will be similar presuppositions regarding the mechanics of encounters. For example, John will assume that when he follows conventions for summoning others into talk, they will allow themselves to be summoned. That once lodged in a state of talk they will give their attention over to it. That they will allow him to complete his turn without "unduly" interrupting him and will take a turn when the prior turn allows or requires it. That topicality will be respected. That a modicum of wariness will be maintained to deal with mis-framings should they seem to occur. That when the encounter is to terminate, all parties will have fair warning. And so forth. (Which is not to say—as Candace West reminds me—that when John is Marsha [i.e., when the person in question is female] these politeness presuppositions will not be qualified by still others regarding the relative weight that the two sexes can anticipate in cross-sex talk.)

More specifically, if the participants can assume that their purpose is solely to use talk in the rational, efficient, instrumental pursuance of some joint enterprise—and presumably this happens occasionally—then something like the Gricean conversational maxims (or rather, admonishments) will apply, establishing normative, not merely cognitive, standards for the exchange of relevant information. What we find in these cases is that cognitive requirements for sustaining staccato, machine-readable communication are underwritten as part of the considerateness the participants owe one another in the circumstances.

Although constraints on the laconic formulation of utterances (whether due to what has not been provided in the text, in the local environment, or in joint experience beyond the situation) do not seem to be entirely of the same order as constraints due to politeness rules, there is one critical way in which they are similar: response to apparent violation. Most literally offensive utterances are not designed to be taken at face value—for example, as malicious or insulting or inconsiderate. Rather, as Lakoff (1973) suggests, a framework of reinterpretation is applied, leading the recipient of the apparent offense to read it as jocularity, inadvertence, or another of our standard discountings. And just as with cognitive presuppositions, if the context supports neither a "literal" interpretation nor a conventional reframing, then some kind of deep mindlessness may have to be imputed.

I have argued that when you ask another what she thought of the movie last night, a variety of constraints can be involved. The question is not merely, How do you cast or frame your utterance so that it will presuppose all the information that is shared by all the participants but no more than is shared? (Although admittedly a principled account of that achievement would be useful to have.) Nor, as already suggested, is the question merely that of maneuvering among the never having been known, the recallable, and the already in mind. For these are all largely cognitive matters. The question is also that of social propriety—presuppositions and presumptions. And central here will be whether the putative speaker is acquainted with the putative recipient, and whether a state of talk already binds them or must be first established.

Consider this: You see a stranger at the movies whose appearance happens to stick in your mind. The next day you see this person on the street. You approach and without further ado ask, "What did you think of the movie last night?" No way. However, if the two of you end up next to each other in a queue that turns out not to be moving at all, and common disgust comes to effect a lowering of mutual barriers, then you can ask (in a properly tentative voice),

Say, didn't I see you at the Regent last night?

The stranger may then reply, quizzically,

Why yes, I was there.

You can then, for example, give an ironic grunt (as if to say that since the queue has made us act as though we were all here on purpose as friends passing the time of day, we might as well act out our forced appearances) and, in a quipping voice, ask,

What did you think of the movie?

the jocular tone providing serious evidence that you appreciate that a "straight" version of your question would be untoward.

But what if it is a friend you saw at the movie who apparently did not see you? Next day, on happening to meet, you ask (in greeting-adjacent slot and in a slight taunting voice),

What did you think of the movie last night?

in which case you will be heard as having played a small trick, inducing in response something like a double take and a dutiful display of mock anger, as in

Hey! Were you there too? Why didn't you tell me?

this being an indirect allusion to the rule that what could have been part of joint experience should have been managed as such from the beginning, which, incidentally, would provide the basis for succinct references later. The unteasing way of going about it would have been to repair the joint biography (preferably in greeting-adjacent slot so as to avoid being trapped into appearing to have been ready to let the matter pass):

YOU: I didn't get a chance to say hello, but I saw you at the movie last night.
FRIEND: Really? Were you there? I wish I'd known you were going.
YOU: So do I. Incidentally, what did you think of it?

Or, alternatively:

YOU: I didn't get a chance to say hello, but I saw you at the movie last night.
FRIEND: Hey! That's funny. I saw you too, but there was no way to say hello.
YOU: Oh, no! By the way, what did you think of it?

Of course, if you saw your friend at the movie and your seeing was seen and acknowledged by a nod (and perhaps a pantomime display of wanting to come together but not being able to—the "natural" way for things to happen—then, the next day during a chat, and at almost any interchange pause during the chat's course, you could jump right in with

What did you think of the movie?

For then each party would not only have had something of the same experience to draw on, know that the other had, and know that this knowing was known to both (as Clark and Marshall [1981] suggest), but also know that this information state could be openly acknowledged—something, incidentally, that might not be felt were the theater a pornographic one. Nor, as suggested, should the situation of John and Marsha be taken to be entirely innocent here. Even if they went to the thing together, some issues would remain. For John to properly get off his "What did you think of the movie last night?" he and Marsha must be in circumstances where, for example, they are seen by each other to be involved in untaxing tasks that allow for the maintenance of a desultory side conversation. It is only under some such circumstances that a question of this sort would make sense. So, for example, upon both returning from the day's work and seeing each other for the first time in nine hours, John cannot march right into "What did you think of the movie last night?"—at least he cannot if his manner does not express that something like irony or hostility is meant. Nor if either has brought home guests can the topic safely be raised precipitously, for under lots of circumstances the guests would not be able to see how they could figure as relevantly present and could well feel they had a right to. At the very least, they would first have to be brought into the picture—both the interactional and the cinematic one.

In sum, then, one can ask, Given that you have something that you want to utter to a particular other, how do you go about getting into the circumstances that will allow you appropriately to do so? (The opposite question is of interest too, namely, How do you go about avoiding the circumstances in which you would be obliged to disclose something you would rather not?) Here, clearly, philosophy and linguistics must give way to sociology.

One answer seems to be found in a stepwise process. At this time, I can catch only a glimmer of a few of the steps:

1. If you are not acquainted with another and are not in a state of talk with that other, is there anything you can properly say flat out, without summons, warning, lead-in, or preliminary arrangement? Differently put, what are the circumstances in our society in which randomly selected individuals can rightly take it that they have the same thing in mind as the next person, and that this same thing allowably can be addressed without preamble?

i. First, unacquainted's greetings. There are lots of environments in our society, even in urban areas, where unacquainted individuals may properly greet one another in passing. Having monitored the other's approach (and the other, yours), consciousness can be assumed to have been readied. Similarly, on arrival at a staging area—an elevator, an entrance way, a waiting room—a newcomer may offer a greeting to a solitary stranger already there.

ii. You are standing next to someone whom you have never seen before. You are both watching what our view of life warrants our defining as a dramatic event: a three-alarm fire, an ambitious display of fireworks, a daring circus event, a very long drive into the stands, an aerial display, precarious construction work. You have the right without preamble to half turn to the other and vent a response:

> Oh, God!
> Did you see that?
> Look at him go!
> Incredible!

to which the other properly responds by displaying that they have not been improperly addressed; they shake their head as evidence of similar wonderment, or possibly reply with a remark such as,

> I'll say!

Or

> Fantastic![6]

(These events occur during purposeful "official" watching; however, unforeseen circumstances can also provide warrant. Thus, should an airplane you are in very sharply jerk or lose altitude, you can unceremoniously exchange exclamations with an unacquainted seatmate, as you can with a fellow pedestrian when you both see that you have both witnessed a sudden near accident.)

Once the interchange is completed, neither of you may feel the need to continue to talk, although it is probably the case that the way has been made a little easier for a second exchange at some later point. You need not feel that any ice has been broken. But when either (or both) of you depart from your vantage point, a departure nod is acceptable. (Throughout social life, when departure is assuredly in progress, a show of bondedness can be afforded, presumably because there is then a guarantee that advantage cannot be taken of it.)

In brief, when jointly faced by what are to be taken as dramatic occurrences, any two individuals in the community can acceptably assume what is in each other's mind, can laconically bridge remarks to it, and will not be seen to presume in doing so. Incidentally, one might be hard put to discover what is the "new" in these expressions of wonderment. Note, too, that whereas the acts earlier considered presuppose a common language—or, rather, knowledge as to whether the language is likely to be common or not—the remarks here considered are almost independent of language. Given that "deeply human" events are felt to be involved, and that such events are felt to strike everyone similarly even though they may perceivedly be of somewhat different culture, and given also that no new information is in any case involved, it is understandable that language itself need not be seen as a barrier. Indeed, among Western people, there are nonvocal gestures which can function as fully equivalent alternatives in these settings. In any case, strangers to the local language well know that at least here they can communicate to the natives.

iii. A further possibility. You are walking along the street. You accidentally bump into someone. Both of you initiate a perfunctory excuse and continue on. (The guilty party, if there very clearly is one, has some obligation to be the more vociferous in verbal apology and to initiate physical remedial actions, if any seem required.) Again, no state of talk need be established in advance and no warning or preamble need be given for the remark. The reference is to something that can be taken to be in both parties' consciousness, and, being there, to be also a proper matter for address by either party. Interestingly, there is considerable variation across societies, and across classes within a society, as to what constitutes excuse-warranting mutual impingement. What is in our minds and can be properly taken to be in our minds during such moments may not qualify as worthy of entering consciousness in other groups. (For example, minor accidental touchings that elicit apologies in pedestrian traffic in our middle-class society routinely pass by unremarked in Brazilian streets.)

iv. Consider another scenario. You go up to a ticket window at the movies and, while fishing for your money, without further ado say to the ticket seller—who, as usual, is a woman,

Two, please.

Following Chafe (1974, p. 112), one can say that your utterance presupposes that tickets are what you want, that the seller will have the possibility that you want tickets in focal consciousness and therefore will not have to canvass her memory to figure out what in the world you have in mind, and that certainly she is obliged to accept the request as appropriate. All the ticket seller will be waiting for, presumably, is a strategic bit of information not otherwise available in the situation, namely, how many. (As a matter of fact, microecology will allow the seller, if she is inclined, to predict how many tickets you want, so your informing words can be merely confirmatory.) Further, the ticket seller will appreciate that she is not being asked to *give* you tickets but to *exchange* them for money.[7] What is special about this scenario, however (and unlike Chafe's [1974, p. 114]), is that no prior state of talk is presupposed; just by walking up to the window, that is, by lodging yourself in current-turn position—the "service post," to use Marilyn Merritt's term (1976, p. 321, n. 14)—you have a right to start flat out with words regarding tickets.

Part of the job of ticket selling, then, is that the performer is obliged to have in mind what it is that will make sense out of cryptic utterances regarding tickets and so orient to any unacquainted other who might approach the service post. And this obligatory matter for consciousness does not come from prior utterances in a conversation but from an institutionalized service arrangement and the probable transactions that will be engineered in its terms. Indeed, the whole transaction can be, and frequently is, consummated silently. Observe that, in some communities, if you treat the transaction as one that requires you first to initiate a state of talk before saying how many (as with, "Excuse me, Miss, could I have . . ."), then the seller may well look to her own behavior and your tone of voice for evidence that a sarcastic reminder of her duties is intended, and (we will soon consider) if she fails to find any such evidence, she may think your head needs tightening.

v. A final matter. The general rule in our society against opening talk with "strangers" seems to be understood as one that should not be sustained too pointedly. The injunction against talking to strangers is merely one part of what we presuppose, another part being that acts which glaringly portray distaste for contact with another should be avoided. Thus, if fortune brings two adults into close and exclusive co-presence for a considerable time, as when an elevator jams with only two riders on it and they are unacquainted, then it may be felt to be improper to refrain from exchanging a few words, in this particular case especially (but not merely) because each can assume the malfunction will be on the other's mind.

2. I have so far touched on some of the social circumstances in our society when an individual without first initiating a state of talk can address an unacquainted other on the basis of what can properly be assumed to be in the other's consciousness, and being there, to be properly available for address. This speaks, of course, to what it is that certain individuals may be *obliged* to accept from unacquainted others by way of unceremonious address. A marginal matter should be considered next, an institution that plays a special role in communication life and has a distinctive role in regard to what it is we must be prepared to bring to mind. I refer to the "summons," that is, a

message conveyed to someone otherwise engaged, directing him to address himself to the speaker in the matter of their establishing a state of talk between them.[8] One deals here with a relationship that pretty much extends to all members of a society, linking every possible pair, and each member both as giver and sender of the signal. For, at least in face-to-face life, it is always possible to imagine *some* circumstances which would provide warrant for communication overture between *any* two individuals within hailing distance of each other.[9] Thus the signals:

Excuse me.
Pardon me.
Sir/Madam [with rising intonation].

Of course, we are not obliged to maintain the possibility of overture ready in our consciousness, merely to bring it to mind when we hear an appropriate signal, especially when followed by an appropriate orienting action on the part of the signaler. Observe, once again, that the use of such signals implies that the user appreciates that we are not to be brought into talk unless given a moment's notice and, incidentally, that we have the right to defer the opening by employing words that request the summoner to place himself on hold while we complete an urgent task. (There is always the possibility of not responding to the summoner at all [or not answering the phone], in which case consciousness is likely to be full of the overture, although no confirming action is forthcoming regarding it.)

3. Summonses aside, consider some of the circumstances in which individuals may feel that to make a statement they must first establish a state of talk to house it in; and, once that is done (or if it already has been done), that an "alert" should be employed, namely, some sort of prefatory warning that information outside of immediate consciousness may well have to be brought to mind.[10]

i. In public places, passing strangers have a right to breach the rule of nonsolicitation to request certain "free goods" of each other, among which is information about direction and places.[11] Of course, there is no obligation on the part of the citizenry to possess the information, merely to countenance a request to search their memory for it. (The obligation of the asker is to approach the potential informant in the situation who might be considered least threatened by the overture.) The request is often prefaced by an excuse for initiating talk and an alert regarding the search—a two-step arrangement:

Excuse me, would you happen to know . . .

Through the same route, passersby can be asked for the time and, under certain circumstances, change for a parking meter or telephone, in which case the free good that is solicited is something other than information, yet something that falls within the domain of matters every citizen must be prepared to address. (Any stranger could be asked what day it is, but few are because it is also assumed that every normally oriented citizen should know that; only very young children can properly tap this resource without doing sheepishness. The *date*, however, can be asked [half apologetically], e.g., whenever the asker can be seen to be filling out legal documents.)

Balancing off the right to elicit a number of free goods, there is the obligation (which can also be a right) to volunteer some others, for example, informing someone that they have dropped something, offering to help with a cumbersome task, and so forth. Here again, a state of talk may well be initiated first, and a warning that the recipient of the summons into talk should check to see what might be a likely reason for the overture. (Apparently you are always supposed to have your mind sufficiently in shape so that if you are told you have dropped something, you can quickly bring to mind that you had this something to drop.)

ii. Pedestrian obligations with respect to being called into talk and being required to bring to mind certain pieces of information, engage in bits of action and the like, are bilateral; individuals who can draw on this corpus of knowledge and action must also be able betimes to make theirs available. There is a contrast here with persons who acquire a specialized role as information givers (and performers of free services), whether formally, as in the case of policemen and information clerks in shops, or informally, as when a news vendor or filling station operator comes to be routinely asked for directions, or a drugstore that is near a bus stop becomes a source of change.

iii. The notion of free goods leads immediately to the issue of what goods, and how much, are to be considered free, and this whether on the part of passersby or specialized providers. A more interesting issue, perhaps, arises when the good is information. Here knowledge, not cost, is felt to be involved.[12] Informational preserves aside, it is as though before making our inquiry, we have to judge how "reasonable" it would be for the addressee to have the information we want, and in making this judgement to conclude that our request has a "respectable" chance of being satisfied. For to ask someone for information they could not "reasonably" be assumed to have is a perceivedly disoriented (and disorienting) thing to do. Which is also to say, of course, that by nicely expressing that we realize how unreasonable our request is, we can get away with making it. Thus locutions such as,

You wouldn't happen to know, would you, where [what, when]. . . .

Contrariwise, the more reasonable the request, the less ritual labor required to ask it. But, of course, these arguments bring the question back to the issue of what is defined as "reasonable." It seems that several principles are involved, all speaking to the issue of the recallable or bringable to mind, of standard stocks of knowledge, not to what ought to be in consciousness at the time.

Take, for example, location information at various removes from the point of inquiry. There is the assumption that persons whose work or domicile fixes them to a given point will have detailed place knowledge of the immediate vicinity. What is asked of suburbanites, news vendors, shopkeepers qualifies here. Of course, "immediate vicinity" (like "reasonableness") itself requires explication, drawing on presuppositions instead of describing them. There is, for example, the question of grid: a salesperson in even the largest department store can be reasonably asked where any particular department is, a filling station attendant where the access point to any neighboring highway is; the first case is on a finer grid than street-place information, the second on a coarser.

In contrast to those perceived as fixed, we have police and cab drivers. They are obliged to take as reasonable a request for information about any "place" in their city; moreover, should they not "know" where the place is (in the sense of being able to direct you or take you), they are under some obligation to recover the facts from a book or a phone call. The citizenry itself can be asked for directions to the city's "leading" grid of downtown streets and landmarks, but hardly for more. Apparently another principle is this: If you feel that your specific request is questionable, you can select a larger segment which (you happen to know) includes your point of interest and ask about this broader area, the assumption being that the greater the distance from your informant's familiar location, the more coarse-grained his grid information. (I might add that if you ask for a place that is within arm's reach, your informant will have to exercise a special tact in informing you; he or she may give, for example, a little sympathetic laugh to show that this sort of blindness is not being taken for what it might be.) So all in all, if you want to fine tune your requests concerning location, it would be a good idea to know in advance just what the answer is going to be.

Interestingly, in replying to a request for location information, the respondent may have to resort to use of other location terms which mark out the route to the asker's destination, but, of course, an asker who does not know one point may not know others on the way. The respondent may have to engage in a probing search procedure, employing "try-markers" to test out various landmarks until one is found that the asker is familiar with. (It need hardly be added that with or without such side sequences the informant's efforts may be insufficient; often she will not be aware of, and hence cannot advise on, all critical decision points that she herself negotiates when following a particular path.)

iv. Return now for a moment to our movie house ticket seller. One finds, of course, that she is not merely exposed to persons who want to buy tickets. A range of other possibilities exists. Potential patrons can come up to the wicket to elicit information about the film: how long will it run, what time does it start or stop, does it have subtitles, is there a cartoon, and so forth. Although these requests for information do not tap what the ticket seller can be presumed to have in the center of her awareness, the presumption can be that she is certain to have access to such information, is obliged to divulge such information, and that a deep search will not be required. Hardly anything by way of an alert need be offered her.

However, with some other matters she can be approached on, ceremony figures differently. As suggested, it can be expected that she knows where particular shops and buildings are in the immediate vicinity of her workplace, and that it is permissible to query her on such matters. Similarly, one can permissibly ask for change for a nearby phone or parking meter. In all these cases of solicited free goods, there is no obligation on her part to provide the service, merely not to take umbrage at its request. Indeed, in the matter of the time, anyone can ask and everyone can expect to obtain an answer.[13] But in all these cases, the asking is often prefaced by a polite alert; certainly such a courtesy is understandable as fitting when it does occur.

I am suggesting that requests that call for dredging or bringing to mind are more likely to be embedded in a perfunctorily established state of talk (along with a polite initiation and close-out) than are requests for tickets. The distinction between what is in consciousness and what is merely recallable is thus reinforced by ceremony; if the ticket seller need only have a matter available to recall, then a request concerning it may well be felt to require first that a state of talk be established. Thus, there is a protective structure to her exposure.

Clearly, the little scenarios we have so far dealt with involve individuals who are allowed to address one another on a very narrow range of topics, all other topics ostensibly forbidden. You are not entitled to ask a ticket seller flat out, without preamble, whether her hair is natural or not, what she thinks about her mother, and a host of other matters she can call to mind and routinely will when talking to intimates. And the same sort of reasoning that applies to asking for information applies to the practice of initiating the divulgence of it, namely, to "reportables." You can tell the ticket seller that you are dying to see the show, and while this might be judged as a little over-sociable, it is perhaps forgivably so. But if you chose the moment of contact with a ticket seller to tell her directly about having to take the car in tomorrow to get a new muffler, that would be considered grounds for imputing strangeness. Obviously, what is reportable "on contact" to a spouse may not be thus reportable to a stranger. And yet, of course, it appears that in certain circumstances strangers can "strike up a conversation"[14] and end by exchanging extensive intimacies, not merely "small talk."[15] And if you are at a ticket wicket that is not busy, and there is a displayable reason for hanging around, you can acceptably lay the groundwork that will supply the perceived relevance and conversational license that is required to allow either her or you to properly report, or inquire about, matters ordinarily precluded.

4. So far I have considered only the circumstances in which we ourselves seek to obtain or reveal information, the question of who in particular we are led to address to this end being of second importance. Omitted, then, have been all those occasions when the asymmetry is on the other foot, and we find ourselves *required* to divulge information about ourselves.

Servers of all kinds have the right to ask those they serve for pertinent biographical information, psychotherapists presumably marking the extreme in this regard. (To seek a service, then, is to expose oneself to questioning.) Agents of social control—police and teachers, for example—exert a somewhat similar claim, except that here the informant may not have sought out any assistance and correspondingly may *more* resent the right of the askers to ask what they do. Rights here, of course, are unilateral. In any case, in coming to a server we ready our thoughts so that the dredging process will be facilitated. The presence of a social control agent may bring certain topics to mind also—commonly ones we would rather avoid.

5. When one shifts from contacts between the unacquainted to those between the acquainted, especially the "socially" or not "merely" acquainted, then, of course, matters get considerably more complicated. Obviously, each party to the relationship will be obliged to recall on sight the name of the other, along with some biographical details, for these may have to be displayed should a greeting occur. Recognizing that certain past experiences, and consequently certain familiarities, will be shared, a base exists to be drawn on anaphorically and deictically. And as suggested, presumably the more fully involved the two individuals have been with each other over time, the richer and more current will be the joint account of known-to-be-known-about available for allusion in setting up an utterance. For example, if Marsha and Mary are adult close friends, then each is likely to know, and be expected to know, critical matters about the other's close others, enough so that each can efficiently report stories involving her own others. I might add that ceremonies of greeting and departure in or society often require reference to these "other person's others," this being a case where what *can* be asked about *ought* to be asked about. Such a rule underlies the insult offered (in *Pride and Prejudice*) by Lady Catherine when, sorely vexed with the marital ambitions of Elizabeth, she departs into her carriage saying:

I take no leave of you, Miss Bennet. I send no compliments to your
mother. You deserve no such attention. I am seriously displeased.

And between close, long-standing workmates or housemates, each party's
preacquaintance past may be reviewed and assimilated somewhat to joint
biography, again so that (or, at least, with the effect that) a recallable framework will be available for anything either party might want to say involving
reference to the past.[16] Correspondingly, there is the important obligation
(and right) to update our associates about any change in our life circumstances—the "closer" the relationship, the more quickly the information is
to be imparted and the less dramatic this information need be. In consequence, one's intimate others will always be properly oriented to receive
reports and make inquiries.

   In brief, what we think of as a relationship is, in one sense, merely a provision for the use of cryptic expressions, a provision of what is required in order
to allude to things economically. Certainly our obligation to keep the names
of our friends in mind, along with other pertinent social facts concerning
them, is more than a means of celebrating and renewing our social relationship to them; it also ensures a shared orientation for reference and hence
talk whenever we come into contact with them. What affirms relationships
also organizes talk.

   6. With this biographical perspective in mind, turn finally from mere and
close acquaintances to the closely intertwined: back to John and Marsha.
They have come into the kitchen for lunch. For a while they will maintain
an open state of talk, that is, the right but not the obligation to utter words.
In consequence, there will be longish silences interspersed with short spurts
of talk. And not a few utterances will receive no other-person uptake of any
kind:

   JOHN [looking in refrigerator]: Marsh've ya seen the mustard. . . . Oh! here
   it is.
   MARSHA. . . .

The general question, then, is, What can be reported on, and what can be
inquired about, with what kind of prefatory work, if any, and what surface
structure evidence will there be of what sorts of matters that are taken for
granted?

   First, there will be the domain of matters than can be addressed flat out
without summons, alerting, or ground laying—in effect, matters taken to be
already in consciousness and in addition permissibly addressable. Included
here is "course of other's action." Marsha can see what John is about (getting
more coffee, rinsing a glass, going to the refrigerator), and in the setting is
licensed to take such doings as the frame of reference for flat-out remarks.

(To help in her tracking of John, Marsha may use John's progress grunts and ostensibly self-directed comments which he may employ in executing his actions.) Observe, John does not have to see that his course of action is seen; he can have his back turned to Marsha, but provided the kitchen is small enough, his doings will provide a graspable tracing of what Marsha has social warrant for assuming is in his mind. Thus, as he gets up to get more coffee, she can laconically say, "Me, too." Further, if the pair are sitting or standing facing each other, Marsha can assume that John is somewhat tracking her course of action (and vice versa), and flat-out requests for specific help or offers of specific help are possible. Indeed, a considerable amount of giving help and getting it will go on without help from words of any kind—enlightened collaboration in spite of total ellipsis. Let me emphasize that one deals here, of course, with social definitions. Thus, in surgery the scrub nurse is obliged to stay "in" the course of action of the surgeon, so that without raising his eyes he can hold out his hand and get what he wants by nakedly naming it; however, she cannot expect him to similarly track her doings. (My pronouns presuppose that the traditional sexual division of labor still typically obtains in surgery; this parenthetical comment, however, involves a statement in this regard, not a presupposition.) Children, to take another example, often feel crowded by their parents, feeling that they cannot complete an act themselves without helpful intervention, both verbal and physical. On the other hand, strangers on the street need to be in fairly dire straits—but not too dire—to allow for unasked-for intercession. (I might add, if you stand at an intersection and look very, very ponderingly in both directions, you may be able to get someone to volunteer the question,

Are you looking for someplace?

But only a very pointed enactment on your part is likely to give Good Samaritans a feeling that they can chance asking before they are asked.) A man seeing a woman (even one not known to him) reaching for a match to light a cigarette can indeed proffer a light; but the reverse still carries more implications than most women might want to risk in the performance of a courtesy. A quarter of a century ago on the Shetland Islands, any man doing outside work would be likely to be asked if he wanted a hand by any male (acquainted or unacquainted) of crofter status who happened to find himself standing about in the vicinity. We do not have this expectation, although when cars get stuck in the snow, volunteers may leave the sidewalk to lend a hand, especially if there has been an extraordinary storm and citizens for a time feel the good-humored will that crises can generate. In other words, appreciating another's course of action is not enough. Helpful intervention on the basis of this cognitive outreaching may require obligation or at least license.

Now return to John and Marsha and their open state of talk in the kitchen. In addition to course-of-current-action as a legitimate window into the consciousness of the other, there will be a set of events entirely external to the current social situation which John and Marsha can assume are salient enough to mutually address without a topic alert or even a cue that talk is to occur. Marsha can break a long pause by saying,

> They seemed to have a good time.

She knows, and correctly, that John will understand she is referring to last night's guests. (Try saying that to a ticket seller.) But, of course, the notion of saliency is only a gloss; one needs a principled analysis. For example, if John and Marsha know they both know that they expect to be involved in an undertaking later that day, it need not be very much on their minds for one to say nakedly into an open state of talk without any lead-in,

> What's-his-name isn't coming 'til two.

In this case a name substitute has been employed that stipulates gender and nothing much else, much as a personal pronoun might, except that here there is recognition that initial mention ought to be a name, not a pronominal substitute.

Further, if a proposed topic (or rather a "mentionable") is perceivedly speaker centred, in the sense of being recognizably relevant primarily to speaker's own involvements, then a special set of alerts seems to be employed in and out of established talk, as if to warn hearer that he or she is going to have to mobilize memory and orientation regarding a yet unnamed theme:

> *Geeze* . . . I waited a long time at the dentist's.
> *Wow*, I didn't sleep much. I feel lousy.
> *Ya Know*, I shouldn't have bought that sweater.[17]

John and Marsha are also likely to employ utterance-initial prosody and utterance-initial vocatives in a manner that informs the hearer immediately whether he or she is being asked to become a sustained sympathetic listener or merely a one-fact informant—someone required to quickly complete a single interchange parenthetical to two ongoing unrelated courses of action.

Also, there will be the range of matters that John and Marsha can introduce into talk by employing standard locater formats, for example:

> Ya remember that green shopping bag we had?

May I add that what one party to the relationship has a right routinely to report to another (given the help of various alerts and the proper activity setting) is not an incidental aspect of what a relationship is, and a far trickier matter than what one party is obliged to report lest the other think that secrets are being kept or that third parties are improperly finding out first. The close study of such reportings takes us right into the banal interiors of intimacy (that domain of which psychotherapists are the absentee land-lords), which might account for the studied neglect of the topic by students of talk.[18]

It might be tempting, of course, to think that there are some relationships, such as the marital one, that allow each member to report anything to the other and inquire into anything about the other. But, of course, there are not. Certainly with intimates each is likely to know enough about the other to know what the other is sensitive to (as we say) and cannot be addressed on except in a roundabout way—for example, only after relevance has been generated by apparently fortuitous events, including a buildup of what can be seen as unconnected mentionings. If the intimates are cross sexed, then there are certainly matters, especially ones defined as quite minor, that each can more easily report to an acquaintance of own sex than to each other. And even when the intimates are of the same sex, and the same everything else that might make for license regarding reportability and inquiry, there will be matters defined as so trivial and fleeting as not to qualify for mention. Again, to closely describe these limits is to closely study the social relations of the people who draw them.

A final comment. Given the speaking arrangements described for John and Marsha, it seems reasonable to raise the question of "misunderstand-ings." We tend to assume that, although persons who do not share the same communication code are prone to genuine misunderstanding of each other ("genuine" in contrast to the many conversational moves based on simu-lated misunderstanding), intimates will at least be spared this source of divisiveness. But if anything, the opposite is true. After all, the domestically entwined can draw cryptically on own and other's course of action, and on a mutually appreciated agenda of impending involvements (both individual and joint); further, in our world they are likely to have ritual license both to initiate a spurt of talk with minimal forewarning and to intrude disjunctive topics with little ceremony during already established states of talk. It is to be expected, then, that in this relationship context, recipients will on occa-sion be in doubt about the reference of utterances and even mis-refer what they hear to a context not intended. And indeed ambiguity and misunder-standing, albeit short-lived, abound in the kitchen, on long drives, and other seats of domestic laconicity. Precisely here, where Marsha feels she can relax and communicate elliptically about "anything" that comes to mind, John may have to invest a certain amount of work in order to keep up with the changing contexts of reference; and so also Marsha with respect to John's utterances. I might add that the properties of these brief domestic hitches in communication have not yet been considered systematically.

In sum, how an individual in talk with us, acquainted or unacquainted, intimate or stranger, can properly lead up to an otherwise intrusive query or a revealing report has never been closely studied; nonetheless, what is involved leads one back to a consideration of the workings of the new and the given. In shifting from considering information about directions or theater tickets to information about oneself—one's social attributes and one's prior experiences—the awful dimensions of the perspective emerge, namely, that conversationally speaking, we are all information storage drums, and for every possible interrogator, there will be an access sequence that allows for entrée to the files. The unilateral access that the police, government officials, credit bureaus, and professional servers of various kinds have to selected stretches of our biography has been considerably pondered, if not studied, by social scientists interested in the question of privacy—although here not particularly in terms of what this sanctioned access implies about the social organization of what people are ready to bring to mind. But I do not think much is known about the distribution of circumstances in which we volunteer reports on ourselves to those whose interest in what we report, incidentally, may extend only to the question of when we are going to finish our turn, so that they can begin their own reporting.

I want to note finally that what has been considered so far is, as it were, a hearer's-ear view of talk, namely, what it is hearer will be able and ready to respond to. Indeed, with small talk, speakers also take this view, rather fully determining what they say according to their view of what it is the hearer can be alive to. But this view gives too much weight to local determination. Speakers have the task of making what they say decipherable and relevant in the circumstances, but why they should have hit on one such particularity instead of some other one equally tailored for the recipient need have nothing at all to do with the latter. For example, John's glance may happen to have fallen on something that reminded him of some preencounter concern he now elects to mention; or something someone else says may fortuitously provide this associative link. And this connection may be totally inaccessible to Marsha. Thus, following an alert by John that breaks a period of silence, Marsha often will not be in a position to know what in the world John is going to say, although, of course, she can be fairly sure that after he has said it, the matter will turn out to qualify as a mentionable between them. (That is why the term "alert" was introduced in the first place.) So, too, in a conversation that is well under way, Marsha's utterance of a topic shift excuse ("Not to change the subject, but . . .") can warn that something not predicted is to be aired. The precise timing of such a shift can be locally determined, and the phrasal warning sufficiently stereotyped to call a "disjunct marker," but even so, just *what* the excuse maker then selects to report on can be a somewhat open matter from the perspective of the listeners. Indeed, speakers can make a point of attempting to conceal the reason for an utterance (as when they "fish" for a compliment, or employ a phrasing that disguisedly presents their real concern as one item in an innocuous-appearing series of questions), and although such an effort takes for granted that utterances will be assessed for the apparent reason for making them, it also assumes that in the last analysis assessors will be cut off from the information required for consistently faultless judgment.

I close with a call to arms. To utter something and to not disconfirm that we are sane requires that our saying be heard to draw appropriately on one array of presuppositions—that sustained by our hearers—and avoid being heard to make others—those which are not, although they may be by persons not present. Responding to another's words, we must find a phrasing that answers not merely to the other's words but to the other's mind—so the other can draw both from the local scene and from the distal, wider worlds of her or his experience. Sociologists recently have not been very helpful here: they reiterate the proposition and provide illustrations. But there is no *analysis* of the taken-for-granted. No framework. Not even a simpleminded classification. The consequence of presuppositions for the surface form and prosody of utterances, on the other hand, has been considerably illuminated by linguists, along with the text-interpretive practices and the repertoire of keyings. The bearing of acquaintanceship and close ties, of the generation and intentional construction of joint biography, of being or not being in a state of talk, of the various locaters we employ to provide a framework for the statements we want to be in a position to utter succinctly—all these critical matters have been little studied. Behind all this, and linking these themes together, is the socially prescribed place of what is taken to be the operation of the mind. A question of who can say what to whom, in what circumstances, with what preamble, in what surface form, and, given available readings, will not be thought mindless in doing so. A question of what we can say and still satisfy Felicity's Condition.

No doubt the most closely examined case is that of "conversation." Anaphora and topical continuity are two examples of what has been considered in the literature. More generally, there is the matter of dialogic or sequence constraints. Given a turn to talk, a next turn will be required and will be examined for how it displays relevance to the now prior one. All kinds of discontinuities will be possible because all kinds of excuses will be available that establish respect for relevance even while failing to provide it substantively. Even one's failure to excuse a failure of uptake will be caught in the interpretive net, being read, for example, as a pointed comment on what has not otherwise been responded to.

But if Felicity's Condition is now best documented within conversations, this should not lead us to worship particularistic structures. To be sure, when John directs an assertion or question to Marsha, and Marsha responds by remaining silent, or changing the topic, or turning from John to direct her own opener to Mary, Marsha's act can be perceived by all three as a behavioral comment, a reply in effect. But analytically speaking, to say that in context no answer is an answer is simplistic. Information derived from Marsha's failure to address John's utterance verbally, that is, canonically, is information given off, not given; it is (on the face of it) expression, not language. As such, this move figures in a special way in regard to what Marsha can be held responsible for having communicated. Whatever John says she meant by her apparent failure of uptake, Marsha has reserved the right to claim otherwise. For she has not *said* anything; she has merely placed participants in a position to draw varieties of conclusion. Should Marsha provide an explicit reply to John's utterance, she can still decline to accept particular readings of its hinted, tacit elements, for these, too, will be expression, not language.

It is true that prior turn is very likely to provide some of the context in terms of which current utterance will be interpreted, of which condition current speakers must demonstrate that they are cognizant. But on the same grounds, prior turn can never be the only such condition current speaker will be required (and allowed) to employ as a frame of reference. In speech act terms, respondents must address themselves to the illocutionary force of what is said to them, and to appreciate this force they will have to have access to a vast array of biographical and cultural understandings—these alone allowing them to make sense out of cryptic allusions. Moreover, matters not even alluded to in prior turn may be available for address by respondents, for in the last analysis it is the situation and circumstances of the prior speaker as these interact with the situation and circumstances of the respondents that the latter must address, the former's speaking merely providing the occasion for doing so.

Further, a conversation is only a conversation after the fact, this being the point when a student can be assured that a continuous stretch of examples can be culled of current turns being followed by contingent next ones. Occasions of one person's talk that lead to no other person's talk perforce fail to end up in the collection. The frequent necessity for speakers to continue beyond a first "transition relevance place" and take in their own washing for want of any volunteer is perhaps not given enough weight. Stops and starts and fitfulness generally are underplayed, as are long stretches of easy silence punctuated by unanswered remarks.[20] And the dynamics of participation are neglected, namely, the formation of subordinated communication (whether in the form of collusion, innuendo, or open byplays), the occurrence of dual or pivotal participation, the movement of participants from one adjacent conversation to another, and the subdividing and recoalescence of encounters (Goffman 1981, pp. 133 ff.). Most important of all, the sense in which current utterance is conditioned by immediately prior turn's talk—when, indeed, there is such talk—does not speak to the many elements of the same current utterance that are not determined in any way by prior turn (or prior utterance in the same turn), yet are nonetheless determined in ways that satisfy Felicity's Condition. In any case, an account of second utterances in terms of their contingency on a first leaves unexplained how there could be any firsts; after all, from where could they draw their design? Conversation could never begin. Or, once begun, would be one utterance away from the end. Tails would know how to wag, but there would be no dogs.

It is true that utterances must display that their makers are appropriately alive to the circumstances *in* which they make the utterance (as well as, of course, to the world *about* which they make an utterance), and must do so at their makers' peril, demonstrating that the minds of the latter are informed by exactly the required presuppositions. And true, too, that speakers can use these constraints as a resource (indeed, are obliged to), allowing them to employ efficient references with the understanding that what they must be mindful of is exactly what their listeners will be mindful of, too. But this informs us about the circumstances in which words are spoken, and these turn out to be very much broader than the circumstances in which conversations are maintained. This is neatly evident, for example, when two individuals are jointly engaged in a physical task and one is directing the other. "Now loosen the other one the same amount" is a deictic utterance whose required context is an immediately prior movement of a wrench, not a larynx, the resulting sequence melding turns at loosening and turns at talk.[21] There occurs an interchange of acts which are sequentially contingent and satisfy Felicity's Condition, but in a fundamental way the interchange is not conversational. A mutually ratified joint focus of attention is here sustained on and through a physical task, a contributory resource for which is an open state of talk.

Nor (it should now be plain) was it right to define Felicity's Condition restrictively in terms of verbal acts. Speech need not figure even in a reduced way for Felicity's Condition to apply: the general constraint that an utterance must satisfy, namely, that it connect acceptably with what recipient has in, or can bring to, mind, applies in a manner to non-linguistic acts in wordless contexts.[22] These acts, too, insofar as they can be perceived by individuals in the vicinity, will have to be styled so as to provide evidence that their doer is engaged in something that perceivers find understandable, even if they are not favored thereby. This paper has dealt only with utterances, but some of what it has dealt with about utterances could almost as well be dealt with about entirely nonlinguistic doings.

In sum, then, whenever we come into contact with another through the mails, over the telephone, in face-to-face talk, or even merely through immediate co-presence, we find ourselves with one central obligation: to render our behavior understandably relevant to what the other can come to perceive is going on. Whatever else, our activity must be addressed to the other's mind, that is, to the other's capacity to read our words and actions for evidence of our feelings, thoughts, and intent. This confines what we say and do, but it also allows us to bring to bear all of the world to which the other can catch allusions.

From "Response Cries"*

The functioning of imprecations raises the question of an allied set of acts that can be performed by singles: *response cries*, namely, exclamatory interjections which are not full-fledged words. *Oops!* is an example . . . Consider now some standard cries.

1. The *transition display*. Entering or leaving from what can be taken as a state of marked natural discomfort—wind, rain, heat, or cold—we seem to have the license (in our society) to externalize an expression of our inner state. *Brr!* is a standard term for wind and cold upon leaving such an atmosphere. (Other choices are less easily reproduced in print.) *Ahh!* and *Phew!* are also heard, this time when leaving a hot place for a cool one. Function is not clear. Perhaps the sounding gives us a moment to orient ourselves to the new climatic circumstances and to fall into cadence with the others in the room, these requirements not ordinarily a taxing matter and not ordinarily needful, therefore, of a pause for their accomplishment. Perhaps the concentration, the "holding ourselves in" sometimes employed in inclement places (as a sort of support for the body), gets released with a flourish on our escaping from such environments. In any case, we can be presumed to be in a state of mind that any and all those already safe might well appreciate—for, after all, weather envelops everyone in the vicinity—and so self-expression concerning our feelings does not take us to a place that is mysterious to our hearers. Incidentally, it appears that, unlike strong imprecations, transition displays in our society are not particularly sex-typed.

2. The *spill cry*. This time the central examples, *Oops!* and *Whoops!*, are well-formed sounds, although not in every sense words, and again something as much (perhaps even more) the practice of females as males. Spill cries are a sound we emit to follow along with our having for a moment lost guiding control of some feature of the world around us, including ourselves. Thus a woman, rapidly walking to a museum exit, passes the door, catches

* First published 1978; these extracts from *Forms of Talk*, 1981, pp. 99–104, 120–2. Reproduced by permission of the University of Chicago Press. © 1983 by The University of Chicago.

her mistake, utters *Oops!*, and backtracks to the right place. A man, dropping a piece of meat through the grill to coals below, utters *Oops!* and then spears the meat to safety with his grill fork.

On the face of it, the sound advertises our loss of control, raising the question of why we should want to defame ourselves through this publicity. An obvious possibility is that the *Oops!* defines the event as a mere accident, shows we know it has happened, and hopefully insulates it from the rest of our behavior, recommending that failure of control was not generated by some obscure intent unfamiliar to humanity or some general defect in competence. Behind this possibility is another: that the expression is presumably used for *minor* failings of environmental control, and so in the face of a more serious failure, the *Oops!* has the effect of downplaying import and hence implication as evidence of our incompetence. (It follows that to show we take a mishap *very* seriously we might feel constrained to omit the cry.) Another reason for (and function of) spill crying is that, a specific vocalization being involved, we necessarily demonstrate that at least our vocal channel is functioning and, behind this, at least some presence of mind. A part of us proves to be organized and standing watch over the part of us that apparently isn't watchful. Finally, and significantly, the sound can provide a warning to others present that a piece of the world has gotten loose and that they might best be advised to take care. Indeed, close observation shows that the *oo* in *Oops!* may be nicely prolonged to cover the period of time during which that which got out of control is out of control.

Note, when we utter *Oops!* as we slip on the ice, we can be making a plea to the closest other for a steadying hand and simultaneously warning others as to what they themselves should watch out for, these circumstances surely opening up our surround for vocalizations. When in fact there is no danger to the self, we may respond to *another's* momentary loss of control with an *Oops!* also, providing him a warning that he is in trouble, a readied framework within which he can define the mishap, and a collectively established cadence for his anticipated response. That some sort of help for others is thus intended seems to be borne out by the fact that apparently men are more likely to *Oops!* for another when that other is a child or a female, and thus definable as someone for whom responsibility can be taken. Indeed, when a parent plucks up a toddler and rapidly shifts it from one point to another or "playfully" swings or tosses it in the air, the prime mover may utter an *Oopsadaisy!*, stretched out to cover the child's period of groundlessness, counteracting its feeling of being out of control, and at the same time instructing the child in the terminology and role of spill cries. In any case, it is apparent that *oopsing* is an adaptive practice with some survival value. And the fact that individuals prove (when the occasion does arise) to have been ready all along to *oops* for themselves or an appropriate other suggests that when nothing eventful is occurring, persons in one another's presence are still nonetheless tracking one another and acting so as to make themselves trackable.

3. The *threat startle*, notably *Eek!* and *Yipe!* Perhaps here is a response cry sex-typed (or at least so believed) for feminine use. Surprise and fear are stated—in lay terms, "expressed"—but surprise and fear that are very much under control, indeed nothing to be really concerned about. A very high open stairwell, or a walk that leads to a precipice, can routinely evoke *yipes* from us as we survey what might have been our doom, but from a position of support we have had ample time to secure. A notion of what a fear response would be is used as a pattern for mimicry. A sort of overplaying occurs that covers any actual concern by extending with obvious unseriousness the expressed form this concern would take. And we demonstrate that we are alive to the fearsome implications of the event, albeit not overthrown by them, that we have seen the trouble and by implication will assuredly control for it, and are, therefore, in need of no warning, all of this releasing others from closely tracking us. And the moment it takes to say the sound is a moment we can use actually to compose ourselves in the circumstances. In a very subtle way, then, a verbal "expression" of our state is a means of rising above it—and a release of concern now no longer necessary, coming after the emergency is really over.

Here an argument made earlier about multiple transformations can be taken up. Precipitous drops are the sorts of things that an individual can be very close to without the slightest danger of dropping over or intent to do so. In these circumstances it would seem that imagery of accident would come to the fore or at least be very readily available. It is this easily achieved mental set that the response cry in question would seem to participate in. Thus the uncompelling character of the actual circumstances can be nicely reflected in the light and almost relaxed character of the cry. One has, then, a warning*like* signal in dangerous*like* circumstances. And ritualization begins to give way to a copy of itself, a playful version of what is already a formalized version, a display that has been retransformed and reset, a second order ritualization.

4. *Revulsion sounds*, such as *Eeuw!* are heard from a person who has by necessity or inadvertence come in contact with something that is contaminating. Females in our society, being defined as more vulnerable in this way than males, might seem to have a special claim on the expression. Often once we make the sound we can be excused for a moment while decontamination is attempted. At other times, our voice performs what our physical behavior can't, as when our hands must keep busy cleaning a fish leaving only the auditory and other unrequired channels to correct the picture—to show that indelicate, dirty work need not define the person who is besmeared by it. Observe, again there is an unserious note, a hint of hyperritualization. For often the contamination that calls forth an *Eeuw!* is not *really* believed to

contaminate. Perhaps only germ contamination retains that literal power in our secular world. So again a protectivelike cry is uttered in response to a contaminatinglike contact.

★   ★   ★

The public utterance of self-talk, imprecations, and response cries constitutes a special variety of impulsive, blurted actions, namely, vocalized ones. Our tacit theory of human nature recommends that these actions are "purely expressive," "primitive," "unsocialized," violating in some way or other the self-control and self-possession we are expected to maintain in the presence of others, providing witnesses with a momentary glimpse behind our mask.

However, the point about these blurtings is not that they are particularly "expressive." Obviously, in this sense of that word, ordinary talk is necessarily expressive, too. Naked feelings can agitate a paragraph of discourse almost as well as they can a solitary imprecation. Indeed, it is impossible to utter a sentence without coloring the utterance with some kind of perceivable affect, even (in special cases) if only with the emotionally distinctive aura of affectlessness. Nor is the point about segmented blurtings that they are particularly unsocialized, for obviously they come to us as our language does and not from our own invention. Their point lies elsewhere. One must look to the light these ventings provide, not to the heat they dispel.

In every society one can contrast occasions and moments for silence and occasions and moments for talk. In our own, one can go on to say that by and large (and especially among the unacquainted) silence is the norm and talk something for which warrant must be present. Silence, after all, is very often the deference we will owe in a social situation to any and all others present. In holding our tongue, we give evidence that such thought as we are giving to our own concerns is not presumed by us to be of any moment to the others present, and that the feelings these concerns invoke in ourselves are owed no sympathy. Without such enjoined modesty, there could be no public life, only a babble of childish adults pulling at one another's sleeves for attention. The mother to whom we would be saying, "Look, no hands," could not look or reply for she would be saying, "Look, no hands," to someone else.

Talk, however, presumes that our thoughts and concerns will have some relevance or interest or weight for others, and in this can hardly but presume a little. Talk, of course, in binding others to us, can also do so for protracted periods of time. The compensation is that we can sharply restrict this demand to a small portion of those who are present, indeed, often to only one.

The fugitive communications I have been considering constitute a third possibility, minor no doubt, but of some significance if only because of what they tell us about silence and talk. Our blurtings make a claim of sorts upon the attention of everyone in the social situation, a claim that our inner concerns should be theirs, too, but unlike the claim made by talk, ours here is only for a limited period of attention. And, simply put, this invitation into our interiors tends to be made only when it will be easy for other persons present to see where the voyage takes them. What is precipitous about these expressions, then, is not the way they are emitted but rather the circumstances which render their occurrence acceptable. The invitation we are free to extend in these situations we would be insane to extend in others.

Just as most public arrangements oblige and induce us to be silent, and many other arrangements to talk, so a third set allows and obliges us momentarily to open up our thoughts and feelings and ourselves through sound to whosoever is present. Response cries, then, do not mark a flooding of emotion outward, but a flooding of relevance in.

There is linguistic point to the consideration of this genre of behavior. Response cries such as *Eek!* might be seen as peripheral to the linguist's domain, but imprecations and self-talk are more germane, passing beyond semiword vocal segregates to the traditional materials of linguistic analysis. And the point is that all three forms of this blurted vocalization—semiword response cries, imprecations, and self-talk—are creatures of social situations, not states of talk. A closed circle of ratified participants oriented to engaging exclusively with one another in avowedly directed communications is not the base; a gathering, with its variously oriented, often silent and unacquainted members, is. Further, all three varieties of this ejaculatory expression are conventionalized as to form, occasion of occurrence, and social function. Finally, these utterances are too commonly met within daily life, surely, to justify scholarly neglect.

Once it is recognized that there is a set of conventionalized expressions that must be referred to social situations, not conversations, once, that is, it is appreciated that there are communications specifically designed for use outside states of talk, then it is but a step to seeing that ritualized versions of these expressions may themselves be embedded in the conventionally directed talk to be found in standard conversational encounters. And appreciating this, then to go on to see that even though these interjections come to be employed in conversational environments, they cannot be adequately analyzed there without reference to their original functioning outside of states of talk.

It is recommended, then, that linguists have reason to broaden their net, reason to bring in uttering that is not talking, reason to deal with social situations, not merely with jointly sustained talk. Incidentally, linguists might then be better able to countenance inroads that others can be expected to make into their conventional domain. For it seems that talk itself is intimately regulated and closely geared to its context through nonvocal gestures which are very differently distributed from the particular language and subcodes employed by any set of participants—although just where these boundaries of gesture-use *are* to be drawn remains an almost unstudied question.

Notes

1   A wonderfully hilarious (and sound) example is provided by Jacques Derrida's 92-page analysis of the presuppositions employed by John Searle in the latter's 10-page reply to Derrida's 25-page critique of speech act theory (Derrida 1977).

2   In this simplified pragmatic view I follow Stalnaker (1973).

3   Austin (1965, pp. 21–3) excludes from infelicities certain ways in which what appears to be a performative really is not, in part because these "parasitic" forms could infect any utterance, not merely a performative; but he admits a clear line cannot be drawn. I follow Searle (1969, p. 61, n. 1) in including these etiolations.

4   Be as informative as is required, but not more so; say only what you believe is true and for which you feel you have adequate evidence; be relevant; avoid ambiguous or obscure expressions or unordered presentation.

5   In a useful paper, Baker (1975) rightly argues that prefatory apologies can be employed to mitigate any dereliction of conversational duty, including, e.g., the violation of any of the Gricean maxims.

6   Individuals situated as herein described teeter on the edge of talk. A "free good" (see n. 11 for definition), e.g., can easily be requested or offered, this in turn giving either party something of a right to extend the crossover with small talk. ("Response cries" can similarly provide an opener, at least for the hearer.) Consequently, someone desirous of offering or requesting a free good might inhibit the impulse, not wanting to risk the possibility that the opening thereby given might be extended by the other into a sustained state of talk.

7   We describe the utterance "Two please" as a *request* for tickets, but in fact the only thing being requested is that an exchange of tickets for money be initiated now. We mean, "Could I buy two tickets now," but we do not say it.

8   "Summonses" were first considered systematically (and under that label) in Schegloff (1968). Sacks (1972, pp. 344–5) used the term "ticket" to refer to warrants for unceremoniously initiating a state of talk. Nofsinger (1975) examines summoning into a state of talk and applying for the right to tell a little story in a state of talk already established, considering both under the term "demand ticket."

9   There is a summons cue that also functions to gain the attention of the head speaker in a meeting, the consequences of which will be a speaker/addressed-recipient exchange within a larger whole. However, such turn requests seem to carry little of the force of the primary kind. After all, those seeking to be ratified as next speaker by head speaker are already engaged in a state of talk—if only as unaddressed recipients—and the person they are trying to make contact with is not in transit beyond their ken.

10   Alerts can be compared to what Jefferson (1978, p. 221) calls "disjunct markers" and "embedded repetition," these being two sequenced devices for gearing a storytelling into a conversation. Disjunct markers, of course ("Incidentally, . . ." "By the way, . . ."), are also employed to show recognition of, and apologize for, other threats to coherence. A general treatment of "speech markers" is available in Schiffrin (1982).

11   I use the term "free good" to refer to those things perceived as ones a possessor can give away at relatively little cost or inconvenience even though they may be urgently needed by the recipient. (I do not, therefore, mean sunshine or public tennis courts, although

these goods could also be called free ones.) Free goods, as here defined, provide an interesting source of social solidarity. Their range varies greatly according to ecology. For example, although fellow pedestrians and fellow motorists ordinarily have quite limited resources of this kind, those who pass each other on isolated desert roads in effect have greater resources and are (in the Southwest) more likely to initiate the offer of them. (Similarly, close neighbors in otherwise isolated areas are well situated to supply each other with a wide range of free goods, and, correspondingly, have a good reason to sustain friendly relations.) All of which is not to deny that free goods are often withheld from those we define as beyond the pale—persons who by their appearance and manner suggest that their need is chronic or even simulated, and that they are systematically exploiting pedestrian charitableness for what can be accumulated through repeated requests. Thus, an affluent-looking stranger may request or be offered an appreciable free good on the assumption, presumably, that no "working" of the system is involved (and, of course, that such a person would be in a position to offer the same level of help to another on a different occasion). A full consideration of the implications of free goods in dealings between cross-sexed strangers is reported in Gardner (1983). A consideration of direction giving is provided in Psathas and Kogloff (1976).

12   In politics, business, and courtship, information can, of course, be strategic and as such anything but free; but this sort of information is not likely to be asked for as if it were a free good. More generally, information about self is a form of personal territoriality and an important ceremonial adjunct to the organization of social relationships (Goffman 1971, pp. 38–40).

13   Not quite everyone, of course. For example (as Bambi Schieffelin has suggested to me), although it is deemed reasonable to wait in line in order to buy a ticket, to do so to elicit a free good might seen odd, perhaps because a free good, after all, is the sort of thing that almost anyone could supply. If the askers are to show they are alive to what they are doing, any marked inconvenience to asking one source should cause them to seek another. Indeed, even in matters cinematic, an asker will be constrained to display a "sense of proportion": to wait in a long line merely to find out who is starring in a film could strike witnesses as strange.

14   For a conversation to have been "struck up," we apparently assume that the participants had been unacquainted (so that to speak of "strangers" doing it is redundant) and that circumstances had positioned them close to each other with evidently "nothing" but waiting to do.

15   Small talk is itself of considerable interest. Topics such as the weather, inflation, television shows, unsafety on the streets, and the like can be seen as "innocuous," meaning here that no offense is likely to be taken by anyone addressed on the matter. But surely more is involved. It is as if society had set aside certain topics as ones that everyone is expected to have an opinion on, that are to be held in relative readiness and to be brought to mind quickly, that are not defined as part of anyone's protected lore (and therefore can be addressed by social inferiors), and that are seen as requiring no special competence or experience. Small-talk topics, then, mark a socially sanctioned opening between minds.

16   The central treatment here is Berger and Kellner (1964).

17   I have also heard "Ya know . . ." used as an alert in small talk among the barely acquainted, the apparent function being to ready hearers for an obiter dictum whose level of generality departs sharply from the conversational particulars that surround it.

18   Labov (1972, p. 370) is almost an exception: "To identify the evaluative portion of a narrative, it is necessary to know why this narrative—or any narrative—is felt to be tellable; in other words, why the events of the narrative are *reportable*." Joel Sherzer reminds me that reportability is very much a cultural matter, citing Cuna Indian

discourse, where, in the replaying of experience, incidental details are routinely reported to a degree we would judge excessive.

19　A beginning is provided by Garnes and Bond (1975) and Grimshaw (1980).

20　It should be noted that this bias is not a necessary result of the Sacks-Schegloff-Jefferson turn-taking model (1974), for the initial formulation leaves ample room for lapses in talk.

21　A useful analysis of reference and task activity is provided in Grosz (1974a, 1974b).

22　A point that Grice (1975, p. 48) himself makes.

References

Austin, J. L. 1965. *How to Do Things with Words.* Edited by J. O. Urmson. New York: Oxford University Press.

Baker, Charlotte, 1975. "This Is Just a First Approximation, But . . ." *Chicago Linguistic Society* 11:37–47.

Berger, Peter L., and Hansfried Kellner. 1964. "Marriage and the Construction of Reality." *Diogenes* 45:1–25.

Chafe, Wallace L. 1974. "Language and Consciousness." *Language* 59:112.

Clark, Herbert H., and Catherine Marshall. 1981. "Definite Reference and Mutual Knowledge." Pp. 10–63 in *Elements of Discourse Understanding*, edited by A. Joshi, B. Webber, and I. Sag. Cambridge: Cambridge University Press.

Derrida, Jacques. 1977. "Limited Inc abc . . ." *Glyph* 2:162–254.

Gardner, Carol. 1983. "Aspects of Gender Behavior in a Small Southwestern City." Ph.D. dissertation, Department of Sociology, University of Pennsylvania.

Garnes, Sara, and Zinny S. Bond. 1975. "Slips of the Ear: Errors in Perception of Casual Speech." *Chicago Linguistic Society* 11:214–25.

Goffman, Erving. 1971. *Relations in Public.* New York: Harper Colophon. —. 1981. *Forms of Talk.* Philadelphia: University of Pennsylvania Press.

Grice, H. Paul. 1975. "Logic and Conversation." Pp. 41–58 in *Syntax and Semantics.* Vol. 3, *Speech Acts*, edited by Peter Cole and Jerry L. Morgan. New York: Academic Press.

Grimshaw, Allen D. 1980. "Mishearings, Misunderstandings, and Other Nonsuccesses in Talk." *Sociological Inquiry* 50:31–74.

Grosz, Barbara J. 1974a. "The Representation and Use of Focus in Dialogue Understanding." Stanford Research Institute Project 1526, Technical Note 90. Menlo Park, Calif.:SRI.

—. 1974b. "The Structure of Task Oriented Dialogues." Stanford Research Institute Project 1526, Technical Note 90. Menlo Park, Calif.:SRI.

Jefferson, Gail. 1978. "Sequential Aspects of Storytelling in Conversation." Pp. 219–48 in *Studies in the Organization of Conversational Interaction*, edited by Jim Schenkein. New York: Academic Press.

Labov, William. 1972. "The Transformation of Experience in Narrative Syntax." Pp. 354–96 in *Language in the Inner City*, by William Labov. Philadelphia: University of Pennsylvania Press.

Lakoff, Robin. 1973 "The Logic of Politeness; or Minding Your P's and Q's." Pp. 292–305 in *Papers from the 9th Regional Meeting, Chicago Linguistic Society*, edited by Claudia Corum et al. Chicago: Chicago Linguistic Society.

Merritt, Marilyn. 1976. "On Questions Following Questions in Service Encounters." *Language in Society* 5:315–57.

Nofsinger, Robert E., Jr. 1975. "The Demand Ticket: A Conversational Device for Getting the Floor." *Speech Monographs* 42:1–9.

Psathas, George, and Martin Kogloff. 1976. "The Structure of Directions." *Semiotica* 17:111–30.

Sacks, Harvey.1972. "On the Analyzability of Stories by Children." Pp. 329–45 in *Directions in Sociolinguistics*, edited by John J. Gumperz and Dell H. Hymes. New York: Holt, Rinehart & Winston.

Sacks, Harvey, Emanuel A. Schegloff, and Gail Jefferson. 1974. "A Simplest Systematics for the Organization of Turn-Taking for Conversation." *Language* 50:696–735.

Schegloff, Emanuel A. 1968. "Sequencing in Conversational Openings." *American Anthropologist* 70:1075–95.

Schiffrin, Deborah. 1982. "Discourse Markers: Semantic Resource for the Construction of Conversation." Ph.D. dissertation, Department of Linguistics, University of Pennsylvania.

Searle, John R. 1969. *Speech Acts: An Essay in the Philosophy of Language*. Cambridge: Cambridge University Press.

Stalnaker, Robert. 1973. "Presuppositions." *Journal of Philosophical Logic* 2:447–57.

14

Frame Analysis of Gender

From "The Arrangement Between the Sexes"*

In modern industrial society, as apparently in all others, sex is at the base of a fundamental code in accordance with which social interactions and social structures are built up, a code which also establishes the conceptions individuals have concerning their fundamental human nature. This is an oft stated proposition, but until recently its awesomely ramified significance escaped us.

★   ★   ★

Now the heart of the matter. It is common to conceive of the differences between the sexes as showing up against the demands and constraints of the environment, the environment itself being taken as a harsh given, present before the matter of sex differences arose. Or, differently put, that sex differences are a biological given, an external constraint upon any form of social organization that humans might devise. There is another way of viewing the question, however. Speculatively one can reverse the equation and ask what could be sought out from the environment or put into it so that such innate differences between the sexes as there are could count—in fact or in appearance—for something. The issue, then, is institutional reflexivity. Consider some examples.

1. Clearly on biological grounds, mother is in a position to breastfeed baby and father is not. Given that recalcitrant fact, it is meet that father temporarily but exclusively takes on such tasks as may involve considerable separation from the household. But this quite temporary biologically-grounded constraint turns out to be extended culturally. A whole range of domestic duties come (for whatever reason) to be defined as inappropriate for a male to perform; and a whole range of occupations away from the household come to be defined as inappropriate for the female. Given these social definitions coalition formation is a natural response to the harsh facts of the world, for only in this way will one be able to acquire what one needs

* Originally published in *Theory and Society*, 1977, 4 (3), pp. 301, 313–19, 324. Copyright © 1977 by Kluwer Academic Publishers. Reprinted by permission of Kluwer Academic Publishers.

and yet not have to engage in labor that is unsuitable for someone of one's kind. Nor is couple formation required only because of gender constraints on task performance. In public life in general women will find that there are things that should be done for them, and men will find that there are things that they should be doing for others, so once again they find they need each other. (So that just as a man may take a wife to save himself from labor that is uncongenial to him, so she can seek him so as to have the company she needs if she is to make full use of public places.) Thus, the human nature imputed to the male causes him to be dependent on a female connection, and the reciprocal condition prevails for women. Who a male finds he needs if he is to act according to his nature is just who needs him so that she can act according to hers. Persons as such do not need one another in these ways, they do so only as gender-based identities.

2.   Consider the household as a socialization depot. Take as a paradigm a middle-class pair of cross-sexed sibs. The home training of the two sexes will differ, beginning to orient the girl to taking a domestic, supportive role, and the boy to a more widely based competitive one. This difference in orientation will be superimposed on a fundamental quality in many matters that are felt to count. So from the start, then, there will be two basic principles to appeal to in making claims and warranting allocations. One is the equality of sibs and beyond this of participating members—the share and share alike theme realized in its strongest form in many wills and in its most prevalent form in turn-taking systems. The other is the accounting by sex, as when the larger portion at mealtime is given to the male "because he's a boy" or the softer of two beds is allocated to the female "because she's a girl," or a male is accorded harsher negative sanctions than a female because his is the coarser nature and it will take more to get through to him. And these accountings by appeal to gender will never cease to be used as a handy device to rationalize an allocation whose basis is otherwise determined, to exclude a basis of allocation that might cause disgruntlement, and, even more, to explain away various failures to live up to expectations.

All of this is perfectly well known in principle, although not adequately explored in detail. What is not well appreciated is that differently sexed children coming under the jurisdiction of the same parental authority and living much of their early lives in one another's presence in the same set of rooms produce thereby an ideal setting for role differentiation. For family life ensures that most of what each sex does is done in the full sight of the other sex and with full mutual appreciation of the differential treatment that obtains. Thus, whatever the economic or class level and however well or badly off a female sees she is when compared to children in other families, she can hardly fail to see that her male sib, equal to her when compared to children in other families and often equal, too, in regard to ultimate claims upon the family resources, is yet judged differently and accorded different treatment from herself by their parents. So, too, a male sib. Thus from the beginning males and females acquire a way of judging deserts and treatment that muffles (by cross-cutting) differences in class and economic power. However superior the social position of a family may be, its female children will be able to learn that they are different from (and somewhat subordinate to) males; and however inferior the social position of a family may be, its male children will be able to learn that they are different from (and somewhat superordinate to) females. It is as if society planted a brother with sisters so women could from the beginning learn their place, and a sister with brothers so men could learn their place. Each sex becomes a training device for the other, a device that is brought right into the house; and what will serve to structure wider social life is thus given its shape and its impetus in a very small and very cozy circle. And it also follows that the deepest sense of what one is—one's gender identity—is something that is given its initial character from ingredients that do not bear on ethnicity or socio-economic stratification, in consequence of which we all acquire a deep capacity to shield ourselves from what we gain and lose by virtue of our placement in the overall social hierarchy. Brothers will have a way of defining themselves in terms of their differences from persons like their sisters, and sisters will have a way of defining themselves in terms of their differences from persons like their brothers, in both cases turning perception away from how it is the sibs in one family are socially situated in a fundamentally different way from the sibs of another family. Gender, not religion, is the opiate of the masses. In any case, we have here a remarkable organizational device. A man may spend his day suffering under those who have power over him, suffer this situation at almost any level of society, and yet on returning home each night regain a sphere in which he dominates. And wherever he goes beyond the household, women can be there to prop up his show of competence. It is not merely that your male executive has a female secretary, but (as now often remarked) his drop-out son who moves up the hierarchy of alternative publishing or protest politics will have female help, too; and had he been disaffected enough to join a rural commune, an appropriate division of labor would have awaited him. And should we leave the real world for something set up as its fictional alternative, a science fiction cosmos, we would find that here, too, males engage in the executive action and have females to help out in the manner of their sex. Wherever the male goes, apparently, he can carry a sexual division of labor with him.

3. In modern times, mating pairs appear naked to each other and are even likely to employ a bathroom at the same time. But beyond this, the mature genitalia of one sex is not supposed to be exposed to the eyes of the other sex. Furthermore, although it is recognized that persons of both sexes are

somewhat similar in the question of waste products and their elimination, the environment in which females engage in this act ought (we in America apparently feel) to be more refined, extensive, and elaborate than that required for males. Presumably out of consideration for the arrangement between the sexes in general, and the female sex-class in particular, it has come to pass, then, that almost all places of work and congregation are equipped with two sets of toilet facilities (a case of parallel organization), differentiated with respect to quality. A case of separate and unequal. Therefore, in very nearly every industrial and commercial establishment, women will be able to break off being exposed to males and their company and retire into an all-female enclave, often in the company of a female friend, and there spend time in toiletry, a longer time presumably, and perhaps more frequently, than males spend in their segregated toilet, and under more genteel environmental conditions. A resting room that is sex-segregated (as many are) may extend this divided realm. There is thus established a sort of with-then-apart rhythm, with a period of the sexes being immersed together, followed by a short period of separation, and so on. (Bars, gyms, locker rooms, pool rooms, etc., accomplish the same sort of periodic segregation, but from the male side, the difference being that whereas female redoubts tend to be furnished more genteely than the surrounding scene, male redoubts [at least in the U.S.] are often furnished less prepossessingly than the surround.) This same pattern seems to be extended outwards from toilets and resting rooms to larger domains. Large stores have floors which merge the sexes but also smaller zones which offer one-sex merchandise patronized very largely by that sex alone. Schools provide coeducational classes, punctuated by gym, sports, and a few other activities that are sex-segregated.

All in all then, one does not so much deal with segregation as with segregative punctuation of the day's round, this ensuring that subcultural differences can be reaffirmed and reestablished in the face of contact between the sexes. It is as if the joining of the sexes were tolerable providing periodic escape is possible; it is as if equality and sameness were a masquerade that was to be periodically dropped. And all of this is done in the name of nicety, of civilization, of the respect owed females, or of the "natural" need of men to be by themselves. Observe that since by and large public places are designed for males (the big exception being large department stores), female facilities have had to be added to ones already established. Predictably, it has been an argument against hiring females that an extra complement of toilet facilities would be necessary and is not available.

Now clearly, if ogling and sexual access is to play the role it does in pair formation in our society, then sequestering of toilet functions by sex would seem to be indicated. And even more clearly, what is thus sequestered is a biological matter in terms of which the sex-classes biologically and markedly differ. But the sequestering arrangement as such cannot be tied to matters biological, only to folk conceptions about biological matters. The *functioning* of sex-differentiated organs is involved, but there is nothing in this functioning that *biologically* recommends segregation; *that* arrangement is totally a cultural matter. And what one has is a case of institutional reflexivity: toilet segregation is presented as a natural consequence of the difference between the sex-classes, when in fact it is rather a means of honoring, if not producing, this difference.

4. Consider now selective job placement. Traditionally in industrial society women have gravitated to, or have been gravitated to, jobs which sustain the note established for them in households—the garment industry, domestic labor, commercial cleaning, and personal servicing such as teaching, innkeeping, nursing, food handling. In these latter scenes, presumably, it will be easy for us to fall into treating the server as someone to help us in a semi-mothering way, not someone to subordinate coldly or be subordinated by. In service matters closely associated with the body and the self, we are thus able to play down the harshness that male servers might be thought to bring.

Women, especially young, middle-class ones, have also, of course, been much employed in clerical and secretarial labor, which work is often defined as a dead-end job to be filled by someone who dresses well and doesn't expect or want to make a career out of the labor. Presumably secretaries are merely marking time until marriage, preferably in a place where opportunity to "meet" men is to be found. In any case, the age and sex difference between secretary and employer allows for some styling in avuncular terms. By removing the relationship from the strict world of business, the superior can suffer being intimately viewed by a subordinate without feeling that he has lost rank by the association. He can also make minor demands beyond the core of the contract, expecting to be seen as someone whose needs should be attended to however varied these might be—as a child would be attended by a mother. In return he can extend family feeling, using a personal term of address (of course asymmetrically), please-and-thank-you brackets around each of the minor discrete services called for, and gallantry in the matter of opening doors and moving heavy typewriters. He can also allow her to use the telephone for personal calls and can respond to pleas for special time off to accomplish the business of her sex.

So, too, one finds in jobs where women "meet the public"—ticket-takers, receptionists, airhostesses, salespersons—that standards of youthful "attractiveness" apply in employee selection. Which practice is, of course, even more marked in selecting women for advertising displays and the dramatic arts. The consequence is that when a male has business contacts with a female, she is more than otherwise likely to be someone whom he might take pleasure in associating with. Again, the courtesy he here extends and receives can carry a dash of sexual interest. (It appears that the higher the male reaches in the hierarchies within business, government, or the professions, the classier will be the women he is required to have incidental dealings with, a sign and symbol of success.)

Finally, note that in almost all work settings established as places for thoroughly masculine labor, one or two women can be found engaged in some sort of ancillary work. It turns out, then, that there are few social settings where males will not be in a position to enact courtesies due to the female sex.

In all, then, one can see that selective employment comes to ensure that males are likely to find themselves rather frequently in the presence of females, and that these women will not only tend to allow a personalization of the contact, but will be relatively young and attractive beyond what random selection ought to allow. In that sense, the world that men are in is a social construct, drawing them daily from their conjugal milieu to what appears to be all-male settings; but these environments turn out to be strategically stocked with relatively attractive females, there to serve in a specialized way as passing targets for sexually allusive banter and for diffuse considerateness extended in both directions. The principle is that of less for more, the effect is that of establishing the world beyond the household as a faintly red-light district where men can easily find and safely enjoy interactional favors. Observe that the more a male contents himself with gender pleasantries—systematically available yet intermittent and brief—the more widely can a preferential category of females be shared by males in general. (Indeed, the traditional dating game can be seen not merely as a means of getting the sexes paired, but as a means of giving a large number of men a little of the company of exemplary women.)

5. Among all the means by which differentiation along sex-class lines is fostered in modern society, one stands out as having a special and an especially powerful influence: I refer to our *identification system*, this involving two related matters, our means of discovering "who" it is that has come into our ken, that is, our placement practices, and our means of labeling what it is we have thus placed.

On the placement side, it is clear that the appearance established as appropriate to the two sexes allows for sex typing at a distance. Although recently this arrangement has developed some potential for error, still the system is remarkably effective at any angle and from almost any distance, saving only that viewing be close enough to allow perception of a figure. Effectiveness of placement by sight is matched by sound; tone of voice alone—as on the phone—is sufficient by and large for sexual identification. Indeed, handwriting is effective, too, although perhaps not as fully as appearance and voice. (Only appreciable differences in age are as effectively betrayed through all three channels; race in America is conveyed through sight and, by and large, through voice but not through handwriting.)

On the naming side, we have a system of terms including proper personal names, titles, and pronouns. These devices are used for giving deference (whether respect, distance, or affection), for specifying who we are addressing or who among those present we are referring to, and for making attributions in written and spoken statements. And in European languages, by and large, except for second-person pronouns, these naming practices inform at least about sex-class, this often being the only matter they do inform about.

Now our placement practices and name practices, taken together as a single system, serve to define who we are to have dealings with and enable these dealings to proceed: and both sets of practices very strongly encourage categorization along sex-class lines. Right from the very start of an inter-action, then, there is a bias in favor of formulating matters in sex-relevant terms, such that sex-class provides the overall profile or container, and particularizing properties are then attributed to the outline by way of speci-fication. This is not a small bias. And note that this identification-naming system is overwhelmingly accounted for by the doctrine that consequent discriminations are only natural, something not to be seen as a product of personal or social engineering but rather as a natural phenomenon.

★　★　★

I have suggested that every physical surround, every room, every box for social gatherings, necessarily provides materials that can be used in the display of gender and the affirmation of gender identity. But, of course, the social interaction occurring in these places can be read as supplying these materials also. Participants in any gathering must take up some sort of microecological position relative to one another, and these positions will provide ready metaphors for social distance and relatedness, just as they will provide sign vehicles for conveying relative rank.

More important, the management of talk will itself make available a swarm of events usable as signs. Who is brought or brings himself into the immediate orbit of another; who initiates talk, who is selected as the addressed recipient, who self-selects in talk turn-taking, who establishes and changes topics, whose statements are given attention and weight, and so forth. As with verbal interaction, so also with joint participation in silent projects such as walking together, arranging objects, and the like. For here, too, organization requires that someone make the decisions and coordinate the activity; and again the opportunity is available, often apparently unavoid-ably so, for someone to emerge as dominant, albeit in regard to trivial matters.

An interactional field, then, provides a considerable expressive resource, and it is, of course, upon this field that there is projected the training and beliefs of the participants. It is here that sex-class makes itself felt, here in the organization of face-to-face interaction, for here understandings about sex-based dominance can be employed as a means of deciding who decides, who leads, and who follows. Again, these scenes do not so much allow for the expression of natural differences between the sexes as for the production of that difference itself.

"Gender Display"*

I

Take it that the function of ceremony reaches in two directions, the affirmation of basic social arrangements and the presentation of ultimate doctrines about man and the world. Typically these celebrations are performed either by persons acting to one another or acting in concert before a congregation. So "social situations" are involved—defining these simply as physical arenas anywhere within which persons present are in perceptual range of one another, subject to mutual monitoring—the persons themselves being definable solely on this ground as a "gathering."

It is in social situations, then, that materials for celebrative work must be found, materials which can be shaped into a palpable representation of matters not otherwise packaged for the eye and the ear and the moment. And found they are. The divisions and hierarchies of social structure are depicted microecologically, that is, through the use of small-scale spatial metaphors. Mythic historic events are played through in a condensed and idealized version. Apparent junctures or turning points in life are solemnized, as in christenings, graduation exercises, marriage ceremonies, and funerals. Social relationships are addressed by greetings and farewells. Seasonal cycles are given dramatized boundaries. Reunions are held. Annual vacations and, on a lesser scale, outings on weekends and evenings are assayed, bringing immersion in ideal settings. Dinners and parties are given, becoming occasions for the expenditure of resources at a rate that is above one's mundane self. Moments of festivity are attached to the acquisition of new possessions.

In all of these ways, a situated social fuss is made over what might ordinarily be hidden in extended courses of activity and the unformulated

* Originally published in *Gender Advertisements: Studies in the Anthropology of Visual Communication,* 1976; reprinted here from the 1979 edition, pp. 1–9. Copyright © 1976 by Erving Goffman. Reprinted by permission of HarperCollins Publishers, Inc.

experience of their participants; in brief, the individual is given an opportunity to face directly a representation, a somewhat iconic expression, a mock-up of what he is supposed to hold dear, a presentation of the supposed ordering of his existence.

A single, fixed element of a ceremony can be called a "ritual"; the interpersonal kind can be defined as perfunctory, conventionalized acts through which one individual portrays his regard for another to that other.

II

If Durkheim leads us to consider one sense of the term ritualization, Darwin, in his *Expression of Emotion in Man and Animals*, leads us, coincidentally, to consider quite another. To paraphrase Julian Huxley (and the ethological position), the basic argument is that under the pressure of natural selection certain emotionally motivated behaviors become formalized—in the sense of becoming simplified, exaggerated, and stereotyped—and loosened from any specific context of releasers, and all this so that, in effect, there will be more efficient signalling, both inter- and intra-specifically.[1] These behaviors are "displays," a species-utilitarian notion that is at the heart of the ethological conception of communication. Instead of having to play out an act, the animal, in effect, provides a readily readable expression of his situation, specifically his intent, this taking the form of a "ritualization" of some portion of the act itself, and this indication (whether promise or threat) presumably allows for the negotiation of an efficient response from, and to, witnesses of the display. (If Darwin leads here, John Dewey, and G. H. Mead are not far behind.)

The ethological concern, then, does not take us back from a ritual performance to the social structure and ultimate beliefs in which the performer and witness are embedded, but forward into the unfolding course of socially situated events. Displays thus provide evidence of the actor's *alignment* in a gathering, the position he seems prepared to take up in what is about to happen in the social situation. Alignments tentatively or indicatively establish the terms of the contact, the mode or style or formula for the dealings that are to ensure among the individuals in the situation. As suggested, ethologists tend to use the term communication here, but that might be loose talk. Displays don't communicate in the narrow sense of the term; they don't enunciate something through a language of symbols openly established and used solely for that purpose. They provide evidence of the actor's alignment in the situation. And displays are important insofar as alignments are.

A version of display for humans would go something like this: Assume all of an individual's behavior and appearance informs those who witness him, minimally telling them something about his social identity, about his mood, intent, and expectations, and about the state of his relation to them. In every culture a distinctive range of this indicative behavior and appearance becomes specialized so as to more routinely and perhaps more effectively perform this informing function, the informing coming to be the controlling role of the performance, although often not avowedly so. One can call these indicative events displays. As suggested, they tentatively establish the terms of the contact, the mode or style or formula for the dealings that are to ensue between the persons providing the display and the persons perceiving it.

Finally, our special concern: If gender be defined as the culturally established correlates of sex (whether in consequence of biology or learning), then gender display refers to conventionalized portrayals of these correlates.

III

What can be said about the structure of ritual-like displays?

1. Displays very often have a dialogic character of a statement-reply kind, with an expression on the part of one individual calling forth an expression on the part of another, the latter expression being understood to be a response to the first.

These statement-response pairs can be classified in an obvious way. There are symmetrical and asymmetrical pairs: mutual first-naming is a symmetrical pair, first-name/sir is an asymmetrical one. Of asymmetrical pairs, some are dyadically reversible, some not: the greetings between guest and host, asymmetrical in themselves, may be reversed between these two persons on another occasion; first-name/title, on the other hand, ordinarily is not reversible. Of dyadically irreversible pairs of rituals, some pair parts are exclusive, some not: the civilian title a male may extend a female is never extended to him; on the other hand, the "Sir" a man receives from a subordinate in exchange for first-name, he himself is likely to extend to *his* superordinate in exchange for first-name, an illustration of the great chain of corporate being.

Observe that a symmetrical display between two individuals can involve asymmetries according to which of the two initially introduced the usage between them, and which of the two begins his part of the mutual display first on any occasion of use.

And symmetry (or asymmetry) itself can be misleading. One must consider not only how two individuals ritually treat each other, but also how they separately treat, and are treated by, a common third. Thus the point about symmetrical greetings and farewells extended between a male and a close female friend is that he is very likely to extend a *different* set, albeit equally symmetrical, to her husband, and she, similarly, a yet different symmetrical set to his wife. Indeed, so deeply does the male-female difference inform our ceremonial life that one finds here a very systematic "opposite number" arrangement. For every courtesy, symmetrical or asymmetrical, that a woman shows to almost anyone, there will be a parallel one—seen to be the same, yet different—which her brother or husband shows to the same person.

2. Given that individuals have work to do in social situations, the question arises as to how ritual can accommodate to what is thus otherwise occurring. Two basic patterns seem to appear. First, display seems to be concentrated at beginnings and endings of purposeful undertakings, that is, at junctures, so that, in effect, the activity itself is not interfered with. (Thus the small courtesies sometimes performed in our society by men to women when the latter must undergo what can be defined as a slight change in physical state, as in getting up, sitting down, entering a room or leaving it, beginning to smoke or ceasing to, moving indoors or outdoors, suffering increased temperature or less, and so forth.) Here one might speak of "bracket rituals." Second, some rituals seem designed to be continued as a single note across a strip of otherwise intended activity without displacing that activity itself. (Thus the basic military courtesy of standing at attention throughout the course of an encounter with a superior—in contrast to the salute, this latter clearly a bracket ritual.) One can speak here of a "ritual transfix" or "overlay." Observe that by combining these two locations—brackets and overlays—one has, for any strip of activity, a *schedule* of displays. Although these rituals will tend to be perceived as coloring the whole of the scene, in fact, of course, they only occur selectively in it.

3. It is plain that if an individual is to give and receive what is considered his ritual due in social situations, then he must—whether by intent or in effect—style himself so that others present can immediately know the social (and sometimes the personal) identity of he who is to be dealt with; and in turn he must be able to acquire this information about those he thus informs. Some displays seem to be specialized for this identificatory, early-warning function: in the case of gender, hair style, clothing, and tone of voice. (Handwriting similarly serves in the situation-like contacts conducted through the mails; name also so serves, in addition to serving in the management of persons who are present only in reference.) It can be argued that although ritualized behavior in social situations may markedly change over time, especially in connection with politicization, identificatory stylings will be least subject to change.

4. There is no doubt that displays can be, and are likely to be, multivocal or polysemic, in the sense that more than one piece of social information may be encoded in them. (For example, our terms of address typically record sex of recipient and also properties of the relationship between speaker and spoken to. So, too, in occupational titles ["agentives"]. In the principal European languages, typically a masculine form is the unmarked case; the

feminine is managed with a suffix which, in addition, often carries a conno-
tation of incompetence, facetiousness, and inexperience.[2]) Along with this
complication goes another. Not only does one find that recognition of
different statuses can be encoded in the same display, but also that a hierarchy of considerations may be found which are addressed sequentially. For
example, when awards are given out, a male official may first give the medal,
diploma, prize, or whatever, and then shake the hand of the recipient, thus
shifting from that of an organization's representative bestowing an official
sign of regard on a soldier, colleague, fellow citizen, etc., to a man showing
regard for another, the shift in action associated with a sharply altered facial
expression. This seems nicely confirmed when the recipient is a woman. For
then the second display can be a social kiss. When Admiral Elmo R.
Zumwalt, then chief of U.S. naval operations, officiated in the ceremony in
which Alene Duerk became the first female admiral in the U.S. Navy's
history (as director of the Navy Nurse Corps) he added to what was done
by kissing her full on the lips.[3] So, too, a female harpist after just completing
Ginastera's Harp Concerto, and having just shaken the hand of the
conductor (as would a male soloist), is free (as a male is not) to strike an
additional note by leaning over and giving the conductor a kiss on the cheek.
Similarly, the applause she receives will be her due as a musician, but the
flowers that are brought onstage a moment after speak to something that
would not be spoken to in a male soloist. And the reverse sequence is
possible. I have seen a well-bred father raise his hat on first meeting his
daughter after a two-year absence, *then* bend and kiss her. (The hat-raise
denoted the relationship between the sexes—presumably "any lady" would
have induced it—the kiss, the relation between kin.)

5. Displays vary quite considerably in the degree of their formalization.
Some, like salutes, are specified as to form and occasion of occurrence, and
failure to so behave can lead to specific sanctions; others are so much taken
for granted that it awaits a student of some kind to explicate what everyone
knows (but not consciously), and failure to perform leads to nothing more
than diffuse unease and a search for speakable reasons to be ill-tempered
with the offender.

6. The kind of displays I will be concerned with—gender displays—have
a related feature: many appear to be optional.[4] In the case, for example, of
male courtesies, often a particular display need not be initiated; if initiated,
it need not be accepted, but can be politely declined. Finally, when failure
to perform occurs, irony, nudging, and joking complaint, etc., can
result—sometimes more as an opportunity for a sally than as a means of
social control. Correlated with this basis of looseness is another: for each
display there is likely to be a set of functional equivalents wherewith something of the display's effect can be accomplished by alternative niceties. At
work, too, is the very process of ritualization. A recipient who declines an

incipient gesture of deference has waited until the intending giver has shown his desire to perform it; the more the latter can come to count on this foreclosure of his move, the more his show of intent can itself come to displace the unfolded form.

7. Ordinarily displays do not in fact provide a representation in the round of a specific social relationship but rather of broad groupings of them. For example, a social kiss may be employed by kin-related persons or cross-sex friends, and the details of the behavior itself may not inform as to which relationship is being celebrated. Similarly, precedence through a door is available to mark organizational rank, but the same indulgence is accorded guests of an establishment, the dependently young, the aged and infirm, indeed, those of unquestionably strong social position and those (by inversion courtesy) of unquestionably weak position. A picture, then, of the relationship between any two persons can hardly be obtained through an examination of the displays they extend each other on any one type of occasion; one would have to assemble these niceties across all the mutually identifying types of contacts that the pair has.

There is a loose gearing, then, between social structures and what goes on in particular occasions of ritual expression. This can further be seen by examining the abstract ordinal format which is commonly generated within social situations. Participants, for example, are often displayed in rankable order with respect to some visible property—looks, height, elevation, closeness to the center, elaborateness of costume, temporal precedence, and so forth—and the comparisons are somehow taken as a reminder of differential social position, the differences in social distance between various positions and the specific character of the positions being lost from view. Thus, the basic forms of deference provide a peculiarly limited version of the social universe, telling us more perhaps, about the special depictive resources of social situations than about the structures presumably expressed thereby.

8. People, unlike other animals, can be quite conscious of the displays they employ and are able to perform many of them by design in contexts of their own choosing. Thus instead of merely "displacing" an act (in the sense described by ethologists), the human actor may wait until he is out of the direct line of sight of a putative recipient, and then engage in a portrayal of attitude to him that is only then safe to perform, the performance done for the benefit of the performer himself or third parties. In turn, the recipient of such a display (or rather the target of it) may actively collaborate, fostering the impression that the act has escaped him even though it hasn't—and sometimes evidentally so. (There is the paradox, then, that what is done for revealment can be partially concealed.) More important, once a display becomes well established in a particular sequence of actions, a section of the sequence can be lifted out of its original context, parenthesized, and used in

a quotative way, a postural resource for mimicry, mockery, irony, teasing, and other sportive intents, including, very commonly, the depiction of make-believe scenes in advertisements. Here stylization itself becomes an object of attention, the actor providing a comment on this process in the very act through which he unseriously realizes it. What was a ritual becomes itself ritualized, a transformation of what is already a transformation, a "hyper-ritualization." Thus, the human use of displays is complicated by the human capacity for reframing behavior.

In sum, then, how a relationship is portrayed through ritual can provide an imbalanced, even distorted, view of the relationship itself. When this fact is seen in the light of another, namely, that displays tend to be scheduled accommodatively during an activity so as not to interfere with its execution, it becomes even more clear that the version ritual gives us of social reality is only that—not a picture of the way things are but a passing exhortative guide to perception.

IV

Displays are part of what we think of as "expressive behavior," and as such tend to be conveyed and received as if they were somehow natural, deriving, like temperature and pulse, from the way people are and needful, therefore, of no social or historical analysis. But, of course, ritualized expressions are as needful of historical understanding as is the Ford car. Given the expressive practices we employ, one may ask: Where do these displays come from?

If, in particular, there are behavioral styles—codings—that distinguish the way men and women participate in social situations, then the question should be put concerning the origins and sources of these styles. The materials and ingredients can come directly from the resources available in particular social settings, but that still leaves open the question of where the formulating of these ingredients, their *styling*, comes from.

The most prominent account of the origins of our gender displays is, of course, the biological. Gender is assumed to be an extension of our animal natures, and just as animals express their sex, so does man: innate elements are said to account for the behavior in both cases. And indeed, the means by which we initially establish an individual in one of the two sex classes and confirm this location in its later years can be and are used as a means of placement in the management of domestic animals. However, although the signs for establishing placement are expressive of matters biological, why we should think of these matters as essential and central is a cultural matter. More important, where behavioral gender display does draw on animal life, it seems to do so not, or not merely, in a direct evolutionary sense but as a source of imagery—a cultural resource. The animal kingdom—or at least certain select parts of it—provides us (I argue) with mimetic models for gender display, not necessarily phylogenetic ones. Thus, in Western society, the dog has served us as an ultimate model of fawning, of bristling, and (with baring of fangs) of threatening; the horse a model, to be sure, of physical strength, but of little that is interpersonal and interactional.[5]

Once one sees that animal life, and lore concerning that life, provides a cultural source of imagery for gender display, the way is open to examine other sources of display imagery, but now models for mimicry that are closer to home. Of considerable significance, for example, is the complex associated with European court life and the doctrines of the gentleman, especially as these came to be incorporated (and modified) in military etiquette. Although the force of this style is perhaps declining, it was, I think, of very real importance until the second World War, especially in British influenced countries and especially, of course, in dealings between males. For example, the standing-at-attention posture as a means of expressing being on call, the "Sir" response, and even the salute, became part of the deference style far beyond scenes from military life.

For our purposes, there is a source of display much more relevant than animal lore or military tradition, a source closer to home, a source, indeed, right in the home: the parent–child relationship.

V

The parent–child complex—taken in its ideal middle-class version—has some very special features when considered as a source of behavioral imagery. First, most persons end up having been children cared for by parents and/or elder sibs, and as parents (or elder sibs) in the reverse position. So both sexes experience both roles—a sex-free resource. (The person playing the role opposite the child is a mother or older sister as much or more than a father or elder brother. Half of those in the child role will be male, and the housewife role, the one we used to think was ideally suitable for females, contains lots of parental elements.) Second, given inheritance and residence patterns, parents are the only authority in our society that can rightly be said to be both temporary and exerted "in the best interests" of those subordinated thereby. To speak here—at least in our Western society—of the child giving something of equivalence in exchange for the rearing that he gets is ludicrous. There is no appreciable quid pro quo. Balance lies elsewhere. What is received in one generation is given in the next. It should be added that this important unselfseeking possibility has been much neglected by students of society. The established imagery is economic and Hobbesian, turning on the notion of social exchange, and the newer voices have been concerned to show how parental authority can be misguided, oppressive, and ineffective.

Now I want to argue that parent–child dealings carry special value as a means of orienting the student to the significance of social situations as a unit of social organization. For a great deal of what a child is privileged to do and a great deal of what he must suffer his parents doing on his behalf pertains to how adults in our society come to manage themselves in social situations. Surprisingly the key issue becomes this: *What mode of handling ourselves do we employ in social situations as our means of demonstrating respectful orientation to them and of maintaining guardedness within them?*

It might be useful, then, to outline schematically the ideal middle-class parent–child relationship, limiting this to what can occur when a child and parent are present in the same social situation.

It seems to be assumed that the child comes to a social situation with all its "basic" needs satisfied and/or provided for, and that there is no good reason why he himself should be planning and thinking very far into the future. It is as though the child were on holiday.

There is what might be called orientation license. The child is tolerated in his drifting from the situation into aways, fugues, brown studies, and the like. There is license to flood out, as in dissolving into tears, capsizing into laughter, bursting into glee, and the like.

Related to this license is another, namely, the use of patently ineffective means to effect an end, the means expressing a desire to escape, cope, etc., but not possibly achieving its end. One example is the child's hiding in or behind parents, or (in its more attenuated form) behind his own hand, thereby cutting his eyes off from any threat but not the part of him that is threatened. Another is "pummeling," the kind of attack which is a half-serious joke, a use of considerable force but against an adversary that one knows to be impervious to such an effort, so that what starts with an instrumental effort ends up an admittedly defeated gesture. In all of this one has nice examples of ritualization in the classical ethological sense. And an analysis of what it is to act childishly.

Next, protective intercession by parents. High things, intricate things, heavy things, are obtained for the child. Dangerous things—chemical, electrical, mechanical—are kept from him. Breakable things are managed for him. Contacts with the adult world are mediated, providing a buffer between the child and surrounding persons. Adults who are present generally modulate talk that must deal with harsh things of this world: discussion of business, money, and sex is censored; cursing is inhibited; gossip diluted.

There are indulgence priorities: precedence through doors and onto life rafts is given the child; if there are sweets to distribute, he gets them first.

There is the notion of the erasability of offense. Having done something wrong, the child merely cries and otherwise shows contrition, after which he can begin afresh as though the slate had been washed clean. His immediate emotional response to being called to task need only be full enough and it will be taken as final payment for the delict. He can also assume that love will not be discontinued because of what he has done, providing only that he shows how broken up he is because of doing it.

There is an obvious generalization behind all these forms of license and privilege. A loving protector is standing by in the wings, allowing not so much for dependency as a copping out of, or relief from, the "realities," that is, the necessities and constraints to which adults in social situations are subject. In the deepest sense, then, middle-class children are not engaged in adjusting to and adapting to social situations, but in practicing, trying out, or playing at these efforts. Reality for them is deeply forgiving.

Note, if a child is to be able to call upon these various reliefs from realities, then, of course, he must stay within range of a distress cry, or within view—scamper-back distance. And, of course, in all of this, parents are provided scenes in which they can act out their parenthood.

You will note that there is an obvious price that the child must pay for being saved from seriousness.

He is subjected to control by physical fiat and to commands serving as a lively reminder thereof: forced rescues from oncoming traffic and from potential falls; forced care, as when his coat is buttoned and mittens pulled on against his protest. In general, the child's doings are unceremoniously interrupted under warrant of ensuring that they are executed safely.

He is subjected to various forms of nonperson treatment. He is talked past and talked about as though absent. Gestures of affection and attention are performed "directly," without engaging him in verbal interaction through the same acts. Teasing and taunting occur, dealings which start out involving the child as a coparticipant in talk and end up treating him merely as a target of attention.

His inward thoughts, feelings, and recollections are not treated as though he had informational rights in their disclosure. He can be queried on contact about his desires and intent, his aches and pains, his resentments and gratitude, in short, his subjective situation, but he cannot go very far in reciprocating this sympathetic curiosity without being thought intrusive.

Finally, the child's time and territory may be seen as expendable. He may be sent on errands or to fetch something in spite of what he is doing at the time; he may be caused to give up territorial prerogatives because of the needs of adults.

Now note that an important feature of the child's situation in life is that the way his parents interact with him tends to be employed to him by other adults also, extending to nonparental kinsmen, acquainted nonkin, and even to adults with whom he is unacquainted. (It is as though the world were in the military uniform of one army, and all adults were its officers.) Thus a child in patent need provides an unacquainted adult a right and even an obligation to offer help, providing only that no other close adult seems to be in charge.

Given this parent–child complex as a common fund of experience, it seems we draw on it in a fundamental way in adult social gatherings. The invocation through ritualistic expression of this hierarchical complex seems to cast a spate of face-to-face interaction in what is taken as no-contest terms, warmed by a touch of relatedness; in short, benign control. The superordinate gives something gratis out of supportive identification, and the subordinate responds with an outright display of gratitude, and if not that, then at least an implied submission to the relationship and the definition of the situation it sustains.

> One afternoon an officer was given a call for illegal parking in a commercial area well off his sector. He was fairly new in the district, and it took him awhile to find the address. When he arrived he saw a car parked in an obviously dangerous and illegal manner at the corner of a small street. He took out his ticket book and wrote it up. As he was placing the ticket on the car, a man came out of the store on the corner. He approached and asked whether the officer had come in answer to his call. When the patrolman said that he had, the man replied that the car which had been bothering him had already left and he hoped the patrolman was not going to tag his car. "Hey, I'm sorry, *pal* but it's already written."
> "I expected Officer Reno, he's usually on 6515 car. I'd appreciate it, Officer, if next time you would stop in before you write them up." The patrolman was slightly confused. . . .
> He said politely and frankly, "Mister, how would it look if I went into every store before I wrote up a ticket and asked if it was all right? What would people think I was doing?" The man shrugged his shoulders and smiled. "You're right, son. O.K., forget it. Listen stop in sometime if I can help you with something." He patted the patrolman on the shoulder and returned to his business [Rubinstein 1973:161–2].

Or the subordinate initiates a sign of helplessness and need, and the superordinate responds with a volunteered service. A *Time* magazine story on female police might be cited as an illustration:

> Those [policewomen] who are there already have provided a devastating new weapon to the police crime-fighting arsenal, one that has helped women to get their men for centuries. It worked well for diminutive Patrolwoman Ina Sheperd after she collared a muscular shoplifter in Miami last December and discovered that there were no other cops—or even a telephone—around. Unable to summon help, she burst into tears. "If I don't bring you in, I'll lose my job," she

sobbed to her prisoner, who chivalrously accompanied her until a
squad car could be found.[6]

It turns out, then, that in our society whenever a male has dealings with a
female or a subordinate male (especially a younger one), some mitigation of
potential distance, coercion, and hostility is quite likely to be induced by
application of the parent–child complex. Which implies that, ritually
speaking, females are equivalent to subordinate males and both are equivalent to children. Observe that however distasteful and humiliating lessers
may find these gentle prerogatives to be, they must give second thought to
openly expressing displeasure, for whosoever extends benign concern is free
to quickly change his tack and show the other side of his power.

VI

Allow here a brief review. Social situations were defined as arenas of mutual
monitoring. It is possible for the student to take social situations very seriously as one natural vantage point from which to view all of social life. After
all, it is in social situations that individuals can communicate in the fullest
sense of the term, and it is only in them that individuals can physically coerce
one another, assault one another, interact sexually, importune one another
gesturally, give physical comfort, and so forth. Moreover, it is in social situations that most of the world's work gets done. Understandably, in all
societies modes of adaptation are found, including systems of normative
constraint, for managing the risks and opportunities specific to social
situations.

Our immediate interest in social situations was that it is mainly in such
contexts that individuals can use their faces and bodies, as well as small
materials at hand to engage in social portraiture. It is here in these small,
local places that they can arrange themselves microecologically to depict
what is taken as their place in the wider social frame, allowing them, in turn,
to celebrate what has been depicted. It is here, in social situations, that the
individual can signify what he takes to be his social identity and here indicate his feelings and intent—all of which information the others in the
gathering will need in order to manage their own courses of action—which
knowledgeability he in turn must count on in carrying out his own designs.

Now it seems to me that any form of socialization which in effect addresses
itself to social situations as such, that is, to the resources ordinarily available
in any social situation whatsoever, will have a very powerful effect upon
social life. In any particular social gathering at any particular moment, the
effect of this socialization may be slight—no more consequence, say, than
to modify the style in which matters at hand proceed. (After all, whether you
light your own cigarette or have it lit for you, you can still get lung cancer.

And whether your job termination interview is conducted with delicacy or abruptness, you've still lost your job.) However, routinely the question is that of whose opinion is voiced most frequently and most forcibly, who makes the minor ongoing decisions apparently required for the coordination of any joint activity, and whose passing concerns are given the most weight. And however trivial some of these little gains and losses may appear to be, by summing them all up across all the social situations in which they occur, one can see that their total effect is enormous. The expression of subordination and domination through this swarm of situational means is more than a mere tracing or symbol or ritualistic affirmation of the social hierarchy. These expressions considerably constitute the hierarchy; they are the shadow *and* the substance.[7]

And here gender styles qualify. For these behavioral styles can be employed in any social situation, and there receive their small due. When mommies and daddies decide on what to teach their little Johnnys and Marys, they make exactly the right choice; they act in effect with much more sociological sophistication than they ought to have—assuming, of course, that the world as we have known it is what they want to reproduce.

And behavioral style itself? Not very stylish. A means of making assumptions about life palpable in social situations. At the same time, a choreography through which participants present their alignments to situated activities in progress. And the stylings themselves consist of those arrangements of the human form and those elaborations of human action that can be displayed across many social settings, in each case drawing on local resources to tell stories of very wide appeal.

VII

I conclude with a sermon.

There is a wide agreement that fishes live in the sea because they cannot breathe on land, and that we live on land because we cannot breathe in the sea. This proximate, everyday account can be spelled out in ever increasing physiological detail, and exceptional cases and circumstances uncovered, but the general answer will ordinarily suffice, namely, an appeal to the nature of the beast, to the givens and conditions of his existence, and a guileless use of the term "because." Note, in this happy bit of folk wisdom—as sound and scientific surely as it needs to be—the land and sea can be taken as there prior to fishes and men, and not—contrary to Genesis—put there so that fishes and men, when they arrived, would find a suitable place awaiting them.

This lesson about the men and the fishes contains, I think, the essence of our most common and most basic way of thinking about ourselves: an accounting of what occurs by an appeal to our "natures," an appeal to the very conditions of our being. Note, we can use this formula both for categories of persons and for particular individuals. Just as we account for the fact that a man walks upright by an appeal to his nature, so we can account for why a particular amputee doesn't by an appeal to his particular conditions of being.

It is, of course, hardly possible to imagine a society whose members do not routinely read from what is available to the senses to something larger, distal, or hidden. Survival is unthinkable without it. Correspondingly, there is a very deep belief in our society, as presumably there is in others, that an object produces signs that are informing about it. Objects are thought to structure the environment immediately around themselves; they cast a shadow, heat up the surround, strew indications, leave an imprint; they impress a part picture of themselves, a portrait that is unintended and not dependent on being attended, yet, of course, informing nonetheless to whomsoever is properly placed, trained, and inclined. Presumably this indicating is done in a malleable surround of some kind—a field for indications—the actual perturbations in which is the sign. Presumably one deals here with "natural indexical signs," sometimes having "iconic" features. In any case, this sort of indicating is to be seen neither as physical instrumental action in the fullest sense, nor as communication as such, but something else, a kind of by-production, an overflowing, a tell-tale soiling of the environment wherever the object has been. Although these signs are likely to be distinct from, or only a part of, the object about which they provide information, it is their configuration which counts, and the ultimate source of this, it is felt, is the object itself in some independence of the particular field in which the expression happens to occur. Thus we take sign production to be situationally phrased but not situationally determined.

The natural indexical signs given off by objects we call animal (including and principally, man) are often called "expressions," but in the sense of that term here implied, our imagery still allows that a material process is involved, not conventional symbolic communication. We tend to believe that these special objects not only give off natural signs, but do so more than do other objects. Indeed, the emotions, in association with various bodily organs through which emotions most markedly appear, are considered veritable engines of expression. As a corollary, we assume that among humans a very wide range of attributes are expressible: intent, feeling, relationship, information state, health, social class, etc. Lore and advice concerning these signs, including how to fake them and how to see behind fakeries, constitute a kind of folk science. All of these beliefs regarding man, taken together, can be referred to as the doctrine of natural expression.

It is generally believed that although signs can be read for what is merely momentarily or incidentally true of the object producing them—as, say, when an elevated temperature indicates a fever—we routinely seek another kind of information also, namely, information about those of an object's properties that are felt to be *perduring, overall,* and *structurally basic,* in short, information about its character or "essential nature." (The same sort of information is sought about classes of objects.) We do so for many reasons, and in so doing presume that objects (and classes of objects) have natures independent of the particular interest that might arouse our concern. Signs viewed in this light, I will call "essential," and the belief that they exist and can be read and that individuals give them off is part of the doctrine of natural expression. Note again, that although some of these attributes, such as passing mood, particular intent, etc., are not themselves taken as characteristic, the *tendency* to possess such states and concerns is seen as an essential attribute, and conveying evidence of internal states in a particular manner can be seen as characteristic. In fact, there seems to be no incidental contingent expression that can't be taken as evidence of an essential attribute; we need only see that to respond in a particular way to particular circumstances is what might be expected in general of persons as such or a certain kind of person or a particular person. Note, any property seen as unique to a particular person is likely also to serve as a means of characterizing him. A corollary is that the absence in him of a particular property seen as common to the class of which he is a member tends to serve similarly.

Here let me restate the notion that one of the most deeply seated traits of man, it is felt, is gender; femininity and masculinity are in a sense the prototypes of essential expression—something that can be conveyed fleetingly in any social situation and yet something that strikes at the most basic characterization of the individual.

But, of course, when one tries to use the notion that human objects give off natural indexical signs and that some of these expressions can inform us about the essential nature of their producer, matters get complicated. The human objects themselves employ the term "expression," and conduct themselves to fit their own conceptions of expressivity; iconicity especially abounds, doing so because it has been made to. Instead of our merely obtaining expressions of the object, the object obligingly gives them to us, conveying them through ritualizations and communicating them through symbols. (But then it can be said that this giving itself has unintended expressive features: for it does not seem possible for a message to be transmitted without the transmitter and the transmission process blindly leaving traces of themselves on whatever gets transmitted.)

There is, straight off, the obvious fact that an individual can fake an expression for what can be gained thereby; an individual is unlikely to cut off his leg so as to have a nature unsuitable for military service, but he might indeed sacrifice a toe or affect a limp. In which case "because of" becomes "in order to." But that is really a minor matter; there are more serious difficulties. I mention three.

First, it is not so much the character or overall structure of an entity that gets expressed (if such there be), but rather particular, situationally-bound features relevant to the viewer. (Sometimes, for example, no more than that the object is such a one and not another.) The notion of essence, character, structure, is, one might argue, social, since there are likely to be an infinite number of properties of the object that could be selected out as the central ones, and, furthermore, often an infinite number of ways of bounding the object from other ones. Thus, as suggested, an attribute which allows us to distinguish its possessor from those he is seen amongst is likely to enter strongly in our characterization of him.

Second, expression in the main is not instinctive but socially learned and socially patterned; it is a socially defined category which employs a particular expression, and a socially established schedule which determines when these expressions will occur. And this is so even though individuals come to employ expressions in what is sensed to be a spontaneous and unselfconscious way, that is, uncalculated, unfaked, natural. Furthermore, individuals do not merely learn how and when to express themselves, for in learning this they are learning to be the kind of object to which the doctrine of natural expression applies, if fallibly; they are learning to be objects that have a character, that express this character, and for whom this characterological expressing is only natural. We are socialized to confirm our own hypotheses about our natures.

Third, social situations turn out to be more than a convenient field of what we take to be natural expression; these configurations are intrinsically, not merely incidentally, a consequence of what can be generated in social situations.

So our concern as students ought not to be in uncovering real, natural expressions, whatever they might be. One should not appeal to the doctrine of natural expression in an attempt to account for natural expression, for that (as is said) would conclude the analysis before it had begun. These acts and appearances are likely to be anything but natural indexical signs, except insofar as they provide indications of the actor's interest in conducting himself effectively under conditions of being treated in accordance with the doctrine of natural expression. And insofar as natural expressions of gender are—in the sense here employed—natural and expressive, what they naturally express is the capacity and inclination of individuals to portray a version of themselves and their relationships at strategic moments—a working agreement to present each other with, and facilitate the other's presentation of, gestural pictures of the claimed reality of their relationship and the claimed character of their human nature. The competency to produce these portraits, and interpret those produced by others, might be said to be essential to our nature, but this competency may provide a very poor picture of the overall relationship between the sexes. And indeed, I think it does.

What the relationship between the sexes objectively is, taken as a whole, is quite another matter, not yet well analyzed.

What the human nature of males and females really consists of, then, is a capacity to learn to provide and to read depictions of masculinity and femininity and a willingness to adhere to a schedule for presenting these pictures, and this capacity they have by virtue of being persons, not females or males. One might just as well say there is no gender identity. There is only a schedule for the portrayal of gender. There is no relationship between the sexes that can so far be characterized in any satisfactory fashion. There is only evidence of the practice between the sexes of choreographing behaviorally a portrait of relationship. And what these portraits must directly tell us about is not gender, or the overall relationship between the sexes, but about the special character and functioning of portraiture.

One can say that female behavioral style "expresses" femininity in the sense of providing an incidental, gratuitous portrait. But Durkheim recommends that such expression is a political ceremony, in this case affirming the place that persons of the female sex-class have in the social structure, in other words, holding them to it. And ethnologists recommend that feminine expression is an indication of the alignment a person of the female sex class proposes to take (or accept) in the activity immediately to follow—an alignment which does not merely express subordination but in part constitutes it. The first points out the stabilizing influence of worshipping one's place in the social scheme of things, the second, the substantial consequences of minor allocations. Both these modes of functioning are concealed from us by the doctrine of natural expression; for that doctrine teaches us that expressions occur simply because it is only natural for them to do so—no other reason being required. Moreover, we are led to accept as a portrait of the whole something that actually occurs at scheduled moments only, something that provides (in the case under question) a reflection not of the differential nature of persons in the two sex classes but of their common readiness to subscribe to the conventions of display.

Gender displays, like other rituals, can iconically reflect fundamental features of the social structure; but just as easily, these expressions can counterbalance substantive arrangements and compensate for them. If anything, then, displays are a symptom, not a portrait. For, in fact, whatever the fundamental circumstances of those who happen to be in the same social situation, their behavioral styles can affirm a contrary picture.

Of course, it is apparent that the niceties of gender etiquette provide a solution for various organizational problems found in social situations—such as who is to make minor decisions which seem better lost than unresolved, who is to give way, who is to step forward, who is to follow, who to lead, so that turns, stops, and moving about can be coordinated, and beginnings and endings synchronized. (In the same way, at the substantive level, the traditional division of labor between the sexes provides a workable solution to the organization of certain personal services, the ones we call domestic; similarly, sex-biased linguistic practices, such as the use of "he" as the unmarked relative pronoun for "individual"—amply illustrated in this paper—provide a basis for unthinkingly concerted usage upon which the efficiency of language depends.) But just why gender instead of some other attribute is invoked to deal with these organizational problems, and how well adapted gender is for doing so, is an open question.

In sum, gender, in close connection with age-grade, lays down more, perhaps, than class and other social divisions an understanding of what our ultimate nature ought to be and how and where this nature ought to be exhibited. And we acquire a vast corpus of accounts to be used as a source of good, self-sufficient reasons for many of our acts (particularly as these determine the allocation of minor indulgences and deprivations), just as others acquire a sovereign means of accounting for our own behavior. Observe, there is nothing superficial about this accounting. Given our stereotypes of femininity, a particular woman will find that the way has been cleared to fall back on the situation of her entire sex to account to herself for why she should refrain from vying with men in matters mechanical, financial, political, and so forth. Just as a particular man will find that his failure to exert priority over women in these matters reflects on him personally, giving him warrant for insisting on success in these connections. (Correspondingly, he can decline domestic tasks on the general ground of his sex, while identifying any of his wife's disinclination here as an expression of her particular character.) Because these stereotypes begin to be applied by and to the individual from the earliest years, the accounting it affords is rather well implanted.

I have here taken a functionalist view of gender display and have argued that what, if anything, characterizes persons as sex-class members is their competence and willingness to sustain an appropriate schedule of displays; only the content of the displays distinguishes the classes. Although this view can be seen as slighting the biological reality of sex, it should not be taken as belittling the role of these displays in social life. For the facilitation of these enactments runs so deeply into the organization of society as to deny any slighting view of them. Gender expressions are by way of being a mere show; but a considerable amount of the substance of society is enrolled in the staging of it.

Nor should too easy a political lesson be drawn by those sympathetic to social change. The analysis of sexism can start with obviously unjust discriminations against persons of the female sex-class, but analysis as such cannot stop there. Gender stereotypes run in every direction, and almost as much inform what supporters of women's rights approve as what they disapprove. A principal means men in our society have for initiating or terminating an everyday encounter on a sympathetic note is to employ endearing terms of address and verbal expressions of concern that are (upon examination) parental in character and profoundly asymmetrical. Similarly, an important ritual available for displaying affectionate concern, emphasizing junctures in discourse, and marking differential conversational exclusiveness is the laying on of the hand, ordinarily an unreciprocatable gesture of male to female or subordinate male.

In all of this, intimacy certainly brings no corrective. In our society in all classes the tenderest expression of affection involves displays that are politically questionable, the place taken up in them by the female being differentiated from and reciprocal to the place taken up by the male. Cross-sex affectional gestures choreograph protector and protected, embracer and embraced, comforter and comforted, supporter and supported, extender of affection and recipient thereof; and it is defined as only natural that the male encompass and the female be encompassed. And this can only remind us that male domination is a very special kind, a domination that can be carried right into the gentlest, most loving moment without apparently causing strain—indeed, these moments can hardly be conceived of apart from these asymmetries. Whereas other disadvantaged groups can turn from the world to a domestic scene where self-determination and relief from inequality are possible, the disadvantage that persons who are female suffer precludes this; the places identified in our society as ones that can be arranged to suit oneself are nonetheless for women thoroughly organized along disadvantageous lines.

And indeed, reliance on the child–parent complex as a source of display imagery is a means of extending intimate comfortable practices outward from their source to the world, and in the wake of this domestication, this only gentling of the world we seem to have, female subordination follows. *Any* scene, it appears, can be defined as an occasion for the depiction of gender difference, and in any scene a resource can be found for effecting this display.

As for the doctrine of expression, it raises the issue of professional, as well as folk, analysis. To accept various "expressions" of femininity (or masculinity) as indicating something biological or social-structural that lies behind or underneath these signs, something to be glimpsed through them, is perhaps to accept a lay theory of signs. That a multitude of "genderisms" point convergently in the same direction might only tell us how these signs function socially, namely, to support belief that there is an underlying reality to gender. Nothing dictates that should we dig and poke behind these images we can expect to find anything there–except, of course, the inducement to entertain this expectation.

Notes

1   *Philosophical Transactions of the Royal Society of London*, Series B, No. 772, Vol. 251 (Dec. 29, 1966), p. 250.
2   See the thorough treatment of "feminizers" in Conners (1971).
3   *International Herald Tribune*, June 3–4, 1972.
4   As Zimmerman and West (1977) remind me, the individual has (and seeks) very little option regarding identification of own sex class. Often, however, there will be choice as to which complement of displays is employed to ensure gender placement.
5   An important work here, of course, is Darwin's *Expression of Emotions in Man and Animals*. In this treatise a direct parallel is drawn, in words and pictures, between a few gestures of a few animals—gestures expressing, for example, dominance, appeasement, fear—and the same expressions as portrayed by actors. This study, recently and rightly resurrected as a classic in ethology (for indeed, it is in this book that displays are first studied in detail in everything but name), is generally taken as an elucidation of our animal natures and the expressions we consequently share with them. Now the book is also functioning as a source in its own right of cultural beliefs concerning the character and origins of alignment expressions.
6   *Time*, May 1, 1972, p. 60; I leave unconsidered the role of such tales in *Time*'s fashioning of stories.
7   A recent suggestion along this line can be found in the effort to specify in detail the difference between college men and women in regard to sequencing in cross-sexed conversation. See Zimmerman and West (1975), Fishman (1975), and West and Zimmerman (1975). The last discusses some similarities between parent–child and adult male–female conversational practices.

References cited

Conners, Kathleen. 1971. Studies in Feminine Agentives in Selected European Languages. *Romance Philology* 24(4):573–98.
Fishman, Pamela. 1975. Interaction: The Work Women Do. Paper presented at the American Sociological Association Meetings, San Francisco, August 25–30.
Huxley, Julian. 1966. A Discussion on Ritualization of Behavior in Animals and Man. *Philosophical Transactions of the Royal Society of London*, Series B, No. 772, Vol. 251:247–526.
Rubinstein, Jonathan. 1973. *City Police*. New York: Farrar, Straus and Giroux.
West, Candace, and Don H. Zimmerman. 1975. Women's Place in Conversation: Reflections on Adult–Child Interaction. Paper presented at the American Sociological Association Meetings, San Francisco, August 25–30.
Zimmerman, Don H., and Candace West. 1975. Sex Role, Interruptions and Silences in Conversation. In *Language and Sex: Differences and Dominance*. Barrie Thorne and Nancy Henley, eds. Pp. 105–29. Rowley, MA: Newbury House.
—— 1977 Doing Gender. Paper presented at the American Sociological Association Meetings, Chicago.

15

Social Interaction and Social Structure

"The Neglected Situation"*

I

It hardly seems possible to name a social variable that doesn't show up and have its little systematic effect upon speech behavior: age, sex, class, caste, country of origin, generation, region, schooling; cultural cognitive assumptions; bilingualism, and so forth. Each year new social determinants of speech behavior are reported. (It should be said that each year new psychological variables are also tied in with speech.)

Alongside this correlational drive to bring in ever new social attributes as determinants of speech behavior, there has been another drive, just as active, to add to the range of properties discoverable in speech behavior itself, these additions having varied relations to the now classic phonetic, phonemic, morphemic and syntactical structuring of language. It is thus that new semantic, expressive, paralinguistic and kinesic features of behavior involving speech have been isolated, providing us with a new bagful of indicators to do something correlational with.

I'm sure these two currents of analysis—the correlational and the indicative—could churn on forever (and probably will), a case of scholarly coexistence. However, a possible source of trouble might be pointed out. At certain points these two modes of analysis seem to get unpleasantly close together, forcing us to examine the land that separates them—and this in turn may lead us to feel that something important has been neglected.

Take the second-mentioned current of analysis first—the uncovering of new properties or indicators in speech behavior. That aspect of a discourse that can be clearly transferred through writing to paper has been long dealt with; it is the greasy parts of speech that are now increasingly considered. A wagging tongue (at certain levels of analysis) proves to be only one part of a complex human act whose meaning must also be sought in the movement of the eyebrows and hand. However, once we are willing to consider these gestural, nonwritable behaviors associated with speaking, two grave embarrassments face us. First, while the substratum of a gesture derives from

* Originally published in *American Anthropologist*, 1964, 66: pp. 133–6. Reproduced by permission of the American Anthropological Association. Not for further reproduction.

the maker's body, the form of the gesture can be intimately determined by the microecological orbit in which the speaker finds himself. To describe the gesture, let alone uncover its meaning, we might then have to introduce the human and material setting in which the gesture is made. For example, there must be a sense in which the loudness of a statement can only be assessed by knowing first how distant the speaker is from his recipient. The individual gestures with the immediate environment, not only with his body, and so we must introduce this environment in some systematic way. Secondly, the gestures the individual employs as part of speaking are much like the ones he employs when he wants to make it perfectly clear that he certainly isn't going to be drawn into a conversation at this juncture. At certain levels of analysis, then, the study of behavior while speaking and the study of behavior of those who are present to each other but not engaged in talk cannot be analytically separated. The study of one teasingly draws us into the study of the other. Persons like Ray Birdwhistell and Edward Hall have built a bridge from speaking to social conduct, and once you cross the bridge, you become too busy to turn back.

Turn now from the study of newly uncovered properties or indicators in speech to the first-mentioned study of newly uncovered social correlates of speech. Here we will find even greater embarrassment. For increasingly there is work on a particularly subversive type of social correlate of speech that is called "situational." Is the speaker talking to same or opposite sex, subordinate or superordinate, one listener or many, someone right there or on the phone; is he reading a script or talking spontaneously; is the occasion formal or informal, routine or emergency? Note that it is not the attributes of social structure that are here considered, such as age and sex, but rather the value placed on these attributes as they are acknowledged in the situation current and at hand.

And so we have the following problem: a student interested in the properties of speech may find himself having to look at the physical setting in which the speaker performs his gestures, simply because you cannot describe a gesture fully without reference to the extra-bodily environment in which it occurs. And someone interested in the linguistic correlates of social structure may find that he must attend to the social occasion when someone of given social attributes makes his appearance before others. Both kinds of student must therefore look at what we vaguely call the social situation. And that is what has been neglected.

At present the idea of the social situation is handled in the most happy-go-lucky way. For example, if one is dealing with the language of respect, then social situations become occasions when persons of relevant status relationships are present before each other, and a typology of social situations is drawn directly and simply from chi-squaredom: high–low, low–high and equals. And the same could be said for other attributes of the social structure. An implication is that social situations do not have properties and a structure of their own, but merely mark, as it were, the geometric intersection of actors making talk and actors bearing particular social attributes.

I do not think this opportunistic approach to social situations is always valid. Your social situation is not your country cousin. It can be argued that social situations, at least in our society, constitute a reality *sui generis* as He used to say, and therefore need and warrant analysis in their own right, much like that accorded other basic forms of social organization. And it can be further argued that this sphere of activity is of special importance for those interested in the ethnography of speaking, for where but in social situations does speaking go on?

II

So let us face what we have been offhand about: social situations. I would define a social situation as an environment of mutual monitoring possibilities, anywhere within which an individual will find himself accessible to the naked senses of all others who are "present," and similarly find them accessible to him. According to this definition, a social situation arises whenever two or more individuals find themselves in one another's immediate presence, and it lasts until the next-to-last person leaves. Those in a given situation may be referred to aggregatively as a *gathering*, however divided, or mute and distant, or only momentarily present, the participants in the gathering appear to be. Cultural rules establish how individuals are to conduct themselves by virtue of being in a gathering, and these rules for commingling, when adhered to, socially organize the behaviour of those in the situation.

Although participation in a gathering always entails constraint and organization, there are special social arrangements of all or some of those present which entail additional and greater structuring of conduct. For it is possible for two or more persons in a social situation to jointly ratify one another as authorized cosustainers of a single, albeit moving, focus of visual and cognitive attention. These ventures in joint orientation might be called *encounters* or face engagements. A preferential mutual openness to all manner of communication is involved. A physical coming together is typically also involved, an ecological huddle wherein participants orient to one another and away from those who are present in the situation but not officially in the encounter. There are clear rules for the initiation and termination of encounters, the entrance and departure of particular participants, the demands that an encounter can make upon its sustainers, and the decorum of space and sound it must observe relative to excluded participants in the situation. A given social gathering of course may contain no encounter, merely unengaged participants bound by unfocused interaction; it may contain one encounter which itself contains all the persons in the situation—a favored arrangement for sexual interaction; it may contain an accessible encounter, one that must proceed in the presence of unengaged participants or other encounters.

Card games, ball-room couplings, surgical teams in operation, and fist fights provide examples of encounters; all illustrate the social organization of shared current orientation, and all involve an organized interplay of acts of some kind. I want to suggest that when speaking occurs it does so within this kind of social arrangement; of course what is organized therein is not plays or steps or procedures or blows, but turns at talking. Note then that the natural home of speech is one in which speech is not always present.

I am suggesting that the act of speaking must always be referred to the state of talk that is sustained through the particular turn at talking, and that this state of talk involves a circle of others ratified as coparticipants. (Such a phenomenon as talking to oneself, or talking to unratified recipients as in the case of collusive communication, or telephone talk, must first be seen as a departure from the norm, else its structure and significance will be lost.) Talk is socially organized, not merely in terms of who speaks to whom in what language, but as a little system of mutually ratified and ritually governed face-to-face action, a social encounter. Once a state of talk has been ratified, cues must be available for requesting the floor and giving it up, for informing the speaker as to the stability of the focus of attention he is receiving. Intimate collaboration must be sustained to ensure that one turn at talking neither overlaps the previous one too much, nor wants for inoffensive conversational supply, for someone's turn must always and exclusively be in progress. If persons are present in the social situation but not ratified as participants in the encounter, then sound level and physical spacing will have to be managed to show respect for these accessible others while not showing suspicion of them.

Utterances do of course submit to linguistic constraints (as do meanings), but at each moment they must do a further job, and it is this job that keeps talk participants busy. Utterances must be presented with an overlay of functional gestures—gestures which prop up states of talk, police them, and keep these little systems of activity going. Sounds are used in this gestural work because sounds, in spoken encounters, happen to be handy; but everything else at hand is systematically used too. Thus many of the properties of talk will have to be seen as alternatives to, or functional equivalents of, extralinguistic acts, as when, for example, a participant signals his imminent departure from a conversational encounter by changing his posture, or redirecting his perceivable attention, or altering the intonation contour of his last statement.

At one level of analysis, then, the study of writable statements and the study of speaking are different things. At one level of analysis the study of turns at talking and things said during one's turn are part of the study of face-to-face interaction. Face-to-face interaction has its own regulations; it has its own processes and its own structure, and these don't seem to be intrinsically linguistic in character, however often expressed through a linguistic medium.

"The Interaction Order"*

Prefatory Note

A presidential address faces one set of requirements, an article in a scholarly journal quite another. It turns out, then, that *ASR*'s policy of publishing each year's ASA [American Sociological Association] address provides the editor with an annual breather. Once a year the lead space can be allocated to a known name and the editor is quit of responsibility for standards that submissions rarely sustain: originality, logical development, readability, reasonable length. For in theory, a presidential address, whatever its character, must have *some* significance for the profession, even if only a sad one. More important, readers who were unable or unwilling to make the trip have an opportunity to participate vicariously in what can be read as the culmination of the meeting they missed.

Not the best of warrants. My expectation, then, was not to publish this talk but to limit it to the precincts in which it was delivered.

But in fact, I wasn't there either. What I offer the reader then is vicarious participation in something that did not itself take place. A podium performance, but only readers in the seats. A dubious offering.

But something would have been dubious anyway. After all, like almost all other presidential addresses, this one was drafted and typed well before it was to be delivered (and before I knew it wasn't to be), and the delivery was to be made by reading from typescript not by extemporizing. So although the text was written as if in response to a particular social occasion, little of it could have been generated by what transpired there. And later, any publication that resulted would have employed a text modified in various ways *after* the actual delivery.

The Interaction Order

For an evening's hour, it is given to each current president of the Association

* Originally published in *American Sociological Review*, 1983, 48, pp. 1–17. Copyright © 1983 American Sociological Association. Reproduced by permission of the American Sociological Association.

to hold captive the largest audience of colleagues that sociology can provide. For an hour then, within the girdle of these walls, a wordy pageantry is reenacted. A sociologist you have selected from a very short list takes to the center of this vasty Hilton field on a hobby horse of his own choosing. (One is reminded that the sociologically interesting thing about Hamlet is that every year no high school in the English-speaking world has trouble finding some clown to play him.) In any case, it seems that presidents of learned societies are well enough known about something to be elected because of it. Taking office, they find a podium attached, along with encouragement to demonstrate that they are indeed obsessed by what their election proved they were already known to be obsessed by. Election winds them up and sets them loose to set their record straight; they rise above restraint and replay it. For Association presidents are led to feel that they are representative of something, and that this something is just what their intellectual community wants represented and needs representing. Preparing and then presenting their addresses, presidents come to feel that they are temporarily guardians of their discipline. However large or oddly shaped the hall, their self swells out to fill it. Nor do narrow disciplinary concerns set limits. Whatever the public issues of the day, the speaker's discipline is shown to have incisive bearing on them. Moreover, the very occasion seems to make presidential speakers dangerously at one with themselves; warmed by the celebration they give without stint, sidetracking their prepared address with parenthetical admissions, *obiter dicta*, ethical and political asides and other medallions of belief. And once again there occurs that special flagrancy of high office: the indulgence of self-congratulation in public. What this dramaturgy is supposed to bring is flesh to bones, confronting the *reader's* image of a person with the lively impression created when the words come from a body not a page. What this dramaturgy puts at risk is the remaining illusions listeners have concerning their profession. Take comfort, my friends, that although you are once again to witness the passion of the podium, ours is the discipline, the model of analysis, for which ceremonies are data as well as duty, for which talk provides conduct to observe as well as opinion to consider. Indeed, one might want to argue that the interesting matter for all of us here (as all of us know) is not what *I* will come to say, but what *you* are doing here listening to me saying.

But I suppose you and I shouldn't knock ritual enterprises too much. Some goy might be listening and leave here to spread irreverence and disenchantment in the land. Too much of *that* and even such jobs as we sociologists get will become empty of traditional employment.

You might gather from this preamble that I find presidential addresses embarrassing. True. But surely that fact does not give me the right to comment at length on my uneasiness. It is a disease of the self, specific to speakers, to feel that misuse of other people's time can be expunged through confessings which themselves waste some more of it. So I am uneasy about dwelling on my embarrassment. But apparently I am not uneasy about my unease about dwelling on my embarrassment. Even though you are likely to be.

I

Apart from providing a live demonstration of the follies I have outlined, what I have to say tonight will be by way of a preachment already recorded more succinctly in the prefaces of the books I've written. It is different from other preachments you have had to listen to recently only by virtue of not being particularly autobiographical in character, deeply critical of established methods, or informed by a concern over the plight of disadvantaged groups, not even the plight of those seeking work in our profession. I have no universal cure for the ills of sociology. A multitude of myopias limit the glimpse we get of our subject matter. To define one source of blindness and bias as central is engagingly optimistic. Whatever our substantive focus and whatever our methodological persuasion, all we can do I believe is to keep faith with the spirit of natural science, and lurch along, seriously kidding ourselves that our rut has a forward direction. We have not been given the credence and weight that economists lately have acquired, but we can almost match them when it comes to the failure of rigorously calculated predictions. Certainly our systematic theories are every bit as vacuous as theirs; we manage to ignore almost as many critical variables as they do. We do not have the esprit that anthropologists have, but our subject matter at least has not been obliterated by the spread of the world economy. So we have an undiminished opportunity to overlook the relevant facts with our very own eyes. We can't get graduate students who score as high as those who go into Psychology, and at its best the training the latter get seems more professional and more thorough than what we provide. So we haven't managed to produce in our students the high level of trained incompetence that psychologists have achieved in theirs, although, God knows, we're working on it.

II

Social interaction can be identified narrowly as that which uniquely transpires in social situations, that is, environments in which two or more individuals are physically in one another's response presence. (Presumably the telephone and the mails provide reduced versions of the primordial real thing.) This body to body starting point, paradoxically, assumes that a very central sociological distinction may not be initially relevant: namely, the standard contrast between village life and city life, between domestic settings and public ones, between intimate, long-standing relations and fleeting impersonal ones. After all, pedestrian traffic rules can be studied in crowded kitchens as well as crowded streets, interruption rights at breakfast as well as in courtrooms, endearment vocatives in supermarkets as well as in the bedroom. If there are differences here along the traditional lines, what they are still remains an open question.

My concern over the years has been to promote acceptance of this face-to-face domain as an analytically viable one—a domain which might be titled, for want of any happy name, the *interaction order*—a domain whose preferred method of study is microanalysis. My colleagues have not been overwhelmed by the merits of the case.

In my remarks to you tonight, I want to sum up the case for treating the interaction order as a substantive domain in its own right. In general, the warrant for this excision from social life must be the warrant for any analytical extraction: that the contained elements fit together more closely than with elements beyond the order; that exploring relations between orders is critical, a subject matter in its own right, and that such an inquiry presupposes a delineation of the several social orders in the first place: that isolating the interaction order provides a means and a reason to examine diverse societies comparatively, and our own historically.

It is a fact of our human condition that, for most of us, our daily life is spent in the immediate presence of others; in other words, that whatever they are, our doings are likely to be, in the narrow sense, *socially situated*. So much so that activities pursued in utter privacy can easily come to be characterized by this special condition. Always of course the fact of social situatedness can be expected to have some consequence, albeit sometimes apparently very minor. These consequences have traditionally been treated as "effects," that is, as indicators, expressions or symptoms of social structures such as relationships, informal groups, age grades, gender, ethnic minorities, social classes and the like, with no great concern to treat these effects as data in their own terms. The trick, of course, is to differently conceptualize these effects, great or small, so that what they share can be extracted and analyzed, and so that the forms of social life they derive from can be pieced out and catalogued sociologically, allowing what is intrinsic to interactional life to be exposed thereby. In this way one can move from the merely situated to the situational, that is, from what is incidentally located in social situations (and could without great change be located outside them), to what could only occur in face-to-face assemblies.

What can be said about the processes and structures specific to the interaction order? I report some glimmerings.

Whatever is distinctive to face-to-face interaction is likely to be relatively circumscribed in space and most certainly in time. Furthermore (as distinguished from social roles in the traditional sense), very little by way of a dormant or latent phase is to be found; postponement of an interactional activity that has begun has a relatively massive effect on it, and cannot be much extended without deeply altering what had been happening interactionally. For always in the interaction order, the engrossment and involvement of the participants—if only their attention—is critical, and these cognitive states cannot be sustained for extended periods of time or much survive forced lapses and interruption. Emotion, mood, cognition, bodily orientation, and muscular effort are intrinsically involved, introducing an inevitable psychobiological element. Ease and uneasiness, unselfconsciousness and wariness are central. Observe, too, that the interaction order catches humans in just that angle of their existence that displays considerable overlap with the social life of other species. It is as unwise to discount the similarity between animal and human greetings as it is to look for the causes of war in genetic predisposition.

A case can be made that the necessity for face-to-face interaction (aside from the obvious requirements of infant care) is rooted in certain universal preconditions of social life. There are, for example, all kinds of unsentimental and uninherited reasons why individuals everywhere—strangers or intimates—find it expedient to spend time in one another's immediate presence. For one, fixed specialized equipment, especially equipment designed for use beyond the family circle, could hardly be economic were it not staffed and used by numbers of persons who come together at fixed times and places to do so—whether they are destined to use this equipment jointly, adjacently, or sequentially. Arriving and departing, they will find it to their advantage to use hardened access routes—sometimes that is much facilitated if they feel they can closely pass each other safely.

Once individuals—for whatever reason—come into one another's immediate presence, a fundamental condition of social life becomes enormously pronounced, namely, its promissory, evidential character. It is not only that our appearance and manner provide evidence of our statuses and relationships. It is also that the line of our visual regard, the intensity of our involvement, and the shape of our initial actions, allow others to glean our immediate intent and purpose, and all this whether or not we are engaged in talk with them at the time. Correspondingly, we are constantly in a position to facilitate this revealment, or block it, or even misdirect our viewers. The gleaned character of these observations is itself facilitated and complicated by a central process yet to be systematically studied—social ritualization—that is, the standardization of bodily and vocal behavior through socialization, affording such behavior—such gestures, if you will—a specialized communicative function in the stream of behavior.

When in each other's presence individuals are admirably placed to share a joint focus of attention, perceive that they do so, and perceive this perceiving. This, in conjunction with their capacity to indicate their own courses of physical action and to rapidly convey reactions to such indications from others, provides the precondition for something crucial: the sustained, intimate coordination of action, whether in support of closely collaborative tasks or as a means of accommodating closely adjacent ones. Speech immensely increases the efficiency of such coordination, being especially critical when something doesn't go as indicated and expected. (Speech, of course, has another special role, allowing matters sited outside the situation to be brought into the collaborative process, and allowing plans to be negotiated regarding matters to be dealt with beyond the current situation, but that is another and forbiddingly complex issue.)

Another matter: The characterization that one individual can make of another by virtue of being able directly to observe and hear that other is organized around two fundamental forms of identification: the *categoric* kind involving placing that other in one or more social categories, and the *individual* kind, whereby the subject under observation is locked to a uniquely distinguishing identity through appearance, tone of voice, mention of name or other person-differentiating device. This dual possibility—categoric and individual identification—is critical for interaction life in all communities except bygone small isolated ones, and indeed figures in the social life of some other species as well. (I will return to this issue later.)

It remains to be said that once in one another's immediate presence, individuals will necessarily be faced with personal-territory contingencies. By definition, we can participate in social situations only if we bring our bodies and their accoutrements along with us, and this equipment is vulnerable by virtue of the instrumentalities that others bring along with their bodies. We become vulnerable to physical assault, sexual molestation, kidnapping, robbery and obstruction of movement, whether through the unnegotiated application of force or, more commonly, "coercive exchange"—that tacit bargain through which we cooperate with the aggressor in exchange for the promise of not being harmed as much as our circumstances allow. Similarly, in the presence of others we become vulnerable through their words and gesticulation to the penetration of our psychic preserves, and to the breaching of the expressive order we expect will be maintained in our presence. (Of course, to say that we are thus made vulnerable is also to say that we command the resources to make others similarly vulnerable to us; and neither argument is meant to deny that there might not be some conventional specialization, especially along gender lines, of threatened and threatener.)

Personal territoriality is not to be seen merely in terms of constraints, prohibitions, and threats. In all societies there is a fundamental duality of use, such that many of the forms of behavior through which we can be offensively treated by one category of others are intimately allied to those through which members of another category can properly display its bondedness to us. So, too, everywhere what is a presumption if taken from us is a courtesy or a mark of affection if we proffer it; our ritual vulnerabilities are also our ritual resources. Thus, to violate the territories of self is also to undermine the language of favor.

So there are enablements and risks inherent in co-bodily presence. These contingencies being acute, they are likely everywhere to give rise to techniques of social management; and since the same basic contingencies are being managed, one can expect that across quite different societies the interaction order is likely to exhibit some markedly similar features. I remind you that it is in social situations that these enablements and risks are faced and will have their initial effect. And it is social situations that provide the natural theater in which all bodily displays are enacted and in which all bodily displays are read. Thus the warrant for employing the social situation as the basic working unit in the study of the interaction order. And thus, incidentally, a warrant for claiming that our experience of the world has a confrontational character.

But I do not claim a rampant situationalism. As Roger Barker reminded us with his notion of "behavioral setting," the regulations and expectations that apply to a particular social situation are hardly likely to be generated at the moment there. His phrase, "standing behavior pattern," speaks to the fact, reasonably enough, that quite similar understandings will apply to a whole class of widely dispersed settings, as well as to particular locations across inactive phases. Further, although a particular behavioral setting may extend no further than any social situation which two or more participants generate in its precincts—as in the case of a local bar, a small shop floor, or a domestic kitchen—other arrangements are frequent. Factories, airports, hospitals, and public thoroughfares are behavioral settings that sustain an interaction order characteristically extending in space and time beyond any single social situation occurring in them. It should also be said that although behavioral settings and social situations are clearly not ego-centric units, some interaction units clearly are: that ill-explored unit, the daily round, is clearly one.

But deeper reasons than these can be given for caution. It is plain that each participant enters a social situation carrying an already established biography of prior dealings with the other participants—or at least with participants of their kind: and enters also with a vast array of cultural assumptions presumed to be shared. We could not disattend strangers in our presence unless their appearance and manner implied a benign intent, a course of action that was identifiable and unthreatening, and such readings can only be made on the basis of prior experience and cultural lore. We could not utter a phrase meaningfully unless we adjusted lexicon and prosody according to what the categoric or individual identity of our putative recipients allows us to assume they already know, and knowing this, don't mind our openly presuming on it. At the very center of interaction life is the cognitive relation we have with those present before us, without which relationship our activity, behavioral and verbal, could not be meaningfully organized. And although this cognitive relationship can be modified during a social contact, and typically is, the relationship itself is extrasituational, consisting of the information a pair of persons have about the information each other has of the world, and the information they have (or haven't) concerning the possession of this information.

III

In speaking of the interaction order I have so far presupposed the term "order," and an account is called for. I mean to refer in the first instance to a domain of activity—a particular kind of activity, as in the phrase, "the economic order." No implications are intended concerning how "orderly" such activity ordinarily is, or the role of norms and rules in supporting such orderliness as does obtain. Yet it appears to me that *as* an order of activity, the interaction one, more than any other perhaps, is in fact orderly, and that this orderliness is predicated on a large base of shared cognitive presuppositions, if not normative ones, and self-sustained restraints. How a given set of such understandings comes into being historically, spreads and contracts in geographical distribution over time, and how at any one place and time particular individuals acquire these understandings are good questions, but not ones I can address.

The workings of the interaction order can easily be viewed as the consequences of systems of enabling conventions, in the sense of the ground rules for a game, the provisions of a traffic code or the rules of syntax of a language. As part of this perspective one could press two accounts. First, the dogma that the overall effect of a given set of conventions is that all participants pay a small price and obtain a large convenience, the notion being that any convention that facilitates coordination would do, so long as everyone could be induced to uphold it—the several conventions in themselves having no intrinsic value. (That, of course, is how one defines "conventions" in the first place.) On the second account, orderly interaction is seen as a product of normative consensus, the traditional sociological view that individuals unthinkingly take for granted rules they nonetheless feel are intrinsically just. Incidentally, both of these perspectives assume that the constraints which apply to others apply to oneself also, that other selves take the same view regarding constraints on their behavior, and that everyone understands that this self-submission obtains.

These two accounts—social contract and social consensus—raise obvious questions and doubts. Motive for adhering to a set of arrangements need tell us nothing about the effect of doing so. Effective cooperation in maintaining expectations implies neither belief in the legitimacy or justice of abiding by a convention contract in general (whatever it happens to be), *nor* personal belief in the ultimate value of the particular norms that are involved. Individuals go along with current interaction arrangements for a wide variety of reasons, and one cannot read from their apparent tacit support of an arrangement that they would, for example, resent or resist its change. Very often behind community and consensus are mixed motive games.

Note also that individuals who systematically violate the norms of the interaction order may nonetheless be dependent on them most of the time, including some of the time during which they are actively engaged in violations. After all, almost all acts of violence are mitigated by the violator proffering an exchange of some kind, however undesired by the victim, and of course the violator presupposes the maintenance of speech norms and the conventions for gesturing threat to accomplish this. So, too, in the case of unnegotiated violence. Assassins must rely on and profit from conventional traffic flow and conventional understanding regarding normal appearances if they are to get into a position to attack their victim and escape from the scene of the crime. Hallways, elevators, and alleys can be dangerous places because they may be hidden from view and empty of everyone except victim and assailant; but again, behind the opportunity that these arrangements provide the miscreant, is his reliance on understandings regarding normal appearances, these understandings allowing him to enter and leave the area in the guise of someone who does not abuse free passage. All of which should remind us that in almost all cases, interaction arrangements can withstand systematic violation, at least over the short run, and therefore that although it is in the interests of the individual to convince others that their compliance is critical to the maintenance of order, and to show apparent approval of their conformity, it will often not be in that individual's interests (as variously defined) to personally uphold the niceties.

There are deeper reasons to question the various dogmas regarding the interaction order. It might be convenient to believe that individuals (and social categories of individuals) always get considerably more from the operation of various aspects of the interaction order than the concomitant restraints cost them. But that is questionable. What is desirable order from the perspective of some can be sensed as exclusion and repression from the point of view of others. It does not raise questions about the neutrality of the term order to learn of tribal councils in West Africa that orderly speaking reflects (among other things) adherence to a rule of rank. Nor that (as Burrage and Corry have recently shown) in orderly ceremonial processions through London, from Tudor to Jacobean times, representatives of the trades and crafts maintained a traditional hierarchy both with respect to their place as marchers and as watchers. But questions do arise when we consider the fact that there are categories of persons—in our own society very broad ones—whose members constantly pay a very considerable price for their interactional existence.

Yet, over the short historic run at least, even the most disadvantaged categories continue to cooperate—a fact hidden by the manifest ill will their members may display in regard to a few norms while sustaining all the rest. Perhaps behind a willingness to accept the way things are ordered is the brutal fact of one's place in the social structure and the real or imagined cost of allowing oneself to be singled out as a malcontent. Whatever, there is no doubt that categories of individual in every time and place have exhibited a disheartening capacity for overtly accepting miserable interactional arrangements.

In sum, then, although it is certainly proper to point to the unequal distribution of rights in the interaction order (as in the case of the segregative use of the local communities of a city), and the unequal distribution of risk (as, say, across the age grades and between the sexes), the central theme remains of a traffic of use, and of arrangements which allow a great diversity of projects and intents to be realized through unthinking recourse to procedural forms. And of course, to accept the conventions and norms as given (and to initiate one's action accordingly), is, *in effect*, to put trust in those about one. Not doing so, one could hardly get on with the business at hand; one could hardly have any business at hand.

The doctrine that ground rules inform the interaction order and allow for a traffic of use raises the question of policing, and policing, of course, once again raises political considerations.

The modern nation state, almost as a means of defining itself into existence, claims final authority for the control of hazard and threat to life, limb, and property throughout its territorial jurisdiction. Always in theory, and often in practice, the state provides stand-by arrangements for stepping in when local mechanisms of social control fail to keep breakdowns of interaction order within certain limits. Particularly in public places but not restricted thereto. To be sure, the interaction order prevailing even in the most public places is not a creation of the apparatus of a state. Certainly most of this order comes into being and is sustained from below as it were, in some cases in spite of overarching authority not because of it. Nonetheless the state has effectively established legitimacy and priority here, monopolizing the use of heavy arms and militarily disciplined cadres as an ultimate sanction.

In consequence, some of the standard forms of interaction life—podium addresses, meetings, processions—not to speak of specialized forms like picket lines or sit-down strikes—can be read by governing officials as an affront to the security of the state and forcibly disbanded on these grounds although, indeed, no appreciable threat to public order in the substantive sense may be involved. And on the other side, breaches of public order may be performed not only for self gain, but as a pointed challenge to the authority of the state—symbolical acts read as a taunt and employed in anticipation of this reading.

IV

I have been speaking in terms that are intended to hold for face-to-face existence everywhere. I have done so at the usual price—the pronouncements have been broad, truistic, and metatheoretical—to use a word that is itself as questionable as what it refers to. A less windy effort, equally general but naturalistically based, is to try to identify the basic substantive units, the recurrent structures and their attendant processes. What sorts of animals are to be found in the interactional zoo? What plants in this particular garden? Let me review what I take to be some basic examples.

1. One can start with persons as vehicular entities, that is, with human ambulatory units. In public places we have "singles" (a party of one) and "withs" (a party of more than one), such parties being treated as self-contained units for the purposes of participation in the flow of pedestrian social life. A few larger ambulatory units can also be mentioned—for example, files and processions, and, as a limiting case, the queue, this being by way of a stationary ambulatory unit. (Any ordering of access by time of application can by extension reasonably be called a queue, but I do not do so here.)

2. Next, if only as a heuristic unit and for purposes of consistency in usage, there is some value in tying down the term *contact*. I will refer thus to any occasion when an individual comes into an other's response presence, whether through physical copresence, telephonic connection or letter exchange. I am thus counting as part of the same contact all those sightings and exchanges that occur during one such occasion. Thus, a passing street glance, a conversation, an exchange of increasingly attenuated greetings while circulating at a sociable gathering, an attendee's-eye-view of a platform speaker—each qualifies as a single contact.

3. Then there is that broad class of arrangements in which persons come together into a small physical circle as ratified participants in a consciously shared, clearly interdependent undertaking, the period of participation itself bracketed with rituals of some kind, or easily susceptible to their invocation. In some cases only a handful of participants are involved, talk of the kind that can be seen as having a self-limiting purpose holds the floor, and the appearance is sustained that in principle everyone has the same right to contribute. Such conversational encounters can be distinguished from meetings in which a presiding chair manages turn taking and relevance: thus "hearings," "trials," and other jural proceedings. All of these talk-based activities are to be contrasted to the many interactive engagements in which

the doings that are interwoven do not involve vocalization, and in which talk, when it figures at all, does so either as a desultory, muted side-involvement or an irregular, intermittent adjunct to the coordination of the doings in progress. Examples of such encounters are card games, service transactions, bouts of love making, and commensalism.

4. Next the platform format: the arrangement found universally in which an activity is set before an audience. What is presented in this way may be a talk, a contest, a formal meeting, a play, a movie, a musical offering, a display of dexterity or trickery, a round of oratory, a ceremony, a combination thereof. The presenters will either be on a raised platform or encircled by watchers. The size of the audience is not closely geared to what is presented (although it is to arrangements which allow for viewing the stage), and the obligation of the watchers is primarily to appreciate, not to do. Modern technology, of course, has exploded this interaction institution to include vast distal audiences and a widened array of materials that can be platformed. But the format itself very much answers to the requirements of involving a potentially large number of individuals in a single focus of visual and cognitive attention, something that is possible only if the watchers are content to enter merely vicariously into what is staged.

5. Finally, one might mention the celebrative social occasion. I refer to the foregathering of individuals admitted on a controlled basis, the whole occurring under the auspices of, and in honor of, some jointly appreciated circumstances. A common mood or tone is likely to develop, tracing a contour of involvement. Participants arrive in a coordinated way and leave similarly. More than one bounded region may function as the setting of a single occasion, these regions connected to facilitate moving, mingling and the circulation of response. Within its compass, a social occasion is likely to provide a setting for many different small focused undertakings, conversational and otherwise, and very often will highlight (and embed) a platform activity. Often there will be a sense of official proceedings, a period before characterized as available to uncoordinated sociability, and a period after that is marked by felt release from occasioned obligations. Typically there will be some preplanning, sometimes even an agenda. There will be specialization of functions, broadly among housekeeping staff, official organizers and nonofficiating participants. The affair as a whole is looked forward to and back upon as a unitary, reportable event. Celebrative social occasions can be seen as the largest interactional unit, being, it seems, the only kind that can be engineered to extend over a number of days. Ordinarily, however, once begun a celebrative occasion will be in continuous existence until its termination.

It is plain that whenever encounters, platform performances, or celebrative, social occasions occur, so also does ambulatory movement and thus the units in which this movement is regulated. It should be just as plain that brief, two- to four-part verbal interchanges serve throughout the interaction order in a facilitative and accommodative way, remedying hitches in coordinated activity and unintended impingements in connection with adjacent, independent activities.

I have touched on a few basic interaction entities: ambulatory units, contacts, conversational encounters, formal meetings, platform performances, and social occasions. A parallel treatment could be provided of interaction processes or mechanisms. But although it is easy enough to uncover recurrent interaction processes of some generality—especially microscopic processes—it is difficult to identify basic ones, except, perhaps, in connection with turntaking in conversation. Something the same could be said of interaction roles.

V

I speak no further of the forms and processes of social life specific to the interaction order. Such talk might only have relevance for those interested in human ethology, collective behavior, public order, and discourse analysis. I want instead to focus my concluding remarks on one general issue of wider bearing: the interface between the interaction order and the more traditionally considered elements of social organization. The aim will be to describe some features of the interaction order, but only those that directly bear upon the macroscopic worlds beyond the interaction in which these features are found.

From the outset a matter that is so obvious as to be taken for granted and neglected: the direct impact of situational effects upon social structures. Three examples might be cited.

First, insofar as a complex organization comes to be dependent on particular personnel (typically personnel who have managed to acquire governing roles), then the daily sequence of social situations on and off the job—that is, the daily round—in which these personages can be injured or abducted are also situations in which their organizations can suffer. Corner businesses, families, relationships, and other small structures are similarly vulnerable, especially those stationed in high crime-rate areas. Although this issue can acquire great public attention in various times and places, it seems to me of no great conceptual interest; analytically speaking, unexpected death from natural causes introduces much the same embarrassment to organizations. In both cases one deals with nothing more than risk.

Second, as already implied, there is the obvious fact that a great deal of the work of organizations—decision making, the transmission of information, the close coordination of physical tasks—is done face-to-face, requires being done in this way, and is vulnerable to face-to-face effects. Differently put, insofar as agents of social organizations of any scale, from states to households, can be persuaded, cajoled, flattered, intimidated, or otherwise influenced by effects only achievable in face-to-face dealings, then here, too, the interaction order bluntly impinges on macroscopic entities.

Third, there are people-processing encounters, encounters in which the "impression" subjects make during the interaction affects their life chances. The institutionalized example is the placement interview as conducted by school counselors, personnel department psychologists, psychiatric diagnosticians, and courtroom officials. In a less candid form, this processing is ubiquitous; everyone is a gatekeeper in regard to something. Thus, friendship relationships and marital bonds (at least in our society) can be traced back to an occasion in which something more was made of an incidental contact than need have been.

Whether made in institutionalized settings or not, what is situational about such processing encounters is clear: Every culture, and certainly ours, seems to have a vast lore of fact and fantasy regarding embodied indicators of status and character, thus appearing to render persons readable. By a sort of prearrangement, then, social situations seem to be perfectly designed to provide us with evidence of a participant's various attributes—if only to vividly re-present what we already know. Further, in social situations, as in other circumstances, deciders, if pressed, can employ an open-ended list of rationalizations to conceal from the subject (and even from themselves) the mix of considerations that figure in their decision and, especially, the relative weight given to these several determinants.

It is in these processing encounters, then, that the quiet sorting can occur which, as Bourdieu might have it, reproduces the social structure. But that conservative impact is not, analytically speaking, situational. The subjective weighting of a large number of social attributes, whether these attributes are officially relevant or not, and whether they are real or fanciful, provides a micro-dot of mystification; covert value given, say, to race, can be mitigated by covert value given to other structural variables—class, gender, age, comemberships, sponsorship network—structures which at best are not fully congruent with each other. And structural attributes, overtly or covertly employed, do not mesh fully with personal ones, such as health or vigor, or with properties that have all of their existence in social situations—looks, personality, and the like. What is situational, then, about processing encounters is the evidence they so fully provide of a participant's real or apparent attributes while at the same time allowing life chances to be determined through an inaccessible weighting of this complex of evidence. Although this arrangement ordinarily allows for the surreptitious consolidation of structural lines, the same arrangement can also serve to loosen them.

One can point, then, to obvious ways in which social structures are dependent on, and vulnerable to, what occurs in face-to-face contacts. This has led some to argue reductively that all macrosociological features of society, along with society itself, are an intermittently existing composite of what can be traced back to the reality of encounters—a question of aggregating and extrapolating interactional effects. (This position is sometimes reinforced by the argument that whatever we do know about social structures can be traced back to highly edited summaries of what was originally a stream of experience in social situations.)

I find these claims uncongenial. For one, they confuse the interactional format in which words and gestural indications occur with the import of these words and gestures, in a word, they confuse the situational with the merely situated. When your broker informs you that he has to sell you out or when your employer or your spouse informs you that your services are no longer required, the bad news can be delivered through a sequestered talk that gently and delicately humanizes the occasion. Such considerateness belongs to the resources of the interaction order. At the time of their use you may be very grateful for them. But the next morning what does it matter if you had gotten the word from a wire margin call, a computer readout, a blue slip at the time clock, or a terse note left on the bureau? How delicately or indelicately one is treated during the moment in which bad news is delivered does not speak to the structural significance of the news itself.

Further, I do not believe that one can learn about the shape of the commodities market, or the distribution of a city's land values, or the ethnic succession in municipal administrations, or the structure of kinship systems, or the systematic phonological shifts within the dialects of a speech community by extrapolating or aggregating from particular social encounters among the persons involved in any one of these patterns. (Statements about macroscopic structures and processes can reasonably be subjected to a microanalysis but of the kind that digs behind generalizations to find critical differences between, say, different industries, regions, short-term periods, and the like, sufficiently so to fracture overall views, and not because of the face-to-face interactions.)

Nor do I subscribe to the notion that face-to-face behavior is any more real, any less of an arbitrary abstraction, than what we think of as the dealings between two corporations, or the distribution of felonies across the weekly cycle and subregions of a New York borough; in all these cases what we get is somebody's crudely edited summaries. I claim merely that forms of face-to-face life are worn smooth by constant repetition on the part of participants who are heterogeneous in many ways and yet must quickly reach a working understanding; these forms thus seem more open to systematic analysis than are the internal or external workings of many macroscopic entities. The forms themselves are anchored in subjective feelings, and thus allow an appreciable role for empathy. The very brief span in space and time of the phenomenal side of many of these events facilitates recording (and replaying), and one has, of course, the comfort of being able to keep one's

own eyes on particular instances throughout the full course of their occurrence. Yet one must see that even within the domain of face-to-face
interaction, what some students accept as the smallest (and in that sense,
ultimate) units of personal experience, others see as already a hopelessly
complex matter requiring a much more refined application of microanalysis.

In sum, to speak of the relatively autonomous forms of life in the interaction order (as Charles Tilly has nicely done in connection with a special
category of these forms) is not to put forward these forms as somehow prior,
fundamental, or constitutive of the shape of macroscopic phenomena. To
do so is akin to the self-centering game of playwrights, clinical psychologists,
and good informants—all of whom fit their stories out so that forces within
individual characters constitute and govern the action, allowing individual
hearers and readers to identify gratefully with the result. Nor is it to speak
of something immutable. All elements of social life have a history and are
subject to critical change through time, and none can be fully understood
apart from the particular culture in which it occurs. (Which is not to say that
historians and anthropologists can often provide us with the data we would
need to do a realistic analysis of interaction practices in communities no
longer available to us.)

VI

I have mentioned direct connections between social structures and the interaction order not because of having anything new or principled to say about
them, but only to establish the appropriate contrast for those interface effects
that are most commonly considered, namely, the Durkheimian ones. You
all know the litany. A critical feature of face-to-face gatherings is that in them
and them alone we can fit a shape and dramatic form to matters that aren't
otherwise palpable to the senses. Through costume, gesture, and bodily
alignment we can depict and represent a heterogeneous list of immaterial
things, sharing only the fact that they have a significance in our lives and yet
do not cast a shadow: notable events in the past, beliefs about the cosmos
and our place in it, ideals regarding our various categories of persons, and
of course social relationships and larger social structures. These embodiments are centered in ceremonies (in turn embedded in celebrative social
occasions) and presumably allow the participants to affirm their affiliation
and commitment to their collectivities, and revive their ultimate beliefs.
Here the celebration of a collectivity is a conscious reason for the social occasion which houses it, and naturally figures in the occasion's organization.
The range in scale of such celebrative events is great: at one end, coron-
ations, at the other, the two-couple dine-out—that increasingly common
middle-class network ritual, to which we all give, and from which we all gain,
so much weight.

Social anthropology claims these various ceremonies as its province, and indeed the best treatment of them in modern communities is Lloyd Warner's *The Living and the Dead*. Secular mass societies, it turns out, have not proven hostile to these celebrations—indeed Soviet Society, as Crystal Lane has recently documented, is rife with them. Benedictions may be on the decline in number and significance, but not the occasions on which they once would have been offered.

And presumably these occasions have consequences for macrostructures. For example, Abner Cohen tells us that the steel-band carnival that began in the Notting Hill area of London as a multi-ethnic block party ended up as the beginning of the political organization of London's West Indians; that what started out as an annual Bank Holiday social affair—quintessentially a creature having merely an interactional life—ended up as an expression of a politically self-conscious group, the expression itself having helped considerably to create the structural context in which it would come to be seen. So the carnival was more the cause of a social movement and its group-formative effects than an expression thereof. Similarly, Simon Taylor tells us that the calendar of political celebrations developed by the national socialist movement in Germany—the calendar being a Hitler-centric version of basic Christian ceremonies—played an important role in consolidating the hold of the Party upon the nation. The key occasion in this annual cycle, apparently, was the Nuremberg Reichsparty-day held in the Zeppelinfield. This place could concentrate almost a quarter of a million people while affording all of them direct visual access to the stage. That number of people responding in unison to the same platform event apparently had lasting influence on some participants; certainly we have here the limiting case of a situational event, and certainly the interesting issue is not how the ritual reflected Nazi doctrines regarding the world, but how the annual occasion itself clearly contributed to the political hegemony of its impresarios.

In these two examples—admittedly both somewhat extreme—one has a direct leap from interactional effect to political organization. Of course, every rally—especially ones involving collective confrontation with authority—can have some long-standing effect upon the political orientation of the celebrants.

Now although it seems easy enough to identify the collectivities which ceremony projects on to a behavioral screen, and to cite, as I have just done, evidence of the critical contribution the shadow may make to the substance, it is quite another matter to demonstrate that *in general* anything macroscopically significant results from ceremony—at least in contemporary society. Those individuals who are in a position to authorize and organize such occasions are often the ones who star in them, and these functionaries always seem to be optimistic about the result. But in fact, the ties and relationships that we ceremonialize may be so attenuated that a periodic celebration is all that we are prepared to commit to them; so what they index is not our social reality but our nostalgia, our bad conscience, and our lingering piety in regard to what is no longer binding. (When friends remove to another town, the celebration of chance conjunctions can become the substance of the relationship not its expression.) Furthermore, as Moore and Myerhoff have suggested, the categories of persons that come together in a ceremony (and thus the structures that are involved) may never come together again, ceremonially or otherwise. A one-time intersection of variously impinging interests may be represented, and nothing beyond that. Certainly celebrative occasions such as this presidential address don't necessarily have the effect of recommitting the members of the audience to the discipline and profession under whose name they foregather. Indeed, all one can hope for is that memory of how the hour was passed will fade quickly, allowing everyone to attend again the following year, willing once again to not not come. In sum, sentiments about structural ties serve more as an involvement resource—serve more to carry a celebrative occasion—than such affairs serve to strengthen what they draw from.

VII

If we think of ceremonials as narrative-like enactments, more or less extensive and more or less insulated from mundane routines, then we can contrast these complex performances with "contact rituals," namely, perfunctory, brief expressions occurring incidental to everyday action—in passing as it were—the most frequent case involving but two individuals. These performances have not been handled very well by anthropology even though they seem much more researchable than the more complex sequences. Indeed, ethology and the ethological conception of ritual, at least in the sense of intention display, turn out to be as germane as the anthropological formulation. The question, then, becomes: what principles inform the bearing of social structures on contact rituals? It is this issue I want to consider in closing.

The events occurring for incidental reasons when individuals are in one another's immediate presence are well designed to serve as micro-ecological metaphors, summaries and iconic symbols of structural arrangements—whether wanted or not. And should such expressions not occur incidentally, local environments can easily be manipulated so as to produce them. Given the selective sensibilities in a particular culture—for example, concern over relative elevation, value placed on right-over left-sidedness, orientation to the cardinal directions—given such cultural biases, some depictive, situated resources will of course be exploited more than others. The question, then, is how will these features of the interaction order be geared or linked into, connected up with, tied into social structures, including social relationships? Here the social sciences have been rather easygoing, sufficiently so on occasion to be content with the phrase "an expression of." Minor social ritual is not an expression *of* structural arrangements in any simple sense; at best it is an expression advanced *in regard* to these arrangements. Social structures don't "determine" culturally standard displays, merely help select from the available repertoire of them. The expressions themselves, such as priority in being served, precedence through a door, centrality of seating, access to various public places, preferential interruption rights in talk, selection as addressed recipient, are interactional in substance and character; at best they are likely to have only loosely coupled relations to anything by way of social structures that might be associated with them. They are sign vehicles fabricated from depictive materials at hand, and what they come to be taken as a "reflection" of is necessarily an open question.

Look, for example, at the bit of our ritual idiom frequently treated in term papers: license to employ reciprocal first-naming as an address formula. Pairs of persons licensed to greet and talk to each other through reciprocal first name can't be taken by evidence of this fact alone to be in a particular structural relation, or to be co-members of a particular social organization or group or category. There is great variation by region, class, and epoch, and these variations do not correspond closely to variation in social structure. But there are other issues. Take persons like ourselves for a moment. We are on reciprocal first name terms with sibs, relatives of same generation, friends, neighbors, early school mates, the newly introduced to us at domestic social gatherings, our office mates, our car salesman, our accountant, and when we gamble privately, the cronies we do it with. I regret to say that in some cases we are also on such terms with our parents and children. The very fact, that in some cases (sibs and spouses for example) first-name terms (as opposed to other proper names) are obligatory and in other relationships optional, suggests the looseness of the usage. The traditional term "primary ties" addresses the issue, but optimistically; it reflects the psychological reductionism of our sociological forefathers, and their wistful memories of the neighborhoods they were raised in. In fact, reciprocal first naming is a culturally established resource for styling immediate dealings: reduced formality is implied and the abjuring of a tone-setting opportunity to stand on one's claim to ritual circumspection. But informality is constituted out of interactional materials (as is formality), and the various social relations and social circles that draw on this resource merely share some affinities. Which is not to say, of course, that a full catalogue of the symmetrical and asymmetrical forms of interactional regard and disregard, of circumspection and ritual ease, that two individuals routinely extend to each other would not appreciably inform us about their structural ties. Nor is it to say that convention can't link some displays to social structures in exclusive ways; in our society the wedding ceremony, for example, employs some forms that advertise the formation of an instance of a particular class of social structure and this alone. Nor is it to say that forms of interaction can't themselves be responsible to the institutional setting in which they occur. (Even apart from *what* is said, turn-taking rules in informal talk differ somewhat from those in family therapy sessions, which are different in turn from those in classroom teaching, and these in turn differ from the practices found in court hearings. And these differences in form are partly explicable in terms of the special tasks undertaken in these several settings, which in turn are determined by extrasituational concerns.)

In general, then, (and qualifications apart) what one finds, in modern societies at least, is a nonexclusive linkage—a "loose coupling"—between interactional practices and social structures, a collapsing of strata and structures into broader categories, the categories themselves not corresponding one-to-one to anything in the structural world, a gearing as it were of various structures into interactional cogs. Or, if you will, a set of transformation rules, or a membrane selecting how various externally relevant social distinctions will be managed within the interaction.

One example. From the perspective of how women in our society fare in informal cross-sexed talk, it is of very small moment that (statistically speaking) a handful of males, such as junior executives, have to similarly wait and hang on other's words—albeit in each case not many others. From the point of view of the interaction order, however, the issue is critical. For one, it allows us to try to formulate a role category that women and junior executives (and anyone else in these interactional circumstances) share, and this will be a role that belongs *analytically* to the interaction order, which the categories women and junior executives do not.

I need only remind you that the dependency of interactional activity on matters outside the interaction—a fact characteristically neglected by those of us who focus on face-to-face dealings—doesn't in itself imply dependency on social structures. As already suggested, a quite central issue in all face-to-face interaction is the cognitive relation of the participants, that is, what it is each can effectively assume the other knows. This relationship is relatively context-free, extending beyond any current social situation to all occasions when the two individuals meet. Pairs constituting intimate structures, by definition, will know considerable about each other, and also know of many experiences they exclusively share—all of which dramatically affects what they can say to each other and how laconic they can be in making these references. But all this exclusive information pales when one considers the amount of information about the world two barely acquainted individuals can assume it is reasonable to assume in formulating their utterances to each other. (Here, once again, we see that the traditional distinction between primary and secondary relations is an insight sociology must escape from.)

The general formulation I have suggested of the relation between the interaction order and the structural ones allows one (I hope) to proceed constructively. First, as suggested, one is encouraged to treat as a matter for discovery just who it is that does it to whom, the assumption being that in almost every case the categories that result will not quite coincide with any structural division. Let me press yet another example. Etiquette books are full of conceptualizations concerning the courtesies that men owe women in polite society. Less clearly presented, of course, is an understanding concerning the kinds of women and the kinds of men who would not be looked to as expected participants in these little niceties. More germane here, however, is the fact each of these little gestures turns out to be also prescribed between other categories: an adult in regard to an old person, an adult in regard to a young person, a host for a guest, an expert for a novice, a native for a visitor, friends in regard to the celebrant of a life turning-point, a well person for a sick one, a whole person for an incapacitated one. And, as suggested, it turns out that what all these pairings share is not something in the social structure but something that a scene of face-to-face interaction allows for. (Even if one were to restrict oneself to one sphere of social life—say activity within a complex organization—a loose coupling between the interaction order and social structure would remain. The precedence one gives one's immediate boss one gives to his or her immediate boss too, and so on to the head of the organization; for precedence is an interactional resource that speaks to ordinal ranking, not to the distance between the rungs.) It is easy enough, then, and even useful, to specify in social structural terms who performs a given act of deference or presumption to whom. In the study of the interaction order, however, after saying that, one must search out who else does it to whom else, then categorize the doers with a term that covers them all, and similarly with the done to. And one must provide a technically detailed description of the forms involved.

Second, a loose-coupling approach allows one to find a proper place for the apparent power of fads and fashions to effect change in ritual practices. A recent example, known to you all, was the rapid and somewhat temporary shift to informal dress in the business world during the latter phases of the hippie movement, accompanied sometimes by a change in salutational forms, all without much corresponding change in social structure.

Third, one can appreciate the vulnerability of features of the interaction order to direct political intervention, both from below and above, in either case bypassing socioeconomic relationships. Thus, in recent times blacks and women have concertedly breached segregated public places, in many cases with lasting consequence for access arrangements, but, all in all, without much change in the place of blacks and women in the social structure. And one can appreciate the purpose of a new regime in introducing and enforcing a practice that strikes at the manner in which broad categories of persons will appear in public, as, for example, when the National Socialists in Germany required Jews to wear identifying arm bands when in public places, or the Soviet government took official action to discourage the wearing of veils by women of the Siberian Khanty ethnic group, or the Iranian government took veils in exactly the opposite direction. And one can appreciate, too, the effectiveness of efforts directly to alter contact interchanges, as when a revolutionary salute, verbal greeting, or address term is introduced from above, in some cases rather permanently.

And finally, one can appreciate the leverage those in an ideological movement can obtain by concentrating their efforts upon salutations and farewells, address terms, tact and indirection, and other junctures for politeness in the management of social contacts and verbal intercourse. Or the fuss that can be made by a doctrine that leads to systematic breaching of standards for seemly public dress. In these matters, American Hippies, and later, "The Chicago Seven," were interesting amateurs; the great terrorists of contact forms were the mid-17th century Quakers in Britain, who managed, somehow, (as Bauman has recently described it) to design a doctrine that struck directly at the then settled arrangements through which social structures and broad official values were given polite due in social intercourse. (To be sure other religious movements of the period employed some of these recalcitrancies too, but none so systematically.) That sturdy band of plain speakers should always stand before us as an example of the wonderfully disruptive power of systematic impoliteness, reminding us once again of the vulnerabilities of the interaction order. There is no doubt: Fox's disciples raised to monumental heights the art of becoming a pain in the ass.

VIII

Of all the social structures that interface with the interaction order, the ones that seem to do so most intimately are social relationships. I want to say a word about them.

To think of the amount or frequency of face-to-face interaction between two related individuals—two ends of the relationship—as somehow constitutive of their relationship is structurally naive, seemingly taking propinquity-related friendship as a model for all relationships. And yet, of course, the link between relationships and the interaction order is close.

Take for example (in our own society) acquaintanceship, or, better still, "knowership." This is a critical institution from the perspective of how we deal with individuals in our immediate, or in our telephonic, presence, a key factor in the organization of social contacts. What is involved is the right and obligation mutually to accept and openly to acknowledge individual identification on all initial occasions of incidentally produced proximity. This relationship, once established, is defined as continuing for life—a property imputed much less correctly to the marriage bond. The social relationship we call "mere acquaintanceship" incorporates knowership and little else, constituting thereby a limiting case—a social relationship whose consequences are restricted to social situations—for here the obligation to provide evidence of this relationship *is* the relationship. And this evidence is the stuff of interaction. Knowledge of another's name and the right to use it in address incidentally implies the capacity to specify who it is one is summoning into talk. Similarly, a greeting owed incidentally implies the initiation of an encounter.

When one turns to "deeper" relationships, knowership and its obligations remain a factor, but now not the defining one. However, other links between relationships and the interaction order appear. The obligation to exchange passing greetings is extended: the pair may be obliged to interrupt their independent courses of action so that a full-fledged encounter can be openly dedicated to display of pleasure at the opportunity for contact. During this convivial pause, each participant is constrained to demonstrate that she or he has kept fresh in mind not only the name of the other but also bits of the other's biography. Inquiries will be in order regarding the other's significant others, recent trips, illness if any, career outcomes, and sundry other matters that speak to the questioner's aliveness to the world of the person greeted. Correspondingly, there will be the obligation to update the other regarding one's own circumstances. Of course these obligations help to resuscitate relationships that might otherwise have attenuated for want of dealings; but they also provide both the grounds for initiating an encounter and an easy initial topic. So one might have to admit that the obligation to maintain an active biography of our acquaintances (and ensure that they can sustain the same in regard to us) does at least as much for the organization of encounters as it does for the relationship of the persons who encounter each other. This service to the interaction order is also very evident in connection with our obligation to retain our acquaintance's personal name immediately in mind, allowing us always to employ it as a vocative in multiperson talk. After all, personal name in utterance-initial position is an effective device for alerting ratified hearers as to which of them is about to be addressed.

Just as the closely related are obliged to enjoy a greeting encounter when they find themselves incidentally in one another's immediate presence, so after a measured time of not having been in contact are they obliged to ensure a meeting, either through a phone call or letter, or by jointly plotting an opportunity for face-to-face contact—the plotting itself providing a contact even if nothing comes of what is plotted. Here, in "due contacts" one can see that encountering itself is borrowed whole cloth from the interaction order and defined as one of the goods mutually provided for in relationships.

IX

Although it is interesting to try to work out the connections between the interaction order and social relationships, there is another matter that more obviously presses for consideration: what in traditional sociology is referred to as diffuse social statuses or (in another version) master status-determined traits. To close my remarks tonight I want to comment on this issue.

In our society, one could say that there are four critical diffuse statuses: age-grade, gender, class, and race. Although these attributes and corresponding social structures function quite differently in society (perhaps race and class being the most closely allied), they all share two critical features.

First, they constitute a cross-cutting grid on which each individual can be relevantly located with respect to each of the four statuses.

Secondly, our placement in respect to all four attributes is evident by virtue of the markers our bodies bring with them into all our social situations, no prior information about us being required. Whether we can be *individually* identified or not in a particular social situation, we can almost always be *categorically* identified in these four ways on entrance. (When not, then sociologically instructive troubles arise.) The easy perceptibility of these traits in social situations is not of course entirely fortuitous; in most cases, socialization, in subtle ways, insures that our placement in these regards will be more evident than might otherwise be. But of course, any trait that is not easily perceptible could hardly acquire the capacity of a diffuse status-determining (or more correctly, status-identifying) trait, at least in modern society. Which is not to say that this perceptibility is of equal importance in the role that each of these diffuse statuses plays in our society. Nor surely that perceptibility alone will guarantee that society will make use of this property structurally.

With this schematic picture of diffuse statuses in mind, turn to one paradigmatic example of the sort of context micro-analysis deals with: the class of events in which a "server," in a setting prepared for the purpose, perfunctorily and regularly provides goods of some kind to a series of customers or clients, typically either in exchange for money or as an intermediate phase in bureaucratic processing. In brief, the "service transaction"—here focusing on the kind that find server and served in the same social situation, in contrast to dealings over the phone, or through the mail, or with a dispensing machine. The institutionalized format for conducting these dealings draws upon a wider cultural complex covering government protocol, traffic rules, and other formalizations of precedence.

In contemporary society almost everyone has service transactions every day. Whatever the ultimate significance of these dealings for recipients, it is clear that how they are treated in these contexts is likely to flavor their sense of place in the wider community.

In almost all contemporary service transactions, a basic understanding seems to prevail: that all candidates for service will be treated "the same" or "equally," none being favored or disfavored over the others. One doesn't, of course, need to look to democratic philosophy to account for the institutionalization of this arrangement: all things considered, this ethic provides a very effective formula for the routinization and processing of services.

The principle of equality of service treatment in service transactions has some obvious implications. In order to deal with more than one candidate for service at a time in what can be perceived as an orderly and fair manner, a queuing arrangement is likely to be employed, this likely involving a first come first served rule. This rule produces a temporal ordering that totally blocks the influence of such differential social statuses and relationships as the candidates bring with them to the service situation—attributes which are of massive significance outside the situation. (Here is the quintessential case of "local determinism" as a blocking device.) Plainly, then, immediately on entering a service arena, customers will find it in their interests to identify the local tracking system (whether numbered slips are to be taken from a machine or spindle, or names logged in a list, or a human queue requiring one's body as a marker, or active orientation to the individual identity of those already present and to the person who enters right after oneself). They will also be expected to manage sorting themselves among sub-queues subtended by multiple servers, all of this as part of their presupposed competence. And of course, if one's place in a queue is to be respected, fellow queuers will have to sustain queuing discipline amongst themselves, apart from relations to the server.

Along with the principle of equality, another rule is everywhere present in contemporary service transactions: the expectation that anyone seeking service will be treated with "courtesy"; for example, that the server will give quick attention to the service request, and execute it with words, gestures, and manner that somehow display approval of the asker and pleasure in the contact. Implied (when taken in conjunction with the equality principle) is that a customer who makes a very small purchase will be given no less a reception than one who makes a very large one. Here one has the institutionalization—indeed the commercialization—of deference and again something that would seem to facilitate the routinization of servicing.

Given the two rules I have mentioned—equality of treatment and courteous treatment—participants in service transactions can feel that all externally relevant attributes are being held in abeyance and only internally generated ones are allowed to play a role, e.g., first come first served. And indeed, this is a standard response. But obviously, what in fact goes on while the client sustains this sense of normal treatment is a complex and precarious matter.

Take, for example, the unstated assumptions in servicing regarding who qualifies as a serious candidate. Situationally perceptible qualifications regarding age, sobriety, language ability, and solvency will have to be satisfied before individuals are allowed to hold themselves as qualified for service. (The order "Cup of coffee to go" might not receive the laconic reply "Cream or sugar?" if it is a street bum who places the order; a polite request at the counter of a West Philadelphia hospital pharmacy for "Twenty 5-milligram valium, please" while submitting the prescription may well evoke the naked reply "How are you going to pay for it?"; and attempted purchases of alcoholic beverages anywhere in this country may well invoke a request to see an age certificate.)

Qualifying rules apart, one is likely to find understandings about the relaxation of queuing constraints. For example, faced by a queue, entering individuals can plea or display extenuating circumstances, beg to be allowed precedence and be granted this special privilege (or have it initiated to them if their need is evident) by the person whose position in the queue will be the first to be set back by the license. The cost to the donor of this license is also borne by all the other members of the queue who are behind the donor, but generally they seem willing to delegate the decision and abide by it. A more common relaxation of the norms occurs when the head of a queue volunteers to change places with the person next in line (or is requested by the latter to do so) because the latter is in an apparent rush or appears to have only a very brief need for the server's time—a switch that does not affect the other parties in the queue.

There are other understandings that must be considered. Service transactions can be carried out in such a manner that the server doesn't even look into the face of the served. (This, indeed, provides the rationale for the generic term "service transaction" rather than "service encounter.") The standard arrangement, however, is for eyes to meet, the mutual obligation of a social encounter accepted, and civil titles used (especially by the server) in the initial interchange, typically in utterance-initial or utterance-terminal position. In our society, this means a gender-marked vocative and a tinting of behavior that is thought to be suitable for the gender mix in the transaction. (Note, titles can almost always be omitted, but if they are used, they must correctly reflect gender.) If the served is a pre-adult, then this too is likely to be reflected in server's vocative selection and "speech register."

If the server and served are known to each other individually by name and have a prior relationship, then the transaction is likely to be initiated and terminated by a relationship ritual: individually identifying terms of address are likely to be used along with the exchange of inquiry and well-wishing found in standard greetings and farewells between acquaintances. So long as these initial and terminal flurries of sociability are sustained as a subordinate involvement during the transaction, so long as other persons present do not feel their movement in the queue is being impeded, then no sense of intrusion into the application of equalitarian treatment is likely to be sensed. The management of personal relationships is thus bracketed.

I have suggested in schematic terms elements of the structure of service transactions that can be taken as institutionalized and official, such that ordinarily when they are seen to apply in a particular service setting, those present feel that nothing marked or unacceptable or out of the ordinary has occurred by way of substance or ceremony. With this in mind, two critical issues can be addressed regarding the management of diffuse statuses in service transactions.

First, note that it is not uncommon that individuals seeking service feel (whether justified or not) that they have been given unequal and discourteous treatment. In point of fact, all the various elements in the standard structure of serving can be "worked," exploited, and covertly breached in almost an infinite number of ways. And just as one customer may be discriminated against in these ways, so another can be unfairly favored. Typically these breaches will take the form of deniable acts, ones whose invidiousness can be disputed by the actor if she or he is challenged openly. And of course, through this route all manner of "expression" can be given to officially irrelevant, externally based attributes, whether these are associated with diffuse social statuses, personal relationships, or "personality." I believe that to understand these effects one must trace them back to the particular point in the framework of servicing at which they occur, and one must see that no simple formulation is possible of the medley of official and unofficial relevancies accorded various attributes of server and served. What will be given recognition at one structural point will be rigorously checked by counterprinciples at another. Again, then, one finds an institutionalized framework (albeit culturally and temporally bound) quite differentiated in its structure which can serve as a resource for accomplishing all manner of ends, one, but only one, of which is informal discrimination in the traditional sense.

The second critical issue is that the notion of "equality" or "fair treatment" must not be understood simplistically. One can hardly say that some sort of objectively based equal treatment ever occurs, except perhaps where the server is eliminated and a dispensing machine is employed instead. One can only say that participants' settled sense of equal treatment is not disturbed by what occurs, and that of course is quite another matter. A sense that "local determinism" prevails doesn't tell us very much as to what, "objectively" speaking, does in fact obtain.

All of this is evident from what has been said about the acceptable ways in which personal relationships can be given recognition in service encounters. The management of queuing provides us with another case in point. What queues protect is ordinal position determined "locally" by first come first placed. But how long one must wait for service depends not merely on one's ordinal position in the queue, but how protracted is the business of each of those ahead of one. Yet, one is obliged to discount this latter contingency. Should the person immediately ahead of one take an inordinate amount of time to service, one will ordinarily be restricted to unofficial, largely gestural, remonstrance. The problem is particularly pronounced in sub-queuing. In banks, supermarkets, and airline check-in counters, the customer may have to select a sub-queue, and then may find once achieving a substantial place in it that switching to the rear of an apparently faster-moving line could entail a strategic loss. Participants can thus find themselves committed to the risk of a line that delivers service with greater than average delay. The normative response to this unequal treatment is a sense of bad luck or personal ill-management of contingencies—something definable as locally generated yet not perceived as a question of invidious treatment by the server.

Sub-queuing can illustrate another point. Large hotels currently provide multiple registration queues each of which is identified with a range of last-name initials. One's last-name initial is certainly a property one brings with one to the situation, not something generated within the situation, but is perceived as having no social significance—something one is not likely to have feelings about. (In state protocol a similar device can be employed to avoid troublesome questions of precedence, namely, allocating priority to the ambassador of longer residence.) A sense of equal treatment in such cases speaks not to the determinants of priority that are employed but to those that are explicitly excluded.

A final example. In service queuing there is the issue of two candidates coming on to the scene at the "same" time. At such junctures of indeterminacy in the queuing rules—junctures where unintended and undesired expressions of inequality may be generated—contestants have a wider set of understandings to draw on a republican form of *noblesse oblige*, whereby the individual who might seem to be the stronger, abler, or superior in social status proffers precedence to the other, as a protector would to the protected. So preferential treatment occurs, but initiated by the individual who would otherwise be in a position to force an opposite outcome. Now there is no doubt that ordinarily such moments hardly form a ripple in the service scene, leaving everyone feeling that no breach of the equality rule has occurred. But of course, categories of individuals receiving such priority courtesy may come to feel patronized and, ultimately, disparaged. Always, a basis of discrimination that the individual may this day accept as of no significance can tomorrow lead to acute reactions of slight or privilege.

In sum, the normal sense that externally based attributes are officially excluded from a role in service dealings, and that local determinism prevails—apart, of course, from covert breaches, real and imagined—is something of a perceptual achievement. Externally based attributes are in fact given routine, systematic "recognition," and various local determinisms apart from first come first served are systematically disattended. "Equal" treatment, then, in no way is sustained by what in fact goes on—officially or unofficially—during service transactions. What can be sustained and routinely is sustained is the blocking of certain externally based influences at certain structural points in the service forework. Out of this we generate a sense that equal treatment prevails.

X

I end this address with a personal bleat. We all agree, I think, that our job is to study society. If you ask why and to what end, I would answer: because it is there. Louis Wirth, whose courses I took, would have found that answer a disgrace. He had a different one, and since his time his answer has become the standard one.

For myself I believe that human social life is ours to study naturalistically, *sub specie aeternitatis*. From the perspective of the physical and biological sciences, human social life is only a small irregular scab on the face of nature, not particularly amenable to deep systematic analysis. And so it is. But it's ours. With a few exceptions, only students in our century have managed to hold it steadily in view this way, without piety or the necessity to treat traditional issues. Only in modern times have university students been systematically trained to examine all levels of social life meticulously. I'm not one to think that so far our claims can be based on magnificent accomplishment. Indeed I've heard it said that we should be glad to trade what we've so far produced for a few really good conceptual distinctions and a cold beer. But there's nothing in the world we should trade for what we do have: the bent to sustain in regard to all elements of social life a spirit of unfettered, unsponsored inquiry, and the wisdom not to look elsewhere but ourselves and our discipline for this mandate. That is our inheritance and that so far is what we have to bequeath. If one must have warrant addressed to social needs, let it be for unsponsored analyses of the social arrangements enjoyed by those with institutional authority—priests, psychiatrists, school teachers, police, generals, government leaders, parents, males, whites, nationals, media operators, and all the other well-placed persons who are in a position to give official imprint to versions of reality.

Bibliography: Erving Goffman's Writings*

1949   Some Characteristics of Response to Depicted Experience. MA Thesis, University of Chicago.

1951   Symbols of Class Status. *British Journal of Sociology* 11 : 294–304.

1952   On Cooling the Mark Out: Some Aspects of Adaptation to Failure. *Psychiatry* 15 (4) : 451–63.

1953a   Communication Conduct in an Island Community. PhD dissertation, University of Chicago.

1953b   *The Service Station Dealer: The Man and His Work*. Chicago: Social Research Inc.

1955   On Face-work: An Analysis of Ritual Elements in Social Interaction. *Psychiatry* 18(3) : 213–231.

1955   Book review of H.R. Service and H.S. Service, *Tobati: Paraguayan town*. *American Journal of Sociology* 61(2) : 186–7.

1956a   *The Presentation of Self in Everyday Life*. Edinburgh: University of Edinburgh Social Sciences Research Centre.

1956b   The Nature of Deference and Demeanor. *American Anthropologist* 58(3) : 473–502.

1956c   Embarrassment and Social Organization. *American Journal of Sociology* 62(3) : 264–71.

1957a   Alienation from Interaction. *Human Relations* 10(1) : 47–59.

1957b   Interpersonal Persuasion. Pp. 117–93 in Bertram Schaffner (ed.), *Group Processes: Transactions of the Third (1956) Conference*. NY: Josiah Macy Jr. Foundation.

1957c   Some Dimensions of the Problem. Pp. 507–10 in D.J. Levinson and R.H. Williams, (eds.), *The Patient and the Mental Hospital*. NY: Free Press.

1957d   Book review of D.R. Cressey, *Other People's Money*. *Psychiatry* 20(3) : 321–6.

1957e   On Some Convergences of Sociology and Psychiatry. *Psychiatry* 20(3) : 201–3.

1957f   Book review of I. Belknap. *Human Problems of a State Mental Hospital*. *Administrative Science Quarterly* 2(1) : 120–1.

1958   The Characteristics of Total Institutions. Pp. 43–84 in *Symposium on Preventive and Social Psychiatry (April 15–17, 1957)*. Washington, DC: Walter Reed Army Institute of Research.

---

* We are indebted to Gregory Smith's and Frances Waksler's bibliography (*Human Studies 12*, 1989) for pointing us to several of Goffman's more obscure writings.

1959a   *The Presentation of Self in Everyday Life.* Garden City, NY: Doubleday, Anchor Books.

1959b   The Moral Career of the Mental Patient. *Psychiatry* 22(2) : 123–42.

1961a   *Asylums.* Garden City, NY: Doubleday, Anchor Books.

1961b   *Encounters: Two Studies in the Sociology of Interaction.* Indianapolis: Bobbs-Merrill.

1961c   On the Characteristics of Total Institutions. In Donald R. Cressey (ed.), *The Prison: Studies in Institutional Organization and Change.* NY: Holt, Rinehart, and Winston.

1963a   *Behavior in Public Places: Notes on the Social Organization of Gatherings.* NY: The Free Press.

1963b   *Stigma: Notes on the Management of Spoiled Identity.* Englewood Cliffs, NJ: Prentice Hall; NY: Touchstone Books, Simon and Schuster, 1986.

1964a   Mental Symptoms and Public Order. *Disorders of Communication.* Association for Research in Nervous and Mental Disease, Research Publications 42 : 262–9.

1964b   The Neglected Situation. *American Anthropologist* 66 : 133–6.

1966   Communication and Enforcement Systems. In Kathleen Archibald (ed.), *Strategic Interaction and Conflict.* Berkeley, CA: Institute of International Studies.

1967   *Interaction Ritual: Essays on Face-to-Face Behavior.* Garden City, NY: Doubleday, Anchor Books.

1969a   *Strategic Interaction.* Philadelphia: University of Pennsylvania Press.

1969b   The Insanity of Place, *Psychiatry* 32(4) : 357–88.

1971   *Relations in Public: Microstudies of the Public Order.* NY: Basic Books.

1974   *Frame Analysis: An Essay on the Organization of Experience.* Cambridge, MA: Harvard University (hardbound); New York: Harper and Row (paperback).

1976a   *Gender Advertisements. Studies in the Anthropology of Visual Communication.* Society for the Anthropology of Visual Communication 3(2).

1976b   Replies and Responses. *Language and Society* 5(3) : 257–313.

1977a   Genderisms. *Psychology Today* 11(3) : 60–3.

1977b   The Arrangement Between the Sexes. *Theory and Society* 4(3) : 301–32.

1978   Response Cries. *Language* 54(4) : 787–815.

1979a   *Gender Advertisements.* Cambridge, MA: Harvard University (hardbound); NY: Harper and Row (paperback).

1979b   Footing. *Semiotica* 25(1/2) : 1–29.

1981a   *Forms of Talk.* Philadelphia: University of Pennsylvania Press.

1981b   A Reply to Denzin and Keller. *Contemporary Sociology* 10(1) : 60–8.

1983a   The Interaction Order. *American Sociological Review* 48 : 1–17.

1983b   Felicity's Condition. *American Journal of Sociology* 89(1) : 1–53.

1983c   Microsociologie et histoire. Pp. 197–202 in Ph. Fritsch, (ed.), *Le Sens de L'ordinaire.* Paris: Editions du Centre National de la Recherche Scientifique.

1989   On Fieldwork. *Journal of Contemporary Ethnography* 18(2):123–32.

Bibliography: Secondary Literature*

Abrahams, R. 1984. Goffman Reconsidered: Pros and Players. *Raritan*, pp. 76–94.

Ashworth, P.D. 1983. A Sartrean Reading of Goffman. *Bulletin of the British Psychological Society* 36:112–22.

Ashworth, P.D. 1985. "L'Enfer, C'est Les Autres": Goffman's Sartrism. *Human Studies* 8:97–168.

Atkinson, Paul. 1989. Goffman's Poetics. *Human Studies* 12:59–76.

Battershill, C.D. 1990. Goffman as a Precursor to Post-Modern Sociology. In Riggins (ed.), *Beyond Goffman*.

Becker, A. 1984. Goffman's Animated Language Game. *Raritan*, pp. 95–112.

Bergesen, A. 1984. Reflections on Erving Goffman. *Quarterly Journal of Ideology* 8(3):51–4.

Bock, Philip K. 1988. The Importance of Erving Goffman to Psychological Anthropology. *Ethos* 16(1):3–20.

Bourdieu, Pierre. 1983. Erving Goffman, Discoverer of the Infinitely Small. *Theory, Culture, and Society* 2(1):112–13.

Bovone, Laura. 1993. Ethics as Etiquette: The Emblematic Contribution of Erving Goffman. *Theory, Culture, and Society* 10(4):25–34.

Burns, Tom. 1992. *Erving Goffman*. London and NY: Routledge.

Chriss, James J. 1992. Habermas and Goffman: Some Suggestions for Future Research. *Perspectives: The Theory Section Newsletter* 15(3):6.

Chriss, James J. 1993. Durkheim's Cult of the Individual as Civil Religion: Its Appropriation by Erving Goffman. *Sociological Spectrum* 13(2):252–75.

Chriss, James J. 1993. Looking Back on Goffman: The Excavation Continues. *Human Studies* 16(4):469–83.

Chriss, James J. 1995. Habermas, Goffman, and Communicative Action: Implications for Professional Practice. *American Sociological Review* 60:545–65.

Chriss, James J. 1995. Role Distance and the Negational Self. In Smith (ed.), *Goffman's Patrimony*.

Chriss, James J. 1995. Some Thoughts on Recent Efforts to Further Systematize Goffman. *Sociological Forum* 10(1):177–86.

Clough, Patricia T. 1990. Reading Goffman: Toward the Deconstruction of Sociology. In Riggins (ed.), *Beyond Goffman*.

---

* We have aimed to provide a comprehensive list of scholarly exegeses of Goffman's ideas. This list does not include the numerous applications of Goffman's thought that currently exist. The line between scholarly presentation and application, however, was not always easy to draw.

Clough, Patricia T. 1992. Erving Goffman: Writing the End of Ethnography. In eadem, *The End(s) of Ethnography*. Newbury Park, CA: Sage.

Collins, Randall, 1980. Erving Goffman and the Development of Modern Social Theory. In Ditton, (ed.), *The View from Goffman*.

Collins, Randall. 1981. Three Stages of Erving Goffman's Sociology. In idem, *Sociology Since Mid Century: Essays in Theory Cumulation*. NY: Academic Press.

Collins, Randall. 1986. The Passing of Intellectual Generations: Reflections on the Death of Erving Goffman. *Sociological Theory* 4(1):106–13.

Collins, Randall, 1988. Theoretical Continuities in Goffman's Work. In Drew and Wooton (eds.), *Erving Goffman: Exploring the Interaction Order*.

Collins, Randall and Makowsky, Michael. 1984. Erving Goffman and the Theater of Social Encounters. In eidem, *The Discovery of Society*, 3rd edn, 230–43. NY: Random House.

Corder, Lloyd E. 1988. *The Utility of Erving Goffman's Theoretical Perspective: Metaphorical Models and "Serious Ethnography" for the Rhetoric and Communication Scholar*. University of Pittsburgh Dept. of Communications.

Coser, Rose Laub. 1966. Role Distance, Sociological Ambivalence, and Transitional Status Systems. *American Journal of Sociology* 72:173–87.

Craib, Ian. 1978. Erving Goffman: Frame Analysis. *Philosophy of the Social Sciences* 8:79–86.

Creelan, Paul, 1984. Vicissitudes of the Sacred: Erving Goffman and the Book of Job. *Theory and Society* 13:649–62.

Creelan, Paul. 1987. The Degradation of the Sacred: Approaches of Cooley and Goffman. *Symbolic Interaction* 10(1):29–56.

Crook, Steve and Taylor, Laurie. 1980. Goffman's Version of Reality. In Ditton (ed.), *The View from Goffman*.

Cuzzort, Ray P. 1969. Humanity as the Big Con: The Human Views of Erving Goffman. In Ray P. Cuzzort and Edith W. King (eds.), *Humanity and Modern Sociological Thought*. NY: Holt, Rinehart, and Winston.

Davies, C. 1989. Goffman's Concept of the Total Institution: Criticism and Revisions. *Human Studies* 12(1–2):77–95.

Dawe, Alan. 1973. The Underworld View of Erving Goffman. *British Journal of Sociology* 24:246–53.

Deegan, Mary Jo. 1978. The Social Dramas of Erving Goffman and Victor Turner. *Humanity and Society* 2(1):33–46.

Denzin, N. and Keller, C. 1981. *Frame Analysis* Reconsidered. *Contemporary Sociology* 10:52–60.

Ditton, Jason (ed.) 1980. *The View from Goffman*. London: Macmillan.

Drew, Paul and Wooton, Anthony (eds.). 1988. *Erving Goffman: Exploring the Interaction Order*. Cambridge: Polity Press.

Erwin, Robert. 1992. The Nature of Goffman. *Centennial Review* 36(2):327–42.

Fine, Gary Alan and Martin, Daniel D. 1990. A Partisan view: Sarcasm, Satire, and Irony as Voices in Erving Goffman's Asylums. *Journal of Contemporary Ethnography* 19:89–115.

Fontana, A. 1980. The Mask and Beyond: The Enigmatic Sociology of Erving Goffman. In J.D. Douglas (ed.), *Introduction to the Sociologies of Everyday Life*. Boston: Allyn and Bacon.

Friedson, Eliot. 1983. Celebrating Erving Goffman. *Contemporary Sociology* 12:359–62.

Gamson, William A. 1985. Goffman's Legacy to Political Sociology. *Theory and Society* 14:605–22.

Gardner, Carol Brooks. 1989. Analyzing Gender in Public Places: Rethinking Goffman's Vision of Everyday Life. *American Sociologist* 20(1):42–56.

Gardner, Carol Brooks. 1991. Stigma and the Public Self: Notes on Communication, Self, and Others. *Journal of Contemporary Ethnography* 20:251–62.

Giddens, Anthony. 1988. Goffman as a Systematic Social Theorist. In Drew and Wooton (eds.), *Erving Goffman: Exploring the Interaction Order*.

Gonos, George. 1977. "Situation" versus "Frame": The "Interactionist" and the "Structuralist" Analyses of Everyday Life. *American Sociological Review* 42:854–67.

Gonos, George. 1980. The Class Position of Goffman's Sociology: Social Origins of an American Structuralism. In Ditton (ed.), *The View from Goffman*.

Gouldner, Alvin W. 1970. Other Symptoms of the Crisis: Goffman's Dramaturgy and Other New Theories. In idem, *The Coming Crisis of Western Sociology*. London: Heinemann.

Grimshaw, A. 1983. Erving Goffman: A Personal Appreciation. *Language in Society* 12:147–8.

Habermas, Jurgen. 1979. Comments of Papers by Ekman and Goffman. In M. von Cranach, K. Foppa, W. Lepenies, and D. Ploog (eds.), *Human Ethology: Claims and Limits of a New Discipline*. Cambridge: Cambridge University Press.

Hall, J.A. 1977. Sincerity and Politics: "Existentialists" vs. Goffman and Proust. *Sociological Review* 25(3):535–50.

Hare, Paul and Blumberg, Herbert H. 1988. *Dramaturgical Analysis of Social Interaction*. NY: Praeger.

Hartland, N.G. 1994. Goffman's Attitude and Social Analysis. *Human Studies* 17(2):251–66.

Hazelrigg, Lawrence, 1991. Reading Goffman's Framing as Provocation of a Discipline. *Human Studies* 15:239–64.

Heath, Christian. 1988. Embarrassment and Interactional Organization. In Drew and Wooton, (eds.) *Erving Goffman: Exploring the Interaction Order*.

Heilman, S.C. 1979. Communication and Interaction: A Parallel in the Theoretical Outlooks of Erving Goffman and Ray Birdwhistell. *Communication* 4:221–34.

Helm, D. 1982. Talk's Forms: Comments on Goffman's *Forms of Talk*. *Human Studies* 5:147–57.

Hood, Th. 1984. Character is the Fundamental Illusion. *Quarterly Journal of Ideology* 8(3):4–12.

Hymes, Dell. 1984. On Erving Goffman. *Theory and Society* 13(5):621–31.

Jameson, Fredric. 1976. On Goffman's *Frame Analysis*. *Theory and Society* 13:119–33.

Kendon, Adam. 1988. Goffman's Approach to Face-to-Face Interaction. In Drew and Wooton (eds.), *Erving Goffman: Exploring the Interaction Order*.

Kuzmics, H. 1991. Embarrassment and Civilization: On Some Similarities and

Differences in the Work of Goffman and Elias. *Theory, Culture, and Society* 8(2):1–30.

Langman, Lauren. 1992. Alienation and Everyday Life: Goffman Meets Marx at the Shopping Mall. In Felix Geyer and Walter Heinz, (eds.), *Alienation, Society, and the Individual*. New Brunswick, NJ: Transaction.

Lanigan, Richard L. 1990. Is Erving Goffman a Phenomenologist? In Riggins (ed.), *Beyond Goffman*.

Levinson, Stephen C. 1988. Putting Linguistics on a Proper Footing: Explorations in Goffman's Concepts of Participation. In Drew and Wooton, (eds.), *Erving Goffman: Exploring the Interaction Order*.

Lofland, John. 1970. Morals are the Message: The Work of Erving Goffman. *Psychiatry and Social Science Review* 4(9):17–19.

Lofland, John. 1980. Early Goffman: Style, Structure, Substance, Soul. In Ditton. (ed.), *The View from Goffman*.

Lofland, John. 1984. Erving Goffman's Sociological Legacies. *Urban Life* 13:7–34.

Lyman, S.M. and Scott, M.B. 1975. *The Drama of Social Reality*. NY: Oxford University Press.

MacCannell, Dean. 1983. Erving Goffman (1922–1982). *Semiotica* 45(1–2):1–33.

MacCannell, Dean. 1990. The Descent of the Ego. In Riggins (ed.), *Beyond Goffman*.

Macintyre, Alasdair. 1969. The Self as a Work of Art. *New Statesman*. March 1969:447–8.

Manning, Peter K. 1976. The Decline of Civility: A Comment on Erving Goffman's Sociology. *Canadian Review of Sociology and Anthropology* 13:13–25.

Manning, Peter K. 1980. Goffman's Framing Order: Style as Structure. In Ditton (ed.), *The View from Goffman*.

Manning, Philip. 1989. Goffman's Revisions. *Philosophy of the Social Sciences* 19:341–3.

Manning, Philip. 1989. Ritual talk. *Sociology* 23:365–85.

Manning, Philip. 1991. Drama as Life: The Significance of Goffman's Changing Use of the Dramaturgical Metaphor. *Sociological Theory* 9(1):70–86.

Manning, Philip. 1992. *Erving Goffman and Modern Sociology*. Stanford, CA: Stanford University Press.

Marx, Gary T. 1984. Role Models and Role Distance: A Remembrance of Erving Goffman. *Theory and Society* 13:649–61.

McGregor, Gaile. 1986. A View From the Fort: Erving Goffman as Canadian. *Canadian Review of Sociology and Anthropology* 23:531–43.

McGregor, Gaile. 1995. Gender Advertisements Then and Now: Goffman, Symbolic Interactionism, and the Problem of History. *Studies in Symbolic Interaction* 17:3–42.

Meyrowitz, Joshua. 1990. Redefining the Situation: Extending Dramaturgy into a Theory of Social Change and Media Effects. In Riggins (ed.), *Beyond Goffman*.

Miller, Thomas G. 1984. Goffman, Social Acting and Moral Behavior. *Journal for the Theory of Social Behavior* 14(2):141–63.

Miller, Thomas G. 1987. Goffman, Positivism and the Self. *Philosophy of the Social Sciences* 16:177–95.

O'Neill, J. 1981. A Preface to Frame Analysis. *Human Studies* 4:259–64.

Oromaner, Mark. 1980. Erving Goffman and the Academic Community. *Philosophy of the Social Sciences* 10:287–91.

Philips, John. 1983. Goffman's Linguistic Turn: A Comment on Forms of Talk. *Theory, Culture, and Society* 2(1):114–16.

Posner, J. 1978. Erving Goffman: His Presentation of Self. *Philosophy of the Social Sciences* 8:67–78.

Psathas, George. 1977. Goffman's Image of Man. *Humanity and Society* 1(1):84–94.

Psathas, George. 1980. Early Goffman and the Analysis of Face-to-Face Interaction in *Strategic Interaction*. In Ditton, (ed.), *The View from Goffman*.

Rawls, Anne. 1984. Interaction as a Resource for Epistemological Critique: A Comparison of Goffman and Sartre. *Sociological Theory* 2:222–52.

Rawls, Anne. 1987. The Interaction Order *sui generis*: Goffman's Contribution to Social Theory. *Sociological Theory* 5 (2):136–49.

Rawls, Anne. 1989. Language, Self and Social Order: A Reformulation of Goffman and Sacks. *Human Studies* 12(1–2):147–72.

Rawls, Anne W. 1990. Emergent Sociality: A Dialectic of Commitment and Order. *Symbolic Interaction* 13(1):63–82.

Rawls, Anne W. 1990. *Interaction vs. Interaction Order: New Directions in the Study of Social Order*. NY: Irvington Press.

Riggins, Stephen Harold (ed.). 1990. *Beyond Goffman: Studies on Communication, Institution, and Social Interaction*. Berlin and New York: de Gruyter.

Rogers, Mary. 1977. Goffman on Power. *American Sociologist* 12(2):88–95.

Rogers, Mary. 1980. Goffman on Power, Hierarchy, and Status. In Ditton (ed.), *The View from Goffman*.

Rogers, Mary. 1984. Watching the Snorers: Erving Goffman and the Ideology of Narcissistic Awareness. *Quarterly Journal of Ideology* 8(3):13–25.

Ryan, Alan. 1978. Maximising, Moralising and Dramatising. In Christopher Hookway and Philip Pettit (eds.), *Action and Interpretation: Studies in the Philosophy of the Social Sciences*. Cambridge: Cambridge University Press.

Schegloff, Emanuel. 1988. Goffman and the Analysis of Conversation. In Drew and Wooton (eds.), *Erving Goffman: Exploring the Interaction Order*.

Scheibe, Karl E. 1985. Historical Perspectives on the Presented Self. In Barry R. Schlenker (ed.), *The Self and Social Life*. NY: McGraw-Hill.

Schudson, Michael. 1984. Embarrassment and Erving Goffman's Idea of Human Nature. *Theory and Society* 13:633–48.

Schwalbe, Michael L. 1993. Goffman Against Postmodernism: Emotion and the Reality of the Self. *Symbolic Interaction* 16(4):333–50.

Schwimmer, Eric. 1990. The Anthropology of the Interaction Order. In Riggins (ed.), *Beyond Goffman*.

Sedgwick, P. 1982. Psycho-Medical Dualism: The Case of Erving Goffman. In idem, *Psycho-Politics: Laing, Foucault, Goffman, Szasz and The Future of Mass Psychiatry*. NY: Harper and Row.

Smith, G.W.H. 1988. The Sociology of Erving Goffman. *Social Studies Review* 3(3):118–22.

Smith, G.W.H. 1989. Snapshots "Sub Specie Aeternitatis": Simmel, Goffman and Formal Sociology. *Human Studies* 12:19–57.

Smith, G.W.H. (ed.), 1995. *Goffman's Patrimony*. London: Routledge.

Srinivasan, Nirmala. 1990. The Cross-cultural Relevance of Goffman's Concept of Individual Agency. In Riggins (ed.), *Beyond Goffman.*

Stein, Michael. 1991. Sociology and the Prosaic. *Sociological Inquiry* 61:421–33.

Stone, G.P. 1962. "Appearance and the Self." In A. Rose (ed.), *Human Behavior and Social Processes.* Boston: Houghton-Mifflin.

Strong, P.M. 1983. The Importance of Being Erving: Erving Goffman 1922–1982. *Sociology of Health and Illness* 5:345–55.

Strong, P.M. 1988. Minor Courtesies and Macro Structures. In Drew and Wooton. (eds.), *Erving Goffman: Exploring the Interaction Order.*

Travers, Andrew. 1991. From "Normal Appearances" to "Simulation" in Interaction. *Journal for the Theory of Social Behavior* 21(3):297–337.

Travers, Andrew. 1992. The Conversion of Self in Everyday Life. *Human Studies* 15:169–238.

Travers, Andrew. 1992. Strangers to Themselves: How Interactants are Other Than They Are. *British Journal of Sociology* 43(4):601–37.

Travers, Andrew. 1994. Destigmatizing the Stigma of Self in Garfinkel's and Goffman's Accounts of Normal Appearances. *Philosophy of the Social Sciences* 24:5–40.

Tseelon, Efrat. 1992. Is the Presented Self Sincere? Goffman, Impression Management and the Postmodern Self. *Theory, Culture, and Society* 9:115–28.

Tseelon, Efrat. 1992. Self-presentation Through Appearance: A Manipulative vs. a Dramaturgical Approach. *Symbolic Interaction* 15(4):501–13.

Verhoeven, J. 1985. Goffman's Frame Analysis and Modern Micro-sociological Paradigms. In H. Helle and S. Eisenstadt (eds.), *Micro Sociological Theory.* New York: Sage.

Verhoeven, J.C. 1993. An Interview with Erving Goffman, 1980. *Research on Language and Social Interaction* 26(3):317–48.

Verhoeven, J.C. 1993. Backstage with Erving Goffman: The Context of the Interview. *Research on Language and Social Interaction* 26(3):307–15.

Vester, Heinz-Guenter. 1989. Erving Goffman's Sociology as a Semiotics of Postmodern Culture. *Semiotica* 76 (3–4):191–203.

Waksler, Frances Chaput. 1989. Erving Goffman's Sociology: An Introductory Essay. *Human Studies* 12:1–18.

Watson, Rod. 1983. Goffman, Talk, and Interaction: Some Modulated Responses. *Theory, Culture, and Society* 2(1):103–8.

Wedel, J.M. 1978. Ladies We've been framed! Observations on Erving Goffman's "The Arrangement Between the Sexes." *Theory and Society* 5(1):113–25.

Weinstein, Raymond M. 1982. Goffman's *Asylums* and the Social Situation of Mental Patients. *Journal of Orthomolecular Psychiatry* 11(4):267–74.

Weinstein, Raymond M. 1994. Goffman's *Asylums* and the Total Institution Model of Mental Hospitals. *Psychiatry* 57:348–67.

Wexler, M. 1984. The Enigma of Goffman's Sociology. *Quarterly Journal of Ideology* 8(3):40–50.

Williams, Robin. 1980. Goffman's Sociology of Talk. In Ditton (ed.), *The View from Goffman.*

Williams, Robin. 1983. Sociological Tropes: A Tribute to Erving Goffman. *Theory, Culture, and Society* 2(1):99–102.

Williams, Robin. 1988. Understanding Goffman's Methods. In Drew and Wooton (eds.), *Erving Goffman: Exploring the Interaction Order.*

Williams, Simon Johnson. 1986. Appraising Goffman. *British Journal of Sociology* 37:348–69.

Winkin, Y. 1983. The French (Re)presentation of Goffman's Presentation and Other Books. *Theory, Culture, and Society* 2(1):109–11.

Winkin, Y. 1988. *Erving Goffman: Les Moments et leurs hommes.* Paris: Minuit.

Young, T.R. 1971. The Politics of Sociology: Gouldner, Goffman and Garfinkel. *American Sociologist* 6:276–81.

Zeitlin, Irving. 1973. The Social Psychology of Erving Goffman. In idem, *Rethinking Sociology.* NY: Appleton-Century-Crofts.

Acknowledgements

We wish to thank, first of all, Simon Prosser, our editor until he returned to London for another position in book publishing. It was he who conceived the idea of this book, then pushed us with such gentle force that we had to make it. Were it nor for him, we might not have enjoyed the several pleasures of reading through all of Goffman, again and again.

We also thank Susan Rabinowitz, Simon's successor at Blackwell, USA, who took up the project and so graciously helped it along to completion.

Charles wishes to thank and acknowledge Edwin Lemert for a life-time of sociological inspiration and avuncular friendship. Edwin Lemert was an acknowledged influence on and intellectual resource for Goffman. Those who know Lemert recognize in him many of the qualities of work and character for which Goffman was known: a brilliant command of the language, an ability to probe beneath the obvious, and a disconcerting readiness to be and do at odds with the officially normal. There should be a book of this sort collecting Edwin Lemert's classic contributions to sociology, criminology, anthropology, and (with the publication of his new book on evil) social philosophy. I would have done it had I thought it proper to perform such a service for a blood kin.

Charles also wishes to thank Karl Scheibe, academic psychology's leading scholar and interpreter of Goffman, of whom he has taught me a great deal. Karl and I have worked together over many years in Wesleyan's Program in Psychology and Sociology. Through the years of work, things between us changed. One day while driving to one of our breakfast meetings I realized that, without knowing just how or when it happened, this man had become a friend. Men cannot often say that of each other, though Karl is among those of whom many do.

Finally, against the usual impression people have of Goffman, but consistent with his abiding commitment to sociology, we dedicate this book to, of all things, an institution. Though we are both native to the Midwest, and obviously share much else in common, we would not have met, as we did a decade ago, had it not been for Wesleyan University's intellectual and cultural style. By various intended accidents of Wesleyan's sometimes unruly purposes, we were brought together, encouraged to be teacher and student, and allowed to become intellectual colleagues and friends. This book is witness to the allowances for true collaboration that Wesleyan first exercised over us.

Charles Lemert
Killingworth, Connecticut
Ann Branaman
State College, Pennsylvania

Index